Lectures on the
Psychology of Women

Lectures on the Psychology of Women

❖

EDITED BY

Joan C. Chrisler
Connecticut College

Carla Golden
Ithaca College

Patricia D. Rozee
California State University at Long Beach

The McGraw-Hill Companies, Inc.
New York   St. Louis   San Francisco   Auckland   Bogotá   Caracas   Lisbon
London   Madrid   Mexico City   Milan   Montreal   New Delhi
San Juan   Singapore   Sydney   Tokyo   Toronto

McGraw-Hill

A Division of The **McGraw·Hill** Companies

LECTURES ON THE PSYCHOLOGY OF WOMEN

This book is printed on acid-free paper.

1 2 3 4 5 6 7 8 9 0 DOC DOC 9 0 9 8 7 6 5

ISBN 0-07-011111-1

This book was set in Palatino by Graphic World, Inc.
The editors were Jane Vaicunas, Beth Kaufman, and John M. Morriss;
the production supervisor was Paula Keller.
The cover was designed by Joan Greenfield.
Project supervision was done by The Total Book.
R. R. Donnelley & Sons Company was printer and binder.

Cover Art : Ink Drawing by Karen Klein, 1995.

Library of Congress Cataloging–in–Publication Data

Lectures on the psychology of women / edited by Joan C. Chrisler.
    Carla Golden, Patricia D. Rozee
        p.   cm.
    Includes bibliographical references and index.
    ISBN 0-07-011111-1
        1. Women—Psychology.   I. Chrisler, Joan C.   II. Golden, Carla.
    III. Rozee, Patricia D. (Patricia Denise)
HQ1206.L415   1996
305.42—dc20   95-40755

Contents

❖

Preface

———— ❖ ————

The three of us have known each other for a number of years, having met through feminist psychology conferences. In the summer of 1992 we were together in Atlanta, Georgia, at a meeting of the leadership of the Association for Women in Psychology. Our conversation eventually turned to our respective psychology of women classes, our favorite lectures, and whether or not we lectured from notes. As we each spoke with excitement about what we considered our best and most interesting lectures, one of us suggested (and the other two of us elaborated and encouraged the idea) that we might invite a number of different feminist psychologists to put into written form their "favorite" lectures to make a psychology reader to accompany psychology of women textbooks. It is from this idea and collaboration that this project grew.

Our discussion ended with a frank talk about the pros and cons of the various textbooks we'd used, and we concluded that all of them could be improved if paired with a good collection of supplementary readings. We then drew up our dream list of contributors, most of whom agreed to participate in the project.

Lectures on the Psychology of Women is not meant to stand alone. It was designed to be a companion to the available texts on the psychology of women, psychology of gender, or gender-role development. We invited our authors to write about topics not normally covered or not covered extensively in the textbooks. Thus, the dual purposes of the lectures are to supplement the main text and to provoke classroom discussion. The lectures are short, and they are not intended to be comprehensive. It is up to the instructor to provide context and commentary.

The lectures are organized to follow the arrangement of topics in several of the standard textbooks, but each is independent of the others, so they can be rearranged and assigned in any order. Some may also be useful assignments for other women's studies or psychology courses.

Each lecture was written by an experienced teacher of the psychology of women. The lectures are written in an informal manner; the authors speak directly to the students on the students' level and address questions that students often ask. The authors involve their readers in the topics by asking questions and by suggesting ideas to consider or exercises to try. Some describe the authors' personal experiences with the topics; others present original data. None of the lectures has been previously published. All were prepared specifically for this collection.

The lectures also serve the purpose of exposing students to some of the experts in the field of feminist psychology. The work of many of the authors is cited in the psychology of women textbooks, so students may already be familiar with their names when they read their lectures or they may be delighted to encounter their work in the text after having read their lectures. The informal tone of the lectures and the biographical statements and photographs are intended to give readers the feeling that they have been "introduced" to the authors.

Working on this book was more than a professional challenge or an intellectual exercise for us. It was a genuine pleasure to collaborate on this project with other feminist psychologists. We got to know each other much better during the two years we spent preparing this book, and we've come to appreciate each other's (and each author's) unique strengths and skills. We're pleased with the results of our work, and we hope you'll enjoy reading *Lectures on the Psychology of Women* as much as we enjoyed editing it.

ACKNOWLEDGMENTS

We'd like first to thank the authors of the lectures for generously agreeing to contribute their ideas to our project, for their willingness to write (and rewrite) in a style other than the usual scientific one, and for responding graciously to our anxious prodding about deadlines. This book would obviously not exist without them!

Our thanks go to our students; we've probably learned almost as much from them as they've learned from us. Our students' needs and our desire to meet them were the inspiration for this book.

Thanks to the Association for Women in Psychology and Division 35 of the American Psychological Association, without whom there would be no organized field of the psychology of women, and without whose activities we would never have met and had the discussion that started this project.

We'd like to thank our colleagues in the Psychology and Women's Studies Departments at Connecticut College, Ithaca College, and the California State University at Long Beach. They provided the supportive atmosphere in which we worked on this project. Thanks to Nancy MacLeod and Sandy Nicolls for their assistance in the preparation of the manuscript.

We would also like to thank the following reviewers for their many helpful comments and suggestions: Judi Addelston, Rollins College; D. Bruce Carter, Syracuse University; Renée A. Lamphere, Aurora University; Catherine S. Murray, St. Joseph's University; Cheryl Rickabaugh, University of Redlands; Michael R. Stevenson, Ball State University; Rhoda Unger, Montclair State University; and Janice D. Yoder, University of Wisconsin, Milwaukee.

Finally, we are grateful to Jane Vaicunas, our editor, for her enthusiastic embrace of our ideas and her vision for this project. Beth Kaufman, Kate Scheinman, and many others at McGraw-Hill were supportive and always ready with helpful advice throughout the preparation of this manuscript.

Joan C. Chrisler
Carla Golden
Patricia D. Rozee

Lectures on the Psychology of Women

Introduction

---------- ❖ ----------

The works in this volume all have one thing in common: They are written by feminist psychologists, all of whom are active and committed teachers of the psychology of women. Because the emphasis is on feminist teachers and teaching, perhaps a definition would be appropriate. Webster's dictionary defines the word "feminist" as: a person (either female or male) who believes in the economic, political, and social equality of women and men. Although all of the writers in this volume are feminists and teachers, they also differ in many ways. They represent a variety of racial, ethnic, and religious backgrounds. They are lesbian, bisexual, and heterosexual in sexual orientation. They are raised in working-class, middle-class, and wealthy families. They live and work in rural, suburban, and urban areas. But these authors are all alike in their belief in both the necessity and importance of gender equality, which includes a commitment to the elimination of all forms of inequality and domination, including sexism, racism, classism, and homophobia.

Certain perspectives on the world are common among feminists. Feminists are concerned with inequality at the personal, cultural, and institutional levels. Patricia Spencer Faunce (1985) describes the feminist worldview from the personal perspective.

Feminism is an advocacy system for women. Feminism insists that women must have personal autonomy and both the freedom to direct and the responsibility for directing all areas of their lives; they must decide for themselves what it means to be a woman; and they must define themselves as independent persons, separate from their relationships. Feminism fosters pride in being female, emphasizes the commonality of the female experience across cultural and socioeconomic lines, and develops a sense of community among women. Feminism holds that all roles are open to all people and that every woman is entitled to the opportunity to develop her potential fully. Feminism recognizes the culturally and experientially based perspective differences between women and men, assumes women and men are more alike than not, and insists that possible differences not be conceptualized in terms of "superiority/inferiority." Finally, feminism strives to equalize personal power, asserts that no person should

1

have noncontractual dominion over another, and encourages equalitarian relationships. (p. 310)

The cultural and institutional aspects of feminism are emphasized by
bell hooks (1981; cited in Ruth, 1995; p. 5), who defines feminism as

A commitment to eradicating the ideology of domination that permeates
Western culture on various levels—sex, race, and class, to name a few—and
a commitment to reorganizing U.S. society, so that the self-development of
people can take precedence over imperialism, economic expansion, and material desires.

As you can see, feminism is a life philosophy, a worldview, a blueprint for justice. Feminists believe that once we remove the patriarchal
lens through which we are accustomed to viewing the world, we are free
to organize our world according to our own priorities. The choices we
make are then made with full knowledge of all available alternatives,
rather than limited to the alternatives predetermined for us by a patriarchal culture. Once we know ourselves, we are in a better position to work
toward changing the cultural and institutional power arrangements that
serve to keep women in their place.

Here are some other common feminist themes you will encounter in
the readings in this book.

SOCIAL CONSTRUCTION OF GENDER

Feminists are interested in how gender is constructed by different societies and at different times in history. By social construction we mean that
the biological reality of being born a woman or a man is differentially em-
bellished in different cultural and situational contexts. The biological
body is not born into a sociocultural vacuum; rather it is influenced by all
kinds of external factors or contexts: cultural expectations, life situations,
institutional pressures, environmental events, and even the presence or
absence of others. Thus, the biological female is shaped into a girl and
then a woman by the culture and time into which she is born. For example, in the nineteenth century, middle-class and upper-class white women
were expected to be frail and weak and to "swoon" or faint regularly. This
was considered very feminine and desirable. Today, however, if we met a
woman who was frail and weak and fainted periodically we would think
she was ill! Indeed we have since learned that those nineteenth-century
fair damsels fainted because they were suffering from a lack of oxygen
caused by too-tight corsets! Claudia Geer and Stephanie Shields' lecture
on "Women and Emotions" deals with the social construction of the emotional female. Alice Eagly also addresses the social construction of gender

as related to differences in helping behavior in her lecture on "Gender and Altruism."

POWER

Feminists argue that it is impossible to examine the psychology of women without considering women's relative position in the power hierarchy. In general, women have less power and status than men. This is true all over the world. Worldwide there is a clear preference for male children (Unger & Crawford, 1992); women are paid less than men for the same work and have fewer opportunities for advancement; men control the U.S. Congress and every state legislature; they hold the top positions in nearly all U.S. corporations, and they are 90 percent of the faculty in U.S. universities; women do nearly all the housework and childcare; women and their children make up the majority of poor people in this country; and violence against women has been characterized as epidemic. The pervasive power differences between women and men in our society, the oppression of women, and the institutionalization of androcentric (male-centered) values are discussed by Ruth Ostenson in her lecture entitled, "Who's In and Who's Out: The Results of Oppression," and by Sandra Bem in her lecture, "Transforming the Debate on Sexual Inequality." The worldwide economic oppression of women is the topic of Bernice Lott's lecture, "Global Connections: The Significance of Women's Poverty." The use of violence to enforce the social control of women is discussed by Patricia Rozee in her lecture "Freedom from Fear of Rape: The Missing Link in Women's Freedom," and by Geraldine Butts Stahly in "Battered Women: Why Don't They Just Leave?".

THE PERSONAL IS POLITICAL

This statement means that what at first appears to be a personal problem is really a social problem with a political solution (Faunce, 1985). We live in a society that tends to blame the victim for her own misfortune. "Victim blaming," as this is called, is a result of our tendency to examine a person's behavior out of context. It is easier to make internal attributions for someone's behavior than to consider all the possible situational factors that may have led to the behavior. For example, one of our students lost a promotion. The reason? Her boss thought she was not committed to her department because she was often late for work. The student explained that she was late because she had to deliver her two small children to daycare on her way to work. Because the daycare center did not open until 7:30 AM and the student had to be at work 20 miles away by 8:00 AM, she often hit traffic and was delayed. So what initially looked like a personal problem, lack of commitment to the job, was actually a social problem, lack of quality childcare, which probably has a political solution—a national childcare policy. Michele Paludi's lecture, "Sexual Harassment in College and University Settings," examines how "the personal is political" operates on campus. The politics of agoraphobia are addressed by Maureen McHugh in her lecture, "A Feminist Approach to Agoraphobia."

THE VALUE OF DIVERSITY

Feminists value the diversities among women, such as those based on race, ethnicity, religion, social class, sexual orientation, age, and physical ability. The consensus among feminist educators (Division 35 National Conference on Education and Training in Feminist Practice, 1993) is that valuing diversity means being appreciative of and open to differences among and between women and recognizing the value of difference. This requires not only receptiveness to and respect for difference but the cultivation and nurturance of different perspectives. Psychology has often presented human experience as male, white, Christian, and heterosexual. But because of the importance of understanding the worldview of *all* women, we believe that these exclusionary practices must be challenged. Therefore, we have included a number of lectures that will expose the reader to the multiple perspectives of women: for example, Connie Chan's lecture, "Sexuality and Sexual Expression among Asian American Women"; Linda Garnets' lecture, "Life as a Lesbian"; Kayla Weiner's lecture, "Appreciating Cultural Difference: On Being an American Jewish Woman"; and Donna Castañeda's lecture, "Gender Issues among Latinas." Valuing diversity includes the consideration of multiple overlapping oppressions. Often it is difficult for a woman of color to know whether discrimination is directed at her because she is a woman, an ethnic minority, or both. Angela Gillem discusses this issue in "Beyond Double Jeopardy: Female, Biracial, and Perceived to Be Black."

VALUING WOMEN AND WOMEN'S EXPERIENCE

Because ours is a society in which males and maleness are more valued than females and femaleness, it is important to feminist psychology to value women and women's experience. Women have long been silenced. Our contributions to society have not been recorded in history books, our experiences have not been heard or valued, and our stories have not been told. In fact, our reality has often been defined by men. For example, most of what was written early on about female sexuality, and even female orgasm, was written by men. If you are a woman, can you imagine writing a book about male orgasm? And without talking to any men about it? Such is the power of patriarchy to define and name. Recognizing women's achievements is discussed by Agnes O'Connell in her lecture, "Women in Psychology as Role Models," and by Beverly Goodwin, "The Impact of Popular Culture on Images of African American Women."

Topics of interest to women, from women's experience, that have generally been ignored by traditional psychology include feminist identity (Judith Worell, "Feminist Identity in a Gendered World"); female friendships (Suzanna Rose, "Who to Let In: Women's Cross-Race Friendships"); women's choices in parenting decisions (Nancy Genero, "The Mothers' Project," and Nancy Felipe Russo, "Understanding Emotional Responses After Abortion"); women in sports (Ruth Hall, "Sweating It Out: The Good News and the Bad News about Women and Sport"); and women's personality development (Carla Golden, "Relational Theories of White Women's Development").

VALUES

An important theme in a feminist psychology of women is values. Each of us grows up with a sense of values instilled by our family, our peers, our social organizations, our community, even our city, state, region, and nation. Often the values we hold dear are not conscious. Like a fish that is unaware that its evironment is wet, we are often unaware of how strongly our values influence our attitudes and behavior (Bem & Bem, 1976). As students of the social and behavioral sciences we have been taught to assume that science is objective and value-free. In psychology we try to design our experiments with control groups, placebos, and double-blind methods to eliminate the effects of our values on the research process.

Nevertheless, feminist psychologists argue that science, including psychology, is not value-free. Psychology is people studying people; it is unlikely that we will be able to completely eliminate the bias infused by the values of the researchers. Our values influence every phase of the research process, from the initial question formulation, through the research design and analysis, to the interpretation.

For example, if scientists think that only women's moods are influenced by hormonal fluctuations, then they might design experiments that study only women. By not studying men and their mood fluctuations, scientists perpetuate the idea that women are controlled by their hormones and men are not. The scientists' own values would then have prevented them from examining mood fluctuations that may occur as a result of varying levels of testosterone in men. Because there is some evidence that the relatively higher levels of testosterone may be related to aggressive behavior in males, this is a serious omission. Joan Chrisler illustrates the limiting effects of androcentric values as she discusses "PMS as a Culture-Bound Syndrome." Christine Smith's lecture on "Women, Weight, and Body Image" confronts the effects of male values on women's comfort with their own bodies.

INCLUSIVE LANGUAGE

There is no longer any doubt that the use of noninclusive, sexist, or male-biased language has negative psychological effects. Our language both contributes to, and is limited by, our conceptualization of the world. Although some people have argued that language is a trivial issue contrived by feminists, those same people are often very offended by "dirty" talk, swearing, and "improper" English. That is because they know that language is powerful.

English—and many other languages as well—use the terms "man" and "he" to describe the whole human race, women as well as men. Studies show, however, that people, from preschoolers through college adults, interpret the word "man" to mean males. For example, when research participants are asked to draw pictures of "early man," their drawings are virtually all of male human beings (Harrison, 1975). Thus the word "man" is not inclusive of woman, as some have argued; it is not the generic "human," but rather the male human that is conceptualized. Little girls will opt out of careers described with such words as "police *man*" or "fire *man*" because they think these are "boy jobs." Yet when the words "police *officer*" or "fire*fighter*" are used, the girls are more likely to see these as careers to which they might aspire. Thus, early in life little girls are limited in their aspirations by their conceptualization of man to mean male (Unger & Crawford, 1992). Feminists see this as a barrier to equality. All the authors in this volume are cognizant of the power of language and are committed to changing language usage, both through example and through institutional changes, such as persuading textbook publishers to adopt inclusive language guidelines.

THE VALUE OF SOCIAL ACTIVISM

Feminists value the collective actions of women, for women, to create social change. We embrace the empowerment of women by both individual and collective actions. Women's collective power to change our status is vast. However, many women do not see either the need for such change or their own power to enact social change. We hope that you will understand both by the time you have finished reading this book.

REFERENCES

Bem, S. L., & Bem, D. J. (1976). Training the woman to know her place: The power of a nonconscious ideology. In S. Cox (Ed.), *Female psychology: The emerging self* (pp. 180–191). Palo Alto, CA: Science Research Associates.

Faunce, P. S. (1985). Teaching feminist therapies: Integrating feminist therapy, pedagogy, and scholarship. In L. B. Rosewater & L. E. A. Walker (Eds.), *Handbook of feminist therapy* (pp. 309–320). New York: Springer.

HARRISON, L. (1975, April). Cro-magnon woman in eclipse. *The Science Teacher,* pp. 8–11.

Proceedings of the Division 35 National Conference on Education and Training in Feminist Practice (1993). Boston: Boston College.

RUTH, S. (1995). *Issues in feminism.* Mountain View, CA: Mayfield.

UNGER, R., & CRAWFORD, M. (1992). *Women and gender: A feminist psychology.* New York: McGraw-Hill.

Patricia D. Rozee
Carla Golden
Joan C. Chrisler

SANDRA LIPSITZ BEM is Professor of Psychology and Women's Studies at Cornell University, where she has also served as Director of the Women's Studies Program. Dr. Bem has taught courses on the psychology of sex roles and the social construction of gender at Cornell and Stanford since 1971. She has been honored by several professional organizations for her many contributions to the literature on the development of gender and sexuality.

Transforming the Debate on Sexual Inequality: From Biological Difference to Institutionalized Androcentrism

❖

Because I am a feminist psychologist, I am frequently asked to lecture on the question, What biological sex differences are there, *really?* This question puts me in an awkward position because I not only don't have the answer to it; I don't even think it's the question we ought to be asking. I'll tell you why.

I begin with a single historical fact: Since the middle of the nineteenth century (and especially during times of intense feminist activity), Americans have been literally obsessed with the question of whether women and men are fundamentally the same as one another or fundamentally different from one another. In other words, the question of biological difference has been the focal point of almost all American discussions of sexual inequality.

This focus on biological difference came into being almost immediately after feminists like Elizabeth Cady Stanton and Susan B. Anthony first started pushing to get women the most basic rights of citizenship, including the rights to vote, own property, speak in public, and have access to higher education. Threatened by these extraordinarily radical proposals for social change, antifeminists tried to argue against them by raising the specter of biological difference. I'll mention just three examples of this antifeminist stance, all by highly regarded scientists and scholars of the period. Paul Broca argued against higher education for women by,claiming that their brains were too small. Edward Clarke argued against higher education by claiming that it would divert women's limited complement of blood from their reproductive organs to their brains; hence, their reproductive organs would atrophy, and they would be unable to bear children. And finally, Herbert Spencer argued against giving women the right to vote on the grounds that they had too much maternal instinct to allow only the fittest in society to survive.

These nineteenth-century arguments against women's equality, I should note, were heavily tinged with racism and classism as well as sexism. With educated white women beginning to have many fewer babies than uneducated women, and with the United States also experiencing a gigantic increase in the number of immigrants from eastern and southern Europe, the feminist proposals for social change were seen as threatening not just to male dominance but to white dominance. When G. Stanley Hall argued that higher education for women would spell "race suicide," it was not the suicide of the human race that he was worried about but the suicide of the white, or European, race.[1]

In response to all of this biological and antifeminist theorizing on the part of some of the most respected scientists of the nineteenth century, by the early twentieth century, many *feminists* were beginning to focus on the question of biological difference as well. I'll give but one example. Beginning in 1903, two of the very first women with PhDs in the new field of empirical psychology took it upon themselves to try to refute all this antiwoman theorizing by doing their own carefully controlled studies of male-female difference on a whole variety of intellectual and other abilities. They also began to publish a whole slew of review articles carefully compiling and evaluating the results of all the research on male-female difference then available.[2] Not only is this work by Helen Thompson Woolley and Leta Stetter Hollingworth recognized today as being among the best science of its time; it is also what started the century-old tradition of psychological research on sex differences, which tries to figure out once

[1]For more on these and other biological theories from the nineteenth and early twentieth centuries, see Jordanova (1989), Russett (1989), and Sayers (1982).

[2]For more on this early feminist work in psychology, see Shields (1975a,b).

and for all what alleged sex differences really exist. Of course, the very existence of this research tradition is itself an example of the American obsession with biological sex difference.

Although our obsession with the question of biological difference died down somewhat after women finally got to vote in 1920, it exploded onto the scene again after the second major wave of American feminism in the late 1960s and early 1970s and has been with us ever since. This modern focus on whether males and females are fundamentally the same or fundamentally different is now so integrated into American culture that you can see it in almost any magazine article on women and men that you happen to pick up at your local supermarket. Here are just a few of the most popular of today's sex difference themes. There's the idea from sociobiology that male dominance (including even the so-called male predisposition to rape) is encoded in our genes. There's the idea from prenatal hormone theory that in-utero testosterone is responsible for male aggression. There's the idea that some kind of a male math gene explains why males do better at mathematics. There's the idea that some difference in brain structure having to do with the corpus callosum makes males "right-brained" and females "left-brained." And finally, there's the idea from a popular stream of modern feminism that says females are naturally concerned about relationships and caring, whereas males are naturally concerned about autonomy and justice—and this is why we have such a hard time relating to one another.

There are two reasons why I am beginning my lecture by pointing out that Americans organize almost all of their discussions about gender and sexual inequality around the issue of biological difference. First, I want to shift your angle of vision a little and have you focus—if only for a moment—on the *question* Americans are always asking instead of the *answer* to that question. Put somewhat differently, I want you to stop taking the focus on sexual difference for granted as something completely natural and unremarkable and instead begin to say to yourself, Why *is* this the question we are always asking? And even more importantly, Is there some *other* question we could or should be asking instead?

Second, I want to set the stage for my major argument, which is that Americans need to shift the focus of their discussion of sexual inequality from *biological difference to institutionalized androcentrism*. That is, we need to reframe our discussion of sexual inequality so that it focuses not on male-female difference per se but on how our androcentric (or male-centered) institutions transform male-female difference into female disadvantage.

My overall argument has two parts. First, I will argue that the focus on biological difference is based on a false assumption and hence is misguided both intellectually and scientifically. Next, I will argue that we need to accept at least a certain level of biological difference as given or axiomatic and thereby shift the starting point of our discussion from difference per se to society's situating of women in a social structure so androcentric that it not only transforms what is really just male-female difference into female disadvantage; it also disguises what is really just a male standard or norm as gender neutrality.

THE FOCUS ON BIOLOGICAL DIFFERENCE IS MISGUIDED

The reason Americans have become so obsessed with the biology of sex differences is that for the last 150 years feminists have been saying that we need to change our society in order to make women more equal—and for that same 150 years, the society has been saying back that our biological differences may not even allow for the kind of equality that feminists like me are always advocating. Implicit in this response, however, is a *false assumption*, which is *that biology is a kind of bedrock beyond which social change is not feasible.* Not only is that assumption false in and of itself; it also leads to the misguided conclusion that the question of biological sex difference is urgent, both politically and scientifically. I disagree. As I see it, social change—or what I would rather call cultural invention—can so radically transform the situational context in which biology operates that the human organism can actually be liberated from what had earlier seemed to be its intrinsic biological limitations. Consider but three examples.

1. As a biological species, human beings require food and water on a daily basis, which once meant that it was part of universal human nature to live as survivalists. But now human beings have invented agricultural techniques for producing food, and storage and refrigeration techniques for preserving food, which means that it is no longer part of universal human nature to live as survivalists.

2. As a biological species, human beings are susceptible to infection from many bacteria, which once meant that it was part of universal human nature to die routinely from infection. But now human beings have invented antibiotics to fight infection, which means that it is no longer part of universal human nature to die routinely from infection.

3. As a biological species, human beings do not have wings, which once meant that it was part of universal human nature to be unable to fly. But now human beings have invented airplanes, which means that it is no longer part of universal human nature to be unable to fly.

As dramatically liberating as these three examples of technological innovation clearly are, the general principle that they illustrate is so mundane and noncontroversial that even sociobiologists would unhesitatingly endorse it. Simply put, *the impact of any biological feature depends in every instance on how that biological feature interacts with the environment in which it is situated.*

Of course, the question that immediately arises is the following: If this whole idea of biology interacting with the social context is right, then why have women and men played such different and unequal roles in virtually every society on earth? The biology-in-context answer is that throughout human history, there have not only been certain indisputable and universal differences between men's and women's bodies, with only women being able to become pregnant and to breast-feed and with men, on average, being bigger and stronger. There have also been certain indisputable and universal features of the environment, with all cultures everywhere having no effective means of controlling fertility, no digestible substitutes for mother's milk, few technological instruments for extending the strength of the human body, and relatively little work that was mental rather than physical.

Now, in that sociohistorical context, the argument continues, the bodily differences between the sexes not only made it likely that most women would be either pregnant or breast-feeding during most of the years from menarche to menopause; they also made it likely that the culture would develop both a division of labor based on sex and an institutionalized system of male political dominance. In the current sociohistorical context, however, those very same bodily differences do not need to impact on people's lives in quite the same way.

But of course, this biology-in-context answer than raises another question that is almost always presented as the ultimate challenge to modern feminism: If cultural invention has now so transformed the situational context of human life that the bodily differences between the sexes are no longer as functionally significant as they once were, then why is it that males and females continue to play such different—and unequal—roles in even a modern technological society like our own, which has not only effective control over fertility and digestible substitutes for mother's milk, but little or no labor for which the sex of the laborer is truly decisive? There is both a short answer to this question and a long answer, both of them historical.

The long answer is spelled out in my book, *The Lenses of Gender: Transforming the Debate on Sexual Inequality* (Bem, 1993). The short answer is that women and men are both politically and economically unequal, even in the United States today, because *we live in an androcentric social structure that continues to invisibly transform what is really just a biological difference between males and females into a massive female disadvantage.* I'll shift in a moment to a discussion of what androcentrism is and how it works, but first I want to make one more point about biology. In particular, I want to answer the question that many of you are silently asking in your minds, which is: Do I really believe that all biology does in the context of sex and gender is produce male and female bodies? Put somewhat differently, Do I really believe there are no biological differences between the sexes beside the very obvious differences in anatomy and physiology?

The truth is that I'm very much an agnostic with respect to this question. For all I know, there may well be a kernel of truth in Alan Alda's (1975) argument that men are more physically aggressive than women because they are suffering from prenatal "testosterone poisoning." There may also be a kernel of truth in Alice Rossi's (1985) argument that women are more maternal than men because of their female hormones. And there may even be a kernel of truth in Camilla Benbow's (1988) argument that males are better at higher mathematics than females because they have some special biological ability to reason mathematically.

But there are three related issues about which I am not at all agnostic, and about which I would not be very likely to become agnostic, even if it should turn out that human males and females differed biologically with respect to any number of specific abilities or predispositions:

1. There would be so much overlap between the sexes in all of these cases that the differences would pale into insignificance next to the bigger and more obvious differences between male and female bodies. Even if they should someday be shown to have a biological component, these differences would thus add little or nothing to our understanding of why it is that women and men have virtually played such different—and unequal—roles in virtually every society on earth.

2. These biological differences would be so poorly matched to the requirements of the jobs that women and men currently hold in American society that they would again add little or nothing to our understanding of why American women and men currently hold the different—and unequal—positions that they do. So, yes, women might well turn out to be more biologically nurturant then men on the average, but that should make them psychiatrists, not secretaries. And, yes, men might also turn out to have a higher aptitude for mathematics than women on the average, but that would not explain why there are so many more women with a high aptitude for mathematics than there are women in careers *requiring* a high aptitude for mathematics. Stated more generally, no matter what subtle biological differences there may someday prove to be between women and men on the average, those differences will never justify the sexual inequality that has, for centuries, been a feature of human social life.

3. No matter how many subtle biological differences between the sexes there may someday prove to be, both the size and the significance of those biological differences will depend, *in every single instance*, on the situational context in which women and men live their lives. The feature of the situational context that I have focused on so far is the

historically universal absence of modern technology. At least as important in the development of sexual difference and sexual inequality, however, is the male-centeredness that has resulted from the institutionalization of male political power in every single culture. And that feature of the environment I'll talk about now.

ANDROCENTRISM

The concept of androcentrism was first articulated in the early twentieth century by Charlotte Perkins Gilman, who wrote in *The Man-Made World; or, Our Androcentric Culture* (1911/1971):

> All our human scheme of things rests on the same tacit assumption; man being held the human type; woman a sort of accompaniment and subordinate assistant, merely essential to the making of people. She has held always the place of a predisposition in relation to man. She has always been considered above him or below him, before him, behind him, a wholly relative existence—"Sydney's sister," "Pembroke's mother"—but never by any chance Sydney or Pembroke herself. . . . It is no easy matter to deny or reverse a universal assumption. . . . What we see immediately around us, what we are born into and grow up with, . . . we assume to be the order of nature. Nevertheless, . . . what we have all this time called "human nature" . . . was in great part only male nature. . . . Our androcentric culture is so shown to have been, and still to be, a masculine culture in excess, and therefore undesirable. (pp. 20–22)

Without actually using the term itself, Simone de Beauvoir brilliantly elaborated on the concept of androcentrism and integrated it more completely into a theory of sexual inequality in *The Second Sex* (1952). According to de Beauvoir, the historical relationship of men and women is not best represented as a relationship between dominant and subordinate, or between high and low status, or even between positive and negative. No, in all male-dominated cultures,

> man represents both the positive and the neutral, as is indicated by the common use of *man* to designate human beings in general; whereas woman represents only the negative, defined by limiting criteria, without reciprocity. . . . It amounts to this: just as for the ancients there was an absolute vertical with reference to which the oblique was defined, so there is an absolute human type, the masculine. Woman has ovaries, a uterus; these peculiarities imprison her in her subjectivity, circumscribe her within the limits of her own nature. It is often said that she thinks with her glands. Man superbly ignores the fact that his anatomy also includes glands, such as the testicles, and that they secrete hormones. He thinks of his body as a direct and normal connection with the world, which he believes he apprehends objectively, whereas he regards the body of woman as a hindrance, a prison, weighed down by everything peculiar to it. . . . Thus humanity is male and man defines woman not in herself but as relative to him; she is not regarded as an autonomous being. . . . She is defined and differentiated with reference to man and not he

with reference to her; she is the incidental, the inessential as opposed to the essential. He is the Subject, he is the Absolute—she is the Other. (pp. xv–xvi)

These quotations make androcentrism pretty clear, but let me describe it a few different ways and then give you some concrete examples to illustrate it. As I see it, *androcentrism is the privileging of males, male experience, and the male perspective.* There are many different ways to describe this privileging. For example, you could say that in the drama of human life males are treated as the main characters around whom all action revolves and through whose eyes all reality is to be interpreted, whereas the females are treated as the peripheral or marginal characters whose purpose for being is defined only in relation to the main—or male—characters. This goes along with Gilman's idea that women are always defined in relation to men. Or you could say that an androcentric viewpoint treats the male as if he were some kind of universal, objective, or neutral representative of the human species, in contrast to the female who is some kind of special case—something different, deviant, extra, or other. This goes along with de Beauvoir's idea that man is the human and woman is the other.

There are lots of examples of androcentrism that you already know about even if you haven't ever thought to label them as such. In language, for example, there's the generic use of "he" to mean "he or she"; "he" is treated as universal, human, genderless, and "she" is specifically female. In the Old Testament story of Adam and Eve, not only is Adam created first (in God's image) and Eve created (out of Adam) to be his helper; but if you recall, only Adam, is explicitly given the power to name every creature on earth from his own perspective. And then, of course, there's Freud's (1925/1959) theory of penis envy, which treats the male body as so obviously being the human norm—and the female body as so obviously being an inferior departure from that norm—that the mere sight of the other sex's genitals not only fills the 3-year-old boy with "a horror of the mutilated creature he has just seen"; it also leads the 3-year-old girl to "make her judgment and her decision in a flash; she has seen it and knows that she is without it and wants to have it" (pp. 190–191).

Let me shift now to some examples of androcentrism that are both more modern and more pertinent to everyday life. As long as we've been talking about the presumed inferiority or otherness of the female body, let's begin with the U.S. Supreme Court's rulings related to pregnancy—in particular, the Court's rulings on whether employees can exclude pregnancy from the package of disability insurance benefits that they provide to their employees. The situation is this: An employer says their insurance benefits will cover you for every medical condition that keeps you away from work, *except* pregnancy and giving birth. Is this exclusion okay? The Supreme Court says yes. But why is it okay to exclude pregnancy if discrimination against women is now illegal? Because, says the Court, although such as exclusion may appear on the surface to discriminate against women, in actuality, it is gender-neutral.[3]

The Court has tried to argue this claim of gender neutrality in a number of different ways. First, says the Court, the exclusion doesn't divide people into the two categories of women and men, but into the two categories of "pregnant women and nonpregnant persons." Second, "there is no risk from which men are protected and women are not. Likewise, there is no risk from which women are protected and men are not." And finally, "pregnancy-related disabilities constitute an *additional* risk, unique to women, and the failure to compensate them for this risk does not destroy the presumed parity of the benefits . . . [that accrue] to men and women alike."

There are some problems with the Court's reasoning here because, as I hope you see, it is androcentrically defining whatever is male as the standard and whatever is female as something "additional" or "extra." Justices Brennan, Douglas, and Marshall came within millimeters of exposing this androcentrism when they wrote in a dissenting opinion,

> By singling out for less favorable treatment a gender-linked disability peculiar to women . . . [while simultaneously giving] men . . . full compensation for all disabilities suffered, including those that affect only or primarily their sex, such as prostatectomies, circumcision, hemophilia, and gout, . . . the State . . . [is creating] a double standard for disability compensation.

Justice Stevens came even closer to exposing the Court's androcentrism when he argued in his dissent,

> It is not accurate to describe the program as dividing "potential recipients into two groups—pregnant women and nonpregnant persons." . . . The classification is between persons who face a risk of pregnancy and those who do not. . . . By definition, such a rule discriminates on the basis of sex; for it is the capacity to become pregnant which primarily differentiates the female from the male. . . .
> Nor is it accurate to state that under the plan "[t]here is no risk from which men are protected and women are not. . . .If the word "risk" is used narrowly, men are protected against the risks associated with a prostate operation whereas women are not. If the word is used more broadly to describe the risk of uncompensated employment caused by physical disability, men receive total protection . . . against that risk whereas women receive only partial protection.

What is going on in these pregnancy cases should be clear. Just like Sigmund Freud himself, the Court is androcentrically defining the male body as the standard human body; hence it sees nothing unusual or inappropriate about giving that standard human body the full insurance coverage that it would need for each and every condition that might be-

---

[3]All legal opinions quoted here can be found in the analyses of *Geduldig v. Aiello* (1974) and *General Electric Co. v. Gilbert* (1976), which appear in Lindgren & Taub (1988).

fall it. Consistent with this androcentric perspective, the Court is also defining equal protection as the granting to women of every conceivable benefit that this standard human body might require—which, of course, does not include disability coverage for pregnancy.

If the Court had even the slightest sensitivity to the meaning of androcentrism, there are at least two truly gender-neutral standards that it would have surely considered instead. In set-theory terms, these are (1) the *intersection* of male and female bodies, which would have narrowly covered only those conditions that befall both men and women alike; and (2) the *union* of male and female bodies, which would have broadly covered all those conditions that befall both men and women separately. In fact, however, the Court was so blind to the meaning of androcentrism that it saw nothing the least bit amiss when, in the name of equal protection, it granted a whole package of special benefits to men and men alone.

Let me now move to a final example of an androcentric law that looked gender-neutral to me until just a couple of years ago. This final example has to do with our culture's legal definition of self-defense, which holds that a defendant can be found innocent of homicide only if he or she perceived imminent danger of great bodily harm or death and responded to that danger with only as much force as was necessary to defend against it. Although that definition had always seemed to have nothing whatsoever to do with gender and hence to be perfectly gender-neutral, it no longer seemed quite so gender-neutral once feminist legal scholars finally pointed out how much better it fit with a scenario involving two men in an isolated episode of sudden violence than with a scenario involving a woman being battered, first in relatively minor ways and then with escalating intensity over the years, by a man who is not only bigger and stronger than she is, but from whom she cannot readily get police protection because he is her husband. The "aha" experience here is the realization that if this woman and this situation had been anywhere near the center of the policymakers' consciousness on the day when they were first drafting our culture's supposedly neutral definition of self-defense, they might not have placed so much emphasis on the defendant's being in imminent danger at the particular instant when the ultimate act of self-defense is finally done.

Of course, it isn't only in the context of insurance and self-defense that the male difference from women is "affirmatively compensated" by American society whereas the female difference from men is treated as an intrinsic barrier to sexual equality. To quote Catharine MacKinnon (1987), who is perhaps the most distinguished feminist lawyer in the United States today:

> Virtually every quality that distinguishes men from women is . . . affirmatively compensated in this society. Men's physiology defines most sports, their needs define auto and health insurance coverage, their socially designed biographies define workplace expectations and successful career patterns, their perspectives and concerns define quality in scholarship, their experiences and obses-

sions define merit, their objectification of life defines art, their military service defines citizenship, their presence defines family, their inability to get along with each other—their wars and rulerships—defines history, their image defines god, and their genitals define sex. For each of their differences from women, what amounts to an affirmative action plan is [thus] in effect, otherwise known as the structure and values of American society. (p. 36)

Of all the androcentric institutions on MacKinnon's list that are typically thought of as gender-neutral, there is perhaps no institution more directly responsible for denying women their rightful share of the United States' economic and political resources than the structure of the American work world. Although that work world may seem to many Americans to be as gender-neutral as it needs to be now that explicit discrimination against women has finally been made illegal, in fact, it is so thoroughly organized around a worker who is not only presumed to be male rather than female, but who is also presumed to have a wife at home to take care of all the needs of his household—including the care of his children—that, as I've said several times already, it "naturally" and automatically ends up transforming what is intrinsically just a male-female difference into a massive female disadvantage.

Imagine how differently our social world would be organized if all of the workers in our work force were women rather than men, and hence most of the workers in our work force—including those at the highest levels of government and industry—were also either pregnant or responsible for childcare during at least a certain portion of their adult lives. Given such a work force, "working" would so obviously need to coordinate with both birthing and parenting that institutions facilitating that coordination would be built into the very structure of the social world. There would thus be not only such things as paid pregnancy leave, paid days off for sick children, paid childcare, and a match—rather than a mismatch—between the hours of the work day and the hours of the school day. There would probably also be a completely different definition of a prototypical work life, with the norm being not a continuous 40 hours or more per week from adulthood to old age, but a transition from less than 40 hours per week when the children are young to 40 hours or more per week when the children are older.

The lesson of this alternative reality should be clear. It is not women's biological and historical role as mothers that is limiting their access to economic and political resources in the United States. It is a social world so androcentric in its organization that it provides but one institutionalized mechanism for coordinating work in the paid labor force with the responsibilities of being a parent, namely, the having of a wife at home to take care of one's children.

Now, to people who don't yet appreciate either what androcentrism is or how it operates institutionally, the suggestion that we need to change our social institutions so that they are more accommodating to women or more inclusive of women's experiences seems completely wrong-headed.

As they would surely describe it, it seems like a move away from gender neutrality and hence in the absolutely wrong direction of where this country ought to be going.

But in fact, American institutions have been so thoroughly organized for so long from an androcentric perspective—that is, they have for so long been taking care of men's special needs automatically while women's special needs have been either treated as special cases or simply left unmet—that *the only way for them to even begin to approximate gender neutrality is for our society to finally begin giving women as complete a package of special benefits as it has always given to men and men alone.*

I want to end my lecture with an analogy that may help you see even more clearly that the gender problem in the United States today isn't about the difference between women and men; it's about the transformation of that difference into female disadvantage by an androcentric social structure that looks not only gender-neutral but even god-given, because we're just so used to it by now that we don't realize that it is, literally, *man-made* until that fact is forced upon us.

This analogy plays on another one of my own nonprivileged attributes, not my femaleness this time, but my shortness. (I am only 4'9" tall.) Imagine, if you will, a whole community of short people just like me. Given the argument sometimes made in our society that short people are unable to be firefighters because they are neither tall enough or strong enough to do the job, the question arises: Would all the houses in the community eventually burn down? Well, yes, if we short people had to use the heavy ladders and hoses designed by and for tall people. But, no, if we (being as smart as short people are) could instead construct lighter ladders and hoses usable by both tall and short people. The moral here should be obvious. It isn't short biology that's the problem; it's short biology being forced to function in a tall-centered social structure.

It should be clear that there are two related morals in both this final story and this whole lecture. The first moral is that as important as the biological difference between the sexes may appear on the surface, the impact of that biological difference depends in every single instance on the environment in which it is situated. This interaction of biology and the situational context can be liberating, as in the case of antibiotics, refrigeration, airplanes, and baby formula. This interaction can also be discriminating, as in the case of women being disadvantaged—and men being advantaged—by a male-centered social structure.

The second moral is that as familiar, comfortable, gender-neutral, and natural as our own culture's institutions may appear to be now that explicit discrimination against women has finally been made illegal, in fact, our institutions are so thoroughly saturated with androcentrism that even those that do not discriminate against women explicitly—like the definition of self-defense—must be treated as inherently suspect.

*R*EFERENCES

ALDA, A. (1975, October). What every woman should know about men. *Ms.,* pp. 15–16.

BEAUVOIR, S. DE. (1952). *The second sex.* New York: Knopf.

BEM, S. L. (1993). *The lenses of gender: Transforming the debate on sexual inequality.* New Haven, CT: Yale University Press.

BENBOW, C. P. (1988). Sex differences in mathematical reasoning ability in intellectually talented preadolescents: Their nature, effects, and possible causes. *Behavioral and Brain Sciences, 11,* 169–232.

FREUD, S. (1925/1959). Some psychological consequences of the anatomical distinction between the sexes. In E. Jones (Ed.), *Sigmund Freud: Collected papers* (vol. 5, pp. 186–197). New York: Basic Books.

GILMAN, C. P. (1911/1971). *The man-made world; or, Our androcentric culture.* New York: Johnson Reprint.

JORDANOVA, L. (1989). *Sexual visions: Images of gender in science and medicine between the eighteenth and twentieth centuries.* Madison, WI: University of Wisconsin Press.

LINDGREN, J. R., & TAUB, N. (1988). *The law of sex discrimination.* St. Paul, MN: West.

MACKINNON, C. A. (1987). Difference and dominance: On sex discrimination (1984). In C. A. MacKinnon (Ed.), *Feminism unmodified: Discourses of life and law* (pp. 32–45). Cambridge, MA: Harvard University Press.

ROSSI, A. S. (1985). Gender and parenthood. In A. S. Rossi (Ed.), *Gender and the life course* (pp. 161–191). New York: Aldine.

RUSSETT, C. E. *(1989). Sexual science: The Victorian construction of womanhood.* Cambridge, MA: Harvard University Press.

SAYERS, J. (1982). *Biological politics: Feminist and anti-feminist perspectives.* New York: Tavistock.

SHIELDS, S. A. (1975a). Functionalism, Darwinism, and the psychology of women. *American Psychologist, 30,* 739–754.

SHIELDS, S. A. (1975b). Ms. Pilgrim's Progress: The contributions of Leta Setter Hollingworth to the psychology of women. *American Psychologist, 30,* 852–857.

*S*UGGESTED READINGS

BEM, S. L. (1993). *The lenses of gender: Transforming the debate on sexual inequality.* New Haven, CT: Yale University Press.

BEM, S. L. (1994, August 17). In a male-centered world, female differences are transformed into female disadvantages. *Chronicle of Higher Education,* pp. B1–B3.

MACKINNON, C. A. (1987). *Feminism unmodified: Discourses on life and law.* Cambridge, MA: Harvard University Press.

TAVRIS, C. (1992). *The mismeasure of woman.* New York: Simon & Schuster.

*R*UTH S. OSTENSON *is Assistant Professor of Psychology at Worcester State College. Ms. Ostenson has taught psychology of women at Worcester and at Roxbury Community College since 1985. She draws on her own life experiences as she writes about oppression and other topics.*

2

Who's In and Who's Out:

The Results of Oppression

❖

*J*ohn Smith, age 40, white, happily married, with two kids, church-going (Christian), physically fit, good-looking, financially well off, . . . Who is this person? This is the most privileged member of our society, the individual who has power and advantages as a member of eight different dominant groups.

If we examine the constructs of modern American society, there are clear divisions between dominants and subordinates (Miller, 1986). Various groups have been viewed *historically* as unequal through the accident of birth: In other words, you are defined by the situation into which you are born. For example, were you born female or male? What is your racial or ethnic identification? Were you born into an economically impoverished environment, or were you born into an upperclass and privileged environment? Were you born physically challenged or physically able? In some cases these divisions may not be entirely permanent. That is, you may attempt to change class membership, or at least economic level; you may choose to change religious affiliation; your physical ableness may actually be temporary; and so on.

According to Miller (1986) the dominants (those in power) label their subordinates as substandard, defective, and inferior. The preferred roles in the culture are reserved for the dominants, and they define the acceptable roles for the subordinates—for example, providing the services that dominants do not want to perform. In addition, the dominants determine the philosophy, values, and morality of the society (Miller, 1986).

It is possible then, to identify specific areas of oppression in our society, where the dominant groups clearly have the power and the subordinate groups have been mistreated. Traditionally, subordination has served as the basis of oppres-

TABLE 1

Components of Oppression

Dominant Group	Subordinate Group	Oppression
Males	Females	Sexism
Whites	People of color	Racism
Early and middle adulthood (i.e., "youthful" adults)	Children and elderly	Ageism
Heterosexuals	Lesbians, gay men, bisexuals, transsexuals, etc.	Heterosexism
Monied/upper class	Poor/working class	Classism
Able-bodied	Disabled	Ableism
Christian	Jewish	Anti-Semitism
"Physically attractive" (as defined by society's ideals)	Very tall, very short, very thin, fat, etc.	Sizism/Looksism

Note: This is an imperfect list. You may care to make additions—political affiliation, individuals labeled mentally ill, etc.

sion. These areas are sexism, racism, ageism, heterosexism, classism, ableism, anti-Semitism, and very possibly an eighth, sizism or looksism. (See Table 1.)

Divisions are often blurred because a person's group membership may be mixed: for example, an African American working-class male or a white disabled lesbian. Being a subordinate in some areas may help to raise consciousness in areas where one is a dominant. It seems, however, that the individuals most resistant to change are those who are dominants on several fronts—like John Smith, mentioned at the opening of this lecture.

When considering the common elements of subordination, it is important to remember that the experiences of individuals are unique and that groups and their members differ tremendously one from another. The purpose here is not to imply that the experiences of all subordinates are the same, but simply to identify some of the commonalities across a broad continuum of experiences. Ideally, a better understanding of any one of the "isms" can be derived by considering it in the context of other areas of oppression.

DEFINING OPPRESSION

Traditional definitions of any oppression include both prejudice and discrimination. Generally a dominant individual or group expresses prejudice and discrimination toward a subordinate individual based on group membership or toward a subordinate group in general. Prejudice is defined as an unfairly negative *attitude* toward members of a particular group. (The root of the word actually means "to prejudge.") Discrimination, on the other hand, refers to a biased *action* toward members of a particular group. In an analysis of dominants and subordinates, I think it is important to include the issue of power because dominants generally have power over subordinates. Therefore, a preferred definition of any "ism" might be prejudice + discrimination + power. Consequently it is difficult for any member of any subordinate group to truly demonstrate any "ism" because subordinates are not in powerful positions. A subordinate could clearly be prejudiced (that is, possess a negative attitude toward a member of the dominant group) but would find it difficult to truly discriminate because the individual is not usually in a position of political, social, or economic power and therefore is not able to systematically engage in a biased action toward a dominant. For example, some believe that it is not possible for a person of color in the United States to be truly racist toward a white person. An individual of color may possess some biased attitudes but, not being in a privileged position in society, he or she cannot discriminate against a white person.

When considering the definitions of oppression, the distinction between individuals and institutions should be noted. A dominant individual may display prejudicial attitudes and discriminatory behavior toward a subordinate individual. Thus we have individual cases of racism, ageism, heterosexism, etc. On the other hand, an institution such as a university, corporation, government agency, or organization may enforce a particular practice or policy that is prejudicial and discriminatory. We have many examples of institutional racism, sexism, etc. The policy may or may not have been intended to be prejudicial and discriminatory; nevertheless, the effect is to restrict the opportunities of subordinates, with harmful consequences. For example, a corporation may hire only college graduates even though a B.A. is not entirely necessary for the job. People of color may have had fewer opportunities to acquire a college education. As a result this company policy decreases the job opportunities for people of color. This is an example of institutional racism.

*H*OSTILITY

The power imbalance between dominants and subordinates may help to explain what Pharr (1988) labels "horizontal hostility." It is common for members of a subordinate group to express hostility in a horizontal direction—toward one's own kind. Clearly, this is safer than expressing hostility toward the oppressor. Consequently, there may be a fair amount of infighting among members of a subordinate group. Says Pharr (1988), "We may see people destroying their own neighborhoods, displaying violence and crime toward their own people, or in groups showing distrust of their own kind, while respecting the power of those that make up the norm" (p. 61).

The perception of vertical hostility is another factor that contributes to oppression. Dominants may believe that they are subject to hostility from those with lower status (subordinates), and the strength of this belief can interfere with their ability to learn about oppression. For example, men may fear false accusations of date rape or sexual harassment from women, and whites may fear hostility from Blacks in the form of crime or verbal attacks. These perceived fears then get in the way of examining one's dominant status. Prominent media coverage of the exceptions tends to perpetuate these misconceptions. For example, the media may focus on the rare case of a false accusation of rape or the uncommon occurrence of Black-on-white violence (most crime occurs within—not between—races).

*P*RIVILEGE

In each area of oppression, the dominant group carries with it certain rights and privileges that are not necessarily available to subordinates. We can talk about male privilege, white privilege, youth privilege, heterosexual privilege, class privilege, able-bodied privilege, Christian privilege, and the privileges that go along with being physically attractive in our society.

These privileges consist of automatic assumptions that the dominant groups generally do not recognize. Obviously, it is easier to identify the privileges of those in power when you are out of power and do not have access to the same privileges. In general, most dominants are unaware of these rights and, in fact, are not particularly interested in becoming conscious of their privilege. As McIntosh (1991) points out, whites are taught not to recognize their privilege; they are meant to be unaware of it. Let's assume, for example, that you are having a problem in a department store and ask to speak to "the person in charge." Most likely this person will not be fat, extremely short, a person of color, disabled, very old or very young, obviously homosexual, etc.—the specific oppressions in operation vary from situation to situation. However, this is just one small example that illustrates the kind of assumptions we make without question. Clearly, there are invisible entitlements at work here.

Let us consider another example. Many heterosexuals do not understand and appreciate the many privileges that go along with being heterosexual. Such entitlements and assumptions include the legal and social benefits of marriage—public acknowledgement of one's union and the accompanying gifts and celebration, the right of the spouse to health care and inheritance, and so on. There are other automatic rights as well: being able to be affectionate in public without fear of harassment, an unquestioned right to have and raise children. We are starting to see changes in some of these areas, but these heterosexual privileges have been rooted in our society for centuries.

SELF-HATRED

One of the most damaging effects of being a member of a subordinate group is self-hatred. It is not unusual for a subordinate at times to feel depressed, to experience despair, and to consider suicide. This is often the result of the internalization of the dominant group's beliefs that those who are subordinates are substandard, defective, and inferior. There are numerous examples of this: The rate of depression of women is two to three times that of men (Matlin, 1993); lesbians and gay men are at greater risk for suicide than heterosexual women and men (Rofes, 1983); many older people experience a sense of despair when they grow old and are no longer considered valued members of society. It is no wonder, then, that movements for social change focus on increased self-esteem and belief in oneself. This is the basis for slogans such as Black is Beautiful and Gay Pride.

PASSING

In our society, there is tremendous pressure on members of minority groups to assimilate, "to drop one's own culture and differences and become a mirror of the dominant culture. This process requires turning one's back on one's past and one's people" (Pharr, 1988, p. 62).

The pressure to assimilate may lead to a member of a subordinate group "passing" as a member of the dominant group. The term "passing" originally referred to "invisible blackness"—the ability of some light-skinned Blacks to assume new identities as white people and gain acceptance in a white world. This was most common between 1880 and 1925 (Williamson, 1980). Although it is not generally viewed as such, I am suggesting that some form of passing takes place in every area of oppression among members of a subordinate group. It may be something as simple as a single act, which is quite temporary, or it may involve a complete change of identity, which has far-reaching consequences.

Passing may also be symbolic; that is, the subordinate group member tries to adopt or be accepted as having the same qualities, values, or personality characteristics as the dominant group. This is commonly labeled "identification with the oppressor" or "imitation of the dominants." An example of this is the Queen Bee syndrome (Matlin, 1987). A Queen Bee is a woman who has achieved considerable success in a male-dominated profession and does not support other women. She has, in essence, become "one of the boys" and has adopted the prevailing male standards for success. She believes, however, that she has reached her success entirely on her own without assistance from other women or the women's movement. She may even deny the existence of sexism in any appreciable way, as she believes that she has never experienced it personally. She is unaware or unwilling to accept the suggestion that the feminist movement may have at least helped her indirectly by paving the way for her success. (Does anyone ever really make it entirely on her own?)

Passing is often the result of deliberate effort on the part of a subordinate who wants to be assumed to be a dominant. It may also be inadvertent in the sense that others simply make assumptions based on general appearances without any effort put forth directly by the subordinate. The issue of passing seems to be more prevalent in the early stages of a social movement and seems to be a result of internalized oppression. It is not pathological. It is often a healthy response to a sick situation or, at least, a survival technique in a situation perceived to be dangerous. Unless it is temporary, passing is in some sense a denial of who one is and, consequently, is damaging to one's self-esteem. The emotional costs may be heavy. As a movement gains more rights and protections, and individuals can safely take more pride in their identities, the incidence of passing seems to be less common.

Because passing is often not emphasized when dealing with the issues of subordination, I have included examples for the eight areas of oppression cited previously. These various examples should underscore the importance of this phenomenon.

There are many cases in which women have assumed a male identity in order to gain acceptance. George Eliot, an English novelist (1819–1880), was born Mary Ann Evans. She was aware of the difficulties women authors encountered in publishing, so she chose to write under a man's name (Moffat & Painter, 1974). Judith Leyster (1609–1660) was a prolific Dutch painter who is now considered to have achieved great excellence. From her death until 1893, however, her work was either ignored or credited to a male painter, Frans Hals (Hofrichter, 1993). Roberta Gibb Bingay, the first woman who tried to run the Boston Marathon in 1966, was officially rejected as an entrant, so she hid in the bushes at the start of the marathon and waited until about half of the runners had passed before entering the race. To disguise her sex, she wore a hooded blue sweatshirt at the start. In 1967, Kathrine Switzer officially entered the race by disguising her name. She entered as K. Switzer and, although unknown to the officials, she was the first woman to be issued an official number in the Boston Marathon (Hosler, 1980).

In the case of people of color, there are many examples of individuals of mixed ancestry who were able to pass as white. Sometimes this involved a deliberate effort on the part of the individual as a survival strategy. "Light mulattoes would simply drop out of sight, move to an area where they were not known, usually north or west, and allow their new neighbors to take them as white" (Williamson, 1980, p. 100). In other cases, people simply made assumptions about the light-skinned individuals who "were often *de facto* white from silence" (Williamson, 1980, p. 101). This is a phenomenon that has affected many ethnic groups. A former student of mine who is Cuban told me that her family had changed their last name after immigrating to this country so as not to appear to be Cuban. She and her family easily assimilated. Increasingly, Asian American teenage girls are having plastic surgery done on their eyes so as to more closely resemble the "white girls."

Women, especially in our society, are encouraged to look younger than their age and never to talk about how old they are. The idea here, of course, is to pass as younger than you are. In the United States profitable industries promote products with "youthful" images in mind—cosmetics, hair products that cover up gray, diet products, and so forth. In addition, plastic surgery is becoming more commonplace, especially face-lifts and tummy tucks. A friend of mine recently showed me an advertisement she received in the mail from an organization called Prevention. The cover of the envelope states, "Old Age Isn't Natural" and goes on to mention ways to reverse the aging process. People often tell me that I look "young for my age." Although this is meant as a compliment, I do not consider it as such. To me it is a denial of who I am. It does not acknowledge my full range of life experience and maturity and, as a 50-year-old woman, I do not care to pass as someone I am not.

With respect to heterosexism, the issue of passing seems to be a daily occurrence. Because lesbians, gay men, and bisexuals have no identifying physical characteristics, there is no way to make this distinction without a verbal acknowledgement. Many heterosexuals seem to be unaware of or simply to ignore the statistic that 10 percent of the population is gay. By this calculation, in a class of 40 students, there will be an average of 4 gay people present. I have been present at many gatherings where it is simply assumed that everyone present is heterosexual. Gay people may intentionally pass by wearing mainstream clothes and keeping silent about their personal lives in order to gain social acceptance and compensate for feeling like an outsider. In some cases, it may be viewed as a necessary survival strategy. It is not unusual for many gay and bisexual professionals to appear to be straight during the workday and to assume their gay and bisexual identities once they arrive home. Thus we have part-time passing on a continual basis.

In the case of classism, there is tremendous pressure in our society to "keep up with the Joneses," to buy the latest technology or gadget, and to live beyond one's means—in other words, to pass as being more wealthy than we are. The easy availability of credit cards contributes to this phenomenon. Many individuals who are continually in debt are eventually forced into bankruptcy. There are other examples of passing that are more related to status, such as those individuals who try to appear to be monied or belonging to an upper class through dress style, language used, mannerisms, driving the "right automobile," being seen in the "right places," living in a "desirable" neighborhood, and so on.

With respect to ableism, able-bodied individuals have historically simply ignored or overlooked those with disabilities. There is tremendous pressure on individuals with disabilities to pass whenever physically possible as not disabled. A deaf student whom I know was forbidden by her parents to learn sign language. Her parents also refused to learn sign language. She was deaf from birth but through extensive speech therapy acquired some language skills. She also communicated with written notes.

According to the young woman, the family did not want to draw attention to themselves and appear to be "different," and as a result she had to rely on lip-reading. This presented a conflict for her, especially when she got involved with a young man who was fluent in American Sign Language (ASL). Rather than allowing her to use all possible resources, her parents were limiting her in the hope that she would appear to be more "normal" and not disabled. Some individuals who experience hearing or sight loss refuse to wear hearing aids or glasses as long as they possibly can. Again, they are passing as being able-bodied.

Franklin D. Roosevelt (1882–1945), the thirty-second president of the United States, offers another example of passing. He was paralyzed by polio at the age of 40 and lost the use of his legs. Although he was usually confined to a wheelchair, he was rarely photographed in it. Roosevelt's disability was well hidden from the American public, and he often passed as being able-bodied.

During Hitler's regime, being able to pass as a gentile was the only hope for survival for many Jews. Many Jewish immigrants to this country had plastic surgery on their noses or changed their surnames. Again, this type of activity, although undertaken for protection and survival, is extremely damaging to one's sense of self because it involves a denial of one's heritage and ethnicity.

In the case of sizism/looksism, individuals who do not meet the physical ideals of our society suffer a great deal. There have been cases of job discrimination as well as personal rejections on many fronts. Overweight people are encouraged to dress in a way that disguises their true body shape (for example, vertical stripes and loose clothing) and to take advantage of liposuction and plastic surgery to change their body shape, breast size, or facial features. The idea here is to permanently alter one's body so as to pass as "physically attractive." In addition, we are encouraged to use a variety of cosmetics, hair dyes, and hair straighteners or permanents to achieve that impossible physical ideal.

*I*MPACT OF SUBORDINATION

The mistreatment and personal wounds of subordinates are quite evident. We as a society need to carefully examine how we deal with the issue of difference. Tavris (1992) points out that women are not the inferior sex, the superior sex, or the opposite sex. By the same token, no subordinate group is inferior, superior, or the opposite of a dominant group. As Miller (1986) suggests, the engagement of difference does not have to lead to difficulty and degradation. Differences are not deficiencies; diversity is not defectiveness. Someone who is different is not "more than" or "less than." We do not need to distrust or fear those who look or act differently from ourselves. A difference is simply a difference. Dealing with difference should be a source of growth. It provides us with the opportunity to interact with others unlike ourselves and to greatly enrich our experiences and our lives.

*R*EFERENCES

HOFRICHTER, F. F. (1993). *Judith Leyster: A Dutch master and her world.* Zwolle, Holland: Waanders Publishers.

HOSLER, R. (1980). The women of Boston. In R. Hosler (Ed.), *Boston: America's oldest marathon* (pp. 50–56). Mountain View, CA: Anderson World.

MATLIN, M. (1987). *The psychology of women.* New York: Holt, Rinehart & Winston.

MATLIN, M. (1993). *The psychology of women* (2d ed.). New York: Holt, Rinehart & Winston.

MCINTOSH, P. (1991, Summer). White privilege: Unpacking the invisible knapsack. *New England Women's Studies Association Newsletter,* pp. 1–5.

MILLER, J. B. (1986). *Toward a new psychology of women* (2d ed.). Boston: Beacon Press.

MOFFAT, M. J., & PAINTER, C. (1974). George Eliot (1819–1880). In M. J. Moffat & C. Painter (Eds.), *Revelations: Diaries of women* (pp. 218–224). New York: Random House.

PHARR, S. (1988). *Homophobia: A weapon of sexism.* Inverness, CA: Chardon Press.

ROFES, E. E. (1983). *"I thought people like that killed themselves": Lesbians, gay men, and suicide.* San Francisco: Grey Fox Press.

TAVRIS, C. (1992). *The mismeasure of woman.* New York: Simon & Schuster.

WILLIAMSON, J. (1980). *New people: Miscegenation and mulattoes in the United States.* New York: The Free Press.

*S*UGGESTED READINGS

MCINTOSH, P. (1991, Summer). White privilege: Unpacking the invisible knapsack. *New England Women's Studies Association Newsletter,* pp. 1–5.

MILLER, J. B. (1986). *Toward a new psychology of women* (2d ed.). Boston: Beacon Press.

MILLER, J. B. (1991). Women and power. In J. V. Jordan, A. G. Kaplan, J. B. Miller, I. P. Stiver, & J. L. Surrey (Eds.), *Women's growth in connection: Writings from the Stone Center.* New York: Guilford Press.

PHARR, S. (1988). *Homophobia: A weapon of sexism.* Inverness, CA: Chardon Press.

BERNICE LOTT *is Professor of Psychology and Women's Studies at the University of Rhode Island, where she has taught a course on the female experience since 1970. Dr. Lott served as President of the American Psychological Association's Division (35) on the Psychology of Women in 1991. She is the author of numerous theoretical and empirical articles and books on issues relevant to women.*

3

Global Connections:

The Significance of Women's Poverty

❖

Similarities among women across cultures can be found in the conditions of our lives. For contemporary women these conditions are situated within patriarchy and sexist institutions and include lesser power relative to men. Among the most devastating indexes of this lesser power is poverty. Examination of this issue, informed by my social-psychological and feminist perspectives, has led me to conclude that the poverty of a particular area is best represented by the economic status of women (and children) and that consideration of the conditions of women's lives is central to the solution of related overall problems. Any program designed to eradicate poverty or hunger must begin with attention to women's lives.

I first began to examine this particular global connection among women during the fall of 1992 when I was teaching a course on women and a course on poverty aboard a ship carrying 525 college students around the world—the University of Pittsburgh's Semester at Sea (SAS) program. In addition to the printed resources I consulted, I was also able to make firsthand observations and visit with informants in 13 countries: Canada, Japan, Taiwan, Hong Kong, China, Malaysia, India, Egypt, Israel, Turkey, Ukraine, Spain, and Venezuela. This examination led me to appreciate the importance of the relationship between the economic resources of a community, infant mortality, and women's literacy, health,

Work on this lecture was begun during the spring semester of 1993 while I was a visiting scholar at the Institute for Research on Women and Gender at Stanford University. Portions have been read at the symposium on Internationalizing the Teaching of Psychology/Sociology, presented at the Fifth International Interdisciplinary Congress on Women, University of Costa Rica, San José, February 26, 1993, and at the March 4, 1994, conference of the Association for Women in Psychology, Oakland, CA.

pregnancies, and work burdens of everyday life. You will find a list of suggested books and articles on these subjects at the end of this lecture.

My primary objective in teaching about poverty is to reduce the psychological distance beween "us" (the middle class and affluent) and "them" (the poor) by helping students understand that the psychological principles and social dynamics that influence attitudes, beliefs, and behaviors are essentially the same for all of us. One exercise I used to further this objective with my SAS students, which I urge you to try, was to ask them if they knew anyone they considered to be poor and, if so, to talk about that person's circumstances and behavior. Students who already identified with "them" and were from poor families were able to enrich the discussion by talking about themselves. Another exercise focused on descriptions of everyday life conditions for poor people. Try to imagine the day-to-day details of the physical and social environments of poor people in some specific place. Think about sounds and smells; about the presence and absence of material objects middle-class people take for granted; about meals eaten; about safety and dangers. Toward the end of the Semester at Sea voyage, I asked small groups of students to imagine themselves as part of a United Nations task force charged with developing a 10-point proposal to end hunger worldwide. Other groups were charged with the task of developing a 10-point plan to end poverty in the United States as part of a hypothetical presidential commission. Put yourself on one of these task forces and see what you come up with; ask a friend to join you.

My experience in classes where poverty is discussed or is the major subject matter is that there is typically great resistance by middle-class students to changing well-learned them-versus-us responses. I have found this to be the case regardless of whether the focus is on poor people in one's home communities or on poor people in foreign lands. Michael Katz (1989) has discussed this phenomenon by noting that those who are not poor identify those who are as "strange." And strangers, of course, remain on the outside. Katz cites Martha Minow, who sees this process as one of reification that defines the line between normality and deviance, ignores the perspective of the powerless, and accepts existing social and economic arrangements as natural. "When we identify one thing as unlike the others," says Minow, "we are dividing the world; we use our language to exclude, to distinguish—to discriminate" (p. 6).

For the most part, the SAS students, like others I have worked with, found it extremely difficult to project themselves into a life of poverty as one of "them." This was true of students who had worked in shelters for the homeless, who had worked among poor farmers or migrant workers in the United States, or who had visited Mother Teresa's clinics in India. Stereotypes about the poor were inevitably evoked in discussions of what students had seen in various ports. Blaming the victim and negative attributions about poor people's character, goals, and behavior were common responses. "If only they would stop having so many children, encourage their kids to go to school, buy more nutritious food," and so on and so on. Regardless of the setting, the students typically saw poverty through their own middle-class eyes. Such eyes, as noted by Michael Katz (1989), view poverty as "a matter of personal responsibility" that could be alleviated by "the acquisition of skills, commitment to the work ethic, or the practice of chastity" (p. 7). Poverty as a social phenomenon primarily related to the distribution of resources or access to them (namely, power) is a discourse or theme that is not expressed readily or with conviction.

It is difficult for middle-class students to understand that poverty is much more than a "personal problem" that can be solved by improving attitudes or motivations or "shaping up." Poverty and hunger are the direct results of social, economic, and political problems that can only be solved by changes in social, economic, and political conditions. That the personal and political are inevitably linked is a primary tenet of feminist analysis in all areas of scholarship and practice. Although this perspective has guided research and application in many areas, even feminist psychologists have tended to ignore poor women. Attention to the lives of poor women and to the ways in which these lives are influenced by structural factors is rare (see, for example Reid, 1993).

The difficulty middle-class students (and others) have in taking the perspective of poor people can be seen in the class discussions or essays about begging by the SAS students who encountered it often in many, many places around the world. The focus of the students' comments was invariably on how it felt to be approached by a beggar; the shame, rage, annoyance, or distrust elicited by the beggar's behavior; and whether or not one should "give." No student ever spontaneously considered begging from the perspective of the beggar, or seemed to find it easy to accept such a perspective either intellectually or affectively. What might the beggar be feeling or thinking? Suppose the beggar is a woman with small children, an often-encountered sight in India and Malaysia, for example? What if we shift our focus to a panhandler in New York City or Chicago or San Francisco?

Because the major brunt of poverty in every country and region of the world is borne by women and children, the problems that arise in teaching about poverty are of clear significance to teaching about women, whether one's primary focus is on women in the United States or on women globally. Few would question the conclusion reached by most experts, and noted by Joni Seager and Ann Olson (1986), that "women everywhere have a smaller share of the pie; if the pie is very small, . . . women's share is smaller still" (p. 7).

Although women around the globe constitute 50 percent of the adult population and one-third of the official work force, and grow 50 percent of the world's food, they own only 1 percent of the world's property and earn only 10 percent of the world's income (*Women Ending Hunger*, no date). Women also comprise two-thirds of the 960 million people who are illiterate (AP/UN report, 1994). The typical woman in India, for example, who represents 75 percent of all women in that country, lives in a village on 1 acre of family land or works for a big farmer. She is illiterate and works in the fields, harvesting, planting, and weeding for half the wages paid to a man for the same work. Elizabeth Bumiller (1990) has described the daily activities of this woman: to make chapati (the traditional flat-bread) she must walk several miles by foot for water; she must harvest her own wheat (using a scythe) and grind it by hand; she must collect fire-wood or make cow-dung cakes for cooking, and feed the cow by collect-ing grasses; she cooks over a small mud stove built into the dirt floor of her hut while breast-feeding one child and watching three others; if the tasks are not done to her husband's liking, he may beat her.

Examples of the smallness of women's share of the pie come from all parts of the world. In the multinational businesses in Malaysia where workers assemble tiny electronic parts and work long hours for low pay under strict regulations and surveillance, 80 percent of the workers are women. Many of the single women, who constitute a ready supply of cheap, expendable labor, live in factory-run hostels where they share beds with others who are on different shifts. Similarly, in the free-trade zones along the U.S.-Mexican border, close to 70 percent of those who work in the U.S.-owned factories (*maquiladoras*) are women. Many work the equiv-alent of double shifts and also care for husbands and children. According to Elizabeth Kadetsky (1994),

> Families can afford no better than shanties, usually with no heat, electricity or running water; clean water must be bought from unreliable trucks that sell it for prices so high that many choose to bathe in the canals, where the sewage and factory runoff flow freely. In company-owned barracks, young single workers—often a hundred women—will share one double-burner hot plate for cooking. (p. 12)

There is no shortage of examples of women's unequal access to eco-nomic resources in all parts of the world. In May 1993 there was a fire at Kader Industrial Company outside of Bangkok, Thailand. It was con-sidered to be the world's worst factory fire; 200 workers died and an-other 500 were injured, almost all of them women. These women earned less than $4 a day making stuffed toys for export to major U.S. compa-nies in a factory that kept its doors locked from the outside and that had no fire alarms or fire escapes ("Thailand," 1993). In post-Commu-nist Russia it is women who are suffering the most severe economic and personal hardships as the country goes through the painful transition to a market economy. In contrast to 1990 when they comprised over half of the work force, women now constitute 70 percent of the unemployed ("Russia," 1993). One final example: Among the continuing number of refugees around the world, more than 80 percent are women and chil-dren. Marcia Ann Gillespie (1992) has written about the conditions of life in refugee camps.

TABLE 1

Comparison of Infant Mortality Rates and Women's Literacy Rates in Selected Countries

| | Infant Mortality Rate | Illiteracy among Women (%) | |
		Age 15–24	Age 25 and over
Japan	5	—	—
Canada	7	—	—
Hong Kong	8	—	—
Taiwan	9	N/A	N/A
United States	10	.6	3.1
Spain	10	1.0	12.3
Israel	12	.4	14.3
USSR (former)	24	—	—
Malaysia	24	16.8	62.2
China	32	17.9	62.3
Venezuela	36	6.3	22.9
Turkey	76	24.7	62.3
Egypt	85	61.9	84.7
India	99	59.7	80.6

Note: All data are the latest available. The most recent data show a drop in the IMR for the United States, to 8.3 in 1993 ("Infant mortality rate drops," 1994).
Source: For Taiwan, see *The Hunger Project* (1985). All other data are from *The World's Women 1970–1990* (1991).

> [They] are usually situated by the host country in bleak, sparsely populated areas close to the border. . . . The newer the camp, the harsher the conditions. Sanitation facilities are often minimal; the stench from latrines and open refuse trenches pollute the air. . . . Many [refugees] arrive in advanced stages of starvation. . . . One study . . . indicated that the nutritional value of refugee rations is less than what dogs are fed in the industrialized world. (p. 20)

One of the most widely accepted measures of poverty (or hunger) used by international agencies is the infant mortality rate—the number of children who die before their first birthday per 1,000 who are born alive. That infant mortality is intimately connected to the living conditions of mothers, to their health, prenatal care, diet, and work burdens is obvious. The physical status of women becomes a key to the analysis of poverty. What is less often considered is the relationship between poverty or hunger and another index of women's situation, the extent to which they can read and write their native language, that is, their rate of literacy. Table 1 presents a list of the countries I visited in the fall of 1992, ranked by infant mortality and women's illiteracy rates. Although the relationship between these two factors is not perfect, it is clear that they show the same pattern. Relatively affluent countries are low in both, whereas poor countries are high in both. Here, then, is another marker of poverty that is situated in the condition of women's lives. It is instructive and depressing to note the high infant mortality rate in some U.S. cities. In 1990 this rate was 20 percent in Washington, D.C., the highest in the country ("D.C. rates highest," 1993).

That direct attention to women's lives is essential in order to reduce or abolish hunger and poverty is a conclusion supported by the following compelling analysis by James P. Grant of UNICEF in his discussion of developing countries.

> A cat's cradle of... synergisms links almost every aspect of development: female literacy catalyzes family planning programmes; less frequent pregnancies improve maternal and child health; improved health makes the most of preschool or primary education; education can increase incomes; ... better incomes or better food reduces infant mortality; fewer child deaths tend to lead to fewer births; smaller families improve maternal health; healthy mothers have healthier babies; healthier babies demand more attention; stimulation helps mental growth; more alert children do better at school ... and so it goes in an endless pattern of mutually reinforcing or mutually retarding relationships. (*The Hunger Project*, 1985, p. 386)

This analysis begins with women's literacy and places women's health at the center of the process required to eliminate poverty and related social problems. A similar analysis, presented in the UN publication *The World's Women* (1991, p. 57), begins with women's state of nourishment. "Malnourished women are sick more, have smaller babies and die earlier. And where infant and child mortality is high, birth rates are also high—increasing the stress on women's bodies and trapping them and their children in a cycle of poor health and nutrition." So women's poor health and nutrition are direct consequences of poverty and contribute to the cycle of its maintenance.

Policymakers in the Clinton administration seem more aware than those in previous administrations of the relationship between the conditions of women's lives and social and economic change. A recent story in *The New York Times* (Greenhouse, 1994) notes that "the emerging policy ... emphasizes not only family planning but also education for women, which by boosting their living standards and independence ultimately increases their power to decide how many children they will bear" (p. 9). Colombia is cited as an example. Colombian women with no education have, on average, 5.4 children, whereas women with some primary schooling have 4.0 children and women who have completed secondary school have 3.2 children. Similarly, in the Indian state of Kerala, which boasts the highest living standard and the lowest birthrate in the country, the women have the highest level of education and the highest rate of literacy. In contrast to India's overall average birthrate of 3.7 in a woman's lifetime, the birthrate in Kerala is 2.0 (Eshoo, 1995).

Those concerned with world population issues now appear to be looking beyond their earlier focus on family planning intervention programs and recognizing the centrality of women. As noted recently by John Bongaarts (1994, p. 774) of the Population Council,

> Improvement in the economic, social, and legal status of women can reduce desired fertility . . . by making nonmaternal roles more important . . . [and by] increas[ing] the willingness of women to make independent reproductive decisions. . . . Empowering women is also likely to lead to reductions in the dominance of husbands, . . . [and] the societal preference for male offspring.

This position received overwhelming support at the August 1994 UN Population Conference held in Cairo. The official draft of proposals submitted to the conference by the UN Population Fund included more than 70 percent of the suggestions that had been offered by the Women's Environment and Development Organization, cofounded by Bella Abzug. These suggestions included giving women

> Equal rights in policy and decision making, expanding the perception of women beyond childbearing and caretaking, eliminating violence against women and insuring women's ability to control their own fertility. ("Keeping alive Cairo goals," 1994, p. 4)

As noted by Hugh O'Haire, a spokesman for the UN Population Fund, "They brought the feminist perspective to prominence and they prevailed" ("Keeping alive Cairo goals," 1994, p. 4). The Cairo conference ended with agreement that the key to population control is the empowerment of women and girls through improved education, health care, and economic status. "Even a little education for women," asserted Timothy Wirth, the U.S. undersecretary of state for global affairs, "pays dividends in every recognized index of social progress and development" ("Aim of conference," 1994, p. A9).

In conclusion, wherever we look, the conditions of women's lives provide primary markers of poverty and hunger. This lecture has focused on places outside the United States, but unfortunately, illustrations could easily have come from within our own country. The relationship between the health and literacy of women and the general economic health of their geographic areas is clear to those who have gathered the relevant data and studied their significance. Policymakers have begun to understand that hunger and poverty cannot be ended by attending primarily to the experiences and needs of men, as has been the case in the past. Viewing men as central to economic and social development ignores women's roles all over the world as producers of wealth through their labor; it also ignores women's key position as childbearers and mothers, a position intimately related to the availability of life-sustaining and life-enhancing resources. Family planners are beginning to appreciate that smaller families are more likely to follow naturally from a program of education for women than from repressive and culturally insensitive technologically based birth control programs. Literate women are empowered women who can make choices about lifestyles, press forward for a more equal share of family and community resources, have fewer and better-educated children, be healthier themselves, and play a larger role in social and political decision making. Knowledge of these relationships enriches our study of women and helps us to understand the varied meanings of global sisterhood.

REFERENCES

Aim of conference: Better lives for women. (1994, September 6). *Providence Journal-Bulletin*, p. A9.

AP/UN REPORT. (1994, August 18). Fast facts. *Providence Journal-Bulletin*, p. A13.

BONGAARTS, J. (1994). Population policy options in the developing world. *Science, 263*, 771–776.

BUMILLER, E. (1990). *May you be the mother of a hundred sons.* New York: Fawcett Columbine.

D.C. rates highest in infant mortality. (1993, January 8). *Providence Journal-Bulletin*, p. A5.

ESHOO, A. (1995, January). Consensus in Cairo. *National NOW Times*, p. 11.

GILLESPIE, M. A. (1992, November/December). No woman's land. *Ms.*, pp. 18–22.

GREENHOUSE, S. (1994, January 23). U.S. to spend more on birth control. *The New York Times*, p. 9.

Infant mortality drops in U.S., government reports. (1994, December 9). *Providence Journal-Bulletin*.

KADETSKY, E. (1994, January/February). The human cost of free trade. *Ms.*, pp. 11–15.

KATZ, M. B. (1989). *The undeserving poor.* New York: Pantheon.

Keeping alive Cairo goals for women. (1994, September 25). *The New York Times*, p. 4.

REID, P. T. (1993). Poor women in psychological research: Shut up and shut out. *Psychology of Women Quarterly, 17*, 133–150.

Russia (1993, May/June). *Ms.*, p. 10.

SEAGER, J., & OLSON, A. (1986). *Women in the world: An international atlas.* New York: Touchstone.

Thailand (1993, July/August). *Ms.*, p. 15.

THE HUNGER PROJECT. (1985). *Ending hunger.* New York: Praeger.

The world's women 1970–1990. (1991). New York: United Nations.

The Hunger Project. Women ending hunger. (no date). San Francisco: Author.

SUGGESTED READINGS

ACOSTA-BELEN, E., & BOSE, C. E. (Eds.) (1990). Women and development in the third world [Special issue]. *Gender & Society, 4*(3).

BENERIA, L., & FELDMAN, S. (Eds.). (1992). *Unequal burden.* Boulder, CO: Westview Press.

KOBLINSKY, M., TIMYAN, J., & GAY, J. (1993). *The health of women: A global perspective.* Boulder, CO: Westview Press.

UNICEF. (1991). *The state of the world's children: 1991.* New York: Oxford University Press.

*A*LICE **H.** E*AGLY* is Professor of Psychology and Women's Studies at Purdue University. Dr. Eagly has taught courses on the psychology of women since the mid-1970s at Purdue, the University of Massachusetts, and the University of Tuebingen (Germany). She has published extensively on attitudes, gender stereotypes, and sex-related differences in social behavior.

4

Gender and Altruism

———— ❖ ————

Does gender influence how helpful people are to one another? The issue I will consider here is the extent to which women and men are different or similar in their tendencies to help others and, more generally, to behave in ways that would be considered altruistic. I hope to convince you that there is no such thing as a sex that is helpful or altruistic. Rather, there are circumstances under which women tend to be more helpful than men and circumstances under which men tend to be more helpful than women. Gender is very important in relation to altruism, but its impact depends on the context and the particular type of altruistic behavior that we examine.

*W*HAT IS ALTRUISM?

Psychologists generally define altruism as behavior that is intended to help or benefit other people. To be considered truly altruistic, this behavior should be performed voluntarily and not be coerced or induced by some external pressure. For example, if you mow your neighbor's lawn and are adequately paid for this service, you would not be altruistic. Also, to be considered altruistic, the helpful act should be performed as an end in itself and not as a means to fulfilling an ulterior personal motive. For example, if you help someone prepare for a math exam only because you want this person to feel obligated to help you write a history paper, your behavior would not be considered altruistic (but expedient or perhaps even manipulative). If you instead help this person merely because you want to be helpful or believe that helping is the "right thing to do," you would be considered genuinely altruistic. Not surprisingly, this definition of altruism contrasts sharply with psychologists' definitions of aggression. Whereas altruism is behavior intended to *help* others, aggression is behavior intended to *harm* others. Altruism and aggression are thus opposites—the good and the bad of interpersonal behavior.

Some psychologists have questioned whether behavior is ever *truly* altruistic if we take seriously the idea that altruistic acts do not fulfill some personal goal of the altruistic person. After all, helpful behavior that does not provide any obvious extrinsic (or external) gain for the helper can provide some intrinsic (or internal) gain. People may feel good or moral when they are helpful and feel bad or guilty when they fail to help. To the extent that people have internalized moral rules about appropriate behavior, they can give themselves internal psychological rewards for conforming to these rules and punishments for deviating from them. Some psychologists maintain that people behave altruistically *in order to* feel good and moral (or avoid feeling bad and guilty) and thus are actually behaving egoistically when they seem to be behaving altruistically. In contrast, other psychologists argue that people can be genuinely altruistic because, at least sometimes, feeling good about oneself is only a by-product of altruistic acts that are intended only to be helpful to others. I will not attempt to resolve this fundamental philosophical and psychological issue but suggest that we consider as altruistic any helpful behaviors that are not coerced or intended to obtain some external reward or avoid some external punishment.

GENDER ROLES' MESSAGES ABOUT ALTRUISM

To understand whether and how altruistic behavior may be shaped by gender in Western society, we need to consider the messages about helping and altruism that are embedded in gender roles. Both the female gender role and the male gender role have the potential to foster altruistic behavior.

Female Gender Role

I will first consider the female gender role because its implications for helpful behavior are probably somewhat more obvious than those of the male gender role. Think for a moment about the female gender role—that is, about society's rules about how to be a good and admirable woman. Do these rules encompass a demand to behave altruistically? Certainly they do—women are expected to be kind, nurturant, compassionate, and caring. Selfishness and lack of compassion are considered serious deficiencies in the character of women. Many social scientists and feminist writers have argued that women are expected to place the needs of others, especially those of family members, before their own. These obligations include caring for the emotional needs of others—being a dedicated listener who bolsters others' morale and sympathizes with their troubles.

These burdens may also include delivering routine forms of personal service, such as doing favors and running errands. More generally, the female role includes the demand to facilitate the progress of other people toward their goals, especially the progress of friends, intimates, and family members.

There is an abundance of empirical evidence that women are expected to be caring and compassionate. In particular, studies of gender stereotypes have shown that women are rated as more helpful than men and also as kinder, more compassionate, and more able to devote themselves to others. This aspect of the female stereotype is prescriptive, as shown by the fact that kind and compassionate personality attributes are rated as *desirable* in women and as more desirable in women than men. In general, people think about women as kind and compassionate and believe that it is a good thing for women to have these characteristics.

Male Gender Role

What about the male gender role? What are its messages about altruism? Although men do not have the burden of being kind, nurturant, and compassionate to the same extent that women do, they are expected to be altruistic in other ways. There are two altruistic themes that are particularly salient to the male gender role: I will refer to these themes as *heroism* and *chivalry.* There also seems to be a demand for men to be helpful in practical ways that involve fixing things and solving certain kinds of practical, technical problems.

Let us first consider heroism because it is a theme that Western culture has long incorporated into its images of ideal male behavior. The ideal man, as described in literature and myth, is very often the noble hero. The hero is someone who engages in the altruistic action of saving others from harm or of fighting for the general good; the hero performs these behaviors at some risk to himself of injury or death. The prototypical hero is the man who takes great risks in battle, especially if he is successful in reaching his objective or in saving others from harm. Although heroes are extremely important in warfare, peacetime offers some opportunities for heroism. Thus, a peacetime hero might rescue others in one of many types of life-threatening situations, such as an auto crash, a house or apartment fire, or a potential drowning.

Direct empirical evidence that men are expected to be heroic is not easy to find, probably because opportunities to be heroic are rare in most people's lives. Most of you will live your whole life without, for example, having an opportunity to rescue someone from a car crash or carry someone from a burning building. Because heroism is by definition unusual behavior carried out in an extreme situation, the term "heroic" does not appear to be stereotypic of men. However, research on gender stereotypes has found that male-stereotypic traits include certain tendencies that would provide a potential for heroic behavior. For example, willingness to take risks, adventurousness, calmness in a crisis, and ability to stand up well under pressure are characteristics that are ascribed to men more than women and are viewed as more desirable in men.

Now, to turn to the second of my two themes about masculine altruism, let us consider chivalry. The term "chivalry" may seem somewhat medieval—wasn't it knights in shining armor who were expected to be chivalrous? The Oxford English Dictionary (1971) defines chivalrous behavior as "characterized by pure and noble gallantry, honor, courtesy, and disinterested devotion to the cause of the weak or oppressed." This definition seems quite dated. The tradition of male chivalry had its origins in the chivalric code taken by medieval knights. These knights took oaths that included vows to protect the weak and defenseless, to respect the honor of women, to fight for the general welfare of all, to live for honor and glory, and so forth. The influence of this chivalric tradition on conceptions of ideal male behavior in Western society has been well documented by historians.

If rules of chivalrous conduct are to some extent alive and well in contemporary society, these rules should induce men to engage in certain specific types of helpful behavior. Particularly relevant to an analysis of gender is the stipulation in the chivalric code that men direct courteous and protective acts toward women because it was presumed that women were weak and defenseless and deserved protection. Of course, the knight in shining armor did not extend his protection to *all* women but to women (or "ladies") of his own social class.

In modern society, where might we observe social norms or conventions that obligate men to be especially protective and respectful of women? Consider commonplace rules about what behavior is polite or courteous. These rules have been written down in twentieth-century etiquette handbooks by such people as the redoubtable Emily Post and Amy Vanderbilt and the more contemporary Miss Manners (whose humorous column on etiquette is carried by many newspapers). These authors describe the sort of behavior that is considered good and proper in "polite society." In these books, you could read that a man is expected to open the car door for a woman, especially when on a date. Emily Post's 1984 statement on this practice is the following: "The custom of a man's opening the door and assisting a woman into a car is still correct—in fact some women feel slighted if the gesture is not made." Is the woman in this situation too weak to perform this action for herself? Well, not exactly. Instead, the man and woman are engaging in a stylized behavior that they probably consider "polite."

Consider too that rules of etiquette say that the man is supposed to walk on the outside of the sidewalk next to the street, ostensibly to protect his female companion from splashes or other dangers that might come from that direction. On this subject, Miss Manners (Martin, 1990) wrote: "When they are walking outdoors, American ladies take the side away from the street." A man is also supposed to help a woman put on her coat; he is supposed to open the doors of buildings for her, and even order for her in restaurants and pay for her meal. Traditionally, men stand up when a woman enters a room and stay standing until she sits down. A woman is not supposed to pour her own alcoholic drink when one or more men are present. On this subject, Miss Manners (Martin, 1990) wrote: "Ladies do not pour their own wine when gentlemen are present. They hold their empty wine glasses casually in front of their noses while staring fixedly at the nearest gentleman, who then falls all over himself to do it for them." Rules such as these have eroded considerably in modern society and were practiced much more fully by people who were higher in the social-class system.

Empirical evidence that these rules of chivalrous conduct are still intact to some extent can be found in a recent questionnaire study by Mary Harris (1992). In this study female and male university students reported on their experiences of giving and receiving courteous behaviors. Harris's findings confirmed that even now it is men rather than women who are expected to engage in at least certain courteous behaviors, particularly opening doors for another person and paying for someone (for example, for the person's meal).

Feminists have often criticized these chivalrous rules of polite conduct. The reasons for this disapproval may be fairly obvious to you. Such rules seem to imply that women are the weaker sex, the sex that needs protection and special favors. These behaviors place men in a more dominant and controlling role—as the person who opens doors, orders in restaurants, initiates dates, and so forth. Merely showing "good manners" in the traditional model may thus help preserve the imbalance of power and authority between the sexes and foster passivity in women.

Do you approve or disapprove of chivalrous courtesy? Although some women agree with feminist objections to chivalrous conduct, other women disagree. In fact, female students who have taken this course in the past have sometimes been very vocal in their support of men's chivalrous behavior. These women often argued that they prefer that men show good manners in these ways because they signify *respect* for a woman. The reasoning is that a man who opens doors, holds a woman's coat, and obeys the traditional rules of polite behavior displays that he is respectful of the women he accompanies. Moreover, many people maintain that these behaviors are merely polite and should be performed equally by both sexes. However, few women in fact hold coats for able-bodied men or open car doors for them.

The Harris questionnaire examined university students' agreement or disagreement with the feminist analysis. Harris found some tendency for these respondents to rate polite behaviors as condescending or patronizing, particularly one sequence of restaurant behavior, namely, having a companion ask you what you want to eat in a restaurant and then order-ing for you. Although regarding courteous behaviors as patronizing would be in keeping with the feminist analysis, Harris's research sug-gested that most students view most courteous behaviors as merely cour-teous and not as condescending or patronizing.

It is easy to get into arguments about chivalry because chivalrous be-havior conveys two kinds of meanings simultaneously: a superiority and dominance on the part of the person who behaves chivalrously and a true helpfulness and respect for the person the act is directed toward. This dual meaning makes many women ambivalent about chivalrous behav-ior. It is thus possible for a woman to both resent *and* appreciate chival-rous behaviors that are directed toward her. In addition, women may dis-approve of chivalry on the job, where gender is supposed to be irrelevent, yet approve of it on a date, where gender is more likely to be important. And many men are aware that women may have reservations about the desirability of these forms of etiquette; therefore, men sometimes express confusion about whether they should follow the traditional rules of polite behavior.

Predictions from Analysis of Gender Roles

Given our analysis of the rules that gender roles convey about altruistic behavior, what might a psychologist predict about sex-related differences in altruistic behavior? I doubt that anyone who thinks about the full range of possible altruistic behaviors would predict that one sex is *generally* more helpful than the other sex. The absence of such a simple, general prediction does not of course mean that gender is unimportant. Rather, gender roles may shape altruistic behavior so that women and men spe-cialize in different types of helpfulness and are especially helpful in dif-ferent types of situations. Consistent with the female gender role, women might tend to be compassionate and self-sacrificing in close relation-ships—with friends, partners, and family members. Women might spe-cialize in nurturing others and caring for their emotional needs. They may more often reach out to people who are ill, depressed, or lonely. Certainly, not all women would behave in these ways, of course; but these tenden-cies may be more common in women than men.

What forms of altruism might be more common in men than women? Men might be self-sacrificing in emergency situations that al-low for heroism. They may be somewhat more willing to place them-selves in danger of physical injury or even death, in order to rescue an-other person. In addition, men might behave in polite, protective ways, especially toward women of their own social group. Men might also be helpful in practical ways—fixing things around the house and solving practical problems.

EMPIRICAL RESEARCH ON ALTRUISTIC BEHAVIOR

Now I will consider empirical evidence that women and men specialize in different forms of altruism. As I will show, some traditions of psychological research tend to display women's helpfulness, and other traditions display men's helpfulness.

Research on Close Relationships Reveals Female Emotional Supportiveness

To find evidence of the helpfulness of women, where might we look? If there is truth to the cultural stereotype that women are kind and compassionate, these tendencies might play out most clearly in friendships, marital and partner relationships, and close relationships more generally. Women might provide more social support and sympathy in such relationships because this is what compassion and kindness are all about.

Evidence of this supportiveness can be found, first of all, in studies of friendship. Many researchers have compared same-sex friendships among women with those among men. They have found that women's friendships with other women tend to be more cooperative, intimate, and emotionally expressive than men's friendships with one another. Men's friendships, in contrast, tend to be built around somewhat competitive activities such as career-related activity and sports to a greater extent than women's friendships are. In men's friendships, trust and empathy are important too, but their priorities seem to be somewhat different than women's, with greater emphasis on shared activities. Thus, the prototype of male friendship is business associates who play golf or tennis together. The prototype of female friendship is women who get together to talk, perhaps at a restaurant or one of their homes. Women tend to spend time with female friends in ways that provide opportunities for lots of talking and sharing of experiences. It follows that women are more likely to provide one another with emotional support and informal counseling for personal problems. This same point about women's supportiveness has also been made by studies of college roommates. Female students report a higher level of social support from their roommates than male students do from their roommates.

In a typical study of same-sex friendships (Davidson & Duberman, 1982), unmarried women and men ranging in age from 18 to 35 described their relationship with their best friend and gave detailed accounts of their typical conversations with the best friend. Although all of the participants in this study were white, they came from all social classes. Analysis of these records showed that the men talked mainly about topical issues, such as current events, work, sports, movies, or politics. The women talked less about topical issues than the men and somewhat more about personal problems and considerably more about the relationship with the best friend. In general, men seem to emphasize companionship and carrying out activities together over self-disclosure and emotional expressiveness.

Psychologists have also examined married couples in order to determine the extent to which spouses provide emotional support to one another. Of course, spouses generally do support each other emotionally, as long as their marriage is not very troubled. However, husbands report more support and affirmation from their wives than wives do from their husbands. It seems that in marriages as in friendships, women are the social-support experts, and people turn to them when they are distressed. The emphasis in the male role on independence, autonomy, and emotional control makes it difficult for men to be providers of social support (see Barbee et al., 1993). Consequently, women apparently rely a good deal on their female friends and relatives for social support and only to some extent on their husbands; married men tend to turn to their wives.

These differences in male and female behavior have also been reflected in studies of self-disclosure—the sharing of intimate, personal information with another person. People differ in the extent to which they share personal information with others and, of course, are generally more willing to share personal details with family members and "best friends." A recent review of research on self-disclosure found that in general women disclosed more intimate information to their female friends than men disclosed to their male friends (Dindia & Allen, 1992). This disclosure of intimate information often contributes to emotional supportiveness in relationships.

Experiments on Helping Behavior Display Male Heroism and Chivalry

Now let's turn to another, very different type of empirical research. For many years, experimental social psychologists have carried out research on what they call *helping behavior*. Although the term "helping behavior" might seem to be quite inclusive, what in fact has been studied by these investigators are mainly two types of behaviors: (1) rescuing or intervention behavior in emergency situations in which another person is in need (sometimes called studies of bystander intervention) and (2) everyday polite behaviors such as opening doors and picking up something that a person has inadvertently dropped. These behaviors have been examined almost exclusively in brief encounters with strangers in field and laboratory situations and not in long-term role relationships within families, small groups, or organizations. These two types of helping behavior, bystander intervention and stylized polite behaviors, should remind you of the two altruistic themes that I have emphasized in relation to the male gender role, namely, heroism and chivalry. The heroic man can be a bystander who intervenes; the chivalrous man is polite in certain specific ways, especially toward women. Given the link between bystander intervention and heroism and between chivalry and polite behaviors, you probably will not be surprised when I show you that in general this type of research tends to display ways in which men tend to be more helpful than women.

Examples of laboratory and field experiments on helping behavior. This tradition of research on helping behavior started with a study by Darley and Latané, which was published in 1968. This experiment was inspired by the case of Kitty Genovese, who was murdered by a man armed with a knife. The attack took place outside of her apartment building in 1964 in a middle-class area of Queens, New York. At least 38 of her neighbors heard or actually watched this attack, which continued for 35 minutes, but none of them called the police until her attacker had departed. This particular tragic incident became famous in part because of an award-winning story about it that appeared in *The New York Times.* Unfortunately, incidents of this type, involving a shocking failure of people to help, have continued to occur from time to time. You have probably read descriptions of such incidents in newspapers.

Darley and Latané conducted a laboratory experiment in order to examine the willingness of bystanders to help someone in need. They designed the experiment to emulate those features of the Kitty Genovese incident that they believed inhibited people from helping. In particular, they thought that having many potential helpers in the situation would decrease helping because no individual would feel uniquely obligated to intervene and in addition each person would reason that someone else must have already taken appropriate action. In the experiment, each subject believed that he or she was a participant in a discussion group whose members were separated in cubicles but listening to one another by means of earphones. Actually they were listening to a recording on which another person who was ostensibly part of the discussion group became very distressed as he went into an epileptic seizure and called for help. The appropriate altruistic action for the subject would be to leave the cubicle and seek out the distressed person. The main finding of interest to Darley and Latané was that the larger the group that was participating in the discussion, the longer it took for the victim to receive help. Their interpretation of this effect of group size was that a *diffusion of responsibility* to help takes place among groups of people. From the perspective of our analysis of gender and altruism, it is important to know that the male subjects were somewhat more likely to help the seizure victim than the female subjects were.

Now let me give you an example of an experiment by Latané and Dabbs (1975) that construed helping as polite behavior, namely, picking up pencils or coins that a person dropped in an elevator. In these field ex-

TABLE 1

Percentages of Bystanders Giving Help to Confederate Who Dropped Coins or Pencils in an Elevator

Sex of Bystanders	Sex of Confederate	Columbus, OH	Seattle, WA	Atlanta, GA
Female	Male	23%	16%	7%
	Female	23%	26%	26%
Male	Male	25%	32%	12%
	Female	32%	39%	70%

Source: Adapted from Latané and Dabbs (1975).

periments, female and male students who were confederates of the researchers went to elevators in office buildings in three cities: Columbus, Ohio; Seattle, Washington; and Atlanta, Georgia. These confederates dropped coins or pencils, seemingly by accident. The other people riding in the elevator became the subjects. The confederates merely kept track of how many people helped pick up these objects; they also recorded the sex of the persons who helped and did not help.

As you should note in Table 1, men helped more than women in this situation, and women received more help, especially from men. However, these trends were weak in Columbus, stronger in Seattle, and very strong in Atlanta. This research examined a helping act that seems to be as appropriate for women as men and that poses no barriers of skill or danger. Still, the study revealed some typically sex-related aspects of findings from field experiments on everyday polite behavior: specifically, this sort of helping is most commonly directed by men toward women and is less common in other types of dyads (that is, directed by men toward men, women toward women, or women toward men). In this experiment, the regional difference in the extent to which these acts were sex-related is remarkable; perhaps the Atlanta data tell us that a more traditional form of gendered politeness prevails in the South (or prevailed when this study was conducted in the 1970s).

Review of research on gender and helping behavior.   Working with Maureen Crowley, I reviewed 172 studies of helping behavior to examine the extent to which these behaviors were sex-related (Eagly & Crowley, 1986). We believed that we would find men somewhat more helpful than women if we averaged across all of these studies because, as I have explained, this research consists primarily of studies of bystander intervention and polite behavior in relationships between strangers. As we have already seen, the helpfulness of women is particularly apparent in close relationships, which are not studied in this particular research tradition.

The experiments that we located examined a very wide array of helping behaviors (and included the studies that I have already mentioned to illustrate this tradition). For example, studies of bystander intervention examined helping a man who fell in the subway, stopping a brutal fight between two subjects, helping a person with car trouble on a busy street, stopping someone from stealing a student's belongings in the library, reporting someone who had shoplifted at a store, helping a woman who was apparently sexually assaulted in a campus building, and helping a female student who was apparently choking on something. Studies of polite behaviors examined helping a woman whose groceries had fallen at a store, helping a woman pick up packages she had dropped, returning the act of opening doors in a building, mailing a stamped letter left in a phone booth, calling a garage for a person with car problems, telling the time to someone who requested it in a public place, and helping a deaf person make a phone call. Other experiments involved donation behaviors such as donating money to the Leukemia Society to a women who comes to the door, giving money to a panhandler on campus, and donating blood to a hemophiliac who has been injured. Still other experiments examined acts of volunteerism: Research participants had opportunities to volunteer to spend time with retarded children, to bake cookies or give money for an ecology project, and to be a subject in a psychology experiment.

As we expected, we found that in general in this research literature men helped more than women did and that people were more helpful to women than men. Especially strong in these studies was the tendency for men to be helpful to women. Nevertheless, the findings of these experiments varied quite a lot. In fact, in 38 percent of the experiments, the sex difference in helping went in the female direction, with women helping more than men, and in the other 62 percent of the experiments, men helped more than women.

As you might guess, certain circumstances fostered the tendency for men to be especially helpful. In some situations, women tended to feel less competent than men to perform the helping act (for example, changing a tire) or thought that some of these acts would put them in danger (for example, picking up a hitchhiker). In our review, we were able to show that the tendency for men to be more helpful than women was stronger to the extent that women felt less competent to help or less comfortable in helping or they believed that they would place themselves in danger if they helped.

There were some other very interesting findings in our review of this research. Specifically, men tended to be more helpful than women to the extent that onlookers were present. Sometimes the helper was merely alone with the victim or person who requested help; sometimes there were onlookers—for example, in a subway car or on a city street. Although the presence of many people may inhibit helping, as suggested by the idea that responsibility can be diffused among a group of people, the presence of an audience seems to foster a sex difference in helping behavior. We believe that tendency for men to be especially more helpful than women with onlookers present makes sense because the presence of an audience should make social norms about helping more powerful influences on behavior. In other words, people are more likely to "do the right thing" if they are under surveillance by others. Because most of these experiments involved behaviors that are mildly heroic or merely polite and the male gender role has particularly salient rules about these types of behaviors, an audience should encourage men to help in ways that are consistent with the masculine role.

Another finding in our review was that men tended to be more helpful than women if the opportunity to help came in the form of a need that presented itself rather than an explicit request. For example, a need is merely present if you observe someone who seems to be ill or has dropped something. In contrast, a request to help might consist of a person asking for a charity donation or asking for someone to make a phone call. In the situation in which a need is present, a helper has to take some initiative or show some assertiveness to intervene, whereas in the situation in which a request is made, the helper can merely acquiesce or be compliant. It is thus possible that this tendency for men to be especially more helpful than women in the presence of a need rather than a request may reflect some greater assertiveness on the part of men.

I have described some of the conditions that make it likely that men help more than women in experimental research on helping behavior. When one or more of these conditions are absent, the tendency for men to be especially helpful weakens and may reverse so that women are more helpful than men. Thus, when women feel at least as competent and comfortable to help as men do and think that the helping situation is not dangerous, they may help as much as or more than men. For example, in particular studies included in our review, women were shown to be more helpful than men in volunteering to spend time with retarded children, helping a man with a neck brace who fell in a campus building, and calling a garage for a person with car trouble.

Awards from the Carnegie Hero Fund Commission Display Male Heroism

I have located some archival data on heroism that yield additional insight into the extent to which heroic behavior is sex-related (see Eagly & Crowley, 1986). These data consist of the records of the Carnegie Hero Fund Commission, which was established by Andrew Carnegie in 1904 to recognize outstanding acts of heroism performed in the United States or Canada. A hero was defined for these purposes as someone who risked or sacrificed his or her life in saving or attempting to save someone's life. These acts of heroism are much more extreme and remarkable than the bystander interventions studied in social psychologists' field experiments. Bystander intervention rarely places a helper in serious danger. In contrast, to win a Carnegie medal, a person must have truly risked his or her life.

The winners each receive a Carnegie Medal and under some circumstances a monetary award or a grant for education or training. It is noteworthy that the Carnegie Hero Fund excludes from awards certain classes of people. Specifically, they exclude people such as firefighters whose duties in their regular vocations require heroism, and they similarly exclude people in military service. Excluded also are parents who rescue family members, except in unusual or very outstanding cases. They also exclude children who are deemed too young to understand the risks that are involved.

Women were explicitly included as potential recipients of these awards from the beginning. Contained in the original charter of the Carnegie Hero Fund Commission was the following statement: "Whenever heroism is displayed by man or woman in saving human life, the Fund applies" (Carnegie, 1907, p. 11). We cannot be sure that these medals were awarded on a gender-fair basis, but it seems that Andrew Carnegie intended that they be so awarded.

Most of the heroic incidents of Carnegie medalists involved acts such as rescuing people from drowning, fires, or physical assault. A typical incident is the following:

> **Carnegie Medal awarded to John Rex Fidler, who saved Paul J. Twyman and others from burning, Bridgeville, California, March 10, 1982.** Paul, 9, and his four brothers and sisters were in their bedroom when fire broke out in an adjoining room. Fidler, 31, mechanic, was alerted and ran to the house, where he broke a window of the bedroom and pulled one of the children out. He entered the room through the window and found three more of the children, whom he handed outside to their father. After climbing outside, Fidler then re-entered the house three more times to search for the fifth child. Dense smoke and intense heat forced him out each time. The fifth child died in the fire; Paul and the other children were not burned. Fidler was treated for smoke inhalation, but he recovered. (*Carnegie Hero Fund Commission Annual Report*, 1983, #6672)

Here is another incident.

> **Carnegie Medal awarded to Helen Gail Shuler, who saved Benjamin E. Wolf from assault, Collegeville, Pennsylvania, August 24, 1982.** A man armed with a 12-inch butcher knife entered a lounge and threatened the five persons present, including Wolf, 54, who required crutches. The others, including Miss Shuler, 36, waitress, fled. Wolf fell as he attempted to flee the assailant, who then poised himself over Wolf, raising the knife. Miss Shuler ran back to the assailant and grabbed his arm and waist, screaming. The assailant broke away, cutting Miss Shuler as he did so. He ran from the lounge. Miss Shuler recovered. (*Carnegie Hero Fund Commission Annual Report*, 1983, #6720)

When I obtained data from the Carnegie Hero Commission in 1986, they informed me that they had awarded 6,955 medals, of which 161 (or 9 percent) had been awarded to women. Men had received 91 percent of the awards. These data suggest that extraordinary heroism is very sex-linked, with men more commonly being the risk-takers. Women do sometimes risk their lives in these ways, but it is less common.

Distributions of the Sexes into Altruistic Social Roles May Display Female and Male Altruism

We have so far looked at altruism that is not part of one's occupational life. However, many people help others because their job requires that they do so. For example, most people who enter burning buildings are ineligible for Carnegie medals because they are firefighters, whose jobs require that they do so. People with occupations involving serious risk of death or injury would include law enforcement officers and members of the armed forces as well as firefighters. Most, if not all, paid occupations that entail a very direct threat to one's life are male-dominated. There has been considerable resistance to allowing women to enter these occupations—for example, to serve in combat roles in the military. In contrast, women are especially well represented in paid occupations that focus on some form of routine personal service. Over half of all women are in clerical and service occupations, and women with professional positions are predominantly in teaching, nursing, and social work.

Whether behavior that is part of one's job should be considered altruistic is an interesting question. Our definition of altruism excluded behavior that brings an external reward. Of course, the fire fighter and nurse receive paychecks, although these occupations are not very highly paid. Physicians *are* highly paid, yet they also help the sick. Should we consider nurses more altruistic than physicians because they are paid considerably less for their efforts? I won't attempt to resolve this kind of question, but I want you to notice that most occupations that require personal service *for relatively low pay* are female-dominated.

When thinking about altruism and social roles, we must remember that the domestic role is highly service-oriented. The occupant of this role devotes herself (or himself) to caring for family members, particularly for children, and keeping the household running for the benefit of a family. Because the role is unpaid, it might be regarded as particularly altruistic. The role of husband and father ordinarily involves a considerably smaller burden of direct, personal service to family members. As we learn when we study the division of labor in the home, housework and childcare are performed mainly by women, even when they are employed outside the home. Yet, among the tasks that husbands and fathers do perform is the occasional "fixing" chore such as repairing the lawn mower or perhaps the toaster or the car. The tendency for people to think of men as helping by carrying out these types of practical chores thus has some basis in fact.

Family roles often encompass caring for family members who are ill. Especially among middle-aged and older adults, these responsibilities may include caring for chronically ill relatives. Women are more common as caregivers for the sick or disabled. For example, a recent study of primary caregivers for family members who were diagnosed with Alzheimer's disease found that 71 percent of the caregivers were female (Schulz, Williamson, Morycz, & Biegel, 1992).

Community service in volunteer roles is also very relevant to understanding altruism. Many citizens perform community service, donate money to altruistic causes, and join organizations that provide public service or engage in advocacy on social issues. Especially in earlier decades, when women were not employed outside the home as commonly as they are now, many women performed substantial amounts of volunteer work. Of course, many employed people also volunteer for community service, and students volunteer as well. Community service remains important to many citizens, men as well as women.

REASONS WHY WOMEN AND MEN SPECIALIZE IN DIFFERENT FORMS OF ALTRUISM

I have reviewed evidence of several types showing that women and men specialize in somewhat different forms of altruistic behavior. Gender is very important in the altruistic domain, even though it is not sensible to claim that there is a general sex difference in altruism. To the extent that people regard men or women as the helpful sex, they are probably bringing to mind particular types of helping behavior and particular types of situations. If they think that women are altruistic, they may be thinking about the emotional supportiveness of friends or the domestic role; if they think that men are altruistic, they may be thinking about heroic or chivalrous behaviors. Yet, the evidence that I have given you that particular forms of altruism are sex-related raises the deeper issue of *why* altruism is gendered. Why don't men specialize in emotional support as much as women do? Why don't women risk their lives as much as men do in emergency situations?

One approach to answering these questions involves taking moral rules into account. When people are truly altruistic, they help others because they believe that helping is the right thing to do. Perhaps the behavioral differences in altruism reflect the fact that men and women define "the right thing" differently; in other words, they may to some extent have a different set of moral principles.

The issue of gender and morality is an old one in psychology. One of Freud's claims was that women have a less-developed superego (or conscience) because girls do not go through the same psychosexual stages that boys do. In a relatively recent analysis of morality, Carol Gilligan proposed that there are two ways of thinking about moral issues: a system of morality based on rights and abstract principles, and a system based on caring and responsibility to others (e.g., Gilligan & Attanucci, 1988). These two systems are sometimes called the *justice* and the *care* perspectives. Gilligan argued that men adopt the justice orientation more often than women do and that women adopt the care orientation more often than men do. Gilligan further argued that these orientations are equally admirable and that neither is superior: A concern with justice does not reflect a higher type of morality than a concern with care, as it did in Kohlberg's system. To support her claim that women are relatively more concerned with care and men with justice, Gilligan examined the decisions of people facing real-life dilemmas, such as women facing a decision about abortion.

Gilligan's work has proven to be quite controversial, with Gilligan and some other psychologists producing research supporting her analysis and other psychologists producing less-supportive research. Whatever the empirical support for the claim that women and men differ in their moral orientations, Gilligan's theory is provocative and relevant to the sex differences that we have observed in altruistic behavior. The care orientation toward morality may underlie women's tendency to be emotionally supportive in close relationships. Moreover, the care orientation may be one determinant of women's tendency to choose social roles that entail direct service to others: for example, the domestic role, helping professions, and community service.

Interesting as Gilligan's analysis is, it may beg the question of why women and men differ in their altruistic behavior because her analysis merely says that women and men differ in their underlying moral orientations. But why should moral orientations be related to gender? Are there more ultimate causes of sex differences in both altruism and morality?

The more ultimate cause that I have emphasized throughout this lecture is *gender roles,* the rules that a society has for behaving as a woman or man. Gender roles convey important messages about altruism—messages that are different for women and men. I regard the moral orientations that Gilligan has described, justice and care, as one aspect of gender roles. Thus, Gilligan's care orientation is consistent with the communal themes of the female gender role, and the justice orientation may be consistent with the agentic themes of the male gender role.

One particularly important aspect of gender roles is the support they lend to a general difference in status and power between the sexes. Because the specific roles that men occupy in organizations and in families have more power and authority than the roles occupied by women, gender roles include rules that encourage men to act as more dominant people and women to act as more submissive people. The messages about status and power that are embedded in gender roles in turn have implications for altruistic behavior. For example, as I have already noted, the patterning of chivalrous behaviors reflects status and power relations between women and men. Men's chivalrous behaviors are dominant and controlling and reflect their higher status. Women's acceptance of these behaviors may reflect their subordination and need for protection.

This analysis in terms of sex differences in power and status is relevant to other aspects of altruism as well. Preserving friendly social relationships, as reflected in women's emotional supportiveness, may be more important to women than men because of women's lesser power. Women may need to cement bonds with others through kindness and compassion, given their relative lack of other forms of power over others. Gilligan's care orientation to morality may also reflect women's lesser power and status rather than gender *per se.*

To explain why women and men specialize in different forms of altruistic behavior, many psychologists would point to socialization. In general, people are socialized to accept the gender role that the society prescribes for them. In particular, many feminist psychologists have argued that female socialization features an emphasis on learning to be caring and responsible to other people (Chodorow, 1978; Miller, 1976). In contrast, male socialization may emphasize assertiveness, which may prepare men for bystander intervention, and chivalrous protectiveness, which may prepare them for certain types of polite behaviors.

Evolutionary psychologists would make still other arguments about the origins of sex-related altruistic behavior. In particular, they would argue that men have the occasional burden of endangering their own lives because they are the more expendable sex in terms of the maintenance of a society. Women must be preserved as the childbearers if the society itself is to be preserved. Another factor underlying the physical risk often required to behave heroically is women's lesser physical strength. The average women is less able than the average man to successfully perform rescuing behaviors that are extremely demanding physically (for example, carrying an adult from a burning building).

There are probably several reasons why altruism is related to gender, and it would be dogmatic to claim that any one reason is the key to understanding why many of these behaviors are correlated with sex. Because we do not know the ultimate reasons why many altruistic behaviors are gendered, it is difficult to predict whether women and men will become more similar in these aspects of their behavior. If these sex differences reflect primarily status and power relations between the sexes, then as women gain more equal status to men, these behaviors should become less sex-related. To the extent that altruistic behaviors reflect more intrinsic sex differences (for example, men's greater physical strength), men and women may continue to specialize in different forms of altruism.

REFERENCES

Barbee, A. P., Cunningham, M. R., Winstead, B. A., Derlega, V. J., Gulley, M. R., Yankeelov, P. A., & Druen, P. B. (1993). Effects of gender role expectations on the social support process. *Journal of Social Issues, 49*(3), 175–190.

Carnegie, A. (1907). Deed of trust. In Carnegie Hero Fund Commission, *Annual report* (pp. 9–11). Pittsburgh, PA: Author.

CHODOROW, N. (1978). *The reproduction of mothering: Psychoanalysis and the sociology of gender.* Berkeley: University of California Press.

DARLEY, J. M., & LATANÉ, B. (1968). Bystander intervention in emergencies: Diffusion of responsibility. *Journal of Personality and Social Psychology, 8,* 377–383.

DAVIDSON, L. R., & DUBERMAN, L. (1982). Friendship: Communication and interactional patterns in same-sex dyads. *Sex Roles, 8,* 809–822.

DINDIA, K., & ALLEN, M. (1992). Sex differences in self-disclosure: A meta-analysis. *Psychological Bulletin, 113,* 106–124.

EAGLY, A. H., & CROWLEY, M. (1986). Gender and helping behavior: A meta-analytic review of the social-psychological literature. *Psychological Bulletin, 100,* 283–308.

GILLIGAN, C., & ATTANUCCI, J. (1988). Two moral orientations: Gender differences and similarities. *Merrill-Palmer Quarterly, 34,* 223–237.

HARRIS, M. B. (1992). When courtesy fails: Gender roles and polite behavior. *Journal of Applied Social Psychology, 22,* 1399–1416.

LATANÉ, B., & DABBS, J. M., JR. (1975). Sex, group size and helping in three cities. *Sociometry, 38,* 180–194.

MARTIN, J. (1990). *Miss Manners' guide for the turn-of-the-millennium.* New York: Simon & Schuster.

MILLER, J. B. (1976). *Toward a new psychology of women.* Boston: Beacon Press.

POST, E. L. (1984). *Emily Post's etiquette* (14th ed.). New York: Harper & Row.

SCHULZ, R., WILLIAMSON, G. M., MORYCZ, R. K., & BIEGEL, D. E. (1992). Costs and benefits of providing care to Alzheimer's patients. In S. Spacapan & S. Oskamp (Eds.). *Helping and being helped: Naturalistic studies* (pp. 153–181). Newbury Park, CA: Sage.

SUGGESTED READINGS

EAGLY, A. H., & CROWLEY, M. (1986). Gender and helping behavior: A meta-analytic review of the social-psychological literature. *Psychological Bulletin, 100,* 283–308.

GILLIGAN, C., & ATTANUCCI, J. (1988). Two moral orientations: Gender differences and similarities. *Merrill-Palmer Quarterly, 34,* 223–237.

HARRIS, M. B. (1992). When courtesy fails: Gender roles and polite behavior. *Journal of Applied Social Psychology, 22,* 1399–1416.

MARTIN, J. (1990). *Miss Manners' guide for the turn-of-the-millennium.* New York: Simon & Schuster.

C *LAUDIA G. GEER recently received her Ph.D. from the University of California at Davis, where she received an award for teaching excellence. Dr. Geer is currently a Lecturer in Psychology at U.C.-Davis and at Cosumnes River College. She studies human emotion as it relates to issues of gender and power.*

S *TEPHANIE A. SHIELDS is Professor of Psychology at the University of California at Davis. Dr. Shields' research interest is human emotion, especially emotion as a quality of consciousness and emotion as a cultural construct. She also writes on the social context of psychological research and is well known for her work on the study of women and gender in the nineteenth century.*

5

Women and Emotion:

Stereotypes and the Double Bind

❖

Pick up any newspaper or magazine article on the differences between women and men and chances are you'll see differences in emotion getting a lot of attention. What's the typical, bottom-line message? "She's emotional. He isn't." In fact, the popular media bombard us with assertions about who is more or less emotional: She experiences more emotion than he does, experiences it more often than he does, and has less control of her emotions than he does. She's emotionally expressive, and he's emotionally inarticulate. After reading these articles it's no wonder we tend to believe that women's and men's emotions are so different.

This more-or-less approach to understanding gender and emotion might be fascinating to newspaper and magazine writers—nourishing arguments that should appeal to those interested in keeping the battle between the sexes in vogue—but it also leaves some interesting and important questions unanswered. For example, why is there a disparity between reports of expressed and felt emotions? We typically use displays of emotion, such as facial expression and gestures, as direct indicators of what we and other people are feeling. Because women are generally seen as more emotionally expressive than men, the assumption is that their feelings must be more intense. Men, on the other hand, are generally viewed as less emotionally expressive, so their feelings must be less intense. Expressed and felt emotion become so conflated in our beliefs about gender and emotion that it's not easy to think about one without the other. But research shows that even though women and men may differ in how they express their emotions, they often report having similar feelings.

The more-or-less approach also falls short in explaining the variability we see in emotional behavior. That is, women and men differ from one another in their

63

emotional expressions, both as individuals and as groups, in ways that don't fit the stereotype. In fact, in some situations, women and men appear to reverse their stereotypical emotional roles. If men are supposed to feel less emotion, less often, and have more control of their emotions, then why are so many "emotionally inarticulate" men so very expressive at the ballpark or in traffic jams? If women are supposed to feel more emotion, more often, and have less control of their emotions, then why are so many "emotionally expressive" women so often inarticulate in their expressions of anger?

An alternative approach to understanding women's and men's emotionality that does address these questions examines our beliefs about gender and emotion and how they combine within social contexts to influence our experiences and expressions of emotion. In taking this approach, we first have to confront the prevailing stereotype about gender and emotion in our culture.

CONFRONTING THE STEREOTYPE

Given the pervasiveness of stereotypes about emotion, it's not surprising that when asked to name the "most emotional" person they know, 80 percent of both women and men college students identify a woman (Shields, 1987). As Agneta Fischer (1993, p. 312) observed, "The general claim that women are more emotional than men tells us more about our cultural stereotypes than about actual sex differences in emotions. The term 'emotional' or 'emotionality' tempts people to think in terms of sex differences." This stereotype represents a culturally shared belief that is learned at a very early age and continues to influence our perceptions of and thoughts about women and men and emotion throughout adulthood.

Research has shown that young children seem to know about emotion stereotypes by the time they're in preschool, and they consistently make associations between particular emotions and the sex of the person expressing those emotions. For example, in studies by Dana Birnbaum and her colleagues (Birnbaum & Chemelski, 1984; Birnbaum, Nosanchuk, & Croll, 1980), preschool children associated anger with boys and men and happiness and fear with girls and women. Later, Richard Fabes (1989) presented children with images of girls and boys expressing an emotion and then asked them to recall what that emotion was and whether the person was a girl or boy. The children in this study were three times more likely to make mistakes in recalling the sex of the person when she or he was expressing a counterstereotypic emotion (for example, the boy is crying) than when the person was expressing an emotion more commonly associated with that sex (for example, the boy is angry). So, how well the children remembered images portraying emotion depended on how well those images conformed to common stereotypes about gender and emotion.

These early distinctions about who has what emotions contribute to the persistence of beliefs we have as adults about sex differences (how females and males differ biologically) and gender differences (culturally defined standards of sex-appropriate behavior) in emotion. For example, Birnbaum and her colleagues (Birnbaum et al., 1980; Birnbaum & Chemelski, 1984; Birnbaum & Croll, 1984) found that college students and working-class parents also associated anger with boys and men and sadness and fear with girls and women. The only difference between the two groups was that the working-class parents attributed the findings to biology—something inherent in the nature of females and males that determines and directs their emotions—whereas the college students attributed the findings to social conditions and expectations and hoped that the standards would change.

Fabes and Martin (1991) found that people apply stereotypes about gender and emotion more strongly to adolescents and adults than to children and that these stereotypes seem to be based on a belief that males don't fully express the emotions they feel. Their results also suggest that stereotypes are emotion-specific. For example, the *experience* of sadness is believed to be similar for both sexes regardless of age, but the *expression* of sadness is believed to decrease significantly as people, especially boys and men, learn to control their emotions. Furthermore, studies on the *experience* of anger suggest that it is similar for both women and men but the overt adult *expression* of anger is associated with being male (Averill, 1982). In general, when people think about socially undesirable emotions, girls and women are believed to experience and express emotions related to internal sources such as guilt or anxiety. Boys and men are believed to experience and express emotions related to external sources such as anger and hate (Fabes & Martin, 1991).

HOW DOES EMOTION DIFFER FOR WOMEN AND MEN?

Stereotypes about emotion seem to suggest the existence of some essential and inevitable difference between the sexes. But, if we look at the research literature, we see a pattern similar to what we've seen before when we looked at other sex-related differences. That is, how big and how stable differences are depend on what we measure and how we measure it. When boys and girls or men and women keep current diaries of their own emotional experiences, researchers find that they report having the same beliefs about emotion, use the same emotional language and expressions, and describe their experiences of emotion in similar ways (see Brody & Hall, 1993; LaFrance & Banaji, 1992; and Shields, 1991a for reviews). Because emotion occurs within socially similar contexts for both sexes, we shouldn't be too surprised by these similarities. After all, both women and men are likely to feel anger when they believe they've been the target of injustice, grief over the loss of a loved one, embarrassment at committing social blunders, and so on, depending on how they evaluate the situation.

However, when women and men are asked to evaluate other women and men or describe their own past emotions in more general terms, their judgments and descriptions tend to be consistent with the stereotypes. Less confidence in our knowledge of others or reliance on our memories of past events leads us to rely more heavily on stereotypes. Differences in emotion are also more likely to occur in contexts that draw attention to social roles and relationships, those contexts in which gender is more pronounced. The conclusions that research seems to reach is that women are more likely than men to give accounts of emotional experiences that involve interpersonal relationships, and women are more likely to express fear and sadness than men, especially when communicating with their friends and family. The expectation that women do not and should not express socially undesirable emotions such as anger is particularly clear. When the emotional experiences of women in the United States are described by others as highly negative, those women are judged to be less likable than men whose emotional experience is described in a similar way (Sommers, 1984). The belief is that the appropriately emotional female is dependent, passive, and sensitive; she is not angry.

Emotion Concepts

Do women and men differ in their understanding of emotion? Do they differ in their perceptions of what brings about an emotional response, the language they use to describe emotions, or the content of those descriptions? Do women and men have different ideas as to why certain emotions occur or about the consequences of emotional episodes? As a matter of fact, descriptions of emotion and knowledge about emotion rarely differ between boys and girls or women and men.

When research participants are asked to make judgments about emotional labels or emotional stereotypes, or when they participate in experiments on mood and memory, very few differences between women and men are found. Even though many jokes and situation comedies on television revolve around the confusion created when women and men apparently perceive a situation differently or interpret the meaning of things differently, consistent gender-related differences have been found in only one area: Women seem more likely than men to emphasize the value of talking about emotion and the significance of emotion in social relationships (Shields, 1991b).

Emotion Expression

Of all research on emotion, the most consistent differences between female and male participants occur in producing facial expressions and judging others' facial expressions of emotion. The majority of studies report girls and women as better at both communicating and interpreting the nonverbal emotional expressions of other people; only a few studies have found men more accurate. Females tend to be more facially expressive and smile more than males (except for little boys). Females establish and maintain more eye contact, approach others more closely (when they're unaware of being observed), and are approached more closely by others. Girls and women are also better at recognizing faces, using nonverbal expressions of emotions, and interpreting the posed or intentional nonverbal cues of others (Hall, 1984). However, when nonverbal cues are unintentional, spontaneous, or expressed through channels other than facial expressions (for example, body posture or tone of voice), differences in the abilities of females and males to interpret others' nonverbal expressions of emotion tend to decrease or disappear altogether.

Although differences in emotional expression do appear when studied in psychology laboratory settings, the size of these differences is moderate at best. This suggests that, when larger gender differences are found, something about the experimental situation may be influencing the results. In an extensive review of this literature, Judith Hall (1987) noted that the contexts in which the behavior was measured tend to be settings that call for gender-appropriate behavior. In particular, research situations that imply or encourage conversation among men and women who are strangers may bring about feelings of self-consciousness, social anxiety, and strong implicit demands to behave in socially appropriate ways. In these situations, people may rely more heavily on expectations for behavior based on gender stereotypes. Rather than focusing on the existence and size of gender-related differences, then, the more important and interesting issue becomes how our assumptions and expectations regarding gender and the expression of emotion exaggerate or attenuate these differences in certain situations.

Emotion Experience

So far, we've seen that women and men have similar ideas and knowledge about emotion and have some differences in their expressions of emotion. But, what happens when we ask people to describe their emotional experiences—their feelings? To get at information about how emotion is experienced, we have to rely heavily on self-report measures; we have to ask people what they feel and when they feel it. It's particularly helpful for subjects to make entries in personal diaries at the time the emotion is occurring, but most often the self-report measures of emotional experience used in studies are in the form of questionnaires. These self-report measures can provide valuable information about the more subjective aspects of emotion only when they are well constructed, carefully used, and appropriately interpreted.

Whether questions are asked about emotion in general or about specific emotions, self-report measures (other than personal diaries) tend to yield gender-related differences. For example, women usually report experiencing emotion more often or more intensely. However, because self-reports reflect beliefs about emotion, participants' responses may reflect what they believe "should" be true, or what is "typically" true, or what they would "like" to be true about themselves rather than what is actually true. Regardless of the topic—emotion or anything else—participants are better at responding accurately and precisely to questions about specific, current, or ongoing experiences and factual occurrences than they are to more general, retrospective questions. The more attention placed on public expressions of emotion rather than private experience, the more social context is embedded in the research question, and the more general rather than specific the questions about felt emotion, the more likely gender-related differences will be found (LaFrance & Banaji, 1992).

THE LINK BETWEEN EXPRESSION AND EXPERIENCE

Earlier we said that because emotional expressions are used as a way of understanding emotional experience, it's hard to think about one without the other. However, emotional expression is not equivalent to emotional experience. We cannot be certain about what another person is feeling unless she or he tells us. On the other hand, emotional expression (or lack of expression) does provide a starting point for evaluating the presence or absence, intensity, and quality of the emotion being experienced. When we see someone else express emotion we make inferences about what that emotion is and what it means. We try to understand what the person may be experiencing based on what we know about our own emotions and our beliefs about what a particular expression might mean. When information is missing or we lack confidence in our inferences, we rely heavily on our understanding of stereotypes regarding gender and emotion to complete the picture.

How we describe our feelings of emotion to others and how we show the emotions we feel depend to a great extent on society's rules about what emotions should and should not be expressed within certain contexts. Children learn very early in life that what a person shows may not match what she or he feels. For example, a child may smile to show public appreciation for a gift that is, in fact, rather disappointing. Girls and boys have similar knowledge of what to show and when to show it, but girls tend to be more skilled at managing their emotional expressiveness at a younger age (Saarni, 1984, 1988).

Which emotions are expressed under which circumstances are affected in much the same way by individual expectations of "gender-appropriate" experience or ideas about what is "gender-appropriate." As an example, feelings of fear and sadness are more strongly associated with females than with males, so outward expressions of fear and sadness are expected (and tolerated) more from girls and women than from boys and men. Similarly, feelings of indignation and rage are more often attributed to males than females, so open expressions of anger are seen as more socially appropriate for boys and men than for girls and women. In general, emotional expressions that deviate too much in quantity or quality from socially sanctioned "rules" meet with disapproval from others (Saarni, 1984).

Just as there are social "display rules" about how to behave and what emotions to show in certain social situations, sociologist Arlie Hochschild (1983) proposes that there are also "feeling rules"—culturally defined guidelines for what kind and how much emotion to experience. When others become aware that our feelings are inconsistent with what is expected and considered appropriate under the circumstances, they pressure us to conform. Someone might ask, "How can *you* feel happy at a time like this?" More important, we become distressed by these misfitting feelings. The question then becomes, "How can *I* feel happy at a time like this?" To relieve the distress of this inconsistency, Hochschild (1983) says that we engage in "emotion work" to change our feelings to fit the socially sanctioned rules of the situation.

*H*OW ARE WOMEN'S EMOTIONS REPRESENTED?

Now, given the prevailing stereotype, how can we go beyond the obvious to identify widely held, implicit, fundamental beliefs about women and emotion? One technique that has been successful in defining cultural standards, conventions, and beliefs about emotion is to examine diaries, marriage manuals, child-rearing manuals, and other sources from a particular period in history. Advice manuals don't reflect actual practices, but they do give us some insight into the ways in which cultural beliefs inform the individual about shared expectations regarding when, where, and how emotion should occur and what the emotion signifies. By looking at how emotion is represented in advice literature aimed at general audiences (or elsewhere in popular culture), we can identify the unspoken assumptions about what emotion is and how it works.

For example, Stephanie Shields and her colleagues (Shields & Koster, 1989; Shields, Steinke, & Koster, in press) looked at the relationship between representations of emotion and gender for family members:

mother, father, son, and daughter. Specifically, they were interested in (1) similarities between adults and children in making sex-specific references to emotion in their descriptions of "mother's emotion" and "father's emotion," (2) beliefs about the nature of and the need for emotional control, and (3) clarification of the sources of gender differences in representations of "mother's emotion" and "father's emotion." More than 50 popular-press books on child rearing published between 1915 and 1980 were examined for passages pertaining to emotion, which were coded by description of the emotion, control and expression of the emotion in the child-rearing situation, and the effects of the emotion on the development of the child.

Shields and her colleagues (Shields & Koster, 1989; Shields, Steinke, & Koster, in press) found little difference in the evaluations of emotions for sons and daughters. However, the emotions of mothers and fathers were evaluated very differently from one another: maternal emotional expressiveness was seen as a potential threat to the child's healthy development, whereas paternal emotional expressiveness was prized. The advice literature portrayed mothers as overflowing with emotion from some internal source that they are barely able to control. If mothers don't exercise sufficient self-restraint, serious consequences may result. Their children may continue to remain dependent on and maintain unrealistic expectations of extravagant displays of attention by other people into adulthood, develop a tense and anxious temperament characterized by the inability to distinguish between ordinary events and potential crises, have difficulty acquiring a sense of appropriate emotional self-control, or exhibit any number of similarly negative effects. The advice literature implies that mothers don't really know what constitutes a reasonable amount of emotional experience or expression. Therefore, they should make every attempt to control their emotional expressions to avoid becoming emotionally inappropriate role models for their children.

On the other hand, societal expectations regarding the mother's emotional role in the family also demand that she is lavish in her emotional expressivity for both her positive and negative emotions. In fact, excessive emotional expression is often considered instrumental to a child's socialization. Large expressions of displeasure or sadness help a child learn quickly what behaviors are dangerous or unacceptable, and exaggerated expressions of delight at a child's accomplishments may help the child develop high self-esteem. So, the emotional expressiveness that is considered to be a defining feature of valued maternal behavior is, at the same time, believed to jeopardize the child's healthy development. This creates an expressive double bind: Faced with these contradictory societal messages regarding their expressions of emotion, mothers are in a position to be damned regardless of what they do.

The advice literature portrays fathers as less emotionally responsive toward their children than mothers, primarily fulfilling the roles of disciplinarian and playful companion. The father's emotional distance from the child is seen as objectivity rather than as insensitivity to the child's emotional needs, and very few passages warn fathers that uncontrolled paternal emotion could be problematic for the child's development. Any potentially harmful emotions expressed by fathers are seen as being against their basic natures, brought about by external situations such as job stress or some violation of their rights, understandable and therefore justified. The characterizations and concerns expressed in the advice literature, then, reflect common and deeply ingrained beliefs about gendered emotionality. In particular, women's emotional expression is thought to be extravagant, reflecting an internal source that is excessive, intense, difficult to contain, and potentially problematic, whereas men's emotional expression is believed to be conservative, reflecting a reasonable amount of controlled passion, and most often observed when provoked by external sources.

*I*S THERE A RIGHT WAY TO "DO" EMOTION?

Our ability to adhere to (or deviate from) the pressures of society in managing emotions suggests that we actively participate in our emotionality. That is, at least to the extent that we regulate our emotional experiences and expressions, we "do" emotion. This view suggests that emotion is a flexible, dynamic, interpersonal process (Shields, 1991a).

Is there an ideal way for women to "do" emotion? Who decides what that is? Are the standards the same for women and men? Our first inclination when considering these questions as feminists is to expect that women's emotions are always somehow devalued. As we've seen from the advice literature, this is not *always* the case; it's quite true that social standards for emotion are hardly value-neutral. Just think about what happens when someone tells you that you are "getting emotional" about something. Most of the time it's not a compliment. In fact, to say someone is emotional usually implies *too much* emotion and is generally an accusation implying lack of control, lack of stability, and lack of reason. But being too emotional isn't always the problem; sometimes the problem is not being emotional enough. Women are expected to be emotionally expressive in their warmth, kindness, sensitivity, and nurturance. Whether women's emotional expressivity is devalued depends a lot on who is doing the evaluating. For example, following the vice-presidential candidates' debate a decade ago, Representative Geraldine Ferraro was seen by her supporters as "cool," "calm," "compassionate," and well-modulated in her presentation, but she was also seen as "annoyed," "bitchy," and expressing "hostility" by her opponents (Shields & MacDowell, 1987).

As feminist psychologists begin to question the basic concepts of emotion, expressivity, and emotion stereotypes, we can move past frustrating and unanswerable questions such as, Who is more or less emotional? and redirect our efforts to answering questions such as, When does gender matter in emotion? Gender's greatest effect lies less in what each sex knows about emotion than in what each sex is likely to do with that knowledge. Instead of being troubled by the inconsistencies in research on gender and emotion, we should focus on them. Then we can begin to understand how beliefs about emotion define its appropriateness, color our views of interpersonal relationships and our evaluations of ourselves and others, and create expectations for our children.

REFERENCES

AVERILL, J. (1982). *Anger and aggression*. New York: Springer-Verlag.

BIRNBAUM, D., & CHEMELSKI, B. (1984). Preschoolers' inferences about gender and emotion: The mediation of emotionality stereotypes. *Sex Roles, 10,* 505–511.

BIRNBAUM, D., & CROLL, W. (1984). The etiology of children's stereotypes about sex differences in emotionality. *Sex Roles, 10,* 677–691.

BIRNBAUM, D., NOSANCHUK, T., & CROLL, W. (1980). Children's stereotypes about sex differences in emotionality. *Sex Roles, 6,* 435–443.

BRODY, L., & HALL, J. (1993). Gender and emotion. In M. Lewis & J. Haviland (Eds.), *Handbook of emotions* (pp. 447–461). New York: Guilford.

FABES, R. (1989, May). *Stereotypes of emotionality*. Paper presented at the Nags Head Conference on Sex and Gender, Nags Head, NC.

FABES, R., & MARTIN, C. (1991). Gender and age stereotypes of emotionality. *Personality and Social Psychology Bulletin, 17,* 532–540.

FISCHER, A. (1993). Sex differences in emotionality: Fact or stereotype? *Feminism & Psychology, 3,* 303–318.

HALL, J. (1984). *Nonverbal sex differences: Communication accuracy and expressive style*. Baltimore: Johns Hopkins University Press.

HALL, J. (1987). On explaining gender differences: The case of nonverbal communication. In P. Shaver & C. Hendrick (Eds.), *Sex and gender: Vol. 7. Review of personality and social psychology* (pp. 177–200). Beverly Hills, CA: Sage.

HOCHSCHILD, A. (1983). *The managed heart*. Berkeley: University of California Press.

LAFRANCE, M., & BANAJI, M. (1992). Toward a reconsideration of the gender-emotion relationship. In M. Clark (Ed.), *Review of personality and social psychology: Vol. 14* (pp. 178–201). Beverly Hills, CA: Sage.

SAARNI, C. (1984). An observational study of children's attempt to monitor their expressive behavior. *Child Development, 55,* 1504–1513.

SAARNI, C. (1988). Children's understanding of the interpersonal consequences of dissemblance of nonverbal emotional-expressive behavior. *Journal of Nonverbal Behavior, 12,* 275–294.

SHIELDS, S. (1987). Women, men, and the dilemma of emotion. In P. Shaver & C. Hendrick (Eds.), *Sex and gender: Vol. 7. Review of personality and social psychology* (pp. 229–250). Beverly Hills, CA: Sage.

SHIELDS, S. (1991a). Gender in the psychology of emotion: A selective research review. In K. T. Strongman (Ed.), *International review of studies on emotion*, Vol. 1 (pp. 227–245). Chichester, England: Wiley.

SHIELDS, S. (1991b, August). *Doing emotion/doing gender*. Paper presented at the meeting of the American Psychological Association, San Francisco, CA.

SHIELDS, S., & KOSTER, B. (1989). Emotional stereotyping of parents in child-rearing manuals, 1915–1980. *Social Psychology Quarterly, 2,* 44–55.

SHIELDS, S., & MACDOWELL, K. (1987, Spring). "Appropriate" emotion in politics: Judgments of a televised debate. *Journal of Communication, 37,* 78–89.

SHIELDS, S., STEINKE, P., & KOSTER, B. (in press). The double bind of caregiving: Representation of emotion in American advice literature. *Sex Roles.*

SOMMERS, S. (1984). Reported emotions and conventions of emotionality among college students. *Journal of Personality and Social Psychology, 46,* 207–215.

RUTH L. HALL is Assistant Professor of Psychology at Trenton State College. Dr. Hall has taught courses on the psychology of women since 1987 and recently introduced a course on the psychology of women of color at Trenton. She maintains a private practice in clinical psychology and consults frequently to agencies and organizations in her areas of expertise: women, people of color, and sport psychology.

6

Sweating It Out:

The Good News and the Bad News about Women and Sport

———— ❖ ————

Contrary to popular belief, the female athlete is not an oxymoron. Yes, we sweat, we grunt, we use our bodies to excel in athletics. Yes, we participate on a recreational and on a competitive level. And yes, we hear about women athletes at least every four years as they surface to gather gold for our country. Why do so many girls decide not to participate in sports or to leave athletics in their early teens? What are the messages to girls that influence their decision to remain in or abandon sport? Why are only 26 percent of all Olympic participants women (WSF, 1994)? Why do only one-third of all Olympic events have women's teams? What's gender got to do with it?

We ignore or minimize the sports participation of women and girls in American culture. Many associate women in athletics with sideline participants (as cheerleaders) and as supporters of the male athletic endeavors. Women can cheer and jeer but are not encouraged to enter the athletic field. The implicit message is that participation in athletics is not for girls and women. But teamwork, camaraderie, and competition are not inherently for men only. Why should muscle tone, cardiovascular fitness, and the athletic use of our bodies (other than for sexual or sensual reasons) be a problem?

Women in sports is both good and bad news. The good news is that thousands of girls and women are involved in sports, love to compete, and enjoy using their minds and bodies as athletes. Sports provide an opportunity to work with other girls and women, to excel in something, to become physically fit, to receive educational scholarships, and to compete. The bad news is that many girls and women have not had the opportunity to participate in athletics, have not been en-

75

couraged to do so, or have been warned that athletics will take away from their "femininity." Of course, some girls and women just don't like sports. That's okay, but look what they're missing!

My lecture will focus on the psychosocial aspects of sports rather than on performance enhancement.[1] I will begin with a discussion of women's athletics as a legal issue and the role of feminism. Second, I will discuss some misconceptions about girls and women who participate in sports and how the media reinforces and perpetuates many myths. Third, I will discuss why girls initially participate in sports, why they remain in sports, and why they leave. Last, I will address two relevant and understudied areas of sport that are in need of further investigation: the role of homophobia in sport, and women athletes of color.

HISTORY OF TITLE IX

In 1972, an amendment of the Higher Education Act, Title IX, made it illegal to deny access to any federally funded programs based on sex (Boutilier & SanGiovanni, 1983; Nelson, 1991). The final revisions and mandated application of Title IX occurred in 1979. These additional funds made sports more available to high school girls and college women, and as a result, more girls and women became active sports participants. Essentially, financial support provided uniforms, equipment, scholarships, and the opportunity to play against other teams.

This victory was relatively short-lived. In 1984, a subsequent ruling diluted Title IX. The *Grove City v. Bell* Supreme Court decision made it legal to limit equity in federal funding to the specific programs that received the funds. That is, if the institution did not use federal dollars in athletic and physical education departments (even if federal funds were supporting other programs within the institution), the monies allocated for athletic departments did not have to be equitable for men's and women's sports. However, the Civil Rights Restoration Act of 1988 completely reinstated Title IX, so that it serves once again as a legal document protecting women athletes. Since passage of Title IX, 2 million women have become involved in interscholastic sports. Before Title IX, only 300,000 women were involved in interscholarstic sports (Cohen, 1993).

Even with the involvement of women, true equity escapes us (Lederman, 1992). According to the data collected by the Women's Sports Foundation (WSF, 1992, 1994), women's college programs receive one-third less scholarship money and have 33 percent fewer athletes than men's. The operating budgets of women's programs are 24 percent less than men's, with 18 percent less money and person power for recruitment. For exam-

---

[1]Performance enhancement refers to the development of skills that will enhance athletic performance. These skills include goal setting, concentration, imagery, and relaxation. Performance enhancement also addresses how to handle "choking," burnout, and athletic injuries.

ple, male athletes receive more than $179 million in scholarship dollars annually; women receive approximately $88 million. Men's athletic teams in Division I and II institutions average 10 more competitions per sport per season than women's teams within the same divisions (WSF, 1994).

Although the consequences of these limitations continue to compromise women's sports, greater access to funding has made coaching women athletes a more attractive employment opportunity for men. More male coaches have become interested in coaching women's teams. In 1972, men coached fewer than 10 percent of women's college teams (Nelson, 1991). Today, men coach 48 percent of women's college teams (WSF, 1994). To no one's surprise, the opposite is not true: women coach fewer than 1 percent of men's teams (Nelson, 1991; WSF, 1994). Because they have more financial resources than before Title IX, women's teams have become magnets for male coaches. But this has resulted in women coaches having access to fewer coaching jobs.

One last note: The impact of the law is significant as it protects the rights of women athletes and provides opportunities for women to participate in sports in larger numbers. However, some women whom we thought would be sources of support did not fully embrace the swell of athletic opportunities for women; the relative absence of mainstream feminist support for women athletes is evident. Clearly, feminists were involved in opening the doors for women athletes. Feminists rallied around the Title IX controversy and a woman's right to participate in athletics. However, once the doors began to open, the push to unite feminism and athleticism seemed to diminish. The problem seems to stem from sport being a male-identified (rather than male-dominated) activity. "It just makes us more like men," one feminist said. Another offered ignorance, "The only part of my body that I was encouraged to use was from the neck up." Are we so fragile that we fear looking at women athletes and focus on less "divisive" topics like sexual assault, child abuse, and battering? Acknowledging and appreciating the differences between women is a tenet of feminism and will not destroy the bond that we as women have.

MYTHS AND MISINFORMATION

The world of women's athletics is filled with myths and lore—myths perpetuated by gender-role stereotypes, misinformation, and fear, and lore by successes, triumphs, and heroines! How many of you have heard of Bonnie Blair (1992 Gold Medalist in speed skating)? Althea Gibson and Billie Jean King (tennis greats)? Boris Becker and Arthur Ashe (tennis stars)? Babe Dedrickson (all round great woman athlete)? Jackie Joyner-Kersee and Carl Lewis (Olympic track stars)? Can you name a "great" in women's golf (LPGA) or men's golf (PGA)? Members of your institution's men's and women's varsity teams? Do you notice any patterns to your knowledge or lack of it? For most of you, I would imagine that the

TABLE 1

Myths about Women in Sport

Myth	Fact
1. Girls will get hurt if they participate in sports.	You can get hurt wearing high heels! Seriously, all athletes run the risk of getting injured, and girls are no different.
2. Sports are for boys.	By whose criteria?
3. Girls aren't good at sport.	By what standards? The standards seem to be more related to opportunity than anything else. Girls are smaller than boys and should have equipment that compliments their build (Eccles & Harold, 1991).
4. Girls will never be as good as boys in sport, so why bother?	In 1992, girls won all three divisions of the All-American Soap Box Derby (WSF, 1992).
5. Sports make girls masculine.	Sports participation tones you, reduces the risk of heart disease, and enhances your self-esteem. Does this sound masculine to you?
6. Boys don't like girls to play sports.	Lots of women athletes date and are in committed relationships with men. Who wants to be involved with a guy who compromises your love for sports? Do you have problems with his interest in sports? Some men can't handle being beaten by a woman in sport.
7. The proper role for girls in sports is cheerleading and supporting the boys.	Girls and boys can both play and both cheer! Yes, there are male cheerleaders too. Are they feminine?
8. Only lesbians play sports.	Lesbians are in every profession, occupation, avocation, and activity. It's no different in sports. No activity or interest can determine your sexual orientation (Nelson, 1991).
9. Supporting women athletes is a financial disaster.	Fully 93 percent of NCAA college football teams lose money annually (WSF, 1992). Is that a waste or disaster?

number of male athletes listed surpasses the number of women. If not, bravo!

Ignorance and misinformation frequently obscure women's history and girls' and women's awareness that sports and athletics are viable options. Myths and misconceptions of female athletes begin in childhood and gain momentum with puberty and womanhood. Society clearly reinforces the persistence of the myths in Table 1. It is our responsibility to dispel the myths that surround girls and women who participate in athletics and provide the misinformed with accurate information.

BRING IN THE REINFORCEMENTS! THE ROLE OF THE MEDIA

When we examine the media, we are examining some negative factors that compromise women's participation in sport (Cohen, 1993). The media recognize and support women athletes marginally at best. When was the last time that you saw coverage of women's sporting events on the evening news? With the exception of women's tennis, the LPGA, and the coverage of the NCAA's collegiate women's basketball finals (which is only a few years old), the media have virtually no coverage of women athletes. Let's take women's golf as an example. Though many believe that most men and women identify more with a woman's golf game, women still do not receive the visibility in the media. The LPGA is third in media coverage and in sponsorship to the PGA and the Men's Seniors Tournaments (Keyes, 1991). Existing media accounts often depict the female golfer as feminine, attractive, and heterosexual rather than talented (Young, 1989). In fact, qualities that enhance women's visibility in sport have little to do with performance and more to do with appearance and controversy (Boutilier & SanGiovanni, 1983). Public exposure to any sport and its players is highly correlated to access to media coverage. For example, more media coverage of the Women's Tour de France (which, by the way, is much shorter than the men's) could result in more female racing cyclists. I believe that watching women race through the French countryside for hours at a time is just as exciting as it is watching men do the same.

Newspaper and magazine coverage of the performance of women athletes is also minimal. Only 3 percent of the 10,000 sport journalists (print and nonprint) are women (WSF, 1994). In addition, we do not see posters, ads in magazines, or feature stories that show women working up a sweat from exercising and participating in a sport. It is a challenge to find motivational posters of women athletes to hang on dorm walls and exercise rooms.

Anita DeFrantz (1991), a member of the International Olympic Committee and the president of the Amateur Athletic Foundation of Los Angeles, directed two studies on gender stereotyping and women's sports coverage in the media. The foundation monitored six weeks of sports coverage on Los Angeles television and in the sports sections of four national newspapers. They discovered that men received 92 percent of televised air time and that the women's television coverage was limited to cheerleading and a story about a Los Angeles woman who liked to run onto the field and kiss baseball players. On the printed page, *USA Today* provided more information about women athletes than other print publications (Kort, 1991). Researchers have conducted similar studies in Canada using four newspapers and one women's magazine. Their findings supported the foundation's conclusions that the media virtually ignores women's sports (Theberge, 1991).

ABC sports producer Eleanor Sanger Keyes (1991) stated that the resources (for example, number of cameras used in televised games, size of the production crew) available for covering men's sports was greater than for covering women's sports. Access to these resources influences the quality of the production (for example, more camera angles) and directly affects the visual representation of women athletes. She also stated that women were referred to by their first names most of the time; among men, African Americans were referred to by their first names. Both male and female commentators called women "girls" and men "men." Keyes also stated that the commentary during professional tennis tournaments implied that men won because of skill and women won because of a weakness in their opponent. In essence, the media does little to support women's athletic endeavors but does a sterling job of reinforcing the stereotype that women, with rare exceptions, are either not particularly good at (or not interested in) athletics (DeFrantz, 1991; Keys, 1991; Kort, 1991; Theberge, 1991).

THE NARROW PARAMETERS OF ACCEPTABLE SPORTS PARTICIPATION

Some sports are seen as appropriate for women, but others are seen as taboo. We perceive individual sports as more feminine than team sports (Boutilier & SanGiovanni, 1983; Sage & Loudermilk, 1979), and we permit women to compete if they remain feminine (Birrell, 1983). The implication is that tennis, figure skating, track, and gymnastics are fine for women, but basketball, rowing, softball, and field events like the shotput are not. Mathes (1978) suggests that sports using more "masculine" skills are less desirable for women than those emphasizing delicacy and gracefulness. She notes that sports that are aesthetically pleasing or use light objects such as racquets are "more feminine" than those that involve body contact or require the application of force or the movement of heavy objects such as boats (Snyder & Spreitzer, 1973).

Thus, women can be athletes, but within a circumscribed framework and at a potential cost. Also, the continued confinement of women to particular sports reinforces an unacceptable construct that femininity is conditional. Such a construct compromises a woman's expressiveness.

SOCIALIZATION OF GIRLS AND WOMEN

The Athletic Footwear Association (1990) surveyed 8,000 students between the ages of 10 and 18 years and asked them why they participated in sport. They found that for both boys and girls having fun was the principal reason for continued sport participation. They also discovered that sports participation decreased with age for both boys and girls, and that dating, television, and socializing with friends were the primary reasons for discontinuing sports. Out of 12 reasons for sport participation, winning ranked last for girls. For boys, winning was eighth. Girls' second and third reasons for remaining in sport were staying in shape and exercise, respectively. For boys, skill enhancement and participation in an activity where they possessed skills were their second and third choices. Even though fun is essential to sport participation for both boys and girls, supplemental enhancers for sport participation vary with gender: girls focus on appearance, and boys on skill enhancement (Greendorfer, 1987).

Adolescence

Both boys and girls begin to drop out of sports during adolescence but at disproportionate rates. For adolescents, regardless of gender, the importance of peer acceptance increases exponentially in adolescence. Adolescents' participation in activities mirrors their quest to achieve social approval within their identified social network—conformist, nonconformist, or counterculture. If the environment for a young woman is nonsupportive of her participation in sport, she may not develop her talent.

An adolescent's environment includes family (nuclear and extended), friends, and classmates, and each environment influences her participation in athletics. The primary motive for an adolescent girl's participation in sports was parental interest (WSF, 1994). The absence of parental support is expressed in a variety of ways: overt lack of interest (for example, not attending her games), stating that she will outgrow her interest in sports, offering support only for her participation in cheerleading or other "feminine activities," or being unwilling (rather than unable) to purchase the proper equipment. Her friends may resent the time that she relegates to athletics and withdraw their support. The person whom she is dating may not support her athletic endeavors and may suggest that she choose between the relationship and her sport. These issues may not influence male athletes in the same manner.

Schools may collude in the process as well and relegate equipment discarded by the boys' teams to the girls' teams (such equipment is tailored to the male body and usually a poor fit for girls and women) rather than purchasing appropriate equipment. Girls' time on the practice field may be at the least opportune times. Girls' teams may not have access to the same resources (assistant coaches, number of games, transportation, etc.) as boys' teams. Girls' teams may be the first cut in a budget crunch.

The additive effect of these events may discourage girls from sport participation. However, we persevere. Although boys outnumber girls 2 to 1 in high school sport participation, 1,940,801 high school girls participated in sports in the 1991–1992 academic year (WSF, 1994). However, the percentage of girls who participate in sports drops steadily in high school (from 30.6 percent to 17.3 percent over the four years). The goal is to provide an environment that is more conducive to girls' continuing with sports.

WHAT DOES THE RESEARCH SAY? THE EARLIER THE BETTER!

In essence, gender role and gender-role expectations can compromise some women and girls and keep them away from athletics, so sports remains a male-dominated field (Gill, 1986; Harris, 1979; Nelson, 1991; Porter & Foster, 1986). Men conduct most of the research, and most of it is on male athletics. Their conclusions assume that the traits, personality, and motivational factors of women athletes are identical to those of men—therefore, separate studies for women or data that include both men and women are not necessary (Duda, 1991). Granted, the similarities between men and women are greater than their differences, but the fact remains that women need to serve as their own reference point (Gilligan, 1982; Harris, 1979; Hill-Collins, 1991) and we may be motivated by different factors than men. The Athletic Footwear Association study found that boys and girls who participate in sports differ along several dimensions. However, Allison (1991) suggests that to overemphasize gender differences does a disservice to women athletes.

Eccles and Harold (1991) conducted a longitudinal study and found that, even in elementary school, boys and girls see sport as something males are better at and more likely to do. Both girls and society place a glass ceiling on girls' sports ability and access to sport experiences. Eccles and Harold believe that when girls see sports as attainable and acceptable, their participation will increase. The need to provide girls with support for and access to athletic participation is critical. If girls do not participate in sports by age 10, there is only a 10 percent chance that they will be active in sports at 25 (WSF, 1994).

It seems obvious that we may actually prevent girls and women from choosing to participate in sports. Perhaps the arbitrary social construction of gender role contributes to low participation of girls and women in sports (Lenskyj, 1986). In her summary of studies on gender-role conflict and female athletes, Allison (1991) made the following observations: Many studies on female athletes are based on the Sage and Loudermilk (1979) instruments and constructs, which suggest that gender-role conflict for women athletes is the salient issue. A few studies (Anthrop & Allison, 1983; Sage & Loudermilk, 1979) suggest that both perceived and experienced gender-role conflict is relatively low (20 to 30 percent). Given the number of women in sports, the percentages may be even lower today. Allison acknowledges the existence of gender labeling and sport activity, but she believes that research design exacerbates this construct. She suggests that there is a difference between the recognition of and internalization of these stereotypes. We do not need to use men as the reference point or believe that to be an athlete is to be male.

Dorothy Harris (1979), a pioneer sport psychologist, suggests that women who continue to participate in sport are women who are stronger and less influenced by societal stereotypes. The experiences of professional business women support her position. Bunker (1995) conducted a survey of women executives in Fortune 500 companies. Of the 280 women who responded to her survey, 86 percent described themselves as tomboys when they were growing up. One of the most important skills that they learned from sport was how to handle victory and defeat. Their only regret is that they missed the opportunities that Title IX provides for girls and women. The 1993 Miller Lite Report on the roles of sport and fitness in the lives of white-collar working women (Sabo & Snyder, 1993) supports Bunker's conclusions. Their study affirms how vital and enriching athletics and fitness are to the lives of professional women. They polled 1,577 women and found that 58 percent participated in sports and fitness training regularly, and that 40 percent believed that sport and fitness training helped them in their professional lives. We can conclude that sport and fitness training contribute not only to the physical well-being of professional women but also to their careers.

THE CONSEQUENCES OF HOMOPHOBIA

"If there's a powerful woman out there in the world and she comes out, it's suddenly, 'Oh, no wonder, she's a dyke'."

Ingrid Sischy, editor-in-chief of Interview

Rotella and Murray (1991) suggest that homophobia (the irrational fear of same-sex sexual orientation) is harmful to everyone, gay, or straight: "Individuals in sport have had a very difficult time openly addressing the issue of homophobia, seemingly preferring to avoid it or pretend it does not exist (men like to pretend it is only in women's sports, whereas women like to pretend it is only present in other women's teams)" (p. 361). Homophobia has the potential to prevent many women from participating in athletics. Homophobia also inhibits many lesbians and bisexual women athletes from coming out to themselves, to their teammates, or to their coaches. Of course, lesbian and bisexual women are active in all levels of sports and athletics. Martina Navratilova and Billie Jean King are two athletes who are well known to us all. Many heterosexual women are accomplished athletes as well, including Chris Everet Lloyd Mills, Althea Gibson, Nancy Lopez, and Jackie Joyner-Kersee. Clearly, any correlation between athleticism and sexual orientation is suspect.

Homophobia compromises team cohesion and unity by emphasizing something other than the goal to pursue optimal performance in all athletes. It is an athlete's ability to perform, not her sexual orientation, that counts! To use people's sexual orientation against them, for any reason, is an unnecessary distraction and destructive to the team and to its members. Martina Navratilova stated:

> The thing in sports that really pisses me off is that women athletes have to prove to the world that they are not lesbians. I was asked the question forever, even before I knew I was gay. They wouldn't ask a male that. The male athletes, the writers protect them. They don't want to shatter the myth, "My God, we can't have a gay football player." It's a macho sport. But the women they attack immediately." (Kasindorf, 1993, p. 35)

Being a feminist and an athlete is especially stigmatizing for women. As one athlete stated, "To be an athlete and a feminist is the kiss of death in sports. Everyone then assumes that you are a lesbian." Clearly, not all strong women are lesbians, and not all lesbians are strong women. Yet the lesbian label often accompanies a powerful or athletic woman.

Coaches who are lesbian fear being fired, and lesbian amateur and professional athletes may lose sponsorships. Consider the consequences that occurred for Billie Jean King! King's affair with a woman (who attempted to sue her for damages) cost her several major endorsements and probably her position as the commentator for televised women's tennis tournaments (Lenskyj, 1986). Penn State Women's Basketball coach Rene Portland (Brownsworth, 1991; Lipsyte, 1991) allegedly had an unspoken policy not to allow lesbians on her team and to bench those lesbians who came out. When sources disclosed Portland's alleged policy, Penn State established a university policy that prohibited discrimination based on sexual orientation. Stories about lesbians benched or losing scholarships and coaching positions abound. It sounds something like the witch hunts in the military. The biggest homophobic fear is that lesbians will recruit straight women, as if anyone else can determine your sexual orientation. No one can make you gay or straight—either you are or you aren't!

Heterosexism provides the basis of our definition of sexuality in the United States. Chodorow (1994) stated that if we use heterosexuality's gender-role stereotypes as the basis for homosexuality, gay men are feminized and lesbians masculinized. What better place to find powerful women than athletics? Pharr (1988) suggests that it is a weapon used to keep women in their traditional gender role, which does not include athletics. At what age do we begin to pathologize women who are tomboys (Lenskyj, 1986)? According to Bunker, tomboys become quite successful adults! Think about it: If women did not fear being called lesbians, no one would be concerned! Athletic participation stretches these arbitrary gender-role boundaries and allows all of us choices based on interest and ability rather than some arbitrary parameters and limitations.

WOMEN ATHLETES OF COLOR

By the year 2000, one-third of the U.S. population will be people of color (Women's Sports Foundation, 1989). But when we talk about women, we are implicitly talking about white women, and when we talk about race, we are implicitly talking about men of color (Anderson, 1992; Lee & Rotella, 1991). The literature has marginalized women of color in race and gender literature, the psychological literature, and the sport psychology literature as well.

The available literature supports the central role that sports play in the lives of women athletes of color. The Women's Sports Foundation (1989) conducted a four-year study of 14,000 high school sophomores, one-quarter of whom were African American and Latino. WSF reported that involvement in sports kept many students in school. Athletes of color did better academically than their nonathlete counterparts but confronted a glass ceiling in obtaining athletic scholarships.

The Miller Lite Report (Sabo & Snyder, 1993) suggests that athletics is also important for professional women athletes of color. The report stated that, although women of color were less likely than white women to participate in sports and fitness training, "Women of color were more likely to believe that sports and fitness help to advance careers and to tap into business networks" than were white women (p. 2).

Additional literature is emerging that addresses the role of culture and racism in sport (Outhouse & Brooks, 1993). A recent study on racial identity and women athletes (Hall, 1993) found that Black players' experiences in cross-racial interactions either affirmed racial pride or reinforced omnipresent racism within our culture (that is, reinforced the feeling of being alienated or stereotyped). White players did not differ significantly in their racial identity with their team's racial composition; for them cross-racial interactions either proved to be educational or fulfilled their stereotypical view of Blacks. It is essential that the impact of culture and racism on the self-concept of women of color be researched further. The results will be useful to determine the role of cultural differences in team cohesion and interpersonal communication. Women of color are

more than the recipients of oppression, and we desperately need literature to address psychosocial forces that may compromise their athletic experience.

POSITIVE ASPECTS OF SPORTS FOR WOMEN

What does participation in athletics offer women? It's a way to get back
in touch with our bodies, to use them, and to keep them fit. Sport is a natural for women: Participating in sports reinforces our sense of sisterhood,
interdependence, and cooperativeness. It also teaches discipline, concentration, goal setting, team building, fitness, leadership, and determination. Participation in sports increases the self-esteem and self-confidence
of girls and women (WSF, 1994). Most of all, its *fun!* Athletics also teaches
risk taking, persistence, empowerment, and assertiveness. Athletes have
experience in putting loss and failure into perspective, in increasing self-
efficacy through skill development, and in using preparation and training
as roads to mastery. Sport has the potential for great comebacks.

WHAT DO WE NEED TO DO?

We need to provide girls and boys with supportive athletic environments
that include emotional support and access to quality coaching, facilities,
and equipment. We need to let girls know when they're young that athletics is a viable option and to offer them the opportunity to participate.
Forty-five percent of the women who responded to a 1985 survey by
Miller Lite stated that their lack of exposure to sports at an early age was
the greatest reason for their lack of participation as adults (WSF, 1994). By
exposing girls to sports, we will increase girls' feelings of competence in
their present abilities and in their careers as adults. The more girls participate in sport, the more we will dispel myths and reinforce the literature
that shows the power and relevance of sports in the lives of girls and
women.

Women athletes provide wonderful role models for all of us. We need
more role models and greater visibility of women athletes. We need to offer women greater opportunities for athletic competition as adults. At
present, there is no future in sports for women except the Olympics
(Gustafson, 1988). This is not true for men! We need posters, ads, and information about women athletes of all races. We need to confront homophobia, sexism, and racism as well.

In closing, remember that National Girls' and Women's Sports Day is
February 4. Make February 4 a memorable day by inviting a woman athlete or coach to speak at your institution. Sponsor a community event for
girls and women to participate in various athletic activities on your campus. Solicit the help of your athletic, physical education, and women's

studies departments (among others). Put posters of women athletes in the library, dormitories, and campus center display cases. Insist that your library purchase books on women and sports. Get involved in your own health and fitness. Share the good fortune that athletics can bring to all of our lives!

R EFERENCES

ALLISON, M. T. (1991). Role conflict and the female athlete: Preoccupations with little grounding. *Journal of Applied Sport Psychology, 3,* 49–60.

ANDERSON, M. B. (1992). Questionable sensitivity: A comment on Lee and Rotella. *Sport Psychologist, 7,* 1–4.

ANTHROP, J., & ALLISON, M. (1983). Role conflict and the high school female athlete. *Research Quarterly, 54,* 104–111.

ATHLETIC FOOTWEAR ASSOCIATION. (1990). *American youth and sports participation.* North Palm Beach, FL: Author.

BIRRELL, S. (1983). The psychological dimensions of female athletic participation. In M. A. Boutilier & L. SanGiovanni (Eds.), *The sporting woman* (pp. 49–92). Champaign, IL: Human Kinetics.

BOUTILIER, M. A., & SANGIOVANNI, L. (Eds.). (1983). *The sporting woman.* Champaign, IL: Human Kinetics.

BROWNSWORTH, V. A. (1991). Penn State basketball coach accused of anti-lesbian policy. *Philadelphia Gay News, 15*(21), 1.

CHODOROW, N. (1994). *Femininities, masculinities, sexualities: Freud & beyond.* Lexington, KY: University of Kentucky Press.

COHEN, G. L. (Ed.). (1993). *Women in sport: Issues and controversies.* Newbury Park, CA: Sage.

DEFRANTZ, A. (1991, February). *Gender stereotyping in sports media.* Paper presented at the Annual Kathleen Ridder Conference, Smith College, Northampton, MA.

DUDA, J. L. (1991). Editorial comment. *Journal of Applied Sport Psychology, 3,* 1–7.

ECCLES, J. S., & HAROLD, R. D. (1991). Gender differences in sport involvement: Applying the Eccles expectancy-value model. *Journal of Applied Sport Psychology, 3,* 7–35.

GILL, D. L. (1986). *Psychological dynamics of sport.* Champaign, IL: Human Kinetics.

GILLIGAN, C. (1982). *In a different voice: Psychological theory and women's development.* Cambridge, MA: Harvard University Press.

GREENDORFER, S. L. (1987). Gender bias in theoretical perspectives: The case of females' socialization into sport. *Psychology of Women Quarterly, 11,* 327–340.

GUSTAFSON, K. (1988, July/August). Women athletes take the field. *Utne Reader,* pp. 22–23.

HALL, R. L. (1993). *Racial identity and racial composition of women's varsity basketball teams.* Paper presented at the meeting of the American Psychological Association, Toronto, Canada.

HARRIS, D. V. (1979). Female sports today: Psychological considerations. *International Journal of Sport Psychology, 10,* 168–172.

HILL-COLLINS, P. (1991). *Black feminist thought: Knowledge, consciousness and the politics of empowerment.* New York: Routlege.

KASINDORF, J. R. (1993, May). Lesbian chic: The bold, brave new world of gay women. *New York, 26*(9), pp. 30–37.

KEYES, E. S. (1991, February). *Respondent: Gender stereotyping in sports media.* Paper presented at the Annual Kathleen Ridder Conference, Smith College, Northampton, MA.

KORT, M. (1991, April). Making waves. *Women's Sports and Fitness,* pp. 56–61.

LEDERMAN, D. (1992, April 8). Men outnumber women and get most of the money in big-time sports programs. *Chronicle of Higher Education,* pp. 37–40.

LEE, C. C., & ROTELLA, R. J. (1991). Special concerns and considerations for sport psychology: Consulting with black student athletes. *Sport Psychologist, 5,* 365–370.

LENSKYJ, H. (1986). *Out of bounds: Women, sport, and sexuality.* Toronto, Ontario: Women's Press.

LIPSYTE, R. (1991, May 24). Gay bias moves off the sidelines. *The New York Times,* p. B11.

MALUMPHY, T. M. (1968). Personality of women athletes in intercollegiate competition. *Research Quarterly, 39,* 610–620.

MATHES, S. (1978). Body image and sex stereotyping. In C. Oglesby (Ed.), *Women and sport: From myth to reality* (pp. 59–73). Philadelphia: Lea & Febiger.

NELSON, M. B. (1991). *Are we winning yet? How women are changing sports and sports are changing women.* New York: Random House.

OUTHOUSE, R., & BROOKS, D. (1993). *Racism in college athletics: The African-American athlete.* Morgantown, WV: Fitness Information Technology, Inc.

PHARR, S. (1988). *Homophobia: A weapon of sexism.* Little Rock, AK: Chardon.

PORTER, K., & FOSTER, J. (1986). *The mental athlete.* New York: Ballentine.

PRAKASA RAO, V. V., & OVERMAN, S. J. (1986). Psychological well-being and body image: A comparison of Black women athletes and nonathletes. *Journal of Sport Behavior, 9,* 79–91.

ROTELLA, R. J., & MURRAY, M. (1991). Homophobia, the world of sport and sport psychology consulting. *Sport Psychologist, 5,* 355–365.

SABO, D., & SNYDER, M. (1993). *Miller Lite report on sports & fitness in the lives of working women.* New York, NY: Miller Brewing Company.

SAGE, G. H., & LOUDERMILK, S. (1979). The female athlete and role conflict. *Research Quarterly, 50,* 88–96.

SNYDER, E. E., & KIVLIN, J. E. (1975). Women athletes and aspects of psychological well-being and body image. *Research Quarterly, 46,* 191–199.

SNYDER, E. E., & SPREITZER, E. (1973). Family influences and involvement in sports. *Research Quarterly, 44,* 249–255.

THEBERGE, N. (1991). A content analysis of print media coverage of gender, women and physical activity. *Journal of Applied Sport Psychology, 3,* 36–48.

WOMEN'S SPORTS FOUNDATION. (1989, October 27). *Minorities in sports. The effect of varsity sports participation on the social, educational, and career mobility of minority students.* New York: Author.

WOMEN'S SPORTS FOUNDATION. (1992, October 27). *Women's sports facts.* New York: Author.

WOMEN'S SPORTS FOUNDATION. (1994, March 1). *Women's sports facts.* New York: Author.

YOUNG, P. (1989, April 10). Belles on the ball (LPGA). *Maclean's,* pp. 68–69.

SUGGESTED READINGS

COHEN, G. L. (Ed.). (1993). *Women in sport: Issues and controversies.* Newbury Park, CA: Sage.

NELSON, M. B. (1991). *Are we winning yet? How women are changing sports and sports are changing women.* New York: Random House.

OUTHOUSE, R., & BROOKS, D. (1993). *Racism in college athletics: The African-American athlete.* Morgantown, WV: Fitness Information Technology, Inc.

PORTER, K., & FOSTER, J. (1986). *The mental athlete.* New York: Ballantine.

C HRISTINE A. SMITH *is a doctoral candidate in social psychology at the University of Pittsburgh. Ms. Smith has taught courses on the psychology of women for four years at Carlow College and Ball State University. Her research interests are women's bodies, feminist self-labeling, and rape empathy.*

7

Women, Weight, and Body Image

❖

The topic of weight concerns (eating disorders, health issues, body image) is a very popular one these days with the general population, the media, and among psychiatrists, psychologists, and feminists. Issues such as body image and eating disorders have received extensive coverage, especially by psychological researchers and feminist theorists. This lecture will deal with several issues, which we will examine from a feminist psychological perspective. What is the feminist psychological explanation for eating disorders and body image disturbance? Why is the current body ideal a thin one? What is the meaning behind the current standard of beauty? Finally, what is the impact on women who strive toward the current ideal, which is perpetually young and perpetually thin, an ideal that is unattainable for most and eventually all women?

PERSPECTIVES ON WOMEN AND WEIGHT

Beliefs about what is attractive or erotic vary from one culture to another and from one historical period to another. What is beautiful? In some cultures facial scarring is attractive; in others, drooping breasts. What is currently beautiful for women in Western culture? If one looks at the media—television, movies, magazines—one sees models who are tall and very thin; they are wrinkle-free, and have small hips and waists, medium to large breasts, and European features. Women in Western cultures are bombarded with images of this unrealistically slim, eternally young, ideal woman. Weights for Miss America winners have consistently decreased since the 1950s, as have weights for fashion models and *Playboy* centerfold models (Freedman, 1986; Garner, Garfinkel, Schwartz, & Thompson, 1980; Wiseman,

Gray, Mosimana, & Ahrens, 1992). These are women who represent ideal female beauty in our society—and they are getting thinner. Marilyn Monroe, who was a sex symbol in the 1950s, would be considered large by today's standards. However, some of the current models bear a striking resemblance to Twiggy, who was popular in the 1960s, another period in which the body ideal was extremely thin. Silverstein and her colleagues (Silverstein, Perdue, Peterson, & Kelly, 1986) analyzed the curvaceousness of women in *The Ladies Home Journal* and *Vogue* from 1901 to 1980 and concluded that the mass media are promoting a thin female ideal. However, they argue, it is not clear whether the media determine cultural ideals or cultural ideals influence media images.

Large women are often treated very poorly in Western society. Individuals often attribute negative characteristics to large people, and more so to large women. People are less likely to want to associate with large people (Millman, 1980; see also Jackson, 1992, for a review). There is extreme pressure on people, especially on women, to be thin. Large women are evaluated more negatively than large men (Stake & Lauer, 1987). Because being physically attractive is more important for women (Bar-Tal & Saxe, 1976), being, or perceiving oneself to be, overweight can result in negative consequences such as social rejection and poor self-esteem for women (Stake & Lauer 1987).

What is the result of this social pressure to be thin? Numerous studies have found that women are obsessed with thinness and unhappy with their weight. For example, Hesse-Biber (1989) found that one-third of her college sample of women expressed a strong concern with dieting, a preoccupation with weight, and an obsession with thinness. Smith and Krejci (1991) found that one-third of their sample of Latina, Native American, and white public high school girls were "always terrified of weight gain," and 22 percent were "never satisfied with body shape." Thomas and James (1988) found in their sample of urban African American women that slightly over one-half were unhappy with their body, and 60 percent thought that they were too fat. Finally, Rosen and colleagues (Rosen et al., 1988) found that 70 percent of the Native American women in their sample were trying to lose weight. A survey in *Glamour* magazine (Wooley & Wooley, 1984) found that the only women who were generally satisfied with their bodies were underweight women, and even some of them believed they were too heavy. Females are generally more dissatisfied than males with their appearance because they believe their bodies are too fat (Fallon & Rozin, 1985; Jackson, Sullivan, & Rostker, 1988).

As a result of feeling overweight, women are going to great lengths to avoid body fat. Hesse-Biber (1989) found that 59 percent of college women in her survey were using extreme and unhealthy measures such as fasting, vomiting, and laxatives to control their weight. Rosen and colleagues (Rosen et al., 1988) found similar percentages in their sample of Chippewa women and girls. It is estimated that as many as 11 percent of young women suffer from some form of anorexia nervosa (Herzog &

Copeland, 1985), which is characterized by loss of at least 25 percent of body fat, preoccupation with food, and extreme fear of becoming fat. Anorexia-like behavior was also documented (Seid, 1989) during the 1920s, when a boyish figure was also stylish. In populations where thinness is mandatory, for example, among dancers and models, eating disorders are common (Garner & Garfinkel, 1978).

The medical community, and even some psychologists, tends to view eating disorders and distorted body images as diseases that can only be diagnosed, treated, and "cured" by a medical professional (Bordo, 1993). Those with eating disorders are seen as abnormal or mentally ill, and the problem is attributed to the individual rather than to some external source. Indeed, much of the research on eating disorders and their treatment is done by doctors, usually psychiatrists.

Certainly, poor eating patterns can result in health problems that require medical attention; however, eating disorders and negative body image may be caused not by physiological problems but by cultural and social pressures to be thin. Some psychologists and feminists argue that such disorders are, in fact, symptoms of a larger "disease," namely the patriarchy, which has an underlying fear of women's power (Chernin, 1981; Freedman, 1986; Wolf, 1991). Although the overt social message may be, "Thinner is fitter is stronger," the effect of the current emphasis on extreme thinness—a nearly unattainable goal for many women—is to keep women's self-esteem low and create a passive and readily exploitable group that will not fight the patriarchal structure (Freedman, 1986). Wolf (1991) maintains that "a cultural fixation on female thinness is not an obsession about female beauty but an obsession about female obedience" (p. 187).

Maybe feminists are overreacting or being paranoid. After all, beauty has "always" been important to women. Women have bound their feet, removed their ribs, and bound their breasts in order to meet standards of beauty. Women have always adorned themselves and performed harsh actions to be beautiful. Rodin and Striegel-Moore (1984; as cited in Rodin, Silberstein, and Striegel-Moore, 1984) found that weight and body image were the central determinants of women's physical attractiveness. Rubin (1979), in her study of women as they age, found that when women were asked to describe themselves in a way that would give a good sense of who they are, they consistently described their bodies rather than their roles or careers. Women aren't doing anything nearly as extreme these days as binding their feet, and besides, thin is healthier, right? But given some estimates that 5 to 10 percent of young women are anorexic and up to six times that many are bulimic (Seid, 1989), that yo-yo dieting is unhealthy and can lead to health problems (Brownell, 1988), and that individuals may have genetically set weights that their bodies will seek to maintain (Nisbett, 1972), thin is not necessarily healthy. Women are going to extremes to lose weight, and many are suffering from anorexia nervosa and bulimia, negative body image and low self-esteem because they have not and cannot meet body ideals.

Many feminist theorists have examined the issue of disordered eating and body image. However, much of the focus in mainstream psychology and medicine has been on diagnosis and treatment and on psychological factors within the individual or family that may have caused the problem (Hesse-Biber, 1989; Jackson, 1992). The medical community has very often attributed the causes and origins to medical or biological factors (for example, chemical disorders in the brain) rather than examining cultural influences. Less focus has been on contributing factors, outside of mental disorders. The issue of mental disorders is an important one. What person in her right mind would starve herself to death? Women get labeled masochistic or mentally ill for performing beauty rituals, but if they don't buy into the beauty ideal, if they don't try to make themselves beautiful and thin, they are still seen negatively because they have failed to conform to or have challenged the role that has been set up for them. What woman in her right mind wouldn't try to be beautiful?

The emphasis on mental disorders became most apparent in 1987, when the revised third *Diagnostic and Statistical Manual of Mental Disorders,* put out by the American Psychiatric Association, added body dysmorphic disorder. This disorder has three aspects: dissatisfaction with appearance of the body; preoccupation with this aspect of appearance; and exaggeration of defects. Fitts, Gibson, Redding, and Deiter (1989) found that 36 percent of college-aged women report strong agreement with all three aspects, with 85 percent reporting strong dissatisfaction, 60 percent strong preoccupation, and 57 percent strong exaggeration. Does this mean that over one-third of college women have a mental disorder regarding their body image? Women tend to exaggerate descriptions of huge thighs and stomachs. Does this mean that they have body dysmorphic disorder? Or does it mean that the message that women must be thin to be attractive, and that attractiveness is what women must have to be valued, is getting through to us very effectively? Women internalize the message to be thin and to get rid of the areas that make them "fat," and then when they do, they are told that they have a mental disorder. Instead of examining social and cultural factors that might be contributing to distorted body image and problem eating, these behaviors are seen as abnormal, and the women who have such concerns are seen as deviant or mentally ill. Yet at least one study (Fitts et al., 1989) suggests that body image distortion and preoccupation may not be abnormal or infrequent at all.

HEALTH ISSUES

In her book, *Never Too Thin,* Roberta Pollack Seid (1989) argues that the medical community has some responsibility in the current obsession with thinness. According to Seid, the medical community promoted thinness by emphasizing the health hazards of obesity but ignoring the hazards associated with thinness and dieting. One of the most common arguments against obesity (or just about any appearance of "excess" body fat) is that it is unhealthy. However, maintaining oneself in a state of semistarvation, which is what it would take for most women to achieve the ideal body (Rodin, Silberstein, & Striegel-Moore, 1984; Wolf, 1991), cannot be considered healthy behavior. Also, few men are in weight loss programs, even though there is evidence that abdominally localized fat (the apple shape more common to men than women) is linked to increased risk of cardiovascular disease, diabetes, hypertension, and cancer (see, Rodin, 1992, for a review of this literature). Seid (1989) discusses medical studies performed in Sweden, the former Yugoslavia, California, and Georgia, all of which found that thin people were not necessarily healthier than their heavier counterparts. But the belief that thinner equals healthier may be so ingrained in the minds of medical professionals that they find it difficult to acknowledge the existence of substantial research that does not support their beliefs. For example, Sorley, Gordon, and Kannel (1980) found that obesity did not affect mortality rates until women were at least 110 percent over their average weight. Also, the weight standard used by many physicians and researchers is the U.S. Metropolitan Life Insurance Company Table, which is based on life insurance applicants in 1959, most of whom were middle- or upper-class white males of East European decent. These tables were never valid for women, and especially for nonwhite, working-class women (Rothblum, 1990). Reuben Andres (1980), former clinical director of the National Institute on Aging, found that the best weights for optimum longevity were 20 to 30 percent above the Metropolitan Life Insurance Company standards and that worst longevity was associated only with weight extremes—the very thinnest and very heaviest of the population. Physicians also fail to recognize that dieting can result in inadequate nutrition, depression, loss of sexual desire, and sudden death from cardiac arrhythmia (Ciliska, 1990).

Because of the medical community's insistence that thin equals healthy, thinness has been argued by both medical professionals and laypeople from the point of view of health, which makes it a matter of "serious" concern, rather than from the "superficial" point of view of aesthetics. Hence, a woman should be thin because it is healthier, not because Western society sees it as more attractive. Because thinness is equated with health, women may be rewarded for starving themselves or engaging in unhealthy behavior such as purging or using laxatives, as long as the end result is a thin body.

But why has thinness been especially emphasized for women if it is a health risk for both sexes? As stated earlier, attractiveness is more important for women (Bar-Tal & Saxe, 1976), and unattractive men are evaluated more favorably than unattractive women. Thinness is currently associated with physical attractiveness, and physical attractiveness and its pursuit are integral to the feminine gender role (Rodin et al., 1984). Certainly thinness is paramount to women's attractiveness (Coward, 1985; Wolf, 1991). And what is beautiful is thin.

FEMININITY AND POWER

Attractive women are perceived as more feminine than unattractive women (Jackson, 1983). Some studies suggest that high femininity corresponds with more negative body image (Jackson, et al., 1988; Kimlicka, Cross, & Tarnai, 1983). Research by Brown, Cross, and Nelson (1990) suggests that college women who have engaged in bulimic behavior tend to be more traditionally feminine than nonbulimic women. Thus, beauty and its pursuit is part of the traditional feminine role, to which most (if not all) of us have been socialized to various degrees.

However, many women who are not traditionally feminine are also concerned about their bodies and may engage in unhealthy eating behaviors and strive toward a thin ideal. Because women have traditionally had access to few avenues of achievement, beauty may be one socially acceptable form of achievement for women because it is part of the traditional feminine role. Losing weight and attaining and maintaining the thin ideal may be a form of achievement for women. Rodin et al. (1984) suggest that "in striving to be thin and beautiful, a woman may both be feminine, thus pleasing society, and experience a sense of agency and control" (p. 292). Garner and Garfinkel (1978) suggest that adolescent women may confuse weight loss with personal accomplishment and achievement. But is this confusion—or a very real and safe form of achievement? The issue of control will be addressed again later, because for women, gaining control of their weight is often linked to gaining control of their lives.

As women achieve more and gain in power, attractiveness may become even more important, as seems to be the case currently. Certainly powerful women are often seen negatively (Lips, 1991). Powerful women threaten those who want to maintain the patriarchy. By being thin, a high-achieving woman may believe she is maintaining her feminine identity (Rodin et al., 1984). It may be a way of saying to society, "Don't worry, I don't want to be a man. See how feminine I look?" Thus, by conforming to social expectations, the powerful woman may be seen as less threatening.

The issue of fear of female power is an important one. What both Black and white women report disliking most about their bodies are those features that are unique to women: rounded hips, thighs, and stomachs (Munter, 1992; Thomas & James, 1988). Women with eating disorders often express a desire to lose all evidence of their womanly bodies. So in their attempts to obtain the ideal body, women are removing their unique physical characteristics to obtain a body that is not womanly but child-like. And many feminist theorists believe that it is not a coincidence that the beauty ideal is childlike. Children are weak and nonthreatening, unlike powerful women (Chernin, 1981). *Newsweek* published a story about the new popular models of the 1990s (Leland & Leonard, 1993), who are "boyish" and "waiflike." This new image of women was deemed to be liberating because frailness and weakness meant that women no longer have to work out to be attractive. But a waif does not ask for equal pay or daycare for her children. A waif is an innocent child, nonthreatening and powerless.

Susan Bordo (1993) discusses how the body reflects social and individual values. We seek to create bodies that project who we are and what our values are. So what a body looks like, how it is shaped, has a meaning in our culture. What meanings might a thin body represent? A thin body may represent weakness, malleability, and conformity to society. It may also represent achievement and control.

In the twentieth century especially during the 1920s, the 1960s, and the current period, the beauty ideal has been extreme thinness. The first wave of the feminist movement in the United States peaked in 1920, when women gained the right to vote. The second wave began in the 1960s after the publication of *The Feminine Mystique* (Friedan, 1963). Finally, a third wave of feminism seems to have emerged in the 1990s. Is it a coincidence that a thin, restrictive beauty ideal, one that reduces women to a childlike appearance—has occurred during the same periods that women have sought to gain power and control?

Childhood is a time of few responsibilities; there is no pressure to be a woman, or a sex object (although younger and younger girls are developing eating disorders and body image disturbances; see, for example, Collins, 1991, and Flannery & Chrisler, 1993). Hence, some women may seek to return to a time that they perceive as less difficult for them, a time when they did not have this womanly body. Women who have very low body fat may stop menstruating, in a sense returning to a child's body.

*H*OW THE MESSAGE WORKS

If the ideal is childlike thinness, how can women be convinced that this is desirable and attainable? Women must be convinced that their self-worth is based on their beauty, that their bodies are inadequate, and that their inadequacy is because they have womanly bodies—large hips, round stomachs. A more childlike, less curvaceous body is therefore more beautiful and desirable. This message comes at a time when women's weights have increased, due to better nutrition (Garner & Garfinkel, 1978).

In actuality, nothing is wrong with women's bodies. What is wrong is that unrealistic and unnatural standards are set up for women, standards that define beautiful women as unnaturally thin, with narrow hips, large breasts, smooth skin—and a society that values what a woman looks like more than who she is or what she does. These are not characteristics of most women's bodies. They are characteristics of prepubescent girls' bodies and men's and boys' bodies with large breasts. The standards also have European features, are able-bodied, and are eternally young. Hence, women of color, disabled women, and older women are excluded from "real" beauty, although all are still expected to be thin. But the message must be that there is something wrong with you, not with the standards. If women fail to internalize the message, it will not serve its ultimate goal: to keep women weak. As Rita Freedman succinctly stated in her book *Beauty Bound* (1987), "a constricted body in turn dictates an equally constricted life" (p. 78). So what is presented to women is only one standard of beauty: a young, able-bodied woman who is thin almost to the point of emaciation and has European features. Occasionally women of color are presented, but they still have all that is "required," including European features and light skin. If beauty were presented in different sizes, ages, colors, and features, then women would think that there are many ways to be beautiful, and they might resist conforming.

The second step is to convince women that this desirable body is attainable. Part of the beauty myth is that any woman can attain it if she can control herself (Seid, 1989; Wolf, 1991). Large women are seen as personally responsible for their size (Maddox, Back, & Liederman, 1968). Body size is one area that women are told they can control, even though 90 percent of dieters regain the weight they lost and may actually *gain* weight as a result of dieting (Chrisler, 1989). Articles on dieting are common in women's magazines (Garner et al., 1980). Advertisements for various weight-loss programs emphasize that anyone (although the commercials target women) can lose weight if they control their eating habits. Chernin (1981) argues that women get the message that if they can control their weight, they can control their lives. Because women have not been able to control much of their lives, the message that women can take control of anything is a powerful one: Job discrimination, violence against women, misogyny will all cease to exist in her life if only she can control her weight. Roth and Armstrong (1990) suggest that control over eating behavior is important for women "because it functions as a metaphor for their sense of control in larger contexts of self-efficacy and interpersonal relationships" (p. 270). Orbach (1978) suggests that by being thin, women can gain control over both traditionally feminine goals, such as attracting men, and traditionally masculine goals, such as competing successfully in the workplace. Hence, this issue of control that women often lack in their lives becomes transferred to control of their bodies. If women can control their bodies, they may think they can control other aspects of their lives.

Some studies suggest that women with eating disorders and body image disturbance are often survivors of sexual abuse (Calam & Slade, 1989; Thompson, 1994). Women who have been sexually abused may feel a need to control their bodies because they could not do so when they were being abused. Also, some women may blame the abuse on their bodies, which caused men to sexualize them. Being a woman means dealing with adult female sexuality. For a girl or woman who has been sexually abused, reducing one's body to a childlike state may be seen as a way to remove oneself from unwanted sexual activity. Hence, removing hips and breasts through dieting and ceasing to menstruate (as many anorexics do) may be a result of an attempt to gain control after sexual abuse. Again, a woman may think that if she can control her body, she can control other aspects of her life, in this case, unwanted sexuality.

Not only must women control their weight, they should also control any signs of aging. The body must be a thin, youthful one. Numerous products are offered to eliminate wrinkles and prevent "signs of aging." Naomi Wolf (1991) writes a scathing review of the cosmetics industry, which feeds on the fear of aging many women have. As she notes, the U.S. Food and Drug Administration, which is responsible for monitoring drugs and cosmetics, has raised few objections to the false claims. Yet women spend $20 billion a year on products that do not work in hopes of holding back aging. These women realize that a woman's worth is still determined by her beauty; as women age, they are perceived as "losing their looks." If the goal is to create a childlike innocence, signs of wisdom and experience, such as laugh lines around the mouth and eyes, are not considered beautiful (Sontag, 1979). In fact, they may be seen as threatening by those who seek naive, easily exploitable, nonthreatening women.

Capitalism also plays a role in convincing women that the current body ideal is desirable and attainable. In a capitalist society, it is profitable to create a problem and then offer a product to solve that problem. But if no problem is perceived, then there is no reason to buy the product. For example, if cellulite were considered desirable, or at least nonproblematic, there would be no need to go to the gym to remove it or buy diet food to reduce fat. If short eyelashes or cellulite or wrinkles or gray hair are "problems," one need only purchase a product or service and the problem can be solved. Again, the message is that women can control their bodies.

What happens to women (eventually, all of us) who do not achieve the ideal body? When individuals repeatedly try to achieve something they are led to believe they can control, and they repeatedly fail, their self-esteem suffers. And this is exactly what our obsession with thinness has done to women. Many studies have demonstrated that women with negative body images have low self-esteem (Cash, Cash, & Butters, 1983; Jackson, et al., 1988; Pliner, Chaiken, & Flett, 1990; Stake & Lauer, 1987). In one experiment, Irving (1990) found that women who were exposed to advertisements with thin models had significantly lower self-esteem than women who were exposed to larger-sized models. This loss of self-esteem was evident in the laboratory after subjects were shown only a few photographs. What happens when women everywhere are exposed to thousands of these thin models?

By emphasizing that anyone can reach an unattainable ideal, and that to be valued as a woman you must be beautiful, women blame themselves for not being able to attain that ideal, rather than seeing the ideal as unrealistic. Women feel like failures, without value. And because they do not look like the ideal, they dislike their own bodies and, therefore, themselves. Their self-esteem suffers because they are labeled as failures, by themselves and by a culture that demands thinness (as well as youth) in women.

It is to the advantage of the patriarchal power structure to keep women's self-esteem low. A woman with high self-esteem will not tolerate pay inequity, sexual harassment, or lack of safe and affordable childcare. As Wolf (1991) states, "the beauty myth generates low self-esteem for women and high profits for corporations as a result" (p. 49). A patriarchal social system can only maintain itself if women are controlled and subordinated. As women gain access to some power structures, the system becomes threatened. By generating self-hatred in women, the system can guarantee that women will not question the system or rise up against it. Also, if women are preoccupied with themselves and channeling all their energies into their bodies, they don't have the time or energy to fight for equal pay, for an end to violence against women, or for reproductive rights. So women will be unwilling or unable to fight misogyny or oppose the patriarchal system.

An unrealistic beauty ideal also creates hatred between women. A recent popular commercial for women's hair coloring portrayed a female model who said, "Don't hate me because I'm beautiful." If beauty is the goal, and it is, then women will be jealous of other women who have reached the goal that they themselves cannot reach. They will be jealous of women who are valued by society. Certainly one of the prime goals of beauty is to be pleasing and valuable to men. Women who have attained the ideal standards of beauty have met that goal (Boskind-Lodahl, 1976). However, if the only goal of the beauty standards was to be pleasing to men, women would only strive to be as thin as men find desirable. But some studies suggest that women overestimate the extent to which men value thinness (Cohn & Adler, 1992; Fallon & Rozin, 1985). And Striegel-Moore, Tucker, and Hsu (1990) found that lesbian college students (who would, presumably, have less interest in being pleasing to men) had similar levels of body image dissatisfaction and disordered eating as a comparison group of heterosexual college females. Hence, there is more to the emphasis on thinness than being aesthetically pleasing to potential male partners.

Beauty is also an arena of competition for women. Women actively compete to be more beautiful than other women, constantly scrutinizing themselves and comparing themselves to other women. This is one area where ambition, a traditionally masculine attribute, is acceptable. Beauty is not only an acceptable ambition for women—it is expected. Women who do not attempt to (or are perceived as not attempting to) fit the beauty ideal are often stigmatized. Because being "overweight" is seen as a sign of weakness in Western society, women who are large are often scorned for daring to reject the thin ideal (even though they may actually desire a thin body) (see Tenzer, 1989, for examples). Feminists have traditionally been criticized for challenging and defying standard images of beauty (see, for example, Richardson, 1982). Chapkis (1986) discusses the challenge feminists have made to the beauty ideal, suggesting (as I do) that feminist defiance to the beauty ideal will lead to liberation from it. Women who defy the beauty ideal are directly challenging the ideal set up for them, and such women are threatening to those who seek to minimize women's power. Note a recent statement by conservative Rush Limbaugh, who suggested that women are feminists because they are too ugly to get a man. Feminists are often perceived as unattractive because it is "unattractive" to challenge the patriarchy and those who seek to keep women weak.

The beauty ideal is being actively challenged by feminist psychologists, not only through theory but also through direct action. Susan Tenzer (1989) discusses a form of group therapy, Fat Acceptance Therapy, aimed at liberating women from the social pressure to be thin and leading to a gain in power and self-esteem. Joan Chrisler (1989) argues that feminist therapists should not counsel clients to lose weight unless their weight presents demonstrable health risks. Because weight loss can damage health as well as self-esteem and because most diets don't work (and to counsel a client to do something at which they are unlikely to succeed is harmful), therapists should instead work on enhancing client self-esteem and feelings of personal power. Hence, it is true that feminism is a threat to the beauty ideal, because the beauty ideal is a threat to women.

CONCLUSION

Recognizing the impact of social standards of weight and body image is of great importance in efforts to empower women. And discussions of eating disorders and body image are incomplete without recognizing why these standards exist and why such pressures are put on women. This lecture has sought to address the specific messages women receive about weight and body image as symptoms of a larger disease, one that seeks to keep women weak. Until the messages are recognized for what they are—attempts to suppress women—women will continue to dislike their bodies and, therefore, themselves. These issues must be recognized as part of the backlash against feminism, which, as Susan Faludi (1991) documents, seeks to convince women that feminism is women's own worst enemy and has only resulted in more misery for women. This is a powerful and dangerous message, especially when so many women are striving for power but hating themselves. How these messages affect our self-esteem, our images of our bodies, and our attitudes toward ourselves cannot be addressed fully by feminists or psychologists without recognition of this backlash.

REFERENCES

AMERICAN PSYCHIATRIC ASSOCIATION. (1987). *Diagnostic and statistical manual of mental disorders.* (3rd ed., rev.). Washington, DC: Author.

ANDRES, R. (1980). Effects of obesity on total mortality. *International Journal of Obesity, 4,* 381–386.

BAR-TAL, D., & SAXE, L. (1976). Physical attractiveness and its relationship to sex-role stereotyping. *Sex Roles, 2,* 123–133.

BORDO, S. (1993). *Unbearable weight: Feminism, Western culture, and the body.* Berkeley, CA: University of California Press.

BOSKIND-LODAHL, M. (1976). Cinderella's stepsisters: A feminist perspective on anorexia nervosa and bulimia. *Signs: Journal of Women in Culture and Society, 2,* 342–356.

BROWN, J. A., CROSS, H. J., & NELSON, J. M. (1990). Sex-role identity and sex-role ideology in college women with bulimic behavior. *International Journal of Eating Disorders, 9,* 571–575.

BROWNELL, K. (1988, January). Yo-yo dieting. *Psychology Today,* 20–23.

CALAM, R., & SLADE, P. (1989). Sexual experience and eating problems in female undergraduates. *International Journal of Eating Disorders, 8,* 391–397.

CASH, T., CASH, D., & BUTTERS, J. (1983). Mirror, mirror on the wall . . .? Contrast effects and self-evaluations of physical appearance. *Personality and Social Psychology Bulletin, 9,* 351–358.

CHAPKIS, W. (1986). *Beauty secrets: Women and the politics of appearance.* Boston: South End Press.

CHERNIN, K. (1981). *The obsession.* New York: Harper & Row.

CHRISLER, J. C. (1989). Should feminist therapists do weight loss counseling? *Women & Therapy, 8,* 27–31.

CILISKA, D. (1990). *Beyond dieting: Psychoeducational interventions for chronically obese women—a non-dieting approach.* New York: Brunner/Mazel.

COHN, L. D., & ADLER, N. E. (1992). Female and male perceptions of ideal body shapes: Distorted views among Caucasian college students. *Psychology of Women Quarterly, 16,* 69–79.

COLLINS, M. E. (1991). Body figure perceptions and preferences among preadolescent girls. *International Journal of Eating Disorders, 10,* 199–208.

COWARD, R. (1985). *Female desires: How they are sought, bought, and packaged.* New York: Grove Press.

FALLON, A. E., & ROZIN, P. (1985). Sex differences in perceptions of body shape. *Journal of Abnormal Psychology, 94,* 102–105.

FALUDI, S. (1991). *Backlash: The undeclared war against American women.* New York: Crown.

FITTS, S. N., GIBSON, P., REDDING, C. A., & DEITER, P. J. (1989). Body dysmorphic disorder: Implications for its validity as a DSM-III-R clinical syndrome. *Psychological Reports, 64,* 655–658.

FLANNERY E. C., & CHRISLER, J. C. (1993, April). *Body esteem, eating attitudes, and gender-role orientation in three age groups of children.* Paper presented at the annual meeting of the Eastern Psychological Association, Arlington, VA.

FREEDMAN, R. (1986). *Beauty bound.* Lexington, MA: D. C. Heath.

FRIEDAN, B. (1963). *The feminine mystique.* New York: W. W. Norton.

GARNER, D. M., & GARFINKEL, P. E. (1978). Sociocultural factors in anorexia nervosa. *Lancet, 2,* 674.

GARNER, D. M., GARFINKEL, P. E., SCHWARTZ, D., & THOMPSON, M. (1980). Cultural expectations of thinness in women. *Psychological Reports, 47,* 483–491.

HERZOG, D. B., & COPELAND, P. M. (1985). Eating disorders. *New England Journal of Medicine, 313,* 295–303.

HESSE-BIBER, S. (1989). Eating patterns and disorders in a college population: Are college women's eating problems a new phenomenon? *Sex Roles, 20,* 71–89.

IRVING, L. M. (1990). Mirror images: Effects of the standard of beauty on the self- and body-esteem of women exhibiting varying levels of bulimic symptoms. *Journal of Social and Clinical Psychology, 9,* 230–242.

JACKSON, L. A. (1983). The perception of androgyny and physical attractiveness: Two is better than one. *Personality and Social Psychology Bulletin, 9,* 405–413.

JACKSON, L. A. (1992). *Physical appearance and gender: Sociobiological and sociocultural perspectives.* Albany, NY: State University of New York Press.

JACKSON, L. A., SULLIVAN, L. A., & ROSTKER, R. (1988). Gender, gender role, and body image. *Sex Roles, 19,* 429–443.

KIMLICKA, T., CROSS, H., & TARNAI, J. (1983). A comparison of androgynous, feminine, masculine, and undifferentiated women on self-esteem, body satisfaction, and sexual satisfaction. *Psychology of Women Quarterly, 7,* 291–295.

LELAND, J., & LEONARD, E. (1993, February 3). Back to Twiggy: The skinny on a surprising revolution in fashion. *Newsweek,* p. 64–65.

LIPS, H. M. (1991). *Women, men, and power.* Mountain View, CA: Mayfield.

MADDOX, G. L., BACK, K., & LIEDERMAN, V. (1968). Overweight as social deviance and disability. *Journal of Health and Social Behavior, 9,* 287–298.

MILLMAN, M. (1980). *Such a pretty face: Being fat in America.* New York: Norton.

MUNTER, C. (1992). Fat and the fantasy of perfection. In C. S. Vance (Ed.), *Pleasure and danger: Exploring female sexuality* (pp. 225–231). London: Pandora Press.

NISBETT, R. E. (1972). Hunger, obesity, and the ventromedial hypothalamus. *Psychological Review, 79,* 433–453.

ORBACH, S. (1979). *Fat is a feminist issue.* New York: Paddington.

PLINER, P., CHAIKEN, S., & FLETT, G. L. (1990). Gender differences in concern with body weight and physical appearance over the life span. *Personality and Social Psychology Bulletin, 16,* 263–273.

RICHARDSON, R. J. (1982). *The sceptical feminist.* London: Penguin Books.

RODIN, J. (1992). Determinants of body fat localization and its implications for health. *Annals of Behavioral Medicine, 14,* 275–281.

RODIN, J., SILBERSTEIN, L., & STRIEGEL-MOORE, R. (1984). Women and weight: A normative discontent. *Nebraska Symposium on Motivation, 32,* 267–307.

ROSEN, L. W., SHAFER, C. L., DUMMER, G. M., CROSS, L. K., DEUMAN, G. W., & MALMBERG, S. R. (1988). Prevalence of pathogenic weight-control behaviors among Native American women and girls. *International Journal of Eating Disorders, 7,* 807–811.

ROTH, D. M., & ARMSTRONG, J. G. (1990). Perceptions of control over eating disorders and social behaviors. *International Journal of Eating Disorders, 10,* 265–271.

ROTHBLUM, E. D. (1990). Women and weight: Fad and fiction. *Journal of Psychology, 124,* 5–24.

RUBIN, L. (1979). *Women of a certain age.* New York: Harper & Row.

SEID, R. P. (1989). *Never too thin: Why women are at war with their bodies.* New York: Prentice-Hall.

SILVERSTEIN, B., PERDUE, L., PETERSON, E., & KELLY, E. (1986). The role of the mass media in promoting a thin standard of body attractiveness for women. *Sex Roles, 14,* 519–523.

SMITH, J. E., & KREJCI, J. (1991). Minorities join the majority: Eating disturbances among Hispanic and Native American youth. *International Journal of Eating Disorders, 10,* 179–186.

SONTAG, S. (1979). The double standard of aging. In J. H. Williams (Ed.), *Psychology of women: Selected readings* (pp. 462–478). New York: Norton.

SORLEY, P., GORDON, T., & KANNEL, W. B. (1980). Body build and mortality: The Framingham Study. *Journal of the American Medical Association, 243,* 1828–1831.

STAKE, J., & LAUER, M. L. (1987). The consequences of being overweight: A controlled study of gender differences. *Sex Roles, 17,* 31–47.

STRIEGEL-MOORE, R. H., TUCKER, N., & HSU, J. (1990). Body image dissatisfaction and disordered eating among lesbian college students. *International Journal of Eating Disorders, 9,* 493–500.

TENZER, S. (1989). Fat Acceptance Therapy (F.A.T.): A non-dieting group approach to physical wellness, insight, and self-acceptance. *Women & Therapy, 8,* 39–47.

THOMAS, V. G., & JAMES, M. D. (1988). Body image, dieting tendencies, and sex role traits in urban black women. *Sex Roles, 18,* 523–529.

THOMPSON, B. (1994). *A hunger so wide and so deep: American women speak out on eating problems.* Minneapolis, MN: University of Minnesota Press.

WISEMAN, C. V., GRAY, J. J., MOSIMANN, J. E., & AHRENS, A. H. (1992). Cultural expectations of thinness in women: An update. *International Journal of Eating Disorders, 11,* 85–89.

WOLF, N. (1991). *The beauty myth.* New York: William Morrow.

WOOLEY, S. C., & WOOLEY, O. W. (1984, February). Feeling fat in a thin society. *Glamour,* pp. 198–252.

SUGGESTED READINGS

FALLON, P., KATZMAN, M. A., & WOOLEY, S. C. (Eds.). (1994). *Feminist perspectives on eating disorders.* New York: Guilford Press.

SEID, R. P. (1989). *Never too thin: Why women are at war with their bodies.* New York: Prentice-Hall.

THOMPSON, B. W. (1994). *A hunger so wide and so deep: American women speak out on eating problems.* Minneapolis, MN: University of Minnesota Press.

WOLF, N. (1991). *The beauty myth.* New York: William Morrow.

J OAN C. CHRISLER *is Associate Professor of Psychology and Associate Dean of the Faculty at Connecticut College. Dr. Chrisler has taught courses on the psychology of women since 1979 at Connecticut and at Mercy College and St. Thomas Aquinas College. She has published extensively on issues of women and gender, especially on women's health, menstruation, weight, and body image.*

8

$\mathcal{PMS}$ as a Culture-Bound Syndrome

❖

When I first began to study changes related to the menstrual cycle in the 1970s, so few studies existed in the literature that I could honestly say that I'd read every word ever written about premenstrual syndrome (PMS). The literature has expanded so dramatically that no one could say that today. When I collected data for my master's thesis on the experience of PMS, most of the women who participated in my study had never heard of it. "Do you mean cramps?", they would ask.

What happened? How did PMS go from a little-known experience of tension in the few days preceding menstruation to a syndrome consisting of dozens of possible symptoms that occur during the weeks preceding menstruation? An experience so common that most women complain about it? An experience so well known that jokes about it appear everywhere? In this lecture we'll consider the sociocultural and political meanings of PMS and how they contributed to its rise from relative obscurity to cultural icon in a mere 20 years.

$\mathcal{W}$HAT IS PMS?

A variety of physiological and psychological changes have been associated with phases of the menstrual cycle. Those changes that occur premenstrually (usually days 23 to 28 of the cycle) have been called premenstrual tension (Frank, 1931) or premenstrual syndrome (Dalton, 1977). The most frequently reported premenstrual change is fluid retention, particularly in the breasts and abdomen. Other symptoms have been classified as follows (Debrovner, 1982):

- *Psychological.*   Irritability, depression, anxiety, lethargy, sleep changes, low morale, crying spells, hostility
- *Neurological.*   Headaches, vertigo, backaches
- *Gastrointestinal.*   Nausea, vomiting, constipation, increased craving for sweet or salty foods
- *Dermatological.*   Acne

It has also been suggested (see Dalton, 1960a, 1960b, 1968), although there is no scientific evidence for this, that premenstrual women have difficulty concentrating, poorer judgment, lack of coordination, decreased efficiency, and lowered school or work performance.

Although the data do indicate that women experience cyclic changes, it is difficult to know how common such changes are. Estimates of the prevalence of premenstrual symptoms, which depend on how the data were collected, have ranged from 2 percent (using the strictest criteria of a 30 percent change in intensity of selected emotional and physical experiences charted daily over three menstrual cycles) to 100 percent (using the loosest criteria, "Have you ever experienced a cyclic change in physiological or psychological state?"). Despite efforts by the Society for Menstrual Cycle Research, the National Institute of Mental Health, and the American Psychiatric Association to produce a standard definition, there is little agreement on how many symptoms must be experienced or how severe the symptoms must be in order to be classified as premenstrual syndrome. So many different definitions exist in the literature that results cannot easily be compared to each other. Even the timing of the premenstrual phase of the cycle is not clear. Some researchers have described it as five to seven days before the start of menstruation; others have described it as the time between ovulation and menstruation (about two weeks). The problem of estimates is made more complicated by the fact that premenstrual experience is highly variable and personal. All women do not experience the same changes, and the experience of any given woman may vary from cycle to cycle. In addition, PMS has been so frequently discussed in recent years that the results of surveys and questionnaire studies have undoubtedly been affected by a response bias in the direction of the cultural stereotype of the premenstrual woman.

What is the cultural stereotype of the premenstrual woman? You probably don't need me to tell you! A recent walk through a shopping mall turned up a bumper sticker ("A woman with PMS and ESP is a bitch who knows everything"), buttons ("It's not PMS, I'm psychotic," "It's not PMS, I'm always bitchy"), greeting cards ("Some special advice for the birthday girl—Never cut your cake during PMS"), a calendar of cartoons about a woman with a particularly bad case of PMS ("Plagued by a raging hormonal imbalance, Melinda devours Hershey, Pennsylvania"), and several "humorous" books (*Raging Hormones: The Official PMS Survival*

Guide, PMS Attacks and Other Inconveniences of Life, and *Hormones from Hell*). Over the years my students have brought me cartoons from magazines and newspapers, greeting cards for every occasion, and even postcards that make fun of premenstrual women. There have been many references to PMS on television and in the movies. Do you remember the episode where Roseanne was premenstrual on Halloween?

Several years ago Karen Levy and I performed a content analysis (Chrisler & Levy, 1990) of 78 articles about PMS that were published in American magazines from 1980 to 1987. The articles described a confusing array of symptoms and contradictory treatment recommendations. No single symptom was mentioned in every article; 131 different symptoms were described, including sallow skin, feeling fat, and changes in the way one's perfume smells. Treatment recommendations included drinking wine and limiting alcohol intake, limiting fluid intake and drinking plenty of water, limiting protein intake and eating a high-protein diet. Although no biochemical differences have yet been found between women who suffer from PMS and women who don't, the journalists implicated hormone levels as the cause of PMS. The menstrual cycle was referred to as the "cycle of misery," a "hormonal roller coaster," the "inner beast," and the "menstrual monster" (p. 98). The premenstrual and menstrual phases of the cycle were described as "weeks of hell" during which women are "hostages to their hormones," and premenstrual women were described as "cripples" and "raging beasts" (p. 98). Among the titles of the articles we read were "Premenstrual Frenzy," "Dr. Jekyll and Ms. Hyde," "Coping with Eve's Curse," "Once a Month I'm a Woman Possessed," and "The Taming of the Shrew Inside of You" (p. 97).

Cartoons about violent women and journalistic representations of frenzied, "raging beasts" could easily make one lose sight of the fact that women commit fewer than 5 percent of all violent crimes. How did this violent image of premenstrual women arise? In 1981 two court cases in Great Britain gained worldwide attention as Sandie Smith and Christine English, on trial for murder, were found not guilty by reason of insanity after Dr. Katharina Dalton testified that they had PMS. When she first began working on PMS in the 1950s, Dr. Dalton did not believe that it was a problem that affected large numbers of women. By the early 1980s she would suggest that most women have PMS, although they might not know it (Rome, 1986). The British trials resulted in an explosion of media interest in PMS. Images of violent premenstrual murderesses merged with ancient images of women as dangerous beings who lured men to their doom, but now there was a "scientific" basis to women's hostility and duplicity—hormones—and everyone was talking about them. Sociologist Sophie Laws (1983) has noted that few people bothered to ask how it is possible that the hormones of millions of women could be out of balance.

*I*S PMS A DISEASE? AN ILLNESS? A SYNDROME?

A disease is defined (Thomas, 1989) as a pathological condition of the body that has clinical signs, symptoms, and laboratory findings that are specific to it and that allow us to discriminate it from normal or other pathological states of the body. PMS is not a disease. There are no laboratory findings that can discriminate PMS sufferers from nonsufferers. The symptoms of PMS are not specific to it; some are common in men and in premenarcheal girls and postmenopausal women. The only clinical sign specific to PMS is that it is generally followed by menstruation. However, there are many menstruating women who don't experience PMS, and some women who don't menstruate (for example, women who have had hysterectomies) do complain of PMS.

In medicine it is common to distinguish between disease and illness. Diseases are tangible and have elements that can be measured. Illnesses are highly individual and personal. When we speak of illness we are generally referring to psychological experiences such as pain, suffering, and distress. For example, a person with hypertension obviously has a disease (chronic high blood pressure), but lacks pain or suffering, and, hence, is not ill (Thomas, 1989). A major problem in treating hypertension is that people often decide to stop taking their medication because they feel fine. People with mental illness, on the other hand, are obviously suffering but may not have evidence of disease; for example, there may be no measurable pathological changes in their bodies. PMS can be categorized as an illness. Those women who have severe symptoms are distressed and may be described as suffering. However, you should consider carefully the definition of an illness before you apply it to yourself. If you experience only a few premenstrual changes that can be described as mild or moderate, are you ill?

Illness behavior refers to "the way in which symptoms are conceived, evaluated, and acted upon by a person who recognizes some pain, discomfort, or other sign of malfunction" (Townsend & Carbone, 1980, p. 230). Illness behavior is significantly affected by society's definition of symptoms and malfunctions and by the roles and expectations society holds for individuals who experience them. Surveys of adults (Meigs, 1961; Siegel, 1963) indicate that at any particular time about 90 percent of the population is aware of some "symptom" that could be seen as clinically serious. Think about this for a moment. Scan your body. Do you have a muscle ache, a stuffy nose, a tickle in your throat, eye strain, a cut or bruise? If 90 percent of adults are experiencing symptoms right now, then statistically, at least, experiencing symptoms is normal. Being ill, you see, is a social process, which we may or may not decide to enter into when we experience a sensation that could be called a symptom.

Cultural images and social roles and stereotypes shape women to notice menstrual cycle–related changes and to label them as pathological rather than as normal. Twenty years ago a woman who was experiencing tension or depression before her menstrual period would have thought to herself, "I'm tense (or blue) today." Now she thinks, "I have PMS." The modern woman engages in illness behavior; she feels ill, tells others that she's ill, and treats her illness (with Pamprin, a day off, etc.). In the past she would have coped in other ways and considered her mood to be part of the normal ups and downs of life. The reason we (Chrisler & Levy, 1990) found 131 different symptoms in our analysis of magazine articles is that the menstrual cycle has become so salient as problematic that American women attribute almost any change to it. If a man has a headache, he may think of several possible reasons for it—work pressure, hunger, or too much beer last night. If a woman has a headache, she could make any of those same attributions, but she's unlikely to do so. Three weeks out of four, she'll probably attribute her headache to her menstrual cycle. Same symptom, very different illness behavior.

A syndrome is a group of symptoms that are related to each other by some anatomical, physiological, or biochemical peculiarity (Thomas, 1989). This definition does not insist that a common cause be known, simply that the symptoms be related in some way. The menstrual cycle is the physiological or biochemical peculiarity that links the "symptoms" of PMS, which appear or are intensified during the premenstrual (luteal) phase. Thus, PMS can be said to meet the definition of a syndrome, although the "symptoms" may never be found to have a common cause.

WHAT IS A CULTURE-BOUND SYNDROME?

To understand PMS we have to take an interdisciplinary approach. So far we've considered evidence from psychology, sociology, and medicine. Now it's anthropology's turn. Anthropologists invented the term "culture-bound syndrome" to help them understand illnesses that occurred in some societies but not in others. Examples of culture-bound syndromes include illnesses that result from voodoo, gypsy curses, and other "magical" spells. Until recently the literature on culture-bound syndromes focused on illnesses in other societies that the Western anthropologists found mystifying because there was no measurable disease process involved. Members of highly technological societies like ours expect that a biomedical cause and cure will ultimately be found for every illness. Now, however, anthropologists are suggesting that the illness behavior that surrounds conditions with which we are very familiar (for example, obesity and menopause) may constitute culture-bound syndromes.

A culture-bound syndrome is a constellation of symptoms that have been categorized as a dysfunction or disease in some societies but not in others. (See Table 1 for a list of requirements for culture-bound syndromes.)

*I*S PMS A CULTURE-BOUND SYNDROME?

I believe that it is, and I'll try to convince you to agree with me. The best way to do this is to take the statements from Table 1 and discuss them one at a time. This way we can decide whether these statements, which appear to Westerners to describe voodoo and gypsy curses, describe PMS as well.

PMS can not be understood apart from its specific cultural or subcultural context. In order to understand PMS one must have, at the most basic level, a concept of menstruation as cyclic, which is necessary in order to anticipate it. Menstruation is a rare event in societies in which women are pregnant or lactating much of their adult lives. Therefore, members of those societies would not develop the same expectations of the menstrual cycle as members of more technologically advanced societies, and they would not have the familiarity with it to notice that certain changes are related to its events. There would thus be no PMS, merely a coping with individual symptoms as they emerged.

Emily Martin (1988) has argued that in order to understand PMS one must live in an industrialized society. Before industrialization people worked in tune with natural rhythms—seasonal for farmers, circadian for skilled laborers. Now that most of us work at jobs in offices and factories that require sustained labor throughout the year and reward discipline of the mind and body, lapses in such discipline are noted. Symptoms on the Menstrual Distress Questionnaire (Moos, 1968) that involve lapses in dis-

TABLE 1

Defining Features of Culture-Bound Syndromes

A culture-bound syndrome is characterized by one or more of the following:

- It cannot be understood apart from its specific cultural or subcultural context.
- The etiology summarizes and symbolizes core meanings and behavioral norms of that culture.
- Diagnosis relies on culture-specific technology as well as ideology.
- Successful treatment is accomplished only by participants in that culture.

Corollaries

- Treatment judged as successful in one cultural context may not be understood as successful from another perspective.
- The symptoms may be recognized and similarly organized elsewhere but are not categorized as the same "disease."

Source: Based on Cassidy (1982) and Ritenbaugh (1982).

cipline include "difficulty concentrating," "confusion," "lowered judgment," "decreased efficiency," and "lowered school or work performance." Martin (1988) has suggested that the women who complain of these "symptoms" may be less willing (as opposed to less able) to discipline themselves as usual when they are premenstrual.

Industrialization may contribute to the belief in many societies that one can and should exercise self-control in order to feel and behave the same way all the time. Our culture encourages people to believe that we can have more control over our lives and bodies than is actually possible (Brownell, 1991; McDaniel, 1988). Premenstrual women often complain of feeling "out of control" because they are irritable, angry at someone, craving chocolate, or not inclined to work as hard as usual—experiences that are considered "normal" in children or men but "pathological" in menstruating women. Control is so important to us that being out of control is frightening (Ritenbaugh, 1982). This belief in control contributes not only to PMS but to eating disorders and compulsive exercise. But that's another lecture. . . .

Finally, there would be no PMS without strong negative attitudes toward menstruation. Many studies (Brooks-Gunn & Ruble, 1986; Clarke & Ruble, 1978; Chrisler, 1988; Golub, 1981; Ruder, Finn, & Rotman, 1981) conducted in the United States have found that both women and men hold negative attitudes toward menstruation. Americans are uncomfortable talking about menstruation and believe that the menstrual cycle has negative effects on women's personality, behavior, and physiology. The most popular measure of menstrual cycle effects is called the Menstrual Distress Questionnaire (Moos, 1968), a title that clearly lets subjects know what kind of responses the researchers are expecting. Margie Ripper (1991) was frustrated in her attempts to study women's experience of the menstrual cycle, a neutral expression, which everyone kept hearing as "women's menstrual problems." Potential subjects would sometimes say to her, "I'd be no use to you; I don't have any problems." In a recent study (Chrisler, Johnston, Champagne, & Preston, 1994) that specifically looked at positive experiences, subjects were startled to learn that anyone thought that the menstrual cycle could be related to any experience that wasn't negative. Negative attitudes are not limited to the general public. A 1979 editorial in the British Medical Journal concluded: "There is nothing pleasant about menstruation. At best it is a physiological inconvenience. At worst it contributes to chronic ill health" (cited in Laws, 1983, p. 30).

PMS summarizes and symbolizes core meanings and behavioral norms of the culture. Among the core meanings and behavioral norms reflected in PMS are mind-body dualism, which contributes to our belief that people are not responsible for emotional or behavioral symptoms of disease (Ritenbaugh, 1982); individuals' need for control and fear of noncontrol; the raging-hormones hypothesis, which promotes the belief that women are emotionally unstable (McDaniel, 1988); and the industrialized society's preference for stability of affect and behavior. Because stability is so highly valued, changeableness, rhythmicity, and emotionality have come to be viewed as inherently "unhealthy" (Koeske, 1983).

PMS also reflects the behavioral norms of the feminine gender role. Women are expected to be soft-spoken, nurturing, patient, and kind. If they are not, there must be something wrong with them. Blaming the "unfeminine" parts of one's personality or behavior on PMS can be a survival strategy for women in that it can allow women to hold onto a self-definition of "good/proper" woman (Laws, 1983). The premenstrual week is the only time of the month some women "allow" themselves to be angry (McDaniel, 1988) because they can attribute their anger to their hormones rather than to any of the many things in the world that could "legitimately" anger them. However, this strategy also works against women. There's nothing more frustrating than expressing anger about something only to hear others say, "She must be on the rag" or "That's PMS talking."

The menstrual cycle provides such a clear distinction between women and men that "its correlates, concomitants, accompaniments, ramifications, and implications have become intrinsically bound up with issues of gender equality" (Sommer, 1983, p. 53). In fact, PMS can be seen as a collection of negative beliefs about women's "nature," a nature that "requires" medical management and the protection of men, who are stronger and "healthier" than menstruating women (Zita, 1988). Don't miss the point: If women are emotionally unstable and inherently unhealthy, it's for their own good and the good of society that women's roles in public life are limited.

Diagnosis of PMS relies on culture-specific technology as well as ideology. To diagnose PMS one must have a knowledge of hormones and their actions and accept the idea that hormones influence affect and behavior. There are no reliable laboratory tests for PMS, but calendars, thermometers, hormone assay techniques, nutrient deficiency measures, and self-report questionnaires have been used in attempts to document its existence. Technology may be involved in the cause as well as the detection of premenstrual symptoms. Landers (1988) has suggested that PMS may be an iatrogenic disease (i.e., an illness caused by medical intervention) because it frequently begins or worsens when a woman is using an IUD or stops using oral contraceptives or after she has had a hysterectomy, a tubal ligation, or an abortion.

The ideologies on which the diagnosis of PMS relies include the raging-hormone hypothesis, an assumption that cyclic change is inherently pathological, an acceptance of stereotypical gender roles as accurate and appropriate descriptions of healthy behavior for women and men, and a social contract between the patient and physician (McDaniel, 1988) that allows patients to trust their physicians as experts who are able to make a diagnosis in a case in which the symptoms are so vague and numerous.

These ideologies are responsible for the fact that many women who experience premenstrual changes diagnose themselves as having PMS.

They then talk about PMS with their friends and thus contribute to giving PMS a legitimacy it doesn't deserve. Such self-diagnosis is dangerous for women because individual acts affect culture as well as being affected by it. When others hear women complaining about PMS, it reinforces these ideologies and persuades others that women cannot be trusted to do important work or to make decisions that have serious implications.

Successful treatment is accomplished only by participants in that culture. The act of being diagnosed has a therapeutic effect for many women who suffer from premenstrual changes, whether or not the symptoms are alleviated (Abplanalp, 1983; McDaniel, 1988). Women are accustomed to having their complaints dismissed by powerful others, and the diagnosis may represent one of the few times someone has listened to the women in a way that made them feel worthy of attention (Abplanalp, 1983). The use of the label PMS indicates that the physician and the patient accept society's standards and the cultural assumptions discussed earlier, which may, in a way, be comforting.

One of the characteristics that women who complain of PMS share is a strong placebo response (McDaniel, 1988). Many cures in Western medicine rely on pills, and patients are accustomed to expect relief from them. A placebo response is a good thing to exhibit if the problem is PMS because there is no effective treatment for it. Women often try a variety of treatments in search of relief or are advised to treat individual symptoms.

Women may be more likely than men to have external health locus of control, that is, to be less likely than men to think that they can affect their health by their own actions. Seeking treatment for PMS, then, can be empowering for women because they will have to be put in charge of their health and self-care. Women will be assigned such tasks as charting symptoms and taking their temperatures daily during the diagnosis phase and then advised to alter their diet, exercise regularly, and learn relaxation strategies. These tasks also have the advantage of causing them to focus on taking good care of themselves and directing their attention away from the people and institutions in their daily lives that make them feel tense, anxious, and depressed (McDaniel, 1988).

Women believed to have PMS are often advised to join self-help groups. Self-help and support groups have become very popular with many Americans in recent years, and one can find such a group for almost any medical or psychological disorder or social situation. People from other cultures would find it very odd to talk about such private matters with a group of strangers and to accept advice from untrained peers!

Treatment judged as successful in one cultural context may not be understood as successful from another perspective. The purpose of treating PMS is to help women to function more smoothly in their traditional, subordinate, "feminine" role "in an uncomplaining, cheerful way" (Rome, 1986). Dalton has suggested that it is a woman's duty and obligation to be treated for PMS (Rome, 1986). Adherence to rigid gender roles may not be seen as a successful treatment even within subcultural contexts of our own society!

Progesterone therapy, which has never been approved by the FDA, has been a popular recommendation for PMS, especially in Great Britain. Side-effects of progesterone include chest pain, yeast infections from vaginal suppositories, diarrhea and cramping from rectal suppositories, excessive drop in blood pressure from sublingual administration (Rome, 1986), continuous bleeding, amenorrhea, menses that are heavier or lighter than usual, dizzy spells, restlessness, gain or loss of weight, uterine cramps, and change in sex drive (Landers, 1988). Sometimes progesterone therapy simply displaces the symptoms to another phase of the cycle. Results of animal studies suggest that progesterone may be addictive and increase cancer risk (Landers, 1988). Thus, the original symptoms may be much milder than the side-effects of the treatment. Is this a cure?

Probably the most serious treatment that has been used to alleviate PMS is hysterectomy plus oophorectomy—the surgical removal of the uterus and ovaries. It is unlikely that interfering so drastically with a woman's body and ending her fertility would be seen as a successful treatment in other cultures.

The symptoms of PMS may be recognized and similarly organized elsewhere but are not categorized as the same dysfunction or "disease." The symptoms associated with PMS are numerous and vague and have considerable overlap with those of other conditions. They could easily be recognized but organized differently. Many of the symptoms—headaches, backaches, irritability, tension, crying spells—are also associated with stress. It is agreed that stress worsens PMS, but perhaps stress actually causes these PMS "symptoms" just as it does in men.

None of the symptoms associated with PMS are unique to menstruation. What seems to be important to Western medicine is cyclicity, which is seen as instability. If cyclic or rhythmic changes were seen as normative or natural, then emotional, behavioral, and physiological changes would be accepted and expected. They would not be pathologized.

Thinking about our premenstrual experience in a different way would also change our illness behavior. Instead of considering yourself as "overreacting," consider yourself "sensitive" (Koeske, 1987). Changing your attributions about premenstrual changes would also make you feel better. If you know you are premenstrual, thinking "Water retention makes my tear ducts feel full" is probably more accurate than thinking "I am depressed and about to cry" (Koeske, 1987). Consider whether some of the changes associated with PMS should even be considered symptoms. If we lived in a society that preferred loose clothing such as robes or saris, then water retention might not even be noticed (Rome, 1986). In our weight-obsessed society the small weight gain from premenstrual fluid retention is actively feared by many women. Probably only in the United States could an occasional urge to eat a candy bar or a salty snack be seen as a sign of a medical condition!

Most of the research on PMS is done by scientists in a few Western countries (Australia, Canada, Germany, Great Britain, the Netherlands, Sweden, and the United States), which share many common cultural beliefs. World Health Organization (WHO) surveys indicate that menstrual cycle–related complaints (except cramps) are most likely to be reported by women living in western Europe, Australia, and North America. Paige (1973) found that the most severe menstrual complaints came from strict Catholics and Orthodox Jews who strongly adhered to the feminine gender role.

WHY HAS PMS BECOME SO SIGNIFICANT?

Why has PMS become so well-known in the last 20 years? With hindsight we can see how the development of interest in PMS coincided with the conservative political shift in the United States and Great Britain in the 1970s and 1980s. It is part of the backlash against feminists so clearly delineated by Susan Faludi (1991). The British women who were tried for murdering their boyfriends must have seemed like a terrible threat to society: What if women everywhere started to treat men the way men treat women? No wonder the British courts accepted the insanity plea. Those women were not normal; oh no, they must have been sick and crazy!

To understand the significance of PMS one must consider who benefits from it. Women? To some extent, yes—if they can excuse behavior others disapprove of by suggesting it was caused by PMS. If physicians or others pay attention to women and take them seriously, women may be said to benefit from seeking help for PMS. Yet, the benefits to women are few, and the drawbacks many. The existence of PMS encourages women to think of themselves as unstable and potentially ill for at least half of each month. It encourages men to think of us that way, too, which limits our opportunities for self-expression and career advancement. Now that the American Psychiatric Association has placed in the fourth edition of their *Diagnostic and Statistical Manual* a mental illness called premenstrual dysphoric disorder, there will be additional ways to stigmatize women and use PMS to our disadvantage.

Emily Martin (1987) has drawn attention to the historical importance of the waves of interest in PMS. Frank "discovered" premenstrual tension around 1930, during the depression, when the economic gains women made during World War I were slipping away. He noted (Frank, 1931) that premenstrual women engaged in foolish and ill-considered actions, and he worried about the consequences these actions might have in the workplace. When she began to study PMS during the 1950s, Katharina Dalton became part of a movement, whether she intended to or not, to convince women to become full-time housewives and leave their jobs to World War II veterans. In the late 1970s, when work on PMS again picked up speed, women had made enormous advances in work, school, and public life thanks to the women's liberation movement. Each time women advance, there's someone there to remind us that we can't go further because of our delicate health.

Who benefits from PMS? The physicians who treat the many women who seek relief from it benefit greatly from the widespread belief that PMS is a disease. Gynecologists and psychiatrists have been battling each other over who has the "right" to treat PMS. Medical researchers and other scientists who work in the biomedical model have benefited greatly from the interest in PMS, as they have been given government and corporate grants to find a cause and cure for PMS. Pharmaceutical companies sponsor research conferences and medical education seminars on PMS in the hope that some drug they can manufacture will be the long-awaited cure (Parlee, as cited in Tavris, 1992). If the publicity about PMS has convinced most women that they have a monthly illness, think what the profits could be on a drug millions of women would buy every month!

The greatest beneficiary of PMS is the status quo. PMS serves to keep women in their place; it is a form of social control. It's a culture-bound syndrome because it is only necessary in societies in which women have made major gains toward equality of rights and opportunities. If women are preoccupied with rhythmic changes in their bodies and emotions instead of preoccupied with winning political power, social institutions are safe.

What do women learn from the label PMS? Karen Levy (1993) believes that it tells women that their problems are internal and individual; warns women not to express the entire range of their emotions because some of their feelings and behaviors are inappropriate; isolates women from the social, cultural, and environmental context of their lives by defining their experience as a medical problem; alienates women from each other and from their collective experience; and silences women from speaking out about the oppressive conditions of their lives.

SOME ADVICE

Stop thinking of menstruation as negative. It has positive aspects, too. Talk about its benefits with your classmates (for example, it's presence is a sign of good health, it is symbolic of our connection to other women, it represents biological maturity, it signifies our ability to bear children or lets us know we are not pregnant). Stop using negative slang to describe menstruation. My friend Ingrid Johnston likes to refer to the menstrual period as AOW, or Affirmation of Womanhood. Try doing that; see how your friends react. Refer to your premenstrual experiences as "changes" rather than "symptoms." A change is a neutral thing. A symptom implies an illness.

Examine your attributions about unpleasant experiences. Never let someone get away with suggesting that your emotions are caused by hormones. Hormonal fluctuations don't make women angry or irritable, although they may intensify those reactions. There are always reasons for your anger, and it's those reasons, not your hormones, that should be discussed. Dalton (1977) noticed that women who live alone are less likely to suffer from PMS than women who live with men. That makes sense to me. After all, it's other people who make us irritable and tense!

The purpose of this lecture was not to suggest that premenstrual changes don't exist. They do, as many women know from personal experience. What I hope you'll do is think about whether your experience of these changes is serious enough to be considered an illness. In most cases, it won't be. And if it's not, don't stereotype yourself and other women by excusing your behavior or by attributing your feelings to PMS. Think about who benefits if you do.

REFERENCES

ABPLANALP, J. M. (1983). Premenstrual syndrome: A selective review. *Women & Health, 8*(2/3), 107–124.

BROOKS-GUNN, J., & RUBLE, D.N. (1986). Men's and women's attitudes and beliefs about the menstrual cycle. *Sex Roles, 14,* 287–299.

BROWNELL, K. (1991). Personal responsibility and control over our bodies: When expectation exceeds reality. *Health Psychology, 10,* 303–310.

CASSIDY, C. M. (1982). Protein-energy malnutrition as a culture-bound syndrome. *Culture, Medicine, and Psychiatry, 6,* 325–345.

CHRISLER, J. C. (1988). Age, gender-role orientation, and attitudes toward menstruation. *Psychological Reports, 63,* 827–834.

CHRISLER, J. C., JOHNSTON, I. K., CHAMPAGNE, N. M., & PRESTON, K. E. (1994). Menstrual joy: The construct and its consequences. *Psychology of Women Quarterly, 18,* 375–387.

CHRISLER, J. C., & LEVY, K. B. (1990). The media construct a menstrual monster: A content analysis of PMS articles in the popular press. *Women & Health, 16*(2), 89–104.

CLARKE, A. E., & RUBLE, D. N. (1978). Young adolescents' beliefs concerning menstruation. *Child Development, 49,* 231–234.

DALTON, K. (1960a). Effects of menstruation on schoolgirls' weekly work. *British Medical Journal, 1,* 326–328.

DALTON, K. (1960b). Schoolgirls' behaviour and menstruation. *British Medical Journal, 2,* 1647–1649.

DALTON, K. (1968). Menstruation and examinations. *Lancet, 2,* 1386–1388.

DALTON, K. (1977). *The premenstrual syndrome and progesterone therapy.* Chicago: Yearbook Medical.

DEBROVNER, C. (1982). *Premenstrual tension: An interdisciplinary approach.* New York: Human Sciences.

FALUDI, S. (1991). *Backlash: The undeclared war against American women.* New York: Crown.

FRANK, R. T. (1931). The hormonal causes of premenstrual tension. *Archives of Neurology and Psychiatry, 26,* 1053–1057.

GOLUB, S. (1981). Sex differences in attitudes and beliefs regarding menstruation. In P. Komnenich, M. McSweeney, J. A. Noack, & N. Elder (Eds.), *The menstrual cycle: Research and implications for women's health* (pp. 129–134). New York: Springer.

KOESKE, R. D. (1983). Lifting the curse of menstruation: Toward a feminist perspective on the menstrual cycle. *Women & Health, 8*(2/3), 1–16.

LANDERS, L. (1988). *Images of bleeding: Menstruation as ideology.* New York: Orlando Press.

LAWS, S. (1983). The sexual politics of premenstrual tension. *Women's Studies International Forum, 6,* 19–31.

LEVY, K. B. (1993). *The politics of women's health care: Medicalization as a form of social control.* Mesquite, TX: Ide House.

MARTIN, E. (1987). *The woman in the body: A cultural analysis of reproduction.* Boston: Beacon.

MARTIN, E. (1988). Premenstrual syndrome: Discipline, work, and anger in late industrial societies. In T. Buckley, & A. Gottlieb (Eds.), *Blood magic: The anthropology of menstruation* (pp. 161–181). Berkeley, CA: University of California Press.

MCDANIEL, S. H. (1988). The interpersonal politics of premenstrual syndrome. *Family Systems Medicine, 6,* 134–149.

MEIGS, J. W. (1961). Occupational medicine. *New England Journal of Medicine, 264,* 861–867.

MOOS, R. H. (1968). The development of a Menstrual Distress Questionnaire. *Psychosomatic Medicine, 30,* 853–867.

PAIGE, K. E. (1973). Women learn to sing the menstrual blues. *Psychology Today, 4* (9), 41–46.

RIPPER, M. (1991). A comparison of the effect of the menstrual cycle and the social week on mood, sexual interest, and self-assessed performance. In D. L. Taylor, & N. F. Woods (Eds.), *Menstruation, health, and illness* (pp. 19–33). Washington: Hemisphere.

RITENBAUGH, C. (1982). Obesity as a culture-bound syndrome. *Culture, Medicine, and Psychiatry, 6,* 347–361.

ROME, E. (1986). Premenstrual syndrome through a feminist lens. In V. L. Olesen, & N. F. Woods (Eds.), *Culture, society, and menstruation* (pp. 145–151). Washington: Hemisphere.

RUDER, FINN, & ROTMAN. (1981). *The Tampax Report.* New York: Author.

SIEGAL, G. S. (1963). *Periodic health examinations: Abstracts from the literature.* Public Health Service publication #1010. Washington, DC: U.S. Government Printing Office.

SOMMER, B. (1983). How does menstruation affect women's cognitive competence and psychophysiological response? *Women & Health, 8*(2/3), 53–90.

TAVRIS, C. (1992). *The mismeasure of woman.* New York: Simon & Schuster.

THOMAS, C. L. (Ed.). (1989). *Taber's cyclopedic medical dictionary* (17th ed.). Philadelphia: F. A. Davis.

TOWNSEND, J. M., & CARBONE, C. L. (1980). Menopausal syndrome: Illness or social role—a transcultural analysis. *Culture, Medicine, and Psychiatry, 4,* 229–248.

ZITA, J. N. (1988). The premenstrual syndrome: "Dis-easing" the female cycle. *Hypatia, 3*(1), 77–99.

SUGGESTED READINGS

GOLUB, S. (1992). *Periods: From menarche to menopause.* Newbury Park, CA: Sage.

LAWS, S. (1990). *Issues of blood: The politics of menstruation.* London: Macmillan.

MARTIN, E. (1987). *The woman in the body: A cultural analysis of reproduction.* Boston: Beacon.

*C*ONNIE S. CHAN *is Associate Professor of Human Services and Co-Director of the Institute for Asian American Studies at the University of Massachusetts at Boston. Dr. Chan has taught an interdisciplinary course on Asian women in America at U. Mass, Wellesley College, and Harvard University since 1987. Her research and writing is focused on the intersection of gender, cultural, and sexual identity in bilingual and bicultural women of color in the United States.*

9

Asian American Women and Adolescent Girls:

Sexuality and Sexual Expression

❖

his lecture addresses the cultural factors that shape and influence sexual expression and sexual identity for Asian American adolescent girls and women. As a group that is bicultural and bilingual to varying degrees, Asian American females confront a sometimes conflicting and confusing set of social and cultural values from their own ethnic and family origin as well as from their exposure to the mainstream "American" culture.

How do Asian American adolescent girls and women make sense of these cues and these values? How do they experience their sexuality, and what models are available to them as they develop their sense of themselves as sexual beings? What is the interaction of these cultural factors upon the choices they make about their sexual expression and sexual identity?

My discussion of these cultural factors is based upon a review of the research in this area and upon my clinical experience working with Asian American teenagers, women, and their families.

Before any discussion of Asian cultural factors, it is important to note that Asians are a very diverse and heterogeneous population, with over 30 separate and distinct ethnic groups, each with their own values, languages, customs, and traditions. To consider combining these very different groups into a single term as "Asian" or "Asian American" requires a certain degree of generalization. This generalization is based upon two assumptions: (1) that Asian groups share a common foundation of cultural values based upon the Confucian and Buddhist

123

philosophies, which stress harmony with others, maintaining the family unit, and the importance of women's familial role as daughter, wife, and mother; and (2) that Americans of Asian descent and immigrants from Asia share a similar experience. This experience is based upon a history of racism characterized by a host of exclusionary laws that institutionalized the prejudice against Asians in this country: laws that severely limited the numbers of Asians allowed into the United States, prohibited Asians from becoming American citizens, kept them from owning property (parents were frequently forced to register their property in the names of their American-born children), and outlawed marriage between Asians and white Americans.

Most non-Asians do not distinguish among the various Asian ethnic groups, and, as a result, tend to treat all Asian Americans in the same manner without regard to individual or ethnic group differences. Although Americans of Asian descent in the United States vary from fourth-generation American citizens to recent immigrants and refugees, they still share a common experience in the reactions they receive from American society.

Although we share some similarities as Asian Americans, our personal assimilation and levels of acculturation are unique and very much influenced by individual and familial experiences—how long we have been in the United States, how much contact we have with hegemonic American culture, what languages we speak at home, how literate we are in English and/or an Asian native language—as well as social and economic factors.

SEXUALITY: A FOUNDATION FOR UNDERSTANDING THE CONCEPTS

With these considerations in mind, let's now look at what the literature provides in understanding the concept of sexuality and sexual identity. First, as Chinese American sociologist Alice Tsui (1985) points out, any open discussion of sexuality or sexual expression is unusual, as sexuality is a very sensitive subject in Asian culture. Even among one's closest friends a discussion about sexuality is considered to be awkward and highly embarrassing at best, and at worst strictly taboo.

This extreme discomfort with open and direct discussion of sexuality is sometimes misconstrued as *asexuality*. Other times it is thought that this discomfort means that Asians are extremely repressed about sex and sexual identity. Both perceptions, although common, are incorrect. Most Asian cultures are neither asexual nor extremely repressed. There is a long history of Asian erotica, both in literature and in art, as well as documentation of private expressions of sexuality and sexual interest in personal journals and in letters. However, what is presented in *public* is very different from what is presented in *private*.

The distinction between the public and private self is a very important concept in most Asian cultures. For women, the public self conforms to the expected gender and familial roles of a dutiful daughter, wife, and mother. A woman is expected to behave in a way that is socially acceptable, and she tries to avoid actions that would bring shame upon herself and her family.

Sexuality, including discussing sexual matters, should only be expressed within the context of one's private self. The private self is never seen by anyone other than a woman's most intimate family and friends. In some cases, an Asian American woman may choose never to reveal her private self to anyone. The dichotomy between the public self and the private self is much more distinct in Asian cultures than in Western cultures.

Why is this private-public split so important in understanding sexuality in Asian cultures? Not only is there very little public expression of sexuality, but private expressions of sexuality may take very different forms than in Western culture. Sexual and erotic behavior may be expressed only in private or in far more subtle and indirect ways in a public setting. Subtle nuances, such as a change in the register of voices of two people having a conversation, minimal physical contact such as the brush of a hand against the other person, a quick glance with the meeting of an eye, and barely discernible language patterns that reflect affection might be misperceived as nonsexual in nature by Westerners. These subtle, very indirect expressions of sexuality may easily be missed by those who are unfamiliar with the cultural cues and norms—not only non-Asians but also Asian American girls who may not see any obvious sexual expression from their parents and other adults.

Lacking role models within their own families for appropriate sexual and erotic behavior, Asian American adolescent girls may search elsewhere for examples of appropriate sexual expression. They may observe non-Asian peers, watch movies and television, and seek out sexually explicit pictures and stories in magazines. Because most of these available models will be Western in culture, Asian American girls may feel caught between the Asian cultural expectation of suppression of sexual expression and the Western expectation of developing a comfort with one's sexual expression.

*A*SIAN CULTURAL EXPECTATIONS OF SEXUAL EXPRESSION

Let's look at Asian cultural expectations. Most Asian cultures take pride in their sense of propriety and good manners in all areas of interaction, including in sexual and general female-male interactions. Sexuality exists, but it is rarely allowed open expression; control of individual sexual gratification and expression is expected. This control is necessary because the Asian cultural system assumes that individual needs are not as important as family and community needs. Thus, suppression of sexual desire is expected, especially for girls and women, because they are not allowed to indulge in individual needs that might bring shame or dishonor to the family. Historically, in Asian cultures, a woman would not be allowed to express her own sexuality and her own desire for sexual activity. If women expressed or acted upon their sexual desires, the custom of arranged marriage based upon social class would be undermined. Traditionally, the value of a young woman to her family was her ability to receive a dowry payment for a suitable marriage. A young Asian woman would have to be pure and chaste to be suitable for an arranged marriage.

Even in modern times, any open expression of sexuality outside of marriage is strictly forbidden. Extramarital sexual activity of any kind would bring great shame upon not only the woman herself but, more importantly, upon her family, clan, and community. Asian adolescent girls and women are expected to remain not only virginal but devoid of sexual desire and expression until their marriages.

These rigid restrictions upon the public and open expression of sexuality should not be mistaken, however, as a denial of sexuality, even for females, within Asian culture. As Alice Tsui (1985) noted, sexuality is considered a very normal part of life and an integral part of one's existence. Though little conscious attention is paid to sexuality, much as one gives very little attention to the normal breathing process, an individual's sexuality is expected to "stay healthy." It is something that one keeps in check and monitors from time to time, but Asian culture does not allow for public sexual expression that might be considered inappropriate.

At first glance, this Asian perception of sexuality as a "very normal part of life" seems to be in contradiction to the reported sexually conservative behavior among Asian Americans, but the two views are actually compatible. Research on Asian American sexual expression, although sparse, does describe "conservative" sexual behavior. Erikson and Moore (1986) indicate that Asian American high school students were significantly less likely to talk about sexual matters than were their white, Latina/o or African American classmates. Thus, what is seen as sexual conservatism may actually be suppression not of sexual desires but of overt verbal and behavioral expression of sexuality. The absence of sexual expression is likely caused by rigid behavioral and expressive restrictions in traditional Asian cultures. As noted by Hirayama and Hirayama (1986), social order and control of emotions and feelings are highly valued among Japanese Americans. Outward displays of emotion are strongly discouraged. In contrast to the Western concept of individualism and independence in one's actions, Asian cultures value family or group unity, especially for females. Children are taught to depend upon the family and to have the utmost respect for their parents' expectations of them. This restraint of emotion and respect for family gives the family a greater degree of control over teenage and adult children. As a result, sexual expression and behavior of adolescents and young adults may be influenced by family values and expectations far more in Asian families than in Western culture.

SEXUAL BEHAVIOR AMONG ASIAN AMERICAN YOUTH

Traditional cultural values such as strong disapproval of marital infidelity and a tendency toward what Erikson and Moore (1986) term "sexually conservative behavior" may help to reduce the risk for HIV and other sexually transmitted diseases. We must be careful, however, not to confuse conservatism in the outward expression of one's sexuality with an absence of sexual activity or with the notion that this will result in less high-risk sexual behavior.

There are indications that when Asian American youth have sex, they engage in high-risk sexual practices to the same degree as do non-Asian youth. Cochran, Mays, and Leung (1991) studied the sexual practices of 153 heterosexual Asian American college students, ages 18 to 25. Asian American students reported unprotected sexual intercourse to the same degree as non-Asian students. Cochran et al. (1991) found no difference between U.S.-born and Asian-born students in their sexual practices.

Another common assumption is that Asian American adolescents and young adults are less sexually active than their non–Asian American peers. There is some evidence, both in the research literature and in clinical experience, that this perception is accurate. Cochran et al. (1991) found that 47 percent of their sample population were sexually active. This finding was significantly lower than among whites in the sample (72 percent), African Americans (84 percent), and Latinas/os (59 percent). Nationally 54 to 57 percent of white 19-year-olds report that they are sexually active. Cochran's study, therefore, supports the notion that either Asian American young adults are less sexually active than their non-Asian peers, or they are less likely to report that they are sexually active.

This finding conforms to my clinical experience and the reports of other clinicians who work with an Asian American population. In my adolescent discussion groups, Asian-born girls, ages 15 to 18, frequently reported that they were responding to explicit demands from both their families and their peers to refrain from expressing their sexuality. They noted that their non-Asian classmates joked and teased about boyfriends and sometimes talked openly about having sex. Within their own Asian peer group, there was an explicit expectation that couples do not engage in sexual activity unless they are "very seriously" involved, that is, engaged or nearly engaged to be married. Until they were convinced of the existence of such a commitment, the Asian American girls tried to avoid sexual activity in their relationships, even if pressured by their boyfriends.

Moreover, Asian American adolescent girls expressed the strong desire to avoid and downplay expressions of their sexuality in any form. They dressed conservatively, used minimal make-up and nonsexual body language, and preferred to be with boys while in groups rather than alone, limiting sexual expression to kissing and holding hands rather than what they termed "bodily contact."

Adolescent Asian American girls also struggle with their own version of meeting the idealized American concept of female beauty. In a 1985 study of 30 Asian American teenage girls, I found this group to be significantly less satisfied with their physical appearance than their non-Asian peers. The Asian American girls reported that they were shorter, smaller, had smaller breasts, and were less physically strong than their white, Black, and Latina classmates. Their lack of satisfaction with their body image is reflected in their sense of self, as their scores on self-esteem scales were also lower than the standardized norm for teenage American girls. These Asian-born 14- to 19-year-old teenage girls also reported feeling more vulnerable in the American social environment. They reported that they had to learn to adapt to new social standards and expectations while still having to fulfill their parents' strict expectations of what is acceptable public behavior for an Asian adolescent girl.

MEDIA IMAGES OF ASIAN AMERICAN FEMALES

An added burden, the Western media often eroticizes and stereotypes Asian women, particularly in visual media. The history of Western colonization of Asian countries, and U.S. involvement in the Philippines, Japan, and China and, more recently, in Korea and Southeast Asia has created the perception in the American public mind that Asian women are prostitutes and sexual objects. This perception has not been restricted to Western soldiers overseas but is portrayed and perpetuated through film and other media in the United States and Europe. Although Asian people were frequently depicted as teeming masses in war movies, Asian women, shown in relation to a Western man, were almost always eroticized as exotic sexual objects. Asian women have suffered from a cultural stereotype of being exotic, subservient, sexy, passive, and available. More recently, the advertisements of Asian women mail-order brides, pictures of sexy Asian women in stocking and perfume ads, and images of competent but beautiful Asian women newscasters and ice skaters have dominated (and limited) the public image of Asian women in the United States. Some adolescents struggle to model these images at the same time that they balance the cultural message from their families to downplay their appearance and sexuality.

JUGGLING CONFLICTING MESSAGES FROM TWO CULTURES

Feeling vulnerable in a country where behavioral expectations and beauty standards are different and having to juggle conflicting cultural demands poses a dilemma for many Asian American girls and young women. Social control of the expression of sexuality comes from three primary sources: (1) from the family, including parents, grandparents, and older siblings; (2) from the adolescent peer group; and (3) from the social environment, including school and community. The greater the influence of traditional Asian cultural expectations, the fewer the choices an Asian American female will believe she has in deciding how she will express her own sexuality.

Within traditional Asian culture, parents play the dominant role in an adolescent girl's understanding of what would be considered appropriate expressions of sexuality. Although open and frank discussion of these issues with parents is unusual, Asian American teenagers consistently report that they receive strong and direct messages from their parents if their appearance or behavior is considered overtly sexual in nature. The parental messages that these Asian American girls receive may not be very different from those expressed by non-Asian parents. However, the difference lies in the relatively greater risk faced by Asian American girls and women if they do not follow the proscribed behavioral, cultural, and gender-role expectations of appropriate sexual expression. Any deviation from the range of acceptable behaviors may result not only in punishment but also in strong expressions of disappointment and shame from family members.

An Asian American adolescent girl or woman who transgresses in the realm of sexual activity, such as being "caught" kissing, hugging, or petting in a car, having premarital sexual intercourse, engaging in homosexual physical contact, contracting a sexually transmitted disease, or getting pregnant can expect to be openly punished and shamed within the family. Given the strong family ties, she might internalize some of the disappointment and shame expressed by family members. She may experience guilt, loss of self-confidence and self-esteem, and feelings of depression. These feelings may be expressed as physical ailments, irritability, eating disorders, lack of concentration, and withdrawal from emotional attachments and social activities.

Asian American adolescent girls may exhibit these classic symptoms of depression when struggling with the conflict between their desire to express their sexuality in a culture that restricts this expression. Western counselors and therapists frequently misunderstand this overwhelming sense of guilt and shame and the bind in which these young women find themselves. The counselors often mistakenly believe that the depression-like symptoms are an overreaction to familial disappointment or to one's own rigid superego or conscience. However, within the context of Asian American culture, reactions of this type are not uncommon among adolescent girls and young women. Rather than being characterological, the symptoms may be situational and based upon a feeling that she has no real options and is caught in a no-win situation. A counselor should help a client in this situation to understand her familial, peer, and internal pressures and work toward identifying viable options, which may not satisfy all parties but will allow her to regain some sense of control and choice in her decisions.

First- and second-generation Asian Americans, both female and male, often feel an extra burden of meeting their family's expectations of the American dream and are caught in these transitional cultural norms. Given their parents' sacrifices to emigrate to the United States, first-generation American-born teenagers often feel a greater burden to meet their family's expectations. They also feel a greater responsibility and guilt if they are unable to live up to these demands. They are in the difficult position of having to maintain the mother culture *and* assimilate into American culture. When these familial and cultural expectations clash, the transitional generation faces the difficult task of finding a comfortable way of integrating conflicting values.

During the teenage years, the struggle often focuses around sexuality and the expression of sexuality for Asian American girls and young women. Each individual finds her own solution to this conflict: Some live double lives, pretending to be dutiful daughters at home, while engaging in more typically American behaviors when away from the family. Others do not risk family disapproval but follow family expectations. Still others, usually those who have been caught transgressing the gender-expectations for "good girls," may rebel and assert their independence from family and traditional cultural norms.

How do Asian American adolescent girls and women make these decisions about their actions and their sexual expression? When they can begin to recognize the conflicting messages of their cultures, their peers, and their families, they may understand that they are caught in an intersection in which varying expectations of their sexual behavior clash. When they do begin to recognize the conflicting messages, then they can understand their bind. After that, they can make informed choices and anticipate the kinds of reactions they might receive to the expressions of sexuality that they choose.

LESBIAN AND BISEXUAL OPTIONS

There are many choices of sexual expression that an Asian adolescent girl or young woman might consider. Such choices might include engaging in homosexual or bisexual activity. On first glance, this might appear to be outside the realm of appropriate behavior, but further examination may show that it is more plausible than it seems.

Given the traditional Asian cultural restrictions against open or public expression of sexuality, identification of *any* sexual identity (whether homosexual, heterosexual, or bisexual) may be unacceptable in traditional Asian cultures. For an Asian woman to identify as a lesbian or as a bisexual would make a private expression of sexuality into a public one. Thus the expression of homosexuality or bisexuality may exist within private expression or even within private identification with a sexual identity, but public expression and public identification as lesbian, gay, or bisexual would be completely out of character with traditional Asian cultural values.

As a result, far fewer Asian American lesbians and bisexuals may openly identify as such. Indeed, there is a common perception that there are proportionately fewer Asian and Asian American lesbian, gay, and bisexual individuals than in the non-Asian population, but there may simply be smaller numbers of openly identified lesbian, bisexual, and gay Asian Americans because of the reluctance to have a public identification of sexuality of any kind. It can also be argued that an Asian American woman who identifies herself as a lesbian or bisexual would have a greater identification with Western cultural influences than with the Asian culture, which values the privacy of one's sexuality. Moreover, with only a minimal identity as an individual distinct from the identity as a member of a family, having a sexual identity may be literally inconceivable except to those who are much more acculturated into a Western identity.

My study of lesbian and gay Asian Americans (Chan, 1989) supports this concept. Much as Oliva Espin (1987) found that Latina lesbians preferred to be affirmed as both lesbian and Latina (see Chapter 12), my study indicated that Asian lesbians felt strongly about keeping both their cultural and sexual identities. Yet, if forced to choose between the two communities, respondents in my study identified more closely with the lesbian community. Although they felt marginalized and somewhat stereotyped within the lesbian community, Asian American lesbians reported feeling even more invisible and invalidated for their sexual orientation within Asian American culture and communities.

Ironically, the restrictions upon open expression of sexuality may actually create less dichotomization of heterosexual versus homosexual behavior. It may also create less rigidly defined sexual identities within Asian cultures. Instead, with the importance of the concept of private expression of sexuality, there could be more allowance of fluidity within a sexual behavior continuum. There may be less public expression but also less necessity for any definition or declaration of sexual orientation. And thus more exploration along the sexual identity continuum may be possible for Asian American girls and women.

At the same time, Asian American adolescent girls report that their parents never directly address the issue of homosexuality or bisexuality with them. However, the teenagers are exposed to both positive and negative images of openly lesbian, gay, and bisexual people in American society. Given this greater exposure to different sexual orientations, it is possible that Asian American females may experience relatively greater flexibility within their private explorations of sexuality but still have more limited restrictions upon their public expressions of sexuality. Within the private self, homosexual or bisexual activity may carry equal weight in comparison to heterosexual activity—after all, it is *sexual behavior* that must be expressed privately—and as a result, homosexual and bisexual behavior may not be as stigmatized as within Western culture.

This concept of the fluidity of sexual behavior does not necessarily mean that Asian cultures are less homophobic or that homosexuality is more tolerated within Asian communities. In fact, Asian American community standards of sexual expression may be *more* restrictive, because any public expression and identification of homosexuality and bisexuality are considered to be taboo.

Clinically, Asian American lesbians and bisexual women have reported that parents frequently have as much difficulty with acknowledging that their daughters are sexually active *at all* as with acknowledging that they are lesbian or bisexual. For some families of Asian lesbians and bisexual women, the issue of engaging in homosexual behavior may be avoided as parents focus primarily upon the taboo of the public expression of sexuality. Families then tend to expend their energy in condemning sexual activity and the inappropriate expression of one's sexual desires.

A case illustration (Chan, 1992, p. 122) may help to clarify this point. Sachiko, 22, is a Japanese American woman who identifies as a lesbian. She came out to her family shortly after becoming sexually involved with another woman. Refusing to accept or to even acknowledge her identity as a lesbian, Sachiko's parents were extremely upset that she was sexually active in any way. They declared that she would never be fit to be married or to be considered part of their family again. No matter how hard Sachiko tried to explain her sexual orientation or identity as a lesbian to her family, they refused to accept that she was anything but a sexually active unmarried woman. By insisting on affirming her own identity, Sachiko was perceived by her parents as having willingly brought shame upon their family. The family forbade her to disclose her lesbian identity to others and tried to convince her to discontinue her relationships with women. Sachiko, however, asserted her independence and insisted on affirming her identity as an Asian American lesbian.

FINDING A BALANCE THAT MAY SHIFT OVER TIME

Sachiko and women like her may choose to assert their independence from cultural restrictions and to express their sexuality more openly. Other Asian American young women may choose to refrain from expressing their sexuality, making individual decisions based upon their cultural pressures and social environments. As a group, Asian American girls and women confront a variety of messages concerning their sexuality and face many restrictions on what is acceptable private and public sexual expression. The traditional Asian cultural influences place a greater demand to restrict open expression of sexuality, whereas mainstream American culture exerts pressure to be more individualistic and openly sexually expressive. At the same time, American culture places greater emphasis upon the dichotomy of choosing either a homosexual or a heterosexual orientation.

Asian American girls and women make sense of these many messages and develop their own sense of themselves as sexual beings in individual ways; each finds her unique balance between Asian and American cultural influences. As with any identity development, sexual identity development is an ever-changing concept, which will integrate different aspects of both cultures over an individual's life span. For adolescent girls, the pressures of parental approval may loom largest and play the most important role in determining their expressions of sexuality. As they mature and become women, Asian American adolescents will develop their own sense of sexuality, which is less tied to their cultural and familial influences and is more reflective of their bicultural social environment.

REFERENCES

CHAN, C. S. (1985). Self-esteem and body image of Asian American adolescent girls. *Journal of the Asian American Psychological Association, 4,* 24–26.

CHAN, C. S. (1989). Issues of identity development among Asian American lesbians and gay men. *Journal of Counseling and Development, 68,* 16–20.

CHAN, C. S. (1992). Cultural considerations in counseling Asian American lesbians and gay men. In S. Dworkin & F. Gutierrez (Eds.), *Counseling gay men and lesbians: Journey to the end of the rainbow* (pp. 115–124). Alexandria, VA: American Association for Counseling and Development.

COCHRAN, S., MAYS, V., & LEUNG, L. (1991). Sexual practices of heterosexual Asian-American young adults: Implications for risk of HIV infection. *Archives of Sexual Behavior, 20,* 381–391.

ERIKSON, P. I., & MOORE, D. S. (1986). *Sexual activity, birth control use, and attitudes among high school students from three minority groups.* Paper presented at the meeting of the American Public Health Association, Las Vegas, NV.

ESPIN, O. (1987). Issues of identity in the psychology of Latina lesbians. In Boston Lesbian Psychologies Collective (Eds.), *Lesbian psychologies* (pp. 35–51). Urbana, IL: University of Illinois Press.

HIRAYAMA, H., & HIRAYAMA, K. (1986). The sexuality of Japanese Americans. *Journal of Social Work and Human Sexuality, 4,* 81–98.

TSUI, A. (1985). Psychotherapeutic considerations in sexual counseling for Asian immigrants. *Psychotherapy, 22,* 357–362.

SUGGESTED READINGS

CHAN, C. S. (1989). Issues of identity development among Asian American lesbians and gay men. *Journal of Counseling and Development, 68,* 16–20.

CHAN, C. S. (1992). Cultural considerations in counseling Asian American lesbians and gay men. In S. Dworkin & F. Gutierrez (Eds.), *Counseling gay men and lesbians: Journey to the end of the rainbow* (pp. 115–124). Alexandria, VA: American Association for Counseling and Development.

COCHRAN, S., MAYS, V., & LEUNG, L. (1991). Sexual practices of heterosexual Asian-American young adults: Implications for risk of HIV infection. *Archives of Sexual Behavior, 20,* 381–391.

*L*INDA **D.** G*ARNETS* is a Lecturer in Psychology and Women's Studies at the University of California at Los Angeles, where she teaches courses on the psychology of gender and the psychology of lesbian experience. Dr. Garnets is a psychotherapist and organizational consultant and specializes in working with nonprofit organizations and with lesbian and gay clients. She has written and lectured widely on lesbian and gay issues.

10

*L*ife as a *L*esbian:

What Does Gender Have to Do with It?

❖

*I*remember the first time I met a lesbian couple. I was beginning to think that I
might really be a lesbian, so I wanted to meet some other people who were
gay. Since I knew very few gay people, I had numerous fantasies about how
they were going to look and act. I vividly remember standing by my front door
waiting for them to arrive and having every possible stereotype about them. I
thought they were going to ride up on motorcycles and have greasy hair and
tatoos. I was shaking. But when I opened the door, there stood two of the most
ordinary-looking women. I thought they must be at the wrong apartment. At dinner, I shared how I expected them to look and act, and we all laughed at how different they were in reality from my stereotypes.

This story reminds us that in the absence of interaction with lesbians, we rely
on stereotypes about them. We have all heard these stereotypes: "Lesbians imitate
men in dress and mannerisms." "Lesbians are unfit parents." "Lesbians are abnormal and sick." "Lesbians are always flaunting their sexuality." "Lesbian relationships are unhappy and dysfunctional." These myths label lesbians as alien,
deviant, and flawed. Social stereotypes define lesbians largely in terms of characteristics that relegate us to unequal status and set us apart from heterosexuals.

Imagine someone asking a heterosexual person any of the following questions: "Is it possible your heterosexuality is just a phase you may outgrow?" "Why
do you heterosexuals feel compelled to seduce others into your lifestyle?" "With
all the societal support marriage receives, the divorce rate is spiraling. Why are
there so few stable relationships among heterosexuals?" "Why do heterosexuals

I am grateful to several colleagues who read and commented on earlier drafts of this article: Jacque-
line Goodchilds, Douglas Kimmel, Barrie Levy, Anne Peplau, and Dorothy Semenow.

place so much emphasis on sex?" "Considering the menace of overpopulation, how could the human race survive if everyone were heterosexual like you?" (Rochlin, 1980). Why do these statements sound so absurd? They assume that homosexuality is natural and superior to heterosexuality, a reversal of what most people actually believe. In fact, all of these questions are often asked about lesbians.

These stereotypes are used to deny lesbians full social participation and civil rights. How is this accomplished? The twin culprits are heterosexism and homophobia. *Heterosexism* is a pervasive set of attitudes akin to sexism and racism. It is defined as "an ideological system that denies, denigrates, and stigmatizes any nonheterosexual form of behavior, identity, relationship, or community" (Herek, 1990, p. 316). This assumption that everyone is or should be heterosexual is epitomized by notions that "for every girl, there is a boy" or "all women are going to marry someday." If someone had told me growing up that "for every girl, there is a girl or a boy," it would not have taken me so long to discover the possibility that I am gay.

By assuming that all people are or should be heterosexual, heterosexism excludes the needs, concerns, and life experiences of lesbians. Lesbians remain excluded from lists of protected categories in most civil rights legislation. As of 1994, except in seven states and a few dozen municipalities, no legal protection exists against overt discrimination against lesbians in employment, housing, or access to public accommodations. The 1992 campaigns in Oregon and Colorado asked voters to amend their state constitutions to forbid adoption of civil rights protections for gay people by any local or state governmental entity and to invalidate the phrase "sexual orientation" in any statute where it currently appeared. These statewide efforts were aimed at legislating gay men and lesbians out of existence.

Such heterosexist bias perpetuates the invisibility of lesbian existence. For example, I am in a 14-year relationship that I know is a life partnership, but it has no legal status because same-gender marriages are illegal. My partner and I cannot be jointly covered by insurance, inheritance laws, or hospital visitation rules. A good friend of ours was dying, and the hospital would only let her partner of 12 years see her if she pretended to be her sister. She was not considered "immediate family" by the hospital's visitation rules.

When the existence of lesbians is recognized, homophobia—defined as hatred and prejudice against lesbians and gay men—leads to institutional and personal hostility toward lesbians: We are hated and despised; we lose our jobs; we lose custody of our children; we face eviction from our homes, verbal harassment and physical attacks, alienation and rejection by our families, friends, and coworkers, and the burden of continually asserting our existence. Homophobic people use stereotypes about lesbians to justify discrimination, harassment, and acts of violence. For example, in a recent case in Virginia, a lesbian couple lost custody of their son to the mother of one of the couple solely because they are lesbians and therefore considered "unfit mothers." Another memorable example occurred in 1988 when a lesbian couple was shot while backpacking on the Appalachian Trail. One woman died, the other was seriously injured. As the surviving member of the couple explained, "He shot from where he was hidden in the woods 85 feet away, after he stalked us, hunted us, spied on us. Later his lawyer tried to assert that our sexuality provoked him. He shot us because he identified us as lesbians. He was a stranger with whom we had no connection. He shot us and left us for dead" (Brenner, 1992, p. 12).

Heterosexism and homophobia create a catch-22 situation for lesbians—between the fear of discrimination and harassment if we disclose our sexual orientation and the invisibility of our true selves if we don't. Many lesbians opt for invisibility as a way to avoid stigma, discrimination, and violence. Because lesbians are diverse and not easily identifiable, most can "pass" as heterosexual. This invisibility of sexual orientation obscures the true diversity of lesbians and contributes to widespread misconceptions about the realities of our lives. Even when lesbians are open about their sexual orientation, we do not automatically invalidate stereotypes about ourselves because each individual can be discounted as an exception to the general pattern.

In my first year of graduate school, after I had just come out, my professor in a psychopathology course invited in two gay men and two lesbians to talk about their lives. When they left the room, the professor spent the rest of the class pointing out each person's pathology and tying it to their being gay. This gave me a powerful message that what I was experiencing was sick and something I should hide.

The good news is that lesbians have shown great resilience in the face of social oppression. As individuals, we typically manage to form a positive sense of self and do not suffer from low self-esteem (Miranda & Storms, 1989). As members of groups, lesbians have worked together to form support networks and communities to facilitate a positive individual and group identity (D'Augelli & Garnets, in press).

GENDER STEREOTYPES AND ANTILESBIAN STEREOTYPES

When we look more closely at the content of antilesbian stereotypes, we discover that it is tied to gender stereotypes, reflecting a link between heterosexism and sexism. The students who take my class in the psychology of the lesbian experience are always a mix of heterosexuals, gay men and lesbians, and bisexual men and women. During the first class, I invite the students to participate in an exercise in which they call out cultural stereotypes for each of the following terms: masculine, feminine, gay man, and lesbian. I then ask them to examine the four lists and see what they notice about the relationships among the concepts. "Masculine" is defined using words suggesting positive and powerful images (dominant, assertive, independent, etc.). "Feminine" is depicted with words denoting power-lessness (passive, submissive, dependent, etc.). The descriptors for "gay man" are on the powerless and feminine side (passive, sissy, nurturant, etc.). In contrast, the list for "lesbian" stereotypes suggests powerful and masculine images but with a heavy negative bias added in (butch, hairy, dominating, man haters, etc.).

This exercise consistently reveals that gender stereotypes are an important aspect of antigay stereotypes. Specifically, lesbians are believed to have characteristics that are culturally defined as nonfeminine. As one lesbian described, "I really put down masculine-acting women until I came out and realized that not all lesbians act that way and that many straight women do" (Troiden, 1989, p. 57).

Let us consider this frequently asked question: Can someone be a "real" man or a "real" woman and be gay? Obviously a great deal depends on our definition of a "real" man or "real" woman. In our society, our masculinity or femininity comprise a core part of our identities, and being a "real" woman means being heterosexual. Because lesbians violate the cultural mandate of heterosexuality, it is assumed we deviate from gender expectations as well.

Lesbians' existence challenges basic assumptions about female role expectations. Stereotypes portray lesbians in relation to men. Lesbians are depicted as failed females who want to be men or who hate men. It is suggested that a woman becomes a lesbian because she has had bad sexual experiences with men or because she cannot get a man. Never mind that these stereotypes find no basis in the reality of lesbian experience, but arise instead from sexist assumptions that define women only in relation to men. A woman without a man is seen as a failure as a woman, and a lesbian is seen as unable to relate to men.

Let's now examine how women's roles and status shape stereotypes about lesbians today. In general, women have less power, less money, fewer job opportunities, fewer social outlets, less social and economic independence, and greater constraints on their autonomy than men. Lesbians share with all women the institutional oppression of sexism, which includes access to fewer material resources. In addition, lesbians face a second kind of discrimination based on their sexual orientation, which includes denial of civil rights and the social stigma of homosexuality.

In this context, heterosexuality can be seen as an institution reflecting male power over women. Men have markedly greater power, rights, and privileges than women. As a lesbian explained, "You have to drop a lot of options. Like economic security. Women don't usually have a lot of money" (Schneider, 1989, p. 128). Women's status and power in this context are linked to their relationships with and dependence on men. Lesbians experience their attractions to women in a social context that devalues both women and gay people.

These attitudes toward lesbians reflect a perceived threat to the traditional patriarchal power structure. Lesbians may be perceived as having greater power than heterosexual women because they live independently of men and do not depend on men for sexual, emotional, or financial support. As one lesbian stated, "You can't turn to men for typical things. You have to depend on yourself and on other women. Men tell you that you can't do things on your own, that you need a man. I don't need a man to help me with anything because I can do it myself. I may depend on other women, but it's not being dependent" (Schneider, 1989, p. 124). Lesbians' autonomy and self-sufficiency may be perceived as challenging both the female's subordinate status and the gender role that defines her identity only in terms of her relationship to men. In other words, "autonomous woman" becomes synonymous with lesbian, leading to accusations toward independent heterosexual women that they are the most hated kind of women: lesbians. And lesbians are "accused" of not being women.

COMING OUT

Now let's discuss a central aspect of lesbian experience: forming and maintaining a positive lesbian identity. Women come to label and construct their own lesbian identity through a process known as "coming out." Coming out is a complex sequence of events through which individuals acknowledge, recognize, and label their sexual orientation and then disclose it to others throughout their lives. In order to form a positive lesbian identity, one must transform the cognitive category "lesbian" from negative stereotypes to positive labels. As one woman explained, "I knew what homosexual meant, it was an in-joke with the kids I knew. So-and-so's bent, queer, a pansy, etc. When you're faced with such negative views of gays, it is not surprising that you are filled with terror at the prospect of acquiring a label . . . how could an ordinary girl like myself possibly be one of a group of sick people?" (Plummer, 1989, p. 206).

This transformation is followed by increased acceptance of the label and commitment to the identity as applied to oneself. Cass (1979) described the growth of self-acceptance in the following terms: "I might be gay, I'm different"; then "I probably am gay"; then "I'm proud I'm gay"; then "I am gay and being gay is one aspect of who I am."

Coming out is considered a rite of passage because forming a positive lesbian identity takes place against a backdrop of difference from the heterosexual mainstream, which, as previously discussed, brings with it not only invisibility but also the prejudice and discrimination directed at women and lesbians. As a lesbian noted, "All around me were girls my own age who were dating guys, who seemed to be enjoying that, and my parents who are heterosexual. I was surrounded by all that. So I felt like there was a part of me that wasn't being acknowledged. That it didn't exist, and it made me feel alone and depressed" (Schneider, 1989, p. 123). Managing one's lesbian identity includes developing strategies to evade the stigma associated with homosexuality and to manage the boundaries between the heterosexual and the gay worlds (D'Augelli & Garnets, in press).

Whenever lesbians meet, sooner or later we get around to telling our coming-out stories. It is a ritual that bonds and affirms our identity. Self-labeling as gay, accepting this label, self-disclosing, and feeling accepted by others have been found to be strongly related to psychological adjustment (Miranda & Storms, 1989).

Today one can also speak about coming in: the realization of having entered into a community and the process of identifying with a larger group of gay and lesbian people (Petrow, 1990). The presence of a lesbian support system has been found to be associated with adaptive coping strategies and positive well-being (Garnets & Kimmel, 1991). Contemporary lesbian communities are composed of networks connected by social and/or political activities. Lesbian community organizations and activities serve as cultural centers, gathering places, and forums for the expression of lesbian culture. The lesbian community has tried to define a uniquely lesbian cultural vision, which is expressed in music and literature and disseminated at national and regional music festivals and conferences (D'Augelli & Garnets, in press).

Our lives are enriched by coming out and living openly as lesbians. As deMonteflores explained (1986, p. 79), coming out "requires an acknowledgment to ourselves of who we are. In this acknowledgment there is a profound self-affirmation." In the course of coming out, many lesbians successfully overcome the threats to psychological well-being posed by heterosexism. We learn to reclaim and value important aspects of ourselves. We recognize that we are not alone, and this leads to a building of community. Coming out appears to provide coping skills that lesbians can subsequently use to face other life challenges.

What role do gender socialization and status differences play in the coming-out experiences of lesbians? Gay men and lesbians are more similar in many respects to heterosexual members of their own gender than to each other. Lesbians and gay men experience the same social pressure to conform to gender expectations as do heterosexual men and women.

What it means not to be heterosexual is different for lesbians than for gay men. For example, in teaching the course "Psychology of the Lesbian Experience" for several years, I have observed that gay men and lesbian students are initially closely aligned; they feel bonded together by the fact that they experience discrimination because of their sexual orientation. As the class progresses, however, the alliances switch: The lesbian and heterosexual women find they share more in common, and the gay and heterosexual men experience greater similarities.

Coming-out experiences appear to follow different developmental patterns for women than for men. During the process of coming out, lesbians are more likely than gay men to define themselves in terms of their total identity and not only their sexual behavior. For example, a lesbian in Sear's (1989) study defined a homosexual as a person who "has intimate love for a person of the same sex." Lesbians more frequently define their sexual identity in terms of affectional preferences (emotional quality or love between partners) or political choices (affirmation of solidarity with all women or breaking with certain traditional standards of behavior for women) than do gay men (Ponse, 1984; Vetere, 1983).

Likewise, before they come out, lesbians and gay men use different stigma-management strategies in order to avoid labeling themselves as lesbian or gay. Consistent with female role expectations, lesbians are more likely than gay men to avoid identifying as lesbian by minimizing the importance of sexuality. For example, lesbians more often report using the "special case" strategy to avoid identifying as gay. They romanticize sexual events and explain them in terms of intense love and feeling for a particular woman: "I never thought of my feelings and our lovemaking as lesbian. The whole experience was too beautiful for it to be something so ugly. I didn't think I could ever have those feelings for another woman" (Troiden, 1989, p. 49). In my own case, it wasn't until there was a "special woman," and then another "special woman," and then still another that I began to think that I might actually be a lesbian.

A predominant pattern for lesbians is to engage in sexual activity as a natural and logical outgrowth of a strong emotional and romantic attachment (Blumstein & Schwartz, 1989). Realization of being in love with or in a relationship with a person of the same gender may serve as a catalyst for solidifying lesbian self-identification. In general, lesbians report having their first sexual experience with a woman in the context of their first meaningful relationship with a woman. One woman described her process of adopting a lesbian identity: "When I was 17, I fell in love with my partner and knew it was right for me though I had never heard the word lesbian. We lived together as lovers in a committed relationship for many years before I came out to myself and then to others and discovered a lesbian community" (Johnson, 1990, pp. 149–150).

These findings fit with data on heterosexual women who are less likely to view sexual acts as a revelation of their true sexual self and who report sexual fantasies and sexual enjoyment in terms of interest in romantic settings and committed partners (Blumstein & Schwartz, 1989).

DIVERSITY AMONG LESBIANS

Let's now examine the overlapping identities and status of gender, race and ethnicity, and sexuality. Recent attention has focused on cultural diversity among lesbians and the important role of culture in shaping and defining the meaning of same-gender sexual and affectional behavior. Different cultural norms and traditions about gender roles, sexuality, and sexual orientation are integrated into the concept of family. Lesbians of color are often perceived as challenging the well-defined gender-role expectations for women in their families and within their ethnic communities. Clear distinctions made between male and female roles in certain cultures may serve to increase the difficulty for lesbians to carve out a nontraditional role.

For example, Latina lesbians challenge many aspects of the well-defined role of women in their cultures: submissiveness, virtuousness, respectfulness toward elders, interdependence, and the expectation to reside within their family until marriage (Espin, 1987). They are perceived as being too independent from the family and not sufficiently feminine. "Being a lesbian is by definition an act of treason against our cultural values. . . . To be a lesbian we have to leave the fold of our family, and seek support within the mainstream white lesbian community" (Romo-Carmona, 1987, p. xxvi). Latino/a communities are less aware of the existence of Latina lesbians than of Latino gay men. Generally, only the openly masculine or "butch" types (that is, those violating gender roles) are recognized as lesbians (Espin, 1984).

Asian Americans often regard sex as a taboo topic and see homosexuality as a threat to marriage and continuity of the family line. Asian communities in the United States, regardless of assimilation, emphasize sharply delineated gender roles and negate or deny the possibility of lesbian existence. If acknowledged, lesbians are perceived as tarnishing the family honor by not being dutiful daughters, by rejecting the role of wife and mother, by rejecting passive reliance on and deference to men, and by rejecting submersion of identity within the family structure (Chan, 1987). As Lin (1978, p. 227) explained:

> The Chinese are very reticent about sex and male-female relationships. Needless to say, female-female relationships (i.e., lesbian relationships) simply do not exist; it would be too shocking to the Chinese conscience to even acknowledge their existence. . . . I didn't even know the Chinese word for "homosexuality" until I was in my late teens. But I have always been aware of my "feelings" for other women since I was four or five years old.

In some cultures it is so important to have a firm identity as a member of the culture or race that a violation of some aspect of the cultural norms may affect one's entire racial identity (as perceived by oneself or by others). For example, African American lesbians may receive negative sanctions for not promoting survival of their people through propagation of the race. Sexuality may be viewed as a natural and positive part of life, and there is relative flexibility in defining gender roles within the family. However, homosexuality is perceived by some African Americans as racial genocide (Greene, 1986).

LESBIAN RELATIONSHIPS

Now let's turn our attention to lesbian relationships. Researchers have investigated the experiences of lesbians by making comparisons among married, cohabiting heterosexual, gay male, and lesbian couples. The same-gender and cross-gender comparisons have provided an opportunity to examine the relative impact of gender and sexual orientation on the factors that characterize intimate sexual relationships of all kinds.

Some major findings about lesbian relationships show that lesbians and gay men bring to love relationships many of the same expectations, values, and interests as heterosexuals of the same gender. Lesbians are more likely than gay men to live with their primary partner and be in a steady relationship (Peplau, 1991). We are more likely to prefer having sex only with partners we care about, view sexuality and love as closely linked, and desire sexual exclusivity (Peplau, 1991). Lesbians place greater importance on emotional intimacy. We are more likely to value and have equality of involvement and equality in power than gay men (Caldwell & Peplau, 1984). These findings fit with data on heterosexual women. Women, regardless of sexual orientation, value emotional expressiveness, sexual exclusivity, and investment in and commitment to maintain relationships more highly than do men (Garnets & Kimmel, 1993).

When people unfamiliar with lesbian relationships try to imagine one, they often resort to a heterosexual frame of reference, attempting to identify the person in the "male" role and the one in the "female" role. In fact, lesbian couples frequently adopt a peer-friendship model of intimate relationships. A lesbian remarked about the most significant factors in her 33-year relationship: "Compatibility. Similar likes in people and other interests. Becoming good friends as well as lovers. Mutual respect" (Johnson, 1990, p. 142). Partners in lesbian relationships show greater equality, reciprocity, and role flexibility than partners in heterosexual relationships. Most lesbian couples value power equality and shared decision making as a goal for their relationships (Peplau, 1991). One partner of a 15-year couple noted, "We don't have to have equal money or do equal things. We need to feel we have equal value, power, and rights in the relationship" (Johnson, 1990, p. 122). Another lesbian in an 11-year relationship stated, "We both are very independent and assume that we will share decisions and responsibilities equally" (Johnson, 1990, p. 123). These findings suggest that a gender-based division of labor is not necessary for relationships to function well.

To understand these findings, it is important to remember that there are no prescribed roles and behaviors to structure such relationships. Because society does not provide explicit or clear models of interaction, lesbian partners rely more on innovative processes for creating idiosyncratic rules, expectations, and division of labor in relationships. This approach may provide lesbians an opportunity for greater creativity in structuring relationships than is true for heterosexuals. Lesbians create intimate relationships based on models that may reduce traditional gender-role power imbalances found in heterosexual relationships.

My stepdaughter was married recently. She told me that she had sought out a relationship with a man who had the elements of reciprocity, equality, and friendship that she had observed between my life partner and me. She wished to avoid the power inequity and role restrictions that she had observed in many heterosexual relationships.

GENDER ROLE FLEXIBILITY AMONG LESBIANS

In examining the impact of gender roles on lesbian identity and relationships, we saw that in many respects gay men are similar to heterosexual men and lesbians are similar to heterosexual women. However, lesbians are often encouraged or permitted by their deviance from accepted norms to explore androgynous gender-role behavior, independence, self-reliance, and educational and occupational options.

The fact that lesbians have no predetermined models about how to interact leads to greater potential for "normative creativity":

> By lacking clear rules about how to be lesbian and gay in the world, we have made up the rules as we go along. . . . Simply being lesbian or gay has been something we have had to invent for ourselves, since whatever roadmaps the dominant culture offered have been full of wrong turns and uncharted territories. [Brown, 1989, pp. 451–452]

They often create patterns of behavior, identity, and relationships that neither mirror nor duplicate heterosexual patterns.

Lesbians neither adhere rigidly to traditional gender roles nor consistently engage in cross-gender behavior. Frequently, lesbians adopt a nontraditional identity that includes nontraditional gender-role norms. Lesbians may be more androgynous than heterosexual women. Comparative studies of heterosexual women and lesbian women found lesbians to be more autonomous, spontaneous, assertive, sensitive to their own needs and fears, unconventional, self-confident, and inner-directed (Morgan & Brown, 1991). Lesbians score higher on scales of masculinity than do heterosexual women, but lesbian women and heterosexual women do not differ on measures of femininity (Kurdek & Schmitt, 1986).

These characteristics of lesbians find plausible explanations in that lesbian communities more readily accept behaviors that would be perceived by the larger society as violations of gender roles. Thus, lesbians often find support within the lesbian communities for flexibility and diversity in their identities as women.

These differences also reflect lesbians' social adaptation to their position in society in which they need to be self-reliant and provide for themselves. In the words of one lesbian, "You have to protect yourself. Straight women think, 'I have a man to protect me,' but for me, it's just me. You've got to stick up for yourself and survive every day—just having the strength and using it" (Schneider, 1989, p. 124). As Morgan and Brown (1991, p. 278) noted:

> From a practical standpoint as well as an ideological one, it makes sense that lesbians as a group would tend toward less gender-role stereotypic behaviors: When women choose to live independent of men, the many household maintenance activities that have traditionally been classified as "men's work" (including the role of breadwinner) still must be done, so gender-role flexibility is a reasonable and necessary adaptive response.

The experience of lesbians provides a unique opportunity to see the impact on identity, behavior, and relationships when the traditional patterns based on gender are reduced or removed. Because traditional roles and stereotypes may limit options for women, gender-role flexibility among lesbians may contribute to their constructing self-images different from heterosexuals. That is, lesbian self-identity may be freer from the bonds of restrictive gender-role constraints.

THE IMPACT OF ANTIGAY ATTITUDES

Fear of being labeled gay is a powerful socialization influence in our society and has negative consequences for both heterosexuals and homosexuals. Women and men who manifest characteristics inconsistent with those culturally prescribed for their gender, regardless of their sexual orientation, are likely to be labeled as gay (Kite, 1994). A woman who does not conform to what is considered feminine runs the risk of being labeled a lesbian. A woman may be labeled a lesbian if she exhibits autonomous or self-assertive behavior, fights for her rights as a woman, enjoys the company of other women, works at a nontraditional job, or says no to violence. This is referred to as "lesbian baiting," which is defined as any attempt to control all women by accusing them of being lesbians because their behavior is not acceptable or appropriate to their gender role (Pellegrini, 1992). As Gloria Steinem (1978) noted:

> The lesson of my experience . . . is that sooner or later, all nonconforming women are likely to be labeled lesbians. True, we start out with the smaller punishments of being called "pushy" or "aggressive," "man-hating" or "unfeminine." But it's only a small step from those adjectives, whether bestowed by men or other women, to the full-fledged epithet of "lesbian."

Homophobia affects heterosexuals, as well as gay men and lesbians, through its enforcement of traditional, rigid gender roles. One significant function of the social stigma of homosexuality is to define limits of acceptable behavior for all men and women. Heterosexuals often restrict their gender-role behavior for fear of provoking the stigmatizing homosexual label. A heterosexual woman may avoid mentioning to friends that she is involved with a feminist organization on campus because she is afraid that they will think that she is a lesbian. Or a heterosexual woman may not confront a heterosexist remark for fear of being identified with lesbians. Or a heterosexual woman may avoid or hide her friendships with lesbians for fear of being labeled one herself.

Attempts to avoid the stigma of being labeled gay inhibit heterosexual men and women from forming close, intimate relationships with members of their own gender. As one heterosexual woman explained, "I've always been physically affectionate with my friends—hugging, kissing them on the cheek, walking arm in arm down the street. I've experienced people assuming we're lesbians because of what we're doing. I've been called "dyke" by people on the street when they saw us being physically affectionate. I've had some friends get nervous and push me off, not wanting to touch anymore" (Elize, 1992, pp. 105–106). Clearly, the interpersonal costs of heterosexism and homophobia are high.

CONCLUSION

We have discussed the ways that women's lives are enhanced by living openly as lesbians. Having an open identity as a lesbian across life contexts is related to positive self-esteem and to overall psychological adjustment. Lesbians often experience a sense of freedom from the bonds of gender role constraints. This includes the ability to create new forms of relationships that reduce the power imbalances sometimes found in traditional heterosexual models and that rely instead on role flexibility, power equality, and shared decision making. As Adrienne Rich (1980, p. xiii) put it:

> I think "coming out"—that first permission we give ourselves to name our love for women as love, to say, I am a lesbian, but also the successive "coming-outs" to the world . . . is connected with power, connects us with power, and until we believe that we have the right not merely to our love but to our power, we will continue to do harm among ourselves, fearing that power in each other and in ourselves.

So, what does gender have to do with it? As we have seen, the life of a lesbian is inextricably bound with being a woman. Our status and socialization as women appear to directly shape our experience as lesbians. Moreover, negative attitudes and stereotypes about lesbians are closely linked to negative attitudes and stereotypes about women's devalued status in society.

Recent evidence suggests that attitudes equating homosexuality with violation of what is normal for women may be changing (Herek, 1990). Changing gender-role expectations for all women may make it possible for lesbians to be seen as "real" women. This benefits lesbians because it reduces homophobic stereotypes and prejudice. Heterosexuals, too, profit from expanded definitions of acceptable behavior—definitions that entitle them to fuller self-expression without fear of being labeled gay. As Charlotte Bunch (1978, pp. 181–182) stated:

> The lesbian is most clearly the antithesis of patriarchy—an offense to its basic tenets. It is woman-hating, we are woman-loving. It demands female obedience and docility; we seek strength, assertiveness, and dignity for women. It bases power and defines roles on one's gender and other physical attributes; we operate outside gender-defined roles and seek a new basis for defining power and relationships.

REFERENCES

BLUMSTEIN, P., & SCHWARTZ, P. (1989). Intimate relationships and the creation of sexuality. In B. Risman & P. Schwartz (Eds.), *Gender in intimate relationships: A microstructural approach* (pp. 120–129). Belmont, CA: Wadsworth.

BRENNER, C. (1992). Survivor's story: Eight bullets. In G. M. Herek & K. T. Berrill (Eds.), *Hate crimes: Confronting violence against lesbians and gay men* (pp. 11–15). Newbury Park, CA: Sage.

BROWN, L. (1989). New voices, new visions: Toward a lesbian/gay paradigm for psychology. *Psychology of Women Quarterly, 13,* 445–458.

BUNCH, C. (1978). Lesbian-feminist theory. In G. Vida (Ed.), *Our right to love: A lesbian resource book* (pp. 180–182). Englewood Cliffs, NJ: Prentice-Hall.

CALDWELL, M. A., & PEPLAU, L. A. (1984). The balance of power in lesbian relationships. *Sex Roles, 10,* 587–600.

CASS, V. C. (1979). Homosexual identity formation: A theoretical model. *Journal of Homosexuality, 4*(3), 219–235.

CHAN, C. S. (1987). Asian lesbians: Psychological issues in the "coming out" process. *Asian American Psychological Association Journal, 12*(1), 16–18.

D'AUGELLI, A. R., & GARNETS, L. (in press). Lesbian, gay, and bisexual communities. In A. R. D'Augelli & C. J. Patterson (Eds.), *Lesbian, gay and bisexual identities across the lifespan.* New York: Oxford University Press.

DEMONTEFLORES, C. (1986). Notes on the management of difference. In T. Stein & C. Cohen (Eds.), *Contemporary perspectives on psychotherapy with lesbians and gay men* (pp. 73–101). New York: Plenum Press.

ELIZE, D. (1992). "It has nothing to do with me." In J. Blumenfeld (Ed.), *Homophobia: How we all pay the price* (pp. 95–113). Boston: Beacon Press.

ESPIN, O. (1984). Cultural and historical influences on sexuality in Hispanic/Latin women: Implications for psychotherapy. In C. Vance (Ed.), *Pleasure and danger: Exploring female sexuality* (pp. 149–163). London: Routledge & Kegan Paul.

ESPIN, O. (1987). Issues of identity in the psychology of Latina lesbians. In Boston Lesbian Psychologies Collective (Eds.), *Lesbian psychologies: Explorations and challenges* (pp. 35–51). Urbana, IL: University of Illinois Press.

GARNETS, L., & KIMMEL, D. (1991). Lesbian and gay male dimensions in the psychological study of human diversity. In J. Goodchilds (Ed.), *Psychological perspectives on human diversity in America* (pp. 137–192). Washington, DC: American Psychological Association.

GARNETS, L., & KIMMEL, D. (1993). *Psychological perspectives on lesbian and gay male experiences.* New York: Columbia University Press.

GREENE, B. (1986). When the therapist is white and the patient is Black: Considerations for psychotherapy in the feminist heterosexual and lesbian communities. In D. Howard (Ed.), *The dynamics of feminist therapy* (pp. 41–65). New York: Haworth.

HEREK, G. M. (1990). The context of anti-gay violence: Notes on cultural and psychological heterosexism. *Journal of Interpersonal Violence, 5*(3), 316–333.

JOHNSON, S. E. (1990). *Staying power: Long-term lesbian couples.* Tallahassee, FL: Naiad Press.

KITE, M. E. (1994). When perceptions meet reality: Individual differences in reactions to lesbians and gay men. *Lesbian and Gay Psychology: Theory, Research, and Clinical Applications, 1,* 206–228.

KURDEK, L. A., & SCHMITT, J. P. (1986). Interaction of sex role concept with relationship quality and relationship beliefs in married, heterosexual cohabiting, gay, and lesbian relationships. *Journal of Personality and Social Psychology, 51,* 365–370.

LIN, Y. (1978). The spectrum of lesbian experience: Personal testimony. In G. Vida, (Ed.), *Our right to love: A lesbian resource book* (pp. 227–229). Englewood Cliffs, NJ: Prentice-Hall.

MIRANDA, J., & STORMS, M. (1989). Psychological adjustment of lesbians and gay men. *Journal of Counseling and Development, 68,* 41–45.

MORGAN, K. S., & BROWN, L. S. (1991). Lesbian career development, work behavior, and vocational counseling. *Counseling Psychologist, 19*(2), 273–291.

PELLEGRINI, A. (1992). S(h)ifting the terms of hetero/sexism: Gender, power, homophobias. In J. Blumenfeld (Ed.), *Homophobia: How we all pay the price* (pp. 39–56). Boston: Beacon Press.

PEPLAU, L. A. (1991). Lesbian and gay relationships. In J. C. Gonsiorek & J. D. Weinrich (Eds.), *Homosexuality: Research findings for public policy* (pp. 177–196). Newbury Park, CA: Sage.

PETROW, S. (1990, May). Together wherever we go. *The Advocate,* 42–44.

PLUMMER, K. (1989). Lesbian and gay youth in England. *Journal of Homosexuality, 17*(1–4), 195–223.

PONSE, B. (1984). The problematic meanings of "lesbian." In J. D. Douglas (Ed.), *The sociology of deviance* (pp. 25–33). Boston: Allyn & Bacon.

RICH, A. (1980). Foreword. In S. J. Wolfe & J. P. Stanley (Eds.), *The coming out stories* (pp. xi–xiii). Watertown, MA: Persephone.

ROCHLIN, M. (1980, October). Heterosexual questionnaire. *Association of Gay Psychologists Newsletter,* 4.

ROMO-CARMONA, M. (1987). Introduction. In J. Ramos (Ed.), *Companeras: Latina Lesbians* (pp. xx–xxix). New York: Latina Lesbian History Project.

SCHNEIDER, M. (1989). Sappho was a right-on adolescent: Growing up lesbian. *Journal of Homosexuality, 17*(1–4), 111–130.

SEARS, J. T. (1989). The impact of gender and race on growing up lesbian and gay in the South. *National Women's Studies Association Journal, 1,* 422–457.

STEINEM, G. (1978). The politics of supporting lesbianism. In G. Vida (Ed.), *Our right to love: A lesbian resource book* (pp. 266–269). Englewood Cliffs, NJ: Prentice-Hall.

TROIDEN, R. (1989). The formation of homosexual identities. *Journal of Homosexuality, 17*(1–4), 43–73.

VETERE, V. A. (1983). The role of friendship in the development and maintenance of lesbian love relationships. *Journal of Homosexuality, 8*(2), 51–65.

*S*UGGESTED READINGS

BLUMENFELD, W. J. (1992). *Homophobia: How we all pay the price.* Boston: Beacon.

FADERMAN, L. (1991). *Odd girls and twilight lovers: A history of lesbian life in twentieth-century America.* New York: Columbia University Press.

GARNETS, L., & KIMMEL, D. (1993). *Psychological perspectives on lesbian and gay male experiences.* New York: Columbia University Press.

GREENE, B. (1994). Lesbian women of color: Triple jeopardy. In L. Comas-Diaz & B. Greene (Eds.), *Women of color: Integrating ethnic and gender identities in psychotherapy* (pp. 389–427). New York: Guilford Press.

K AYLA MIRIYAM WEINER *is a psychotherapist in private practice in Seattle. Dr. Weiner has lectured frequently on women's issues at schools and universities in the Pacific Northwest as well as in China and Israel. She is editor of* Jewish Women Speak Out, *a book of papers based on presentations at the First International Conference on Judaism, Feminism, and Psychology: Creating a Shelter in the Wilderness, which she coordinated in 1992.*

11

Appreciating Cultural Difference:

On Being an American Jewish Woman

❖

I am a Jew. I have never denied my roots. Yet, it is only as I have become aware of how anti-Semitism has had an influence on my own identity development that I have begun to make my Jewish identity consciously visible as a means of healing myself and educating others.

I was born during World War II, the years of the Holocaust, a time in which 6 million of my people were killed because they were born or identified by others as Jewish. I have come to understand how anti-Semitism—really anti-Jewishness—has had an impact on every thought I have had and every action I have taken in my life. To stand before you and say "I am a Jew" strikes a chord of fear in my inner being. The historic and modern oppression of Jews is directed at Jews because we are Jews and for no other reason. Anti-Semitism historically has been cyclical in nature, allowing times of apparent peace for Jews before being used as the scapegoat for the ills of the country in which we are living. Anti-Semitism may abate, but it never reaches the point of zero. In much the way that every woman knows at her deepest core that she is always in danger of rape and carries that fear with her, I believe every Jew at some level of consciousness wonders when, not if, the next holocaust will occur.

Because many of us are in social service fields and because many psychological theorists—for example, Freud and Adler—were Jewish, one would think that the psychology of Jewish people would have been well researched and reported, but this is not the case. Here I intend to demonstrate why it is necessary specifically to study the psychology of Jews. I will enumerate some of the major reasons it is difficult to understand the Jewish culture and address what elements in society have the most impact on the psychological development of Jewish women.

It is impossible to talk about Jewish women and not talk about Jewish men because we cannot be separated from our Jewish culture: Our oppression as Jews is separate from, and in addition to, the oppression we face as women. We are faced with the added burden of being oppressed within the Jewish culture. I will describe the ways in which we are directly and indirectly confronted with anti-Semitism within the women's movement and explore the interrelationship of sexism, racism, heterosexism, and anti-Semitism.

I believe that just by virtue of being raised in the American culture we are all, men and women, sexist. We are all racist, we are all heterosexist, and we are all anti-Semitic. We live in a toxic environment, and it is impossible to avoid contamination. When Mt. St. Helens erupted in 1980, the volcanic ash spread over my home and land in Montana. Although I cleaned everywhere, years later I could turn over a board or move a piece of equipment and find remnants of ash. I'm sure I could still find some today. It is each person's willingness to acknowledge the presence of prejudice and hate within herself, and commit herself to purge these conditions whenever they surface, that facilitates healing and understanding among people. It is our collective commitment to work to mitigate the effects of oppression that brings about change. The purpose of this lecture is not to assess blame or to evoke guilt in Jews or non-Jews. The intent is to raise issues; dispel myths, stereotypes, and misconceptions; and provide a framework for examining the issues significant to being an American Jewish woman.

JEWISH DIVERSITY

If I ask you to visualize a tree, each person would likely come up with a different image: One might see an oak, another an apple, another a pine. Although each is different, they have in common a root system, a large strong trunk, multiple branches, and some form of leaf. Trees can be classed as ornamental, protective, or food-bearing; these classifications are separate yet interrelated. The Jewish community is as strongly related, and as clearly diverse, as the trees in nature.

Most people understand that Judaism is a religion. This is true; but it is not the whole truth. A very large percentage of people clearly and proudly identify themselves as ethnic Jews; that is, they feel connected to the culture and traditions of the Jewish people, yet have no religious practice. In addition, there are those who do not identify with the culture, the ethnicity, or the religion but are born to Jewish parents and are therefore defined as Jewish. It is essential to hold this triple perspective when trying to understand Jewish people. Although there are differences in Jewish culture that are related to religious creed, the experience of being Jewish involves numerous other components, including, but not limited to, individual and collective history as well as time and space considerations. If you focus on religion, you miss the point—but you cannot avoid religion as a consideration.

Jews who observe religious practices fall into five general categories or communities, ranging from Orthodox (the most fundamental), to Conservative, Reform, Reconstructionist, and, more recently, the Jewish Renewal movement. There are secular or cultural Jews who may do no more than attend an occasional family event, but they are emphatically Jewish. And there are Jews by choice—people who have converted to Judaism as adults. The great differences in the way each of these groups interprets Judaism influences the individuals within the group. An Orthodox person would probably never acknowledge the legitimacy of a woman as a rabbi. A woman who belongs to a modern religious community that treats women and men equally would probably be unwilling to sit behind the curtain that separates women from men at an Orthodox service. Because no woman is permitted to say the prayer for the dead in an Orthodox synagogue, but would have to hire a man to do so for her, a feminist would find herself very unwelcome and most likely very uncomfortable in an Orthodox synagogue.

To complicate matters even more, Jews come from different parts of the world and have many differences based on their country of origin. There are three main cultural groups of Jews: the Ashkenazi, who are generally from northern and eastern Europe; the Sephardic, who were expelled from Spain in 1492 and settled in countries throughout the Mediterranean region; and the Mizrachi, loosely defined as of Asian heritage. Someone who marries outside her group, even if it is to someone from another Jewish group, is considered to have entered a mixed marriage. Intermarriage between Jewish communities can create unique problems. For example, it is traditional for an Ashkenazi Jew to name her child after someone who has died to honor the dead relative; to name a child after someone alive is considered a death sentence for the elder. Yet, among the Sephardic community, children *must* be named after someone living. The largest percentage of Jews in the United States are of Ashkenazi descent, and the experience or knowledge that most non-Jews have about Jews is primarily based on the Ashkenazi culture. Time and space limitations do not permit a lengthy explanation of the Sephardic or Mizrachi cultures, and it should be noted that what I present is through my personal filter as a second-generation Ashkenazi Jew of East European descent. Jews of color inside the United States have a different psychosocial experience than Jews of European descent.

The psychological development of the individual Jew will be influenced by her relationship to the Holocaust: whether she was born before or after the Holocaust; was in the United States, Europe, Asia, or the

Middle East; was in hiding in Europe; was in the camps; lost members of her family or is the child of a survivor. For example, one woman who was the child of a Holocaust survivor, had heard all her life of the travails of her parents. She thought she had no right to feelings of sadness because her parents had endured so much, and consequently she repressed all of her feelings (Epstein, 1982).

Diversity within the Jewish community makes it difficult to make generalizations about any individual or the group as a whole. As a useful guideline, do not assume you know what being a Jew means, but rather, inquire of each person what it means to that person.

STEREOTYPES, MYTHS, AND MISCONCEPTIONS

Three major areas of myth and stereotype that have created a tremendous amount of pain and confusion for Jewish Americans are women, money, and education. Although separate topics, they are very interrelated, and they will be addressed along with other misconceptions about the behaviors of Jewish people.

Women

Jewish men and women have been taught to be ashamed of their mothers. It is difficult to honor our mothers when books, movies, and psychological professionals negate or demean them. Rather than see Jewish mothers as caring and loving as well as frugal and efficient, we have been taught to see them as enmeshed, overinvolved, and insensitive, not to mention dominating and compulsive. In *The Jewish Woman in America*, Charlotte Baum, Paula Hyman, and Sonya Michel (1977) describe the role of the Jewish woman in the *shtetl* (Jewish community in Europe) and then her migration to the United States as one way of understanding the behavior of Jewish mothers. In the *shtetl* the woman was expected to maintain the family so that the man could devote himself to the study of the religious texts. When European Jews came to this country, the woman's role remained the same. In addition, because jobs were difficult for men to acquire, as was true with all immigrant groups, the Jewish woman had to provide the money for the family and creatively manage the family resources for the survival of the family (Baum et al., 1977). The "perfect Jewish woman" was "clear, patient, hardworking and silent, submissive to God and her husband, devoted to her children . . . her own well being was unimportant" (McGoldrick, Pearce, & Giordano, 1982, p. 373). The structure of gender in the Jewish culture has had devastating effects on the individual and the community. I will return to this later.

Along with the high value placed on the family is the emphasis upon geographical and emotional closeness (McGoldrick et al., 1982). Traditionally, there is a high expectation in most Jewish families for closeness and connection. Jewish women are often criticized and maligned for encouraging family closeness. This culturally determined practice puts her in conflict with Western, non-Jewish, male-conceived theories of appropriate family dynamics. For a people who have had their children taken from them, never to be returned, as happened most recently during the Holocaust, this should not be hard to understand; parents need to know their children are healthy and safe.

The reemergence of the term Jewish American Princess, or JAP, a pejorative term for Jewish women with material wealth, is demeaning and destructive to the self-esteem of Jewish women. This term surfaced after World War II and has obvious racist implications. The epithet attacks Jewish women for displaying materialism, which, in reality, is at the core of American culture, albeit denied by the culture. It seems that it is okay to have money but not acceptable to show it if you are a Jewish woman. A report by the Anti-Defamation League (Ross, 1988) notes that at least one nationally distributed and widely read guide to campuses, *The Insider's Guide to Colleges,* refers to the prevalence of JAPs at certain schools. Small groups of campus rowdies at Syracuse University have been known to declare their hangouts "JAP-free zones" marked off with swastikas. A joke floating around the Syracuse campus suggests that JAPs and pizzas are alike in that they belong in an oven.

Money

The negative association of Jews and money must be viewed in a historical context. Until recent generations, Jews all over the world were restricted in varying degrees from owning land, getting an education, or entering a profession. In Europe they were limited by law to being merchants and money lenders and then judged as evil for the positions they were required to fill. The immigrants who came to this country at the turn of the century came with nothing and lived in poverty. Knowing that there was a time when the men could not provide for their families in this country, it is then easy to understand that when men were able to provide for their families they often restricted the work of the women and then showered them with material possessions as a sign of their own accomplishment. It is a sad irony that Jewish women are reviled as JAPs for their material possessions by Jewish men as well as by the non-Jewish community.

It is important to remember that the Jewish people have a long history of being displaced, dating back to biblical times. The Sephardic Jew may carry the collective memory of expulsion first from Spain and then from one country after another. Knowledge of the pogroms of Russia and the

Nazi Holocaust, comparatively recent in Jewish history, breeds a sense of fear and insecurity in most Jews today, even those with no direct personal involvement with these atrocities. It is a common practice of many Jewish people to keep money or other negotiables, as well as a current passport, hidden but always available, "just in case" they need to flee. Material possessions, although a measure of success and acceptance in the greater society, mean survival and a means of escape in times of danger for Jews. Some people simultaneously condemn Jews as communists and as malevolent capitalists plotting to take over the world. But control of personal money is significantly different from control of public money: The major financial institutions are in actuality primarily controlled by non-Jewish white men. Ultimately, the Jew is in a classic double bind: to achieve financial success is to be visible and therefore in danger; not to achieve it is to have no means of escape and protection when they are needed.

Education

The study of religious texts is a requirement of the Jewish religion. Traditionally, men were expected to study at all times (hence women's need to provide financial support, as noted above). This predisposition to study has crossed into the secular culture and become an integral part of the Jewish psyche. Jews, women as well as men in the modern era, are usually expected to acquire an education. The message transmitted by one generation to the next is that an education is something that cannot be taken away and is completely portable if the need to flee arises. Again there is the double bind: to speak up and demonstrate one's knowledge is to be considered "pushy"; to be quiet is to ignore one's ability and one's culture.

Other Misconceptions

A Jewish religious belief is that one has a direct connection with God and the right—even the obligation—to question God. This belief has been transmitted to the secular life of many Jews, so we consider it appropriate to question all things and all people. Non-Jews may see intense and emotional interchanges between individuals as dissension; most Jews perceive such exchanges as a way to seek the truth. What is often described as Jewish "intensity" creates difficulty for Jews living in the dominant culture because that intensity is often perceived as wrong by non-Jews, and the Jew is made to feel that the behavior, and hence the self, is bad. This is particularly true for Jewish women who face the twin oppressions of sexism and anti-Semitism, which both require them to be quiet and submissive. "Feminist process," which requires each woman to sit quietly and wait her turn to speak, has often proved difficult for Jewish women.

"Interrupting" or "talking over" one another is a form of Jewish discourse, and the enthusiasm and excitement generated in a discussion is considered useful and valuable in exploring any question. Personally I have found living in the "mellow" Northwest a challenge because any expression of emotion seems to be considered strange here. I often feel I must be more reserved in order to belong.

Tikkun olum, which means approximately "to heal, repair, and transform the world," is a basic philosophy of Judaism that requires each Jew to make the world a better place. Right living and social action is considered more important than religious faith. The child of a Holocaust survivor noted,

> I am in awe of my parents. I often wonder if I could have survived myself and I doubt whether I could have. Being their child has given me a certain depth, a seriousness about life that most people can't possibly have. I'm aware of the evil in the world and I'm not complacent. I feel it requires an active struggle to prevent a revival of the sort of thing that led to the murder of my family.
> [Epstein, 1982, p. 31]

Jews are often chided for being too serious or for being too involved in social action and too concerned about world problems. This puts us in conflict with cultural, religious, and family values and the dominant societal values (Weiner, 1990).

Stereotypes, myths, and misconceptions set Jews apart and make us "other" when "other" is bad. This contributes to a poor sense of self for the individual and creates a very fragile sense of safety for the community.

ANTI-SEMITISM AND THE JEWISH PSYCHE

The most obvious act of anti-Semitism in our generation is the Holocaust, a clear and overt attempt at a "final solution" to rid the world of Jews. Before World War II, anti-Semitism was generally accepted in the United States. As I was growing up in the 1940s and 1950s, there were still neighborhood restrictions and quotas in universities to limit Jewish access. By the 1960s many of the more obvious barriers had come down, and it was no longer acceptable to be openly anti-Semitic. However, the roots and foundations of anti-Semitism are present and exist everywhere in our society today. A poll conducted by the Anti-Defamation League (Ross, 1988) notes that almost 40 million people in the United States have "strongly anti-Semitic attitudes." According to the 1993 *Audit of Anti-Semitic Incidents* (Anti-Defamation League, 1994), the number of anti-Semitic incidents—assaults, threats, and harassments—in the United States increased to the second highest level in the 15-year history of the report. The rise of groups such as the Aryan Nation and the skinheads and the revitalization of the Ku Klux Klan and other militaristic neofascist groups in this country are chilling reminders to Jews that anti-Semitism is alive and well and thriving throughout the world.

These examples of anti-Semitism are only the most obvious ways Jewish women are made to feel vulnerable. There are far more subtle ways that dramatically influence the psychological development of the Jew. What is the message to a Jew when she is forced to miss high school activities because they occur on Friday night when she is home with her family for the beginning of the sabbath? What is the message when she learns there is a Christian prayer at the beginning of each legislative session? What does she think when fish is served in school cafeterias on Friday (to respect traditional Catholic beliefs), yet pork is served every day (ignoring traditional Jewish beliefs)? What is she to think when told that Christmas is a "national" holiday and she is making a fuss or is too "pushy" if she objects to its intrusion in her life? The message is that Christianity is institutionalized in this country, and she, the Jew, is invisible.

As women, and/or as lesbians, and/or as women of color, we know that to be rendered invisible is an attack on our being, an affront to our values, and a negation of our existence. Invisibility creates a fear that contributes to the internalization of oppression and the destruction of self-worth for Jews in general, and for Jewish women in particular, because of our multiple oppressions. To be invisible is to be silent, to be silent is to be powerless, and to be powerless can mean death.

To help understand the pervasiveness of anti-Semitism, even in places one would not expect to find it, I will share two personal examples. In the first instance, two major peace foundations were planning a training for local peace groups, which happened to include a large percentage of Jewish women. When the person from the fund called to announce the schedule he noted, "By the way, it will be on Yom Kippur. That's okay isn't it?" It wasn't that he didn't know that this is the most important holy day of the year for Jewish people. He did know, and yet he apparently did not feel the need to accommodate the Jewish women involved.

The other incident concerns the summer I chose to share a house with a woman I had met at a conference. She was a refugee from an East European country, held a doctorate in a physical science, had been married to a Jewish man, and we seemed to have a lot in common. Throughout our time together she said things that I identified as anti-Semitic yet, with a sick feeling in my stomach, I tried to explain away or excuse. One Saturday she began shouting at me hysterically and I immediately told her I intended to move. On Sunday evening she came up behind me while I was washing dishes and made a number of demands that she followed with, "You better watch out, Jew. We goyim know how to take care of you." My earlier feelings of sadness at the separation and anger at her abuse totally disappeared: I was left with unmitigated fear to my deepest core. The event I had been trained all my life to expect had finally occurred. It wasn't a politician; it wasn't a fanatic. It was someone I trusted and for whom I cared. Nothing, not even fear of rape, was as frightening as hearing her heavily accented voice tell me she "knew what to do with me."

ASSIMILATION AS A RESPONSE TO ANTI-SEMITISM

I believe the pervasiveness of anti-Semitism breeds a subconscious and constant sense of fear and alienation in most Jews and causes us to vacillate between a need to be invisible to be safe and a need to be visible to belong. Jews from all the diverse cultural groups in some ways find ourselves taking on the values, ideas, and characteristics of the dominant culture. For example, because we are made to feel guilty about being emotionally expressive, we may restrict our communication. Because our foods are different and often judged negatively, old family recipes may be lost from one generation to the next. To fit in with the dominant culture, parents may not teach the cultural languages: Yiddish for the Ashkenazi, Ladino for the Sephardic. So-called Jewish facial features are not judged beautiful in the dominant culture, so many Jews, primarily women, feel forced to get plastic surgery to adjust their appearance. The observance of meaningful Jewish holy days, Rosh Hashanah and Yom Kippur (the Jewish New Year and the Day of Atonement) is ignored, and Jews feel forced to celebrate less important days such as Hanukkah to create the illusion of belonging.

Many Jews internalized negative images and learned to feel shame; many thought assimilation would provide a measure of safety. The Jewish perception that a chameleon nature is necessary for physical and emotional survival causes great psychological distress because of the loss of identity and alienation from self. There is tremendous loss and alienation for Jews who have moved away from our heritage, our identities, and our traditions to be accepted by the dominant culture, only to realize that we are never truly accepted.

The gender structuring mentioned earlier in this presentation proves to be a difficult barrier for Jewish feminists wanting to be a part of our community of origin. Those who marry and have children are often able to stay within the community structure, but their role frequently becomes one of revolutionary leader bringing changes to the community. Those women who choose to remain single or child-free often find that there is no place for them within the Jewish family-oriented culture. Lesbians in particular often find no comfortable community. Many Jewish women in the past two decades have turned to the women's community for a sense of family. However, we have not always felt welcome there either.

In the 1970s and 1980s the United Nations sponsored conferences in several nations to explore the condition of women throughout the world. The official and unofficial treatment of Jewish women at the Mexico and Copenhagen women's conferences were chilling. As Naomi Chazan

(1984) stated, "The trauma of Copenhagen cannot be forgotten by those who attended the conference. . . . They left Copenhagen with the distinct impression, verified by their own experiences, that anti-Semitism was rampant in the international women's movement" (p. 9). "In Copenhagen," said Sonja Johnson, "I heard people say that Gloria Steinem, Betty Friedan, and Bella Abzug all being Jewish give the American Women's Movement a bad name. I heard 'The only good Jew is a dead Jew.' I heard, 'The only way to rid the world of Zionism is to kill all Jews'" (Pogrebin, 1982, p. 48). Chiae Herzig reported, "A UN staff person said to me, 'Denmark is wonderful, but the Germans take it over in the summer and I hate them. They only did one thing right; they killed the Jews.' I made choking sounds. 'Oh, did I hurt your feelings?' she asked. 'Are you German?'" (Pogrebin, 1982, pp. 48-49).

As a result of these and similar incidents, many Jewish feminists have limited their involvement with the larger women's movement in order to feel safe. We have begun to establish new Jewish communities that eliminate what is patriarchical from the Jewish culture and incorporate an egalitarian, feminine spirit into our prayers, practices, and politics.

CONCLUSION

It is important to understand the powerful effect of anti-Semitism on Jewish women's identity development and to realize the interrelationship of anti-Semitism with other forms of oppression, specifically sexism, racism, and homophobia. Susan Griffin (1981) states:

> The contents of the racist mind are fundamentally pornographic. . . . And when we turn to pornography we discover that just as the racist is obsessed with a pornographic drama, the pornographer is obsessed with racism. . . . *Hustler* magazine displays a cartoon called "Chester the Molester" [part of a series depicting child molestation as humor], in which a man wearing a swastika on his arm hides behind a corner, holds a bat, and dangles a dollar bill on a wire to entice a little girl from her parents. The child and her parents all wear yellow stars of David; each member of the family is drawn with the stereotypical hooked nose. Nazi memorabilia, helmets, SS uniforms, photographs of the atrocities of concentration camps, swords, and knives are sold as pornographic thought and racist ideology is neither casual nor coincidental. . . . If we look closely at the portrait which the . . . racist draws of a man or a woman of color, or that the anti-Semite draws of the Jew [or, I might add, the homophobe draws of the lesbian], we begin to see that these fantasized figures resemble one another. For they are the creations of one mind. This is the chauvinist mind, a mind which projects all its fears in itself onto another; a mind which defines itself by what it hates. (p. 126)

German propagandists flooded Poland with pornography before the German army invaded. The obvious hatred of women was intended to stimulate and encourage hate for Jews. Hatred leads to an abandonment of self that leaves one unable to resist authority, in this case that of the Nazis.

A protest sign at the Houston Women's Conference in 1977, organized to prepare for the international women's conference scheduled for 1980 in Copenhagen, read: "Kill All Dykes, Kikes, Commies, and Abortionists" (Beck, 1982, p. 126). Describing her objection to the equal rights amendment, one woman said, "The next time you read something about a rally supporting the ERA or see something on your TV news, take a good look at the demonstrators. You will probably see fat, ugly, stringy-haired lesbians in droopy T-shirts, fanatical Jewesses and loudmouthed minorities." (Wolk, 1980, p. 2).

So, you may ask, "Why is all of this important to me?" If it is not that you will someday work with Jewish women and therefore need to know as much about us as possible in order to help us; if it is not to improve your relationships with individuals in your life; then it is important to remember that the oppression of Jews serves as a model of oppression for other groups. Once oppression of one group is tolerated, it can easily be applied to other groups.

We are all asked to assess our responsibility and examine our role in making change. Jews must carefully examine our internalized oppression to allow ourselves to live more full and happy lives. Jews and non-Jews alike must make themselves knowledgeable about the issues and be prepared to speak out and educate others. We must be aware of the connections among sexism, racism, heterosexism, and anti-Semitism in our institutions in order to facilitate action for change.

A German minister, the Reverend Martin Niemoller, arrested by Hitler stated, "When they came to get the Jews, I was not Jewish, so I did not protest. When they came to get the Catholics, I was not Catholic, so I did not protest. When they came to get the trade unionists, I was not a trade unionist, so I did not protest. When they came for me, there was no one left to protest."

If we don't learn to live together, we will die together. Cultural illiteracy will be the destruction of the planet; cultural competency can save us.

REFERENCES

ANTI-DEFAMATION LEAGUE. (1994). Annual report as cited in the *Jewish Transcripts* Feb. 24, 1995.

BAUM, C., HYMAN, P., & MICHEL, S. (1977). *The Jewish woman in America.* New York: New American Library.

BECK, E. T. (1982). *Nice Jewish girls: A lesbian anthology.* Trumansberg, NY: Crossing Press.

CHAZAN, N. (1984). *Anti-Semitism and politics in the international women's movement.* Paper presented at the International Conference on Politics and Anti-Semitism in the Women's Movement, Paris, France.

EPSTEIN, H. (1982). *Children of the Holocaust.* New York: Penguin.

GRIFFIN, S. (1981). *Pornography and silence.* New York: Harper & Row.

McGOLDRICK, M., PEARCE, K., & GIORDANO, J. (1982). *Ethnicity and family therapy.* New York: Guilford.

POGREBIN, L. C. (1982, June). Anti-Semitism in the women's movement. *Ms.,* pp. 45–68.

ROSS, J. (1988, February). JAP baiting on American campuses. *Anti-Defamation League Bulletin,* p. 3.

WEINER, K. (1990). Anti-Semitism in the therapy room. In R. J. Siegel & E. Cole (Eds.), *Jewish women in therapy: Seen but not heard* (pp. 119–126). New York: Haworth Press.

WOLK, R. S. (1980, July). Anti-Semitism in America: Prophecy or paranoia? *Lilith* (No. 7), pp. 1–3.

*S*UGGESTED READINGS

BECK, E. T. (1982). *Nice Jewish girls: A lesbian anthology.* Trumansberg, NY: Crossing Press.

POGREBIN, L. C. (1991). *Deborah, Golda, and me.* New York: Crown.

SIEGEL, R. J., & COLE, E. (1990). *Jewish women in therapy: Seen but not heard.* New York: Haworth Press.

VON KELLENBACH, K. (1994). *Anti-Judaism in feminist religious writings.* Atlanta: Scholars Press.

DONNA CASTAÑEDA *is Assistant Professor of Psychology at San Diego State University. Dr. Castañeda has taught gender-related courses at San Diego State and at the University of California at Davis. Her work focuses on close relationships among Latinas/os, health promotion in Latina/o communities, and sexual risk behavior among Latina women.*

12

Gender Issues among Latinas

❖

*D*IVERSITY AMONG LATINAS

*A*s an undergraduate in the late 1970s and early 1980s looking for published work specifically focused on Latinas, I found very little. A silence regarding these women exists in the larger society that is reflected in their invisibility in the social science literature. But the situation is improving and certainly there is much more information available now than in the past. Much of this newer work has been done by Latinas themselves. I think one of the most important elements in this emergent literature is the emphasis on the diversity present among Latina women. Much of the available research deals with Mexican American women because they are the largest Latina group. There is, however, growing interest in and concern for distinctions in socioeconomic class, degree of Spanish language usage, sexual orientation, acculturation, and race both within and across differing Latina groups, such as Puerto Rican, Dominican Republican, Central and South American, and Cuban women.[1]

Each unique constellation of the above elements has very different implications for the lived experience of individual Latina women. Consider the case of two women, one a Dominican Republican woman of African descent who has recently arrived in the United States to work in a factory in New York City, the other

Special thanks to Elida Lopez for helpful comments on this paper.
[1]For the purposes of this paper, the term "Latina" refers to women of Mexican, South American, Central American, Puerto Rican, Dominican Republican, or Cuban descent. It does not indicate immigration status. The terms Latina/o and Latinas/os refer to both women and men.

a woman who came from Mexico to the United States and has worked, married, and raised a family in the Central Valley of California (a largely agricultural region) over the last 30 years. Both would be considered immigrants and Latinas, and although their lives would contain certain commonalities, their circumstances and experience would be quite different. U.S.-born Latinas would also have a different experience from that of these two women. Their first language is likely to be English, they may be second-, third-, or even fourth-generation Latinas, and their personal and cultural identity will be related to their experience of growing up in the United States rather than in a different country.

Even college-educated Latinas can come from differing backgrounds. At the university where I teach there is a sizable Latina student population. Most of the women in my classes are the first in their families to attend college, and they tend to come from working-class backgrounds. However, there are some whose parents are professionals and who have a history of higher education in their families. Because the campus where I teach is located at the U.S.-Mexico border, many of the Latina students are bilingual, but even in this location there is still variability in Spanish-language ability among the Latina students, with some who speak Spanish fluently and others who do not.

A DEMOGRAPHIC PICTURE OF LATINAS

Before examining gender-related issues I think it is helpful to have a clear demographic picture of Latinas in the United States. Latinas/os overall are one of the fastest-growing ethnic groups, and they make up approximately 10 percent of the total U.S. population. The largest group of Latinas/os in the United States are those of Mexican descent (61 percent), second are those of Puerto Rican descent (12 percent), and third are those of Cuban descent (5 percent). There are, however, sizable populations of persons of Central American (6 percent), Caribbean (2 percent), and South American (5 percent) descent. Across all Latina/o subgroups, women make up 49 percent of the total Latina/o population, whereas non-Latina women make up 51 percent of the non-Latina/o population. Latinas are younger than non-Latina women in the general population. The median age for Latina women is 26 years, compared to 34 years for non-Latina women. Although the popular perception of Latinas is that they are primarily immigrants, in fact over two-thirds of both Latina/o women and men have been born in the United States (U.S. Bureau of the Census, 1993a).

A significant element that affects the lives of Latinas is poverty. Almost a third of Latinas, 32 percent, are living below the poverty line. This number jumps to 49 percent for those who are single parents (U.S. Bureau of the Census, 1993b). Reasons for high rates of poverty among Latinas are related to gender and ethnic discrimination, lack of educational opportunities, and the type of employment in which Latina women are concentrated. For example, only 51 percent of Latinas have had four or more years of high school, compared to 67 percent of African American women, and 80 percent of white women (U.S. Bureau of the Census, 1992). In 1989, only 3 percent of Latina women were enrolled in colleges and universities, compared to 44 percent of non-Latina women (Garwood, 1992).

A smaller percentage of Latinas than non-Latina women (57 percent versus 71 percent) work in white-collar or pink-collar jobs. Latinas who do work in these sectors tend to be concentrated at the low end of the pay scale; few are in management or professional positions. On the other hand, more Latina women work in blue-collar and service-sector jobs: 42 percent, compared to 28 percent of non-Latina women (Hispanic Almanac, 1990).

WHAT'S IN A NAME?

It is important to understand the labels Latinas use to describe themselves. Because Latinas are a diverse group, a great deal of complexity surrounds the use of these labels. For example, women of Mexican descent in this country may call themselves Chicanas, Mexican Americans, Hispanas, Tejanas, Mexicanas, Spanish Americans, or Hispanics. Each of these terms has its own history and regional specificity. In addition, how an individual names herself can contain political connotations. Many times these political connotations lead to strong feelings about which term should be used to describe Latinas. For example, the term "Chicana/o" was appropriated by activists in the Chicana/o movement in the late 1960s and early 1970s as a term indicating pride in a Mexican heritage, particularly a pre-Columbian Indian heritage, and a rejection of the implicit assimilationist connotations of the term Mexican American. Thus a woman who uses this term to describe herself would also be understood to hold these values. On the other hand, the term "Hispanic" is often viewed as a politically conservative label. It was coined by the government to indicate all persons of Mexican, Caribbean, Central American, or South American descent in the United States. A woman who prefers this term to describe herself would then be understood to hold politically conservative views regarding the role of ethnicity.

Currently, when referring to women of Mexican, Puerto Rican, Cuban, Dominican Republican, Central and South American descent in the United States, the term "Latina" is preferred. Even though it glosses over the diversity among these groups of women, it is a term that originated among Latinas themselves, and it connotes a sense of community across the many Latina subgroups.

At times, the norms surrounding labels developed in academic circles can be at odds with those used by Latinas themselves. Zavella (1993), in describing how her New Mexican informants characterized their ethnic identity, found that these women often had difficulty trying to describe themselves with a single label. They typically had to contextualize their answers to her question about ethnic identity by explaining where they were from, where their parents were from, to whom they were related, their religion, and traditional family activities. Or, as one woman said in response to that question, "I don't know, I'm just me" (p. 64). When Zavella reported her results at a conference using the term which the women had themselves used, "Spanish American," her academic colleagues angrily objected to it because they thought it was too politically conservative and racially inaccurate.

Labels are seen as important indicators of individuals' sense of their own ethnic identity. However, to me it seems that one's ethnic identity can rarely be summarized in a one-word label. The region where one has grown up, family and community norms, whether one has a mixed heritage, such as Latina and European American, immigration status (even the region where an immigrant is from), how long one has lived in the United States, level of acculturation, and political outlook (that is, assimilationist versus nonassimilationist)—all of these go into one's sense of ethnic identification. Of course, there are commonalities among Latinas, but there are multiple Latina experiences, and these often defy simple categorization. In order to understand an individual's sense of ethnic identity it is important to go beyond labels and understand an individual's personal history. When Latinas meet each other for the first time, the interactions often include finding out in either direct or indirect ways a woman's background, where she is from, where she has lived, her work, and her Spanish language proficiency. This is one of the ways that Latinas themselves determine understandings of each other.

GENDER AND FAMILY ROLES

The first gender-related issue I want to talk about is gender and family roles among Latinas. In general, gender roles among Latinas/os have been depicted as highly stylized and male-dominated. Women are thought to be submissive to, and controlled by, their male partners. This stereotype, however, obscures the multidimensional and dynamic quality of gender roles among this group. There is no question, of course, that patriarchy and gender oppression exist in Latina/o families and societies. However, more recent research on gender roles stresses the heterogeneity within this group by including an analysis of class, urban-rural, region, and generational differences, and how these internal differences impinge on gender roles within Latina/o families.

The stereotype of dominant male and submissive female roles in the family is not held up in research that includes the factors mentioned above, and a more complex picture emerges. In one study (Hurtado, Hayes-Bautista, Burciaga Valdez, & Hernandez, 1992) both Latina/o women and men rejected a solely male-dominated family structure (that is, one where a wife should do whatever a husband wants, husbands should make all important decisions, only girls should do housework, and only men should provide for the family). The strength of this rejection varied by generational status. Among first-generation Latinas/os fewer than half endorsed a husband-dominated family structure; the percentages continued to decline for second- and third-generation women and men, although women tended to reject this family structure more than men at all generational levels.

The Latina/o family has been undergoing, and continues to undergo, many changes in its structure and functions. Because of this, Latinas, like women from other cultural and ethnic groups, are attempting to redefine or create new roles and identities for themselves in relation to their male partners and families. For Latinas such processes may contain costs and strains owing to expectations that limit their growth and autonomy, from both inside and outside the family. For example, one woman in my class described how both her immediate and extended family, after being generally supportive of her efforts to complete her college education, stepped up pressures for her to get married after she graduated. *"Now* why aren't you getting married, they say, as if there is something wrong with me." That she may want to follow a different path is never questioned.

According to a study by Williams (1988), social class is an important factor that influences Latina women's ability to change gender roles and expectations for their behavior in the family. A key issue for working-class Mexican American women was the need to develop new social and personal identities separate from husbands, something they had never done before. Attempts to do this, however, caused strain with husbands who continued to insist on maintaining control over women's behavior and activities. These women used both direct and indirect techniques to negotiate this strain. For example, one woman who wanted to join coworkers at Friday evening "happy hours" encountered resistance from her husband. He believed that women who went to bars unaccompanied by their husbands were "loose." This woman persisted, however, and she convinced her husband to change his beliefs, thus allowing her to attend happy hours with coworkers. At other times, working-class women used indirect methods that avoided direct confrontations. For example, if they know their husbands will object to their autonomous behavior, they may do something first and then inform husbands of what they have done afterward.

Mexican American business and professional women, on the other hand, took for granted the notion of both public and private identities that did not rely on their husband's status. For these women, conflicting demands of children, work, and husbands were sources of strain. Each of these domains were important to these women, and they coped with conflicting demands by keeping separate, or compartmentalizing, their public and private identities. By doing so, business and professional women were able to give high priority to both family and work. On the other hand, there were still costs associated with being part of the public domain and having a career. Husbands and family continued to expect them to shoulder the greater share of housekeeping and childcare. As one woman said, "It's unfair. Women have to do things that they are expected to do, hold on to housekeeping responsibilities. We are supermoms. I teach, and as a mother I work all night" (Williams, 1988, p. 210). Furthermore, the few Mexican American women who had more prestigious careers and made more money than their husbands had to downplay these for the sake of husbands. As Williams (1988) says, "One woman carefully avoided emphasizing her own career or monetary success because this made her husband feel threatened; he conceded that he had difficulty accepting his wife's role in having a successful career and being chief wage earner of the family" (p. 211).

A common factor that influenced the roles of both working-class and business and professional women in this study was discrimination in the community and in the workplace. Cultural traditions give men greater authority over women in the Mexican American community, and discrimination based on gender *and* ethnicity in the workplace constrained women's efforts at refashioning their work and public roles. In the workplace these women encountered negative stereotypes of Mexican Americans that were expressed both subtly and directly. As one woman says, "They [Anglo Americans] do not care for Mexican Americans. They will call you anything" (Williams, 1988, p. 211). The business and professional women were more likely to experience more subtle discrimination such as negative stereotypes that were carried into the workplace (for example, that Mexican Americans are less competent).

CLOSE HETEROSEXUAL RELATIONSHIPS

The development of close heterosexual relationships presents Latinas with dilemmas surrounding cultural maintenance, identity, and women's changing roles. In one instance, for example, Mexican American women pursuing a higher education who were strongly ethnically identified and who preferred Mexican American partners in close relationships experienced stress because of their perception that Mexican American men feared high-achieving women. As Gonzalez (1988) suggests, college-educated Mexican American women may "experience conflict as their behavior is changing more rapidly than their sex role attitudes and the attitudes of their male partners" (p. 378). This situation may be particularly pronounced for Latinas with advanced degrees. As a friend of mine who has a Ph.D. told me, "Finding Latino men who are not afraid of talented and educated Latinas is really hard. They talk the talk, but when it really comes down to it they want to marry their secretaries."

Another study (Castañeda, 1993) identified a componential definition of romantic love among heterosexual Mexican American college students. Although women were as likely as men to indicate that trust, communication, shared values and attitudes, and honesty were part of a definition of love, they significantly differed in their likelihood of indicating mutual respect as part of a definition of love. Women were more likely to identify mutual respect as a component of romantic love than were men. Open-ended responses revealed that mutual respect meant a willingness for each partner to listen to the other and to consider the partner's opinions to be important and valid. For the women in this sample, unlike the men, these elements could not as readily be taken for granted in heterosexual relationships. As one woman in this study says, "We don't have to agree on everything but I want respect for my opinions and beliefs. I guess listening is important in a love relationship."

Heterosexual relationships for Latina women are arenas of both satisfaction and struggle, but the burden of adaption to changing gender-role expectations falls primarily on them. This situation is similar to the situation of all women who are struggling to develop nonoppressive heterosexual relationships, but the unique historical, cultural, and class conditions of Latinas may result in the development of different strategies in response to different conditions. For example, Latinas must navigate and balance changing gender expectations, meet the needs of partners, children, and other family members, uphold the cultural integrity of Latinas/os as a whole, and resist racism while also meeting their own needs for positive growth and validation in close relationships. Many Latinas I know express that they are not getting their needs met in their relationships with men. They are frustrated with the lack of understanding received from male partners, but there are few places to turn for help and advice. There are few models for successfully resolving these frustrations that are culturally consistent and personally satisfying. Instead, there is a strong model of female self-sacrifice, obedience, and caring for the needs of others in Latina/o cultures. Because of this, focusing on oneself and getting needs met in a mutually satisfying way can be difficult for Latinas. As one woman describes this process, "since in the Anglo [European American] culture the Catholic church is not the predominant religious institution, women believe in the right to self-improvement. They do not only believe in it, but they struggle for it, whereas in our Latin American culture if a woman speaks out for her rights she is immediately branded, labeled" (Colindres, 1989, p. 77).

*H*ETEROSEXUAL SEXUALITY AND LATINAS

There are a number of contradictory myths regarding Latina sexuality. First, there is the notion of the woman who remains chaste and virginal until married, unsullied by sexual desire of any kind. If a woman is married, she is viewed as a mother figure who is happy having many children, but who is not particularly interested in sex. Instead, she merely "submits" to a partner's sexual desires. (The partner being, of course, a "Latin lover" with insatiable sexual demands.) Finally, there is the myth of the "sexy señorita with smoldering eyes" who is always ready for sex. Certainly, there is little consciousness of Latina lesbian sexuality. None of these myths reflect the reality of Latina sexuality, but there has been no public or private vision of Latina sexuality in between or outside of these extremes. Latinas have few realistic or positive images of their sexuality reflected in the media, art, literature, or in the Latina/o or non-Latina/o culture.

A small number of empirical studies of Latina sexuality exist in the literature, but they are limited in their scope and interpretive power. These studies have found that Latina (and Latino) university students tend to be less knowledgeable about sexuality (Padilla & O'Grady, 1987) and more conservative in their sexual behavior (Baldwin, Whiteley, & Baldwin, 1992; Padilla & O'Grady, 1987) and in their attitudes toward sexuality (Padilla & O'Grady, 1987) than European American students. This situation also appears to be the case among Latina adolescents (Padilla & Baird, 1991; Scott, Shifman, Orr, Owen, & Fawcett, 1988).

The picture is somewhat different when community samples of Latinas are studied. Latinas in drug treatment were found to be quite willing and able to broach the subject of condoms to their male partners and to convince them to use them (Kline, Kline, & Oken, 1992). In another study (Amaro, 1988), Latina women did not endorse the notion that the purpose of sexuality was solely reproduction. However, this sample expressed a high level of dissatisfaction with the quality of their current sexual relationships.

To date, the most interesting and provocative work on Latina sexuality is to be found not in the social sciences but in literature, art, and poetry (for example, Alarcon, Castillo, & Moraga, 1989; Trujillo, 1991). A common theme in this work is the historical repression of Latina sexuality within the family and larger Latina/o culture. This repression has served to silence women and leave them with inadequate knowledge of their own sexuality. Catholicism, and its pervasiveness in Latina/o culture, has played a central role in keeping Latinas from full knowledge of their sexuality. As Castillo (1991) writes, "Sexuality for the Catholic woman of Latin American background has, at best, been associated with her reproductive ability (or lack of it) and otherwise, repressed" (p. 40). In Catholicism the Virgin Mary, and the qualities she embodies, is upheld as the model for all women to emulate. These qualities include self-abnegation, motherhood, and above all, sexual purity. This model, which may not be articulated by individual women, is clearly implicated in the stress on virginity until marriage for women within Latina/o cultures. In addition, although the reality of Latina sexuality indicates otherwise (e.g., the rates of teen pregnancy and sexually transmitted diseases), Latinas are still subjected to cultural expectations that emphasize a double standard in which men's sexuality is positively viewed and encouraged, whereas that of women is negatively viewed and discouraged.

All of these factors, the myths, Catholicism, repression, and the double standard directly influence the development of sexuality among Latinas. In some cases, sexual enjoyment itself can be conflictual for Latinas. In order to see themselves as virtuous some women may, as Espín (1985) says, "shun sexual pleasure" (p. 156) and "even express pride in their own lack of pleasure or desire" (p. 156).

Despite the greater restrictions on Latinas' expression of their sexuality, my experience has been that, given the appropriate context, Latinas have much to say about sexuality and will do so openly. In a study I did (Castañeda, 1985) to examine mediation of sexuality during menstruation among a sample of Mexican farm-working women (certainly a topic many would consider too "taboo" for this group!), I found that these women could easily speak about this topic. They also had much to say about related topics, such as birth control, courtship, and gender relations. Given a space to do so, Latinas can express a multiplicity of sexual views, forms, and experiences.

*L*ATINA LESBIANS

To a large extent lesbianism is invisible within Latina/o communities. Lesbians and gay men are generally negatively viewed and may be ostracized by their families if their sexual orientation is known. Because of this, Latina lesbians may not be out about their lesbianism with family members, even if they are out in other contexts of their lives.

On the other hand, I have seen a number of instances where, even though it may not be openly acknowledged, a Latina's lesbianism may be tacitly accepted by her family and her community. This may be one way that lesbian women can, at least to a small extent, exist in Latina/o communities. In these cases, Latinas are able to maintain connections with their community, their family, *and* their lesbian identity.

Because Latinas/os grow up in a context that stresses family bonds and connection to community, to be ostracized from these is particularly distressing for Latinas. To live solely in a non-Latina context, even though it may be one where an individual Latina's lesbianism is accepted and validated, is generally not preferable. However, unlike Latina heterosexuals or non-Latina lesbians, Latina lesbians must often make the decision to separate two fundamental elements of the self: ethnicity and lesbianism. Individual Latina lesbians make this decision in ways that work for each of them, but the decision can be fraught with ambivalence and even anger that they must confront such a decision. One Cuban woman describes these feelings well by saying, "it is a very painful question because I feel that I am both, and I don't want to have to choose. Clearly, straight people don't even get asked this question and it is unfair that we have to discuss it" (Espín, 1987, p. 47).

Another factor that affects the experience of Latina lesbians is that a much larger percentage of Latinas are poor. To establish and live a lesbian lifestyle is much more difficult for a Latina lesbian who is also poor (Castillo, 1991). The lives of all poor women are more difficult than those of middle-class women, but when one is poor, subject to racism in the larger society, part of a culture that censures lesbianism, and where even definitions of heterosexual Latinas' sexuality are obscured by myth, the options for expression of a lesbian identity are more restricted. Because of this, many Latina lesbians may opt for a heterosexual lifestyle by marrying and having children, and they may either not acknowledge their awareness of their lesbianism or practice it in secrecy. In addition if one's lesbian identity is expressed, the alternatives available for safety, both physical and emotional, are also limited if one is poor and Latina.

Unfortunately, there is very little published information regarding Latina lesbian sexuality. As mentioned above, the silence surrounding Latina lesbian sexuality has been broken with the publication of various literary works, but these represent the work of educated and highly articulate women. The sexual lives of Latinas outside this small circle are not well represented, particularly in the social sciences. How Latina lesbians create, define, and live out their sexuality, its commonalities and differences from non-Latina lesbian sexuality, and how that intersects with factors affecting lesbian and ethnic identity are important issues for future research.

SPOUSAL AND INTIMATE-PARTNER VIOLENCE

Now I would like to turn to the issue of spousal or intimate-partner violence. What I mean by this is violence that Latinas experience from a husband or boyfriend. Little research has been done on family violence in general among Latinas/os in the United States. Available data show that Latina women are less likely to be victims of homicide by a spouse or intimate partner than either African American or white women (UCLA-CDS, 1985, cited in Sorenson & Telles, 1991). In one study (Sorenson & Telles, 1991) that included both Latina/o women and men, Latinas/os overall did not differ from non-Latinas/os in reported rates of spousal or intimate-partner violence. There were, however, differences between immigrant and nonimmigrant Latinas/os. Immigrant Latinas/os were significantly *less* likely to report spousal or intimate-partner violence (5.6 percent) than non-Latinas/os (10.5 percent). On the other hand, U.S.-born Latinas/os (15.2 percent) were *more* likely to report spousal or partner violence than either immigrant Latinas/os or non-Latinas/os. Furthermore, Latinas/os who spoke primarily English were more likely than those who spoke primarily Spanish to report spousal and intimate-partner violence.

There are a number of possible reasons for these differences. Immigrant Latinas/os may be less likely to report such incidents; Latinas/os who show higher rates of spousal or partner violence may be less likely to emigrate to a new country; and Mexico and other countries from which Latinas/os emigrate may simply be less violent societies than the United States. There may also be differences in definitions and tolerance for spousal or intimate-partner violence among these different groups. Immigrant Latinas may, for example, be less aware that violence from a partner should be unacceptable and not tolerated.

Another factor that may play a role is that U.S.-born Latinas/os may experience greater cultural conflict because they must negotiate two sets of cultural and social demands (Sorenson & Telles, 1991). Furthermore, U.S.-born Latinas/os show higher rates of drug and alcohol use than immigrant Latinas/os (Amaro, Whitaker, Coffman, & Heeren, 1990; Markides, Ray, Stroup-Benham, & Treviño, 1990). All these elements, either singly or interactively, may be operative in the higher rates of spousal and intimate partner violence seen among U.S.-born Latinas/os.

SEXUAL ASSAULT

Another form of violence I want to talk about is sexual assault. The study of sexual assault among Latinas is, again, an area in which little research has been done. In one study (Sorenson & Siegel, 1992) using a community sample in Los Angeles which included both women and men, Latinas/os were found to have a lower overall prevalence of sexual assault, 8.1 percent, compared to 19.9 percent among non-Latinas/os. A previous study that included analyses by immigration status found that although Latinas/os overall show a lower prevalence of sexual assault, the prevalence of sexual assault among U.S.-born Latinas/os, 11.4 percent, approaches that of U.S.-born non-Latinas/os, 16.2 percent (Sorenson & Telles, 1991). This study included both women and men, but within every ethnic, age, and education level women reported a higher prevalence of sexual assault than men. Although Latinas/os were not significantly different from non-Latina/os in likelihood to resist rape, to report specific emotional reactions to a sexual assault, to develop mental disorders due to the assault, or to talk to someone about the assault, they were less likely to talk to a psychotherapist about the assault than were non-Latinas/os (Sorenson & Siegel, 1992).

Looking at only women, Sorenson and Telles (1991) found that Latina women overall reported lower rates of sexual assault, 8.6 percent, than non-Latina women, 22 percent. Again, immigrant Latinas reported lower rates, 4.2 percent, than U.S.-born Latinas, 14.3 percent. However, when immigrant women were sexually assaulted, almost one-third of the time, 31 percent, the perpetrator was a husband or intimate partner. This was the case among only 13 percent of non-Latina women.

The reasons for lower rates of intimate-partner and sexual violence reported by immigrant Latinas are still unclear. These data should not lead to a sense that these women are somehow "protected" or safer from violence than U.S.-born Latinas or non-Latina women. In many ways these women are quite vulnerable. They live and work in some of the most unsafe areas of U.S. cities, they must use public transportation at all hours to travel to and from work, they work in conditions where they are susceptible to sexual coercion, and those who are in the United States illegally have little recourse for protection from the police or legal system. The high rate of sexual assault from husbands or intimate partners among immigrant women suggests that these women may be particularly vulnerable to violence within the family.

SERVICES FOR LATINA VICTIMS OF VIOLENCE

Although rates of spousal and intimate partner violence and sexual assault among Latinas are important to understand, perhaps more important than these is the development of appropriate and accessible services for Latinas who experience these types of violence. Many rape crisis centers and battered women's shelters make efforts at outreach to Latinas, but these services are often underutilized by Latinas and those who may need help may not receive it. Such programs need to consider language, cultural, and economic issues that may impact their accessibility to Latinas in the community. For example, service agencies should have bilingual and bicultural staff persons, should understand that Latinas may believe sacrifice for the family and keeping the family intact is important, that Latinas' economic dependence may make them less able to take action, and that Latinas may fear that the social stigma of rape or intimate partner violence, if it is known, will affect not only them but their family as well. Furthermore, immigrant women may fear deportation or incarceration themselves if they take complaints to legal authorities.

CONCLUSION

For Latinas, each of these topics intersects with other issues such as poverty, the secondary status of Latinas/os in U.S. society, and mandates for women's behavior derived from two sources, Latina/o cultures and the larger U.S. society. These are all inseparable elements of the lived experience of Latinas. For Latinas, being poor is equally as oppressive as discrimination based on race and ethnicity, or being subjected to sexism either by Latino or non-Latino men. The limited number of Latinas in higher education, for example, is due not just to racism; it is also due to living and growing up in poor communities with inadequate schools and to the secondary status of women in Latina/o and non-Latino/a society.

Researchers are only beginning to uncover how these elements interactively influence the development, mental and physical well-being, and behavior of Latinas.

The diversity inherent in the Latina population has been a thread running throughout this lecture. Latinas are from various countries of origin; they are workers, students, scholars, activists, mothers, lesbians and heterosexuals, immigrants and nonimmigrants. There are factors that separate them from non-Latina women as well as ones that lead to internal divisions such as skin color, level of acculturation, and country of origin. Because of this diversity, and because they must essentially navigate two cultures, they cross multiple contexts, or "borders," everyday (Anzaldúa, 1990). At times Latinas must cross borders that are alienating, even denigrating, such as when they must interact with health, mental health, or educational institutions that are hostile to them or prefer to exclude them. However, being able to work well in many contexts can also lead to greater strength and a more insightful understanding of oneself. Mainstream psychology has not yet been able to adequately represent this reality.

The notion of border crossing has a deep resonance for me each time I go home to visit my family. In a family of seven children I have been the only person to go to college, and on top of that I went on to get a Ph.D. As the eldest daughter in a family that places great value on children (I have many nieces and nephews), not only do I not have any children, but I am also unmarried! Each homecoming is like moving from one world into another, from one self to another. The transitions are now much smoother for me than in earlier years, but only after a process of coming to understand that at any point in time I am more than one person, one dimension.

Currently, gender meanings and gender relations among Latinas/os are in flux. Instead of using stereotypes to explain gender-related behavior, researchers are either questioning their veracity or even moving beyond them to develop explanatory frameworks that are in greater touch with the multifaceted experience of Latinas. As more researchers, particularly Latina researchers, become involved in the study of gender issues among Latinas/os, a more viable image of this group of women is emerging. Although the diversity and complexity of Latina lives present challenges to researchers, developing a psychology of Latinas can also lead to a more integrative and truly representative discipline of psychology.

REFERENCES

ALARCON, N., CASTILLO, A., & MORAGA, C. (Eds.).(1989). *Third woman: The sexuality of Latinas.* Berkeley, CA: Third Woman Press.

AMARO, H. (1988). Women in the Mexican-American community: Religion, culture, and reproductive attitudes and experience. *Journal of Community Psychology, 20,* 6–20.

AMARO, H., WHITAKER, R., COFFMAN, G., & HEEREN, T. (1990). Acculturation and marijuana and cocaine use: Findings from the HHANES 1982–1984. *American Journal of Public Health, 80,* 54–60.

ANZALDÚA, G. (1990). La conciencia de la mestiza: Towards a new consciousness. In G. Anzaldúa, (Ed.), *Making face, making soul, haciendo caras: Creative and critical perspectives by feminists of color* (pp. 377–389). San Francisco: aunt lute books.

BALDWIN, J. D., WHITELEY, S., & BALDWIN, J. I. (1992). The effect of ethnic group on sexual activities related to contraception and STDs. *Journal of Sex Research, 29,* 141–167.

CASTAÑEDA, D. (1985). *Mediation of sexuality during menstruation among Mexican farmworking women: An analysis of differing levels of variables.* Unpublished manuscript.

CASTAÑEDA, D. (1993). The meaning of romantic love among Mexican-Americans. *Journal of Social Behavior and Personality, 8,* 257–272.

CASTILLO, A. (1991). La macha: Toward a beautiful whole self. In C. Trujillo (Ed.), *Chicana lesbians: The girls our mothers warned us about* (pp. 24–48). Berkeley, CA: Third Woman Press.

COLINDRES, C. (1989). A letter to my mother. In N. Alarcon, A. Castillo, & C. Moraga (Eds.), *Third woman: The sexuality of Latinas* (pp. 73–79). Berkeley, CA: Third Woman Press.

ESPÍN, O. M. (1985). Influences on sexuality and Hispanic/Latin women. In C. S. Vance (Ed.), *Pleasure and danger: Exploring female sexuality* (pp. 149–164). Boston, MA: Routledge & Kegan Paul.

ESPÍN, O. M. (1987). Issues of identity in the psychology of Latina lesbians. In Boston Lesbian Psychologies Collective, (Ed.), *Lesbian psychologies* (pp. 35–55). Chicago, IL: University of Illinois Press.

GARWOOD, A. N. (Ed.). (1992). *Hispanic Americans: A statistical sourcebook.* Boulder, CO: Numbers and Concepts.

GONZALEZ, J. T. (1988). Dilemmas of the high-achieving Chicana: The double-bind factor in male/female relationships. *Sex Roles, 18,* 367–380.

HISPANIC POLICY DEVELOPMENT, INC. *Hispanic Almanac* (2d ed). (1990). New York: Author.

HURTADO, A., HAYES-BAUTISTA, D. E., BURCIAGA VALDEZ, R., & HERNANDEZ, A. (1992). *Redefining California: Latino social engagement in a multicultural society.* Los Angeles, CA: UCLA Chicano Studies Research Center.

KLINE, A., KLINE E., & OKEN, E. (1992). Minority women and sexual choice in the age of AIDS. *Social Science and Medicine, 34,* 447–457.

MARKIDES, K. S., RAY, L. A., STROUP-BENHAM, C. A., & TREVIÑO, F. (1990). Acculturation and alcohol consumption in the Mexican American population in the southwestern United States: Findings from the HHANES 1982–1984. *American Journal of Public Health, 80,* 42–46.

PADILLA, A. M., & BAIRD, T. L. (1991). Mexican American adolescent sexuality and sexual knowledge: An exploratory study. *Hispanic Journal of Behavioral Sciences, 13,* 95–104.

PADILLA, E. R., & O'GRADY, K. E. (1987). Sexuality among Mexican Americans: A case of sexual stereotyping. *Journal of Personality and Social Psychology, 52,* 5–10.

SCOTT, C. S., SHIFMAN, L., ORR, L., OWEN, R. G., & FAWCETT, N. (1988). Hispanic and Black American adolescents' beliefs relating to sexuality and contraception. *Adolescence, 23,* 667–688.

SORENSON, S. B., & SIEGEL, J. M. (1992). Gender, ethnicity, and sexual assault: Findings from a Los Angeles study. *Journal of Social Issues, 48,* 93–104.

SORENSON, S. B., & TELLES, C. A. (1991). Self-reports of spousal violence in a Mexican-American and non-Hispanic white population. *Violence and Victims, 6,* 3–15.

TRUJILLO, C. (Ed.). (1991). *Chicana lesbians: The girls our mothers warned us about.* Berkeley, CA: Third Woman Press.

U.S. BUREAU OF THE CENSUS. (1992). *Educational attainment in the United States: March 1991 and 1990.* (Current Population Reports, Series P-20, No. 462). Washington, DC: Government Printing Office.

U.S. BUREAU OF THE CENSUS. (1993a). *Persons of Hispanic origin in the United States, 1990* (CP-3-3). Washington, DC: U.S. Government Printing Office.

U.S. BUREAU OF THE CENSUS. (1993b). *Poverty in the United States: 1992.* (Current Population Reports, Series P60-185). Washington, DC: Government Printing Office.

WILLIAMS, N. (1988). Role making among married Mexican American women: Issues of class and ethnicity. *Journal of Applied Behavioral Science, 24,* 203–217.

ZAVELLA, P. (1993). Feminist insider dilemmas: Constructing ethnic identity with "Chicana" informants. *Frontiers, 13,* 53–76.

*S*UGGESTED READINGS

ANZALDÚA, G. (Ed.).(1990). *Making face, making soul, haciendo caras: Creative and critical perspectives by feminists of color.* San Francisco, CA: aunt lute books.

HURTADO, A., HAYES-BAUTISTA, D. E., BURCIAGA VALDEZ, R., & HERNANDEZ, A. (1992). *Redefining California: Latino social engagement in a multicultural society.* Los Angeles, CA: UCLA Chicano Studies Research Center.

TRUJILLO, C. (Ed.). (1991). *Chicana lesbians: The girls our mothers warned us about.* Berkeley, CA: Third Woman Press.

BEVERLY J. GOODWIN is Associate Professor of Psychology at Indiana University of Pennsylvania. Dr. Goodwin has been teaching courses on the psychology of African American women since 1977 at IUP and the University of Pittsburgh. She is a clinical psychologist, and is best known for her work on victimization, textbook evaluation, and issues in clinical supervision.

13

The Impact of Popular Culture on Images of African American Women

❖

Writing on African American[1] women for a psychology of women reader is quite an overwhelming task because much of what is considered the psychology of women is, in reality, "a psychology of white, middle-class, American women" (Hyde, 1985, p. 380). Black women have received limited, disjointed, and sometimes biased treatment in many psychology of women courses and textbooks (Brown, Goodwin, Hall, & Jackson-Lowman, 1985; Brown-Collins, 1988; Goodwin, 1990; Goodwin, 1991a; Goodwin, 1991b; McHugh & Goodwin, 1991). As a result it is difficult to produce a review article on the psychology of African American women without appearing too disperse.

When my colleagues (Brown et al., 1985) and I reviewed psychology of women textbooks for the inclusion of material on African American women for a course we were designing, we found that the following content areas dominated the literature: "the black matriarchy and female-headed households; black women and feminism; economic roles, occupational status, and educational levels of black women; racism versus sexism; female-male relationships; self-esteem, black women, and femininity; and socialization of black women" (p. 34).

---

[1]The term used to identify those born and raised in the United States who can trace their ancestry to the continent of Africa has changed over the years. For the purposes of writing this document, I have settled on the labels African Americans and Blacks and have used both terms interchangeably throughout this document.

Our review found that omissions abound and that Black women had been excluded from, included in a restricted way, or treated in a negative fashion in most of the textbooks surveyed. In addition the activist role was downplayed, and the victim role was highlighted (Collins, 1990; Giddings, 1983; Lerner, 1972). What the writers failed to recognize was the vast diversity among Black women—a diversity too comprehensive and exhaustive for essential characteristics to be summarized.[2] What the writers also did not understand was that some of us do not see our history as being filled with pathos and victimization and, as a result, do not embrace the victim role (e.g., Giddings, 1983; Hine, 1993; Hull, Scott, & Smith, 1982; Lerner, 1972; Morton, 1991; Rodgers-Rose, 1980; Sharp, 1993). We have not depended on nor have we identified with dominant images in the psychology of women, media, or popular culture for self-definition (Collins, 1990), especially when some of the images could be viewed as prejudiced (Brown et al., 1985; Goodwin, 1990; Torrey, 1979).

This lecture explores the impact of media images on African American women by considering several particular ways we have resisted representations (hooks, 1994) of narrow and often negative portrayals of us in popular culture (hooks, 1992; Jewell, 1993; Null, 1975; Turner, 1994). This is accomplished by sharing incidences in which Black women have challenged media images by daring to create a contrary representation. This lecture concludes with attention to the efforts of African American women at self-definition and image transformation. My hope is that this lecture can at least prompt you to question what you read about Black women, and thereby make it possible to change the way the psychology of women is presented and taught.

I have a long-standing interest in film. I was born in Los Angeles, surrounded by the influence of Hollywood. In addition, both my grandmother, Ruby Berkley Goodwin, and my father, Robert L. Goodwin, were actors and writers in Hollywood. Many of their friends were in the industry too. My grandma Ruby had little opportunity to play more than maid roles, and my father talked often and openly about his efforts to change the images of Blacks in film. For a number of years he was blacklisted for not compromising on his ideals. At an early age I was introduced to the significance of character development and encouraged to read scripts. As a child I did not passively consume television or movies, and I realized the power of popular culture in shaping American society.

Wilson (1994) points out that "part of the territory which goes with being black and female is that of contending or being confronted, from time to time, with other people's, often wrong, ideas of who we are as black women. We have been particularly plagued by the stereotype of myth, because historically we have tended to be invisible" (p. 6). It is safe to say that African American women have not faired well in popular cul-

---

[2]The intent of writing this chapter is not to critique the authors who represent this line of work. Instead the objective is to encourage revisionist and proactive efforts by focusing on activities not persons.

ture (cf., Bogle, 1973; Brown et al., 1985; hooks, 1992; Jewell, 1993; Null, 1975; Turner, 1994; Walker, 1994; Wallace, 1990). We have been victimized on several levels. We have been belittled, discredited, ignored, silenced, and stereotyped (Bogle, 1973, 1988; Boyd, 1993; Collins, 1990; Lorde, 1995). We have been made fun of because of our attitudes, physical features, and demeanor. For African American women the dominant images in popular culture have been overwhelmingly negative and narrow.

Michele Wallace (1990) sees African American women as experiencing the "invisibility blues." When Blacks are being considered, the analysis often does not include gender. When women are being considered, the analysis often does not include race or ethnicity. Elizabeth Spelman (1995) calls this the "ampersand problem" or the "additive perspective," and Sapiro (1994) refers to this as the "distinct components model." This predicament is manifested when the experiences of a Black woman are not considered apart from her gender or race. We can then add on other characteristics including but not limited to class, religion, sexual orientation, or geography. For example, she is *either* a Black, a woman, or a working-class woman, but seldom a Black working-class woman. Unique characteristics of being Black, female, and of a particular social class cannot be appreciated simultaneously. Regardless, Black women are missing from many disciplines and institutions (Hull et al., 1982). We are absent from pop culture and feminist theory, from the media and the classroom.

Nowhere do we witness the notion of invisibility more than in the movies with descriptions of familial relations involving Black females. hooks (1992) notes, "The emphasis on film is so central because it, more than any other media experience, determines how blackness and black people are seen and how other groups will respond to us based on their relation to these constructed and consumed images" (p. 5).

What are the images of Black women in situation comedies, dramas, or documentaries? Any similarities? Is she multidimensional? What are her dominant personality characteristics? What about physical characteristics? The dominant characterizations of African American women in film are narrow and excessive. There is little variety. She is either an asexual mother figure or a sexpot. There is little in between. "From early adolescence to adulthood, women of color are inundated by media and social contacts that serve to instill the belief that to be different is societally unacceptable," says Boyd (1990). "It is obvious that commercial media present images of women with flowing hair and strong European features as ideals of Western beauty" (pp. 151–152).

The self-concept and self-esteem of African American women are challenged. Patricia Turner (1994) in her book *Ceramic Uncles & Celluloid Mammies: Black Images and Their Influence on Culture* has observed that "in television, as well as other vehicles of popular culture, images of African Americans have been limited and are often one-dimensional" (p. xii). The one-dimensional nature of Black women on film is usually relegated to a racial- and gender-stereotyped role—for example, as submissive women who work hard for a living and are paid minimal wages to clean, cook, and care for white people. Her primary responsibility is nurturing somebody other than members of her family or friends. Those outside of her race get her best; her family and friends get what is left. Probably she is a domestic. But this role has recently been updated to other kinds of service worker, civil servant, or best friend—someone who is generally supportive of a non-Black character.

These qualities have been selected and fostered by the dominant culture. Why? Some would say that they are intended to "offend and hurt" (Boyd, 1993, p. 11). Selfish needs are met. Entertainment occurs. The net result has been the objectification of Black women (Collins, 1990). In Patricia Hill Collins's (1990) book *Black Feminist Thought: Knowledge, Consciousness, and the Politics of Empowerment* there is a chapter called "Mammies, Matriarchs, and Other Controlling Images." She identified four pervasive images of Black women in the media: they are the mamma, the matriarch, the welfare mother, and the Jezebel (the sexually aggressive woman, including the whore). Of the four controlling images listed above, the first three have received the most recognition in the media. In explaining the importance of the caricature of Black mothers, Turner (1994) notes that, "no image exceeds the popularity and diversity of the smiling, overweight, copiously dressed figure referred to alternately as mamma or auntie" (p. 41). Donald Bogle (1973), in his definitive manuscript on the African American presence in Hollywood, added to this discussion by identifying five dominant images: Toms, coons, mulattoes, mammies, and bucks. Again, the Mamma character was identified. In describing the Mamma character, Bogle wrote:

> She is representative of all-black woman, overweight, middle-aged, and so dark, so thoroughly black, that it is preposterous even to suggest that she be a sex object. Instead she was desexed. (pp. 14–15)

Each description is slightly different but in essence describes the same character:

> She made her debut around 1914 when audiences were treated to a black face version of *Lysistrata.* The comedy, titled *Coon Town Suffragettes,* deals with a group of bossy mamma washerwomen who organized a militant movement to keep their good-for-nothing husbands at home. (p. 9)

Cornel West (1994) also sees the Aunt Jemima actress as "the sexless, long-suffering nurturer" (p. 119). This character was not meant to elevate or inspire Blacks; movies including her were a "powerful medium of propaganda" (Null, 1975, p. 7) that have been influential in forming public policy, limiting opportunities for Black women, and dictating interpersonal relationships (Greene, 1990; Jewell, 1993).

Blacks have scrutinized, cross-examined, and expelled Mamma as a degrading character and an embarrassment to her race. The political aspects of the character cannot be overlooked because "it has been almost impossible to keep politics and aesthetics apart" (Bogle, 1973, p. xi). Her primary role has been to nurture whites and to keep Blacks in their place. She is the quintessential Black woman.

Bogle (1973) implores us to review Mamma and other Black fictional characters as "cultural ancestors" and to "put black films and black personalities in their proper historical perspective" (p. xi) because it is his belief that no African American actor can escape playing stereotyped roles. What is most important is not the stereotyped role but what a skilled actor can do with the stereotype.

Perhaps no one took more heat, played the role better, or was more identified with playing Mamma roles than Hattie McDaniel. She was the first African American to win an Academy Award for acting. Her name became synonymous with "the good old South," and she played the Mamma character in over 300 films (Jackson, 1990). As historian Darlene Hine (1993) wrote:

> Character actress Hattie McDaniel presents a troubling figure on the landscape of American race relations. On the one hand, she had a fruitful career in the competitive industry of Hollywood cinema in the 1930s and 1940s. . . . On the other hand, she became famous for portraying mamma-like figures and thus perpetuated one of the most hated stereotypes of Black women. . . . It is also impossible to reconcile these two opinions, because McDaniel was so firmly defined by a paradoxical nature. (p. 768)

Carlton Jackson (1990), Hattie's biographer, recognized the confounding image she has in the history of the civil rights movement and Blacks in Hollywood too. She worked to gradually change Hollywood and the working conditions for Blacks there. She thought that the role of Mamma could evolve into a less stereotypic character for herself and other Black actresses. Her capstone character was "Beulah"—a character she played on the radio. She was no longer one-dimensional. She was intelligent and happy. She was content being single. Yes, she was still overweight but she saw losing a few pounds as desirable. This was the late 1940s. This was a major departure from other Mamma roles. For instance, she was able to compromise with directors to play the Mamma role as a smart woman, without a Southern dialect; she wore the uniform of the maid but one designed by top fashion designers (Jackson, 1990). Eventually the NAACP and the Urban League made positive and supportive remarks regarding her roles.

When Hattie's health began to deteriorate, her public was told that she was ill. She received letters, cards, and prayers. This is what Grandma Ruby said (as cited in Jackson, 1990), when she was interviewed about Hattie's health.

> I believe every faith in the country prayed for her. . . . Old people at Jewish homes for the aged wrote while Hattie was ill, and said they were offering special prayers. Catholic friends told of burning candles for her, and Protestant churches remembered her in their services and broadcasts. "Miss Mac"

was universally loved, and her life and career transcended political and religious boundaries. (p. 160)

When Hattie died on October 26, 1952, she was mourned by both Blacks and whites alike. Many Americans felt as if a family member had passed. This obituary was not intended to magnify the woman or her contributions to Blacks in the media. She did not live an easy life; she had many problems. Some of her problems were similar to those Mamma encountered. She was a giver and a pleaser. She was always taking care of others, and her own needs were seldom being met. But her accomplishments did not make her happy. She suffered from depression throughout her career and even attempted suicide. Jackson (1990) described her as behaving in a "manic-depressive manner" at times (p. 144). She took care of many without taking care of herself. She contributed her money and efforts to those in need. Sometimes she was taken advantage of when she opened doors for other Black entertainers. She even invited several to live in her mansion while they searched for employment, and sometimes they used her for her prestige and resources. She was harassed by the national president of the NAACP for many years, and he encouraged Blacks to boycott several of her movies. She took his admonishments personally and eventually became overly defensive and irritable. She was married four times, never had any children, was rumored to be bisexual, and indulged in too much drink, food, and partying (Jackson, 1990).

In recognizing her contributions, Jackson, her biographer, noted:

> Beyond being a wonderful movie star, Hattie was also a grand person. In her best form she could thrill and delight, not for her own self-aggrandizement, but to make people around her feel important. Making others realize their own value and significance is no small accomplishment. Perhaps that trait was the most important legacy Hattie McDaniel left to the world. (p. 161)

My grandmother was her best friend, confidante, and personal secretary. And Grandma Ruby played her share of Mamma roles. My grandmother did not live her life without controversy either. When she wasn't acting, she was writing. She kept busy writing a syndicated column, "Hollywood in Bronze," a regular entry on the happenings among Black entertainers (Jackson, 1990; E. G. Jordan, personal communication, September 16, 1994). As a trusted insider, Grandma Ruby produced writings on the importance of the Black presence in Hollywood—opening the doors for better and less stereotypic roles. She was viewed as a traditionalist and a traitor by some.

She received much criticism for her autobiography, *It's Good to Be Black* (Goodwin, 1953). The title offended some Blacks, especially the leadership of several civil rights organizations, but my family took pride in being Black. Story upon story was shared of family life and triumphs. Taking pride in being Black seemed incomprehensible to some. To most Blacks at that time, the reference name was "Negro" or "Colored." To be called Black was an insult. Presenting the Berkley family and the towns-people of Du Quoin, Illinois, particularly her parents, as victors in life up-set others. My father used to say that Blacks were told to boycott this book. Her alma mater, Southern Illinois University, reprinted her book in 1976, and I cherish my copy.

When I discussed Hattie's impact on my grandmother and the Goodwin family with my Aunt Ethel, Grandma Ruby's only daughter, (E. G. Jordan, personal communication, September 16, 1994), I learned some surprising information. She saw Goodwin family life as changing dramatically when Hattie and Grandma Ruby became friends. Aunt Ethel saw 1939 as the year the Goodwin family moved into a new era. That year Hattie won the Academy Award. Aunt Ethel saw this change as one that caused family life to deteriorate, not improve. There was much more ac-tivity, much more interest in visibility, much more interest in being a bet-ter entertainer or writer. The children took dance and music lessons. Things no longer revolved around the family, but around Grandma Ruby's work and her commitment to Hattie's career. My great-grandparents, Grandma Sophie and Grandpa Braxton, and my grand-father, Grandpa Lee, raised the five kids (James, my father, Robert, Ethel, Paul, and Phillip) because Grandma Ruby had to finish a story, or write a speech or letter for Hattie, or make a movie, or go to New York to play summer stock. Aunt Ethel saw her father, Grandpa Lee, as being totally devoted to her mother. Whatever work she did took priority over any-thing and everything, including the children.

As her granddaughter I have loving memories of my visits to her house on West 39th Street. I can't remember a time when my grandmother and I were alone because siblings and cousins were always around. But I do remember her library and her office. As a child I was overwhelmed by all those books and pictures. She wrote several of the books in her library. I wanted to learn to read so badly because I wanted to read what she had written. It was there where I learned to read. It was there where I learned to love a good story and listen to adults talk about the good life. It was there where I was told, "You must be Ruby's grandbaby because you look so much like her." That observation has come my way many times since then.

My Grandma Ruby was nothing like that character; she was much more loving and nurturing. The nurturing Mamma was only one side of her life, but the American public never knew her as a creative person. She had limited opportunities not only because of her race and gender but be-cause she was born at the beginning of this century.

In all, I guess to me she was more Mamma-like than any movie could have made her. She died at the age of 56 in 1961 after a long battle with breast cancer. I'm sorry I didn't know her better or fully appreciate her contributions to Black women in Hollywood during her lifetime. I would have loved to have had her assistance in preparing this lecture by asking her the many questions I had as I did the research for this paper and to share stories from that time, usually referred to as the "golden age of Hollywood."

Both Hattie and my grandmother were born at the turn of this century when racial segregation was the law of the land. As my Grandma Ruby (Goodwin, 1976) wrote in her autobiography,

> Until I once argued with a psychology teacher, I didn't know that all Negro children grow up with a sense of frustration and insecurity. . . . The philosophy behind this remark, however, I have since found implied in most books about Negroes. . . . I have learned to resent this implication much as I earlier resented the flat remark of the psychology teacher. As a result I have felt impelled to write of life as I have lived it. (p. 7)

She put forth a particular perspective on living, a particular worldview that was not especially popular at that time. She didn't profess to be an expert on the lives of all Black women or the "African American experience." But she did know something about being a Black woman and the way the media affected her. So did Hattie. She did know that in the media there is a narrow acceptable range of physical and personality characteristics in actresses, and particularly for Blacks. And she used her writings and her acting to challenge the images.

What about now? Have things changed for actresses? One might speculate that there are no more Mamma characters played by popular present-day actresses. Don't we live in a time of political correctness? Whoopi Goldberg, probably the most influential Black actress of today, has played her share of Mamma-like characters in her short movie career. The most recent characterization is a movie just released at the time of this writing, *Corrina, Corrina*.

Also, singer Gladys Knight has been selected to be a spokesperson for Aunt Jemima products (Associated Press, 1994). To quote Bob Hilarides, brand manager of Aunt Jemima for Quaker Oats: "The Aunt Jemima symbol stands for quality and trust and nurturing and good cooking and making breakfast special. . . . It's so woven into our family traditions that it becomes and has become something that links families across generations" (p. B-9).

These two recent representations of Mamma may be considered degrading or a devaluation of Black women. Hattie died more than a generation ago, yet Hollywood has not given up on the Mamma image. Although her image has outgrown that of her creators, it no longer debilitates the subject. In an era in which nurturance is lacking in the lives of so many, Mamma has grown to represent something grander, something more powerful—a subject, no longer an object. Alice Walker (1994) calls her a Goddess.

> I was in the presence of the Goddess, she who nurtures all, and that no matter how disguised, abused, ridiculed She may be, even white supremacists have been unable to throw Her away. She is with us still. Furthermore, I realized I loved Her. (p. 23)

Hattie, Grandma Ruby, and all the other countless Black women who have played and have lived the role of Mamma have elevated her to an icon and an archetype. She is a woman who "will neither reject nor judge you" (Walker, 1994, p. 22). Many household utensils and product containers were covered with Mamma images. Some are now quite valuable collectibles. Alice Walker (1994) wrote lovingly of the Mamma image representing *all* Black women by saying

> It occurred to me that the black woman is herself a symbol of nourishment, and that these women throughout all their incarnations in this country, and for millennia before they arrived, would have been standing or sitting just so, in whatever tribe or clan, being sure that everyone was fed. In other worlds, what I was seeing, as if for the first time, was a very ancient image that the modern world, quite without knowing why, had found impossible to do without. (pp. 22–23)

What Walker is speaking of is the Black Madonna image found throughout the world. She was a creation of a white patriarchal culture, but now she is recognized and worshipped everywhere. When she is around, people feel protected and safe. She can nurse you back to health and solve any problem you have. Maybe we have Hattie, Grandma Ruby, and all the other Black women out there to thank for transforming Mamma from a one-dimensional fictionalized character to a thinking, breathing, loving woman with a distinct personality. Isn't this what self-definition is all about (Collins, 1990)?

Probably some of you are saying that college students taking psychology of women classes are different; they do not view Black women as Mamma. Let me share with you an experience I had regarding this matter. The last day of the fall semester in 1994, I asked my students what I considered to be a simple, yet broad and unbiased question to guide their thinking: "If you were to pose one question to an individual who is an expert on the psychology of African American women, what would you ask?"

My students generated questions that asked for basic information on the quality of life of African American women. They asked questions about Black women being burdened by countless problems of living simply because they are Black and female, powerless, and poor. Some of my students' questions related to the unidimensionality of Black women and the perceived lack of diversity among African American women. They seemed to assume that Black women share many commonalities—they are monolithic, they come from an "underclass" or lower-class group, and they are all heterosexual.[3] Demographics, lifestyles, or any other distinguishing qualities were not considered. In all, little distinctiveness among

---

[3]Heterosexism is obvious in the tone of many of the questions and in many of the references surveyed for this paper. The assumption implicit by many is that *all* Black women are heterosexual; bisexuals and lesbians are ignored.

African American females was noted, and those similarities that were observed seemed stereotypic.

Specifically, my students characterized Black women as encountering and having to deal with (not listed in any particular order) racism, sexism, the criminal justice system, discrimination, unemployment, underemployment, gang violence, sexual violence, biased treatment in the media, drug addiction, neglectful parents, the generational cycle of teen pregnancy and public assistance, low self-esteem, undesirable role models at home and in the media, antagonism in intraracial male-female relationships, anger toward white females who are partners in interracial dating and marriage, feelings about interracial dating, being matriarchs, and emasculating Black males. What a list! Did they overlook any other less-than-flattering qualities?

Most of their questions signaled that Black women have monstrous, towering, and enormous problems, and they possess few, if any positive attributes. The questions portrayed African American women as victims of society and the people in their lives, especially family members. My students saw African American women as being burdened by many forms of oppression including the weight of racism, sexism, and classism. In addition, they saw these systemic forces as contributing to bleak and depressing life situations. The gist of their questions was "What's wrong with Black women?" and "Why don't they do something about their lives?" My students indicated that Black women are autonomous, independent, and active participants and creators of their own conditions. Their questions sounded very much like victim-blaming. One thing I did realize was that their questions had not come from me or from the writers whose works I selected for them to read.

I was not prepared for the litany of oppressions identified. Is that the particular reality of Black women? I don't think so. I had hoped for something different, something more uplifting. My students had just spent the entire semester studying the psychology of *all* women. The diversity of experiences was stressed at every opportunity. Many topics of relevance to the understanding of some of the psychological experiences of African American women were covered. A concerted effort was made to give my students an affirming glimpse into the lives of some of the African American women I have known, interviewed, and studied. Also, the class was taught by me, an African American woman, and I presented stories of Black women whom I admired. Success stories were shared. I talked about family members and what it was like being raised in Los Angeles. Yet, instead of viewing us as survivors, my students still saw us as victims.

This experience demonstrated the pervasiveness of media images of Black women. I was struck by the similar mind-set of my students. Writer upon writer shared a particular vision of African American women, that of "problem Black women." Thus, my students received many of the same media messages, and they brought those messages with them into the classroom. I have come to realize that for my students and many

Americans television is the major source of disseminating current events. As Sapiro (1994) notes, most of what we know and we

> receive about the world around us does not come from direct experience. Our knowledge about human life is gained secondhand from the mass media of communication—radio, television, newspapers, and magazines—or from the artistic media of communication such as the performing, graphic, and literary arts. For this reason the collective normative power of the people and organizations who manage these media is enormous. (p. 209)

Furthermore, as Else Barkley Brown (1989/1990) stated in her assessment of the interaction between minority instructors teaching nonminority students topics related to minority subjects:

> One of the central problems that confronts those of us who attempt to teach or write about nonwhite, non-middle-class, non-Western persons is how to center our work, our teaching, in the lives of the people about whom we are teaching and writing. As researchers, this is a persistent problem, but as teachers, it is perhaps an even more enormous problem. No matter how much prior preparation they have had, in large measure our students come to us having learned a particular perspective on the world, having been taught to see and analyze the world in particular ways, and having been taught that there are normative experiences and that they are those of white, middle-class, Western men and women. (pp. 9–10)

Also, I had to admit that the worldview of "white, middle-class, Western men and women" is vastly more powerful and influential than mine and that of most other Blacks. Movie production is one place where image development of Black women has been profound. Can the same be said regarding the psychology of women? We are vulnerable and dependent on others to recognize us and tell our stories. The media have created images of Black women for several hundred years (Turner, 1994). With such narrow images, opportunities are limited, and Black women are faced with multiple problems not of their making. If the same message is repeated enough times, the listener begins to believe it to be fact. If Blacks continue to be shown as dysfunctional beings, violent individuals, lazy parents, victims, and victimizers of society, the self-fulfilling prophecy will be realized.

The mass distribution of audiovisual and print media have refined the images of African American women. The images are slick, and the messages are subtle. Although there continue to be remnants of a past full of negative and insulting images, some Americans have become sophisticated in decoding the messages (Smith, 1995).

All is not lost or bleak. Resistance and activism have been recurring themes in the history of Black women (Collins, 1990; hooks, 1994; Hull et al., 1982; Morton, 1991). Introspection and self-reflection have and are aiding Black women in expanding the images and the messages representing us (Lorde, 1995). We have taken control of our images. Out of this morass has come a new set of images of African American women that are

visible and clearly understood. There are several activities that have contributed to Black women resisting and redefining our images. A few noteworthy efforts are the development of support groups (hooks, 1993), self-
development information and exercises (Boyd, 1993; Myers, 1980;
Vanzant, 1992), journal writings (Bell-Scott, 1994), and survival activities
(Scott, 1991). Also, the meaning of work has been reconceptualized, as
May Madison stated.

> One very important difference between white people and black people is that
> white people think you are your work. ... Now a black person has more sense
> than that because he [sic] knows that what I am doing doesn't have anything
> to do with what I want to do or what I do when I am doing for myself. Now,
> black people think that my work is just what I have to do to get what I want.
> [Gwaltney, 1980, p. 174]

African American women have *historically* rejected the "doormat status" (Smith, 1995, p. 156). Although Paula Giddings (1984) saw us as the
original feminists and Barbara Smith (1995) referred to us as possessing
"innate feminist potential" (p. 156), we have received little recognition for
the ways we have been able to balance public and private lives. Black
women have been fully integrated in major functions both inside and outside of the family dating back to precolonial West Africa (Rodgers-Rose,
1980). Sharp (1993) chronicles this system as being in existence for at least
7,000 years. Without the participation of Black women, the survival of her
family, group, and culture would have been in jeopardy. There was order
and purpose and women were socially and economically secure not because of whom they married, but because of what work they performed.
This was neither "anti-male nor pro-female; it was a system of organization that allowed for orderly succession of power and continuity within
the community" (Sharp, 1993, p. 109). Some Black women have been empowered as a result of knowing that history and living that life. As a
friend of Grandma Ruby once remarked, "to be born black is more than
to be persecuted; it is to be privileged" (Goodwin, 1976, p. 8). Some pity
us, still others see us as having been conquered by myriad societal forces.
Few see us as having resiliency. As Grandma Ruby (1976) wrote, "we have
probably been overlooked by writers because it is much easier to drama-
tize the brutal and the sordid than the commonplace" (p. 7).

REFERENCES

ASSOCIATED PRESS. (1994, September 17). Gladys Knight to pitch for Aunt Jemima
    products. *Pittsburgh Post-Gazette*, p. B-9.
BELL-SCOTT, P. (Ed.). (1994). *Life notes: Personal writings by contemporary Black
    women.* New York: W. W. Norton.
BOGLE, D. (1973). *Toms, coons, mulattoes, mammies, and bucks: An interpretive history
    of Blacks in American films.* New York: Viking Press.

BOGLE, D. (1988). *Blacks in American films and television: An encyclopedia.* New York: Garland.

BOYD, J. A. (1990). Ethnic and cultural diversity: Keys to power. In L. A. Brown & M. P. P. Root (Eds.), *Diversity and complexity in feminist therapy* (pp. 151–167). New York: Harrington Park Press.

BOYD, J. A. (1993). *In the company of my sisters: Black women and self-esteem.* New York: Dutton.

BROWN, A., GOODWIN, B. J., HALL, B. A., & JACKSON-LOWMAN, H. (1985). A review of psychology of women textbooks: Focus on the Afro-American woman. *Psychology of Women Quarterly, 9,* 29–38.

BROWN, E. B. (1989/1990). African-American women's quilting: A framework for conceptualizing and teaching African-American women's history. In M. R. Malson, E. Mudimbe-Boyi, J. F. O'Barr, & M. Wyer (Eds.), *Black women in America: Social science perspectives* (pp. 9–18). Chicago: University of Chicago Press.

BROWN-COLLINS, A. (1988). Integrating third world womanism into the psychology of women course. In P. A. Bronstein & K. Quina (Eds.), *Teaching a psychology of people: Resources for gender and sociocultural awareness* (pp. 102–111). Washington, DC: American Psychological Association.

COLLINS, P. H. (1990). *Black feminist thought: Knowledge, consciousness, and the politics of empowerment.* New York: Routledge.

GIDDINGS, P. (1983). *When and where I enter: The impact of Black women on race and sex in America.* New York: William Morrow.

GOODWIN, B. J. (1990, August). *Inclusion of Black women in the teaching of the psychology of women.* Paper presented at the meeting of the American Psychological Association, Boston, MA.

GOODWIN, B. J. (1991a, August). *Inclusion in the curriculum: Psychology as a case study.* Paper presented at the meeting of the American Psychological Association, San Francisco, CA.

GOODWIN, B. J. (1991b, March). *Is it soup yet? The integration of diversity in psychology textbooks.* Paper presented at the meeting of the Association for Women in Psychology, Hartford, CT.

GOODWIN, R. B. (1976). *It's good to be Black.* Carbondale, IL: Southern Illinois University Press.

GREENE, B. A. (1990). What has gone before: The legacy of racism and sexism in the lives of Black mothers and daughters. In L. A. Brown & M. P. P. Root (Eds.), *Diversity and complexity in feminist therapy* (pp. 207–230). New York: Harrington Park Press.

GWALTNEY, J. L. (1980). *Drylongso: A self-portrait of Black America.* New York: Vintage.

HINE, D. C. (Ed.). (1993). *Black women in America: An historical encyclopedia.* New York: Carlson.

HOOKS, B. (1992). *Black looks: Race and representation.* Boston: South End Press.

HOOKS, B. (1993). *Sisters of the yam: Black women and self-recovery.* Boston: South End Press.

HOOKS, B. (1994). *Outlaw culture: Resisting representations.* New York: Routledge.

HULL, G. T., SCOTT, P. B., & SMITH, B. (1982). *All the women are white, all the Blacks are men, but some of us are brave: Black women's studies.* Old Westbury: Feminist Press.

HYDE, J. S. (1985). *Half the human experience: The psychology of women* (3d ed.). Lexington, MA: D. C. Heath.

JACKSON, C. (1990). *Hattie: The life of Hattie McDaniel.* Laham, MD: Madison Books.

JEWELL, K. S. (1993). *From Mammy to Miss America and beyond: Cultural images and the shaping of U.S. social policy.* New York: Routledge.

LERNER, G. (1972). *Black women in white America.* New York: Vintage.

LORDE, A. (1995). The transformation of silence into language and action. In S. Ruth (Ed.), *Issues in feminism: An introduction to women's studies* (pp. 151–153). Mountain View, CA: Mayfield.

McHUGH, M. C., & GOODWIN, B. J. (1991, March). *Who is the woman in the psychology of women?* Paper presented at the meeting of the Association for Women in Psychology, Hartford, CT.

MORTON, P. (1991). *Disfigured images: The historical assault on Afro-American women.* New York: Praeger.

MYERS, L. W. (1980). *Black women: Do they cope better?* Englewood Cliffs, NJ: Prentice-Hall.

NULL, G. (1975). *Black Hollywood: The Negro in motion pictures.* Secaucus, NJ: Citadel Press.

RODGERS-ROSE, L. F. (1980). The Black woman: A historical overview. In L. F. Rodgers-Rose (Ed.), *The Black woman* (pp. 15–25). Beverly Hills: Sage.

SAPIRO, V. (1994). *Women in American society: An introduction to women's studies* (3d ed.). Mountain View, CA: Mayfield.

SCOTT, K. Y. (1991). *The habit of surviving: Black women's strategies for life.* New Brunswick, NJ: Rutgers University Press.

SHARP, S. (1993). *Black women for beginners.* New York: Writers & Readers.

SMITH, B. (1995). Myths to divert Black women from freedom. In S. Ruth (Ed.), *Issues in feminism: An introduction to women's studies* (pp. 154–162). Mountain View, CA: Mayfield.

SPELMAN, E. V. (1995). Gender & race: The ampersand problem in feminist thought. In S. Ruth (Ed.), *Issues in feminism: An introduction to women's studies* (pp. 24–36). Mountain View, CA: Mayfield.

TORREY, J. W. (1979). Racism and feminism: Is women's liberation for whites only? *Psychology of Women Quarterly, 4,* 281–293.

TURNER, P. A. (1994). *Ceramic uncles & celluloid mammies: Black images and their influence on culture.* New York: Anchor Books.

VANZANT, I. (1992). *Tapping the power within: A path to self-empowerment for Black women.* New York: Harlem River Press.

WALKER, A. (1994, May/June). Giving the party: Aunt Jemima, Mamma, and the Goddess within. *Ms.,* pp. 22–25.

WALLACE, M. (1990). *Invisibility blues: From pop to theory.* London: Verso.

WEST, C. (1994). *Race matters.* New York: Vintage Books.

WILSON, M. (1994). *Crossing the boundary: Black women survive incest.* Seattle: Seal Press.

SUGGESTED READINGS

BELL-SCOTT, P. (Ed.). (1994). *Life notes: Personal writings by contemporary Black women.* New York: W. W. Norton.

Bogle, D. (1973). *Toms, coons, mulattoes, mammies, and bucks: An interpretive history of Blacks in American films.* New York: Viking Press.

Brown, A., Goodwin, B. J., Hall, B. A., & Jackson-Lowman, H. (1985). A review of psychology of women textbooks: Focus on the Afro-American woman. *Psychology of Women Quarterly, 9,* 29–38.

Sharp, S. (1993). *Black women for beginners.* New York: Writers & Readers.

*A*NGELA **R. G**ILLEM *is Assistant Professor of Psychology at Beaver College. Dr. Gillem previously taught psychology of women at Pennsylvania State University. She maintains a private practice in clinical psychology and is committed to integrating issues of gender and other aspects of human diversity into her teaching, writing, and practice of psychotherapy.*

14

Beyond Double Jeopardy:

Female, Biracial, and Perceived to Be Black

❖

Biracial women who are the offspring of one African American parent and one European American parent are the focus of this lecture. Although more has been written about biracial people and about African American women's issues in recent years than in the past, very little has been done to explore the interface of gender and race as it impacts on biracial women. This lecture will consider whether biracial women are in multiple jeopardy, being Black (according to the "one-drop rule" that governs how race is constructed in the United States), female, and the product of a union of members of two antagonistic groups. Given the dearth of research specific to biracial women, I will attempt to construct an answer to this question through a discussion of the relevant theory and research on African American women, biracial people, and the social construction of race. Drawing on the paradigm of triple jeopardy that has been proposed by Greene (1994) to describe the multiple oppressions experienced by lesbians of color, I will develop a similar paradigm that may apply to the multiple oppressions that biracial women must manage in their lives. Recognizing that multiple oppressions have more than an additive effect on people's lives, I will call my paradigm triple jeopardy.

The ideas in this paper were developed through presentations at the 101st Annual Convention of the American Psychological Association in Toronto, Ontario, Canada, August 21, 1993, and at the Annual Conference of the Association for Women in Psychology in Oakland, California, March 5, 1994.
I would like to thank those students who, through their candid, joyous, and often painful sharing, inspired me to begin my exploration of what it is to be biracial. I especially want to thank Erica Freeman and Joy Zarembka. I would also like to acknowledge those friends and colleagues who have spent their valuable time and energy in helping me to develop my ideas and express them understandably, particularly Ruth Hall, Beverly Greene, Marianne Miserandino, and Ruth Seymour.

THE DOUBLE JEOPARDY OF AFRICAN AMERICAN WOMEN

Beverly Greene (in press) has stated: "Gender and race constitute two major dimensions around which most people organize themselves and which influence both their understanding of the world and of their relative place in it." Mary Church Terrell stated in 1904 that "not only are colored women . . . handicapped on account of their sex, but they are almost everywhere baffled and mocked because of their race. Not only because they are women, but because they are colored women" (quoted in King, 1988, p. 42). Smith and Stewart (1983) have developed a model that suggests that racism and sexism provide contexts for each other that produce not only a cumulative or parallel effect on Black women's lives, but also an interactive effect. This has been referred to as "double jeopardy" by a number of authors (Fleming, 1983; King, 1988; Smith & Stewart, 1983). The interaction of the two oppressions may lead to the development of psychological strengths to cope with adversity in some areas of Black women's lives; but in other areas there may be negative effects, accounting, for example, for Black women's low socioeconomic status and proneness to depression. Thus, Smith and Stewart (1983) suggest that this complex interaction of oppressions may produce a qualitative difference between the effects of racism on Black men and women and between the effects of sexism on Black women and white women.

Fleming (1983) and Allen (1992) have noted the double-jeopardy phenomenon in Black college women. Fleming found that the racially adverse conditions of predominantly white colleges encouraged self-reliance and enhanced coping and survival skills, articulateness, Black ideological consciousness, and assertiveness in African American women but contributed to lower academic performance and greater negative feelings and dissatisfaction with their college experience. On the other hand, she found that the academically supportive atmosphere of Black colleges enhanced academic motivation, confidence, and performance, but apparently the presence of large numbers of African American men encouraged passivity, reduced social assertiveness, and increased shyness, submissiveness, and fear of confrontation—all stereotypical, and often problematic, feminine characteristics. These findings have been fairly consistent across a number of studies that involve Black college women (Allen, 1992; Fleming, 1983; Smith, 1982).

In comparison, Allen (1992) found that it has been consistently advantageous, both academically and psychologically, for Black men to attend Black colleges. Further, despite higher scholastic achievement than Black men in high school and overall lower fear of success than white women (Smith, 1982), Black women had lower career aspirations in college than did Black men. Most aspired to stereotypical female jobs with lower prestige, less power, and lower pay (Allen, 1992; Smith, 1982) than their Black male counterparts were seeking. These lower aspirations lead Black women to the bottom of the occupational pyramid in low-status service jobs (Fleming, 1983), where they earn a median income of $3,897 less than Black men and $2,179 less than white women (U.S. Bureau of the Census, 1994). Over 60 percent of African American women hold jobs in the service economy with little chance of advancement (Matlin, 1993). It's no wonder, then, that Black women report lower psychological well-being than Black men and white men and women, and are two to three times more likely than Black men to experience depression in their lives (Matlin, 1993). In contrast, however, Smith (1982) has found that Black women have a positive sense of themselves despite the double jeopardy of racism and sexism. It would appear that Black women develop strength in the face of racial adversity but pay a high price for it academically and professionally. On the other hand, they gain academically in a racially supportive atmosphere but lose strength in their relationships with Black men, as white women do with white men.

The strengths that Black women display in some contexts often lead to stereotypes of Black women as domineering matriarchs. Because of this stereotype, African American women have been blamed for everything from the deterioration of the Black family (the "normal" role of dominance being reserved, of course, for men) to the "castration" of Black boys and men, which ultimately leads to their imprisonment and endangerment. Black women have also been stereotyped as not being in need of the kind of emotional support and physical help that white women supposedly deserve. This was eloquently addressed in Sojourner Truth's famous "Ain't I a Woman?" speech. Fleming (1983) has concluded that the concept of the Black matriarchy is a myth despite the strength that many African American women evidence in some contexts. In fact, research on Black families has demonstrated that African American marriages are, on the whole, more egalitarian than white marriages (Boyd-Franklin, 1989). Instead, Fleming (1983) interprets this strength not in terms of Black women being more domineering than Black men, but in terms of Black women being less passive and dependent than white women because of a long history of self-reliance and an orientation to serving the family. Thus, one ought not confuse strength with dominance (Ladner, 1971, cited in Smith, 1982).

Thus, theory and research point to the existence of double jeopardy for African American women with regard to the dual oppressions of racism and sexism, as well as in their adaptive and maladaptive responses to those oppressions. Although I have found no references on this issue with regard to biracial women, I suspect that many biracial women are subject to similar jeopardy, particularly if they self-identify as Black or are perceived as Black because of physical appearance. Research on biracial people in general may provide a clue to yet a third level of oppression that may interact with race and gender oppression to enhance the social and psychological jeopardy of biracial women.

BIRACIAL RESEARCH AND THE SOCIAL CONSTRUCTION OF RACE

I became interested in issues concerning biracial people as a result of my interaction with a group of biracial college students during a pre-freshman orientation program for students of color. During an extended discussion with students of mixed heritage I learned of both the joys and sorrows of growing up biracial in the United States. I heard them speak of feeling "torn," "split," guilty, and without a community. But I also heard them speak of feeling more sensitive, unique, and happy in their inherent diversity; challenged and lucky at having two cultural heritages; and pleased to represent a "coming together of differences," "a point of connection, a link."

Much of what has been written about biracial people has been related to racial identity and self-concept development. These have been of particular interest to many researchers primarily because of the way that race is constructed in our society. Maria Root (1990) has suggested that racial identity development and self-concept are especially difficult for biracial people because of the tension between the two racial components of the self, and she asserts that rejecting either part of their heritage represents internalized oppression for biracial people. Sebring (1985) says that adopting a monoracial identity can lead to "massive guilt" and "feelings of disloyalty" (pp. 6–7), and many biracial people themselves have indicated that being forced to adopt a monoracial identity is emotionally damaging (Watts, 1991).

To understand this potential for damage, we need to consider the racial history of the United States. The practice of monoracial assignment of biracial people in the census is rooted in a long history of discrimination against people of African descent. According to the one-drop rule, anyone with "one drop" of African blood is considered African American (Davis, 1991; Spickard, 1992). This hierarchical typology of race, which was developed by Europeans, places Caucasians, Asians, Native Americans, and Africans, respectively, in descending order of evolutionary development (Curchack, 1991; Spickard, 1992). The majority of scientists now agree, however, that the concept of race is itself a myth and that all human populations are racially mixed and have been mixing for thousands of years (Curchack, 1991; Davis, 1991). Thus, this typology has been used to create and justify boundaries between races that are based on phenotype (physical appearance), not genotype (genetic inheritance) (Davis, 1991). For biracial people this has meant being assigned exclusively to the racial group with the lowest social status. Spickard (1992) suggests that this has been done so that whites could maintain absolute and undiluted economic, social, and political power in the United States. The one-drop rule is simply a social fiction with no biological legitimacy. Its use continues to benefit whites at the expense of African Americans by maintaining a social, political, and economic hierarchy. As the Reverend Joseph Lowery has stated, "What's implied in labeling everybody black who has any black blood…is that you are contaminated" (quoted in Watts, 1991, p. A10).

This social fiction and the historical antagonism of whites toward Blacks in the United States have given rise, in many African American communities, to a range of strict rules for determining who is Black and who is not. One of these rules is reflected in a "you're either with us or against us" attitude: Pressure is placed on those who are biracial to identify as Black in order to expand numbers, to increase political strength, and to avoid dilution of what little political power Blacks have managed to gain. In this context, claiming an exclusively Black identity is presumed to establish racial loyalty. Claiming a biracial identity is deemed suspect. However, imposing a Black monoracial identity on biracial persons carries the danger of perpetuating the one-drop rule and not respecting the dual heritage of biracial people.

I am *not* saying that Black and biracial people should not join forces politically. However, to be unified, they need not be the same. In fact, making sameness a requirement of unity only serves to pressure biracial persons to deny half of their heritage. This may be psychologically damaging as it imposes an additional layer of racial discrimination.

The difference between the social context of miscegenation in the late 1800s and the context of interracial relationships today is important in further understanding this potential for psychological jeopardy. In the 1800s most of those who were biracial were mixed race as the result of sexual exploitation of Black women by white slave owners (Davis, 1991; Williamson, 1984). Thus, rejection of their white heritage was consistent with rejection of the illicit, immoral, exploitative means by which it occurred, and thus was adaptive. Today, however, biracial offspring are most often the result of a consensual union between a Black person and a white person based on mutual attraction. (A discussion of whether or not social or economic exploitation exists in these relationships is beyond the scope of this paper). Case studies suggest that the better the parents handle their interracial marriage, the more accepting their children are of their parents' relationship (Teicher, 1968). For children of a consensual interracial union, compulsory rejection of a part of their racial heritage may represent rejection or betrayal of the parent of that race; conversely, a child's racial rejection of either parent may be a reflection of the child's rejection of that racial part of themselves, and thus may be maladaptive.

Root (1990) asserts that because of racial inequality in our society, biracial people "begin life as marginal people" (p. 185) and experience severe stress in identity development. Sommers (1964) found that identity problems in biracial people tend to result from lack of a secure parental relationship, from society's messages about their parents' social status (for example, that the Black parent has lower status), and from conflicting social and cultural loyalties. These conflicting loyalties can arise out of societal pressures to identify with the "race" of only one parent; and when that one parent is Black, developing a positive self-concept is even more complex because of the negative information and stereotypes about Black people that are both expressed and implied by our society's treatment of race (Brandell, 1988; Gibbs, 1989; Lyles, Yancey, Grace, & Carter, 1985). In fact, Arnold's (1984) research indicated that biracial children with a Black identity had lower self-concept scores than those with white or biracial identities. Thus, for some Black-identified people, acceptance of the one-drop rule can be a reflection of internalized racism. This is defined as the incorporation and acceptance by African Americans of idealized stereotypes of white Americans and devalued stereotypes of African Americans.

As an alternative to forcing a choice between Black and white heritage, current research and theory suggests that we might do better to support the identification of biracial people with both sides of their heritage in order to have a positive biracial identity and a healthy psychological adjustment. Those who identify as biracial have been found to have fewer emotional and psychological problems; have a stronger, more positive sense of identity; and have greater self-confidence than those who adopt a monoracial label (Arnold, 1984; Watts, 1991). Research has also shown that being raised in interracial families that provide minority status consciousness (Lyles et al., 1985; Miller & Miller, 1990; Wardle, 1987), parental support with regard to encounters with racism (Brandell, 1988; Gibbs & Hines, 1992), and interracial self-labeling (Jacobs, 1978; McRoy & Freeman, 1986) is associated with positive self-concept and identity in biracial people. Root (1990) has suggested that however biracial people identify—whether they take on the minority identity assigned by society, identify with both Black and white heritage, identify with only one self-chosen part of their racial heritage, or identify as a new biracial or mixed group—they must always accept both sides of their heritage, make their own uncoerced choices, and develop ways to deal with others' perceptions and reactions to them. They need to learn to adjust and function within mainstream society without sacrificing the integrity of their cultural identities (Brown, 1990). Many researchers have suggested that by doing so, biracial people become more tolerant and less biased individuals (Brandell, 1988) and develop the ability to function within diverse, and even antagonistic, cultural environments (Sebring, 1985; Wardle, 1987). We must remember, however, that our society has not yet gotten beyond racial hierarchy and the one-drop rule. Those who are biracial must often struggle to attain the level of personal integrity that these authors prescribe. For example, one biracial woman reported that despite the fact that her upbringing fit the above-described ideal, she still always feels that, in both Black and white settings, she is "adopting experiences that are not her own." She reports that "if I try to be rooted in either culture, my perceptions are never totally genuine" (personal communication, August 17, 1994). She believes that she is both but neither.

BIRACIAL WOMEN: TRIPLE JEOPARDY?

Sandoval (quoted in Root, 1992) has placed the racial hierarchy into a gendered context in which "the final and fourth category [after white men, white women, and men of color in descending order] belongs to women of color who become survivors in a dynamic which places them as the final 'other' in a complex of power moves" (p. 5). Root (1992) has suggested that biracial men and women would be fifth and sixth, respectively, in this power hierarchy (p. 5). However, as suggested by Smith and Stewart's (1983) model discussed earlier, multiple oppressions have more than just an additive effect; they have very complex interactive effects on people's lives. For example, Johnson (1992) explains that "the biracial child has a dual minority status both within the larger society as a member or partial member of a devalued racial group and often within the African American community due to perceived lack of 'full' affiliation" (p. 45). The experience of being caught between two antagonistic cultural worlds—not being either, but being both—would seem to compound for biracial women the double jeopardy found in Black women's lives in which the oppressions of racism and sexism have a multiplicative, not merely additive, relationship (King, 1988).

Jeopardy is multiplied by the stereotypic characterizations of biracial women as exotic, passionate, sexually promiscuous, "Anglicized" versions of Black women (Nakashima, 1992). Root (1990) has suggested that biracial women may be less of a threat to whites than monoracial (Black) women, perhaps because of assumptions of Anglicization. Thus, for example, we see Madison Avenue and Hollywood "diversifying" their ads by using light-skinned or biracial models and actresses to represent Black women, virtually ignoring the other end of the skin color spectrum among Black women. This often makes biracial women the target of resentment from darker-skinned African American women.

Gibbs's (1989) clinical experience with biracial adolescent girls indicates that they are especially likely to feel ashamed of their Black physical traits and are more likely than boys to feel anxiety about social acceptance. I suspect that the pressure in our society on all women of color to live up to a white standard of beauty, which, as we all know, is often unrealistic even for white women, may cause some biracial women to be more prone to reject the African American part of their heritage. One biracial college woman, who had resisted rejecting her Black heritage and who reported having achieved a good level of self-esteem, wondered why other Blacks didn't value their hair and skin color as much as they did hers. She eventually "realized that people valued my hair and skin because it is 'good' or closer to white. Of course it was easy for me to accept myself when everybody always told me how beautiful I was and when everybody wanted to play in my hair" (personal communication). She was learning through socialization that her "white features" were especially valuable, whereas "Black features" were not as valuable. It was on this socialization that her good level of self-esteem was based.

Funderburg (1994) suggests that the overvaluing of skin color and physical features in our society makes biracial people especially prized by some as romantic partners; however, the exoticized and Anglicized perception of biracial women can have a negative impact on dating experiences. Many have reported feeling used or mistreated by Black men, as did Jeana Woolley, "to reinforce their legitimacy in terms of the majority population" (quoted in Funderburg, 1994, p. 193) and to get revenge against white men who, many Black men think, have deprived them of power and self-respect. In this sense, as Sandy Shupe suggests, biracial women become a trophy in the struggle between Black and white men (Funderburg, 1994).

Root (1992) suggests that dating for biracial women may be difficult both because of the sexual stereotypes and Anglicized perceptions and because all dating for biracial women is interracial dating. A recent incident at a high school in Alabama exemplifies this dilemma. When the principal of the high school attempted to ban interracial couples from the prom, a biracial student, Revonda Bowen, asked him, "Who am I supposed to go with?" He responded that she was a "'mistake' he wanted to prevent others from making" (Smothers, 1994, p. A16). Other biracial women have reported being perceived as white and resented by Blacks when they date Blacks (Funderburg, 1994), or they are perceived as trying to pass when dating whites. Whites often reject biracial women's involvement with white men, particularly if they "appear Black," because they are violating the taboo against interracial dating. Sonia Trowers, who was raised to identify as mixed, attended a predominantly white school and started having problems only when dating became an issue among her all-white set of friends: "I just knew that these white guys in this group I associated with wouldn't have any interest in me" (quoted in Funderburg, 1994, p. 37). When her friends actually started dating, she decided to transfer to a more racially mixed public school to escape the uncomfortable feeling of being left out.

CONCLUSION

The multiple oppressions that biracial women face may have a negative effect on their self-esteem, psychological adjustment, social relations, and identity formation. They are routinely confronted with racism and sexism from white-supremacist society. They encounter sexism and internalized racism within the African American community. They may experience guilt about rejecting their white heritage, and their white parent, if they submit to the one-drop rule. On the other hand, they may experience similar conflicts about rejecting Black heritage, and their Black parent, if they identify as white. They may elicit confused, distrustful, or even hostile reactions from both the Black and white communities if they adopt a biracial, mixed, or multicultural identity. Thus, there is good reason to believe that biracial women may be in triple jeopardy with regard to both the types of discrimination that they experience and their responses to that discrimination.

In conclusion, we must consider the possibility that many women who identify themselves as Black in clinical and research settings (often because of a forced choice that does not allow other than a monoracial identity) are in fact biracial. When we fail to consider this phenomenon, we lose a sense of the richness of their diverse experiences, and we lose accuracy in our data. Furthermore, we need to understand the clinical implications of different life experiences, special stressors and vulnerabilities in biracial women, and their effects on their functioning. Finally, we need to develop models of healthy racial identity development for biracial women that take their unique status into account. As race and gender interact in complex ways in Black women, we need to know more about how they interact in equally complex, and perhaps different, ways in biracial women who may be caught between the rock of gender and the hard place of race.

REFERENCES

ALLEN, W. R. (1992). The color of success: African-American college student outcomes at predominantly white and historically black public colleges and universities. *Harvard Educational Review, 62*(1), 26–44.

ARNOLD, M. L. (1984). The effects of racial identity on self-concept in interracial children (Doctoral dissertation, Saint Louis University, 1984). *Dissertation Abstracts International, 45,* 3000A.

BOYD-FRANKLIN, N. (1989). *Black families in therapy: A multisystems approach.* New York: Guilford.

BRANDELL, J. R. (1988). Treatment of the biracial child: Theoretical and clinical issues. *Journal of Multicultural Counseling and Development, 16,* 76–187.

BROWN, P. M. (1990). Biracial identity and social marginality. *Child and Adolescent Social Work, 7*(4), 319–337.

CURCHACK, M. P. (1991, November). *Race, language, and culture: Some forgotten anthropological lessons.* Paper presented at the conference on The Inclusive University: Multicultural Perspectives in Higher Education, Oakland, CA.

DAVIS, F. J. (1991). *Who is black? One nation's definition.* University Park, PA: Pennsylvania State University Press.

FLEMING, J. (1983). Black women in black and white college environments: The making of a matriarch. *Journal of Social Issues, 39*(3), 41–54.

FUNDERBURG, L. (1994). *Black, white, other: Biracial Americans talk about race and identity.* New York: William Morrow.

GIBBS, J. T. (1989). Biracial adolescents. In J. T. Gibbs & L. N. Huang (Eds.), *Children of color: Psychological interventions with minority youth* (pp. 322–350). San Francisco: Jossey-Bass.

GIBBS, J. T., & HINES, A. M. (1992). Negotiating ethnic identity: Issues for black-white biracial adolescents. In M. P. P. Root (Ed.), *Racially mixed people in America* (pp. 223–238). Newbury Park, CA: Sage.

GREENE, B. (1994). Lesbian women of color: Triple jeopardy. In L. Comas-Diaz & B. Greene (Eds.), *Women of color: Integrating ethnic and gender identities in psychotherapy* (pp. 389–427). New York: Guilford.

GREENE, B. (in press). African American women: Derivatives of racism and sexism in psychotherapy. In E. Tobach & B. Rosoff (Eds.), *Challenging racism and sexism: Alternatives to genetic determinism*. New York: Feminist Press.

JACOBS, J. H. (1978). Black/white interracial families: Marital process and identity development in young children. *Dissertation Abstracts International, 38;* 5023B.

JOHNSON, D. J. (1992). Developmental pathways: Toward an ecological theoretical formulation of race identity in black-white biracial children. In M. P. P. Root (Ed.), *Racially mixed people in America* (pp. 37–49). Newbury Park, CA: Sage.

KING, D. K. (1988). Multiple jeopardy, multiple consciousness: The context of a black feminist ideology. *Signs, 14*(1), 42–72.

LYLES, M. R., YANCEY, A., GRACE, C., & CARTER, J. H. (1985). Racial identity and self esteem: Problems peculiar to biracial children. *Journal of the American Academy of Child Psychiatry, 24*(2), 150–153.

MATLIN, M. W. (1993). *The psychology of women* (2d ed.). New York: Harcourt Brace Jovanovich.

McROY, R. G., & FREEMAN, E. (1986). Racial-identity issues among mixed race children. *Social Work in Education, 8,* 164–174.

MILLER, R. L., & MILLER, B. (1990). Mothering the biracial child: Bridging the gaps between African-American and white parenting styles. *Women & Therapy, 10*(1), 169–179.

NAKOSHIMA, C. L. (1992). An invisible monster: The creation and denial of mixed-race people in America. In M. P. P. Root (Ed.), *Racially mixed people in America* (pp. 162–178). Newbury Park, CA: Sage.

ROOT, M. P. P. (1990). Resolving "other" status: Identity development of biracial individuals. In L. S. Brown & M. P. P. Root (Eds.), *Diversity and complexity in feminist therapy* (pp. 185–205). New York: Haworth.

ROOT, M. P. P. (1992). Within, between, and beyond race. In M. P. P. Root (Ed.), *Racially mixed people in America* (pp. 3–11). Newbury Park, CA: Sage.

SEBRING, D. L. (1985). Considerations in counseling interracial children. *Journal of Non-White Concerns, 13,* 3–9.

SMITH, A., & STEWART, A. J. (1983). Approaches to studying racism and sexism in black women's lives. *Journal of Social Issues, 39*(3), 1–15.

SMITH, E. J. (1982). The black female adolescent: A review of the educational, career, and psychological literature. *Psychology of Women Quarterly, 6*(3), 261–288.

SMOTHERS, R. (1994, March 16). Principal causes furor on mixed-race couples. *The New York Times,* p. A16.

SOMMERS, V. S. (1964). The impact of dual-cultural membership on identity. *Psychiatry, 27*(4), 332–344.

SPICKARD, P. R. (1992). The illogic of American racial categories. In M. P. P. Root (Ed.), *Racially mixed people in America* (pp. 12–23). Newbury Park, CA: Sage.

TEICHER, J. D. (1968). Some observations on identity problems in children of Negro-white marriages. *Journal of Nervous and Mental Disease, 146*(3), 249–256.

U.S. BUREAU OF THE CENSUS. (1994). *Statistical abstract of the United States: 1994.* Washington, DC: U.S. Government Printing Office.

WARDLE, F. (1987, January). Are you sensitive to interracial children's special identity needs? *Young Children,* pp. 53–58.

WATTS, R. A. (1991, December 1). Not black, not white, but biracial. *The Atlanta Journal and The Atlanta Constitution,* pp. A1, A10.

WILLIAMSON, J. (1984). *New people: Mulattoes and miscegenation in the United States.* New York: New York University Press.

SUGGESTED READINGS

COMAS-DIAZ, L., & GREENE, B. (Eds.). (1994). *Women of color: Integrating ethnic and gender identities in psychotherapy.* New York: Guilford.

FUNDERBURG, L. (1994). *Black, white, other: Biracial Americans talk about race and identity.* New York: William Morrow.

ROOT, M. P. P. (Ed.). (1992). *Racially mixed people in America.* Newbury Park, CA: Sage.

ZACK, N. (1993). *Race and mixed race.* Philadelphia, PA: Temple University Press.

*S*UZANNA ROSE *is Associate Professor of Psychology and Women's Studies at the University of Missouri-St. Louis. Dr. Rose has taught courses on the psychology of women, female sexuality, and women and mental health at Missouri and at the University of Pittsburgh since 1974. Her current research focuses on how gender, race, and sexual orientation affect the development of friendships and romantic relationships.*

15

Who to Let In: Women's Cross-Race Friendships

❖

*S*ilently or explicitly, we all have been taught "who to let in and who to keep out" as friends (Pratt, 1991, p. 19). A color line often divides the group of eligibles from ineligibles in friendship, although the line may be disguised or denied. The line separating Black people from whites in terms of friendship appears to be especially effective. Own-race friendships are the norm; most adults show a clear preference for friends of the same race, gender, age, and class (Duck, 1991). Women seem to be more able to transcend the race barrier than men. First, women tend to be more intimate and affectionate with their friends than men do (Duck, 1991). Their capacity for intimacy perhaps enables them to empathize more easily with women of other races. Second, women of all races share a common oppression based on gender that, if acknowledged, may enhance a sense of sisterhood. However, women and girls do not appear to choose cross-race friendships more often than men and boys (Clark & Ayers, 1992).

What inhibits cross-race friendship? The lack of attention to this topic among social scientists is surprising given the strong racial tensions present in the United States and the need for greater racial tolerance. The neglect of the topic within the psychology of women is also surprising, given that building alliances among women has been one of the feminist principles guiding research in the field. Few empirical studies have specifically examined cross-race friendships. As a result, little is known about how common they are or how they operate.

Gratitude is extended to Randy A. Page, members of the St. Louis Anti-Racism Group, and the Association for Women in Psychology for many of the ideas expressed in this chapter and for providing the motivation to change. Many thanks also to the students who participated.

The difficulties in establishing and maintaining cross-race friendships became apparent to me on a personal level through my involvement in feminism. Though I and other white feminists professed to be entirely open to and desirous of cross-race friendships, our friendship and political networks were mostly white. My participation in numerous antiracism trainings, the St. Louis antiracism group, and many discussions with women of color made me seek to understand the dynamics of the racial divide. It also made me aware of the tremendous potential rewards of cross-race friendships. These experiences provided the motivation for me to investigate the nature of cross-race friendship through my teaching.

In this lecture, we will explore the cross-race friendships of psychology of women students. The intent is to illustrate the racial attitudes that inhibit women's cross-race friendships, as well as the education and motivation needed to facilitate them. Friendships between Black and white women will be emphasized because the participants represented only these two racial groups; however, the processes described here may apply equally well to other cross-race friendships.

RACISM AND RACIAL IDENTITY

Racism is the most powerful barrier to establishing cross-race friendship. Although many white people today consciously reject racist beliefs, asserting that Blacks and whites should be treated equally, psychological research indicates that a majority of whites hold negative attitudes about Blacks (Carter, White, & Sedlacek, 1987; Pope-Davis & Ottavi, 1994). Racist attitudes and behaviors discourage cross-race friendship. For example, many whites agree that it would upset them personally if Blacks moved into their neighborhood or that Blacks in this country have tried to move too fast to attain their rights (Pope-Davis & Ottavi, 1994). In terms of Black women specifically, Weitz and Gordon (1993) found that white college students ascribe more negative traits to Black women than to American women in general. Almost all (95 percent) described Black women as threatening (argumentative, loud, stubborn, "bitchy," or dishonest). About 28 percent endorsed "welfare mother" traits (for example, too many children, fat, and lazy) as describing Black women and 19 percent selected traits associated with a good mother/wife/daughter image (for example, intelligent, family-oriented, loyal to family ties). In contrast, traits selected by the white women and men for "American women in general" were uniformly more positive, including intelligent, sensitive, attractive, sophisticated, emotional, ambitious, career-oriented, independent, talkative, imaginative, and kind. These results suggest that many white women regard Black women as unlikely candidates for friendship.

Do Black people hold racist views of whites that result in whites being perceived as undesirable as friends? According to the dictionary definition of racism, Blacks can be *prejudiced* against whites, but cannot accurately be labeled *racist*. Prejudice refers to unreasonable or hostile feelings, opinions, or attitudes directed against a racial, religious, or national group or behaviors that discriminate against individuals of such a group. In contrast, racism has two components: (1) the *belief* that one's race is superior and has the right to rule others, and (2) a *policy* of enforcing such rights or a *system of government* based on them (Mallon, 1991, p. 115). White people have the power in the United States to put their racial prejudices into action in terms of governmental and institutional policies as specified by this definition; Black people do not.

Black people who are prejudiced against whites often develop racial hostility in response to the racism they experience. They frequently operate from three major assumptions (Sue, 1990). First, there is a common saying among Black Americans: "If you really want to know what White folks are thinking or feeling, don't listen to what they say, but how they say it" (p. 427). A second assumption held by many people of color is that all whites are racist because they actively or passively participate in racist institutions and benefit from them. Third, they believe that most whites will go to great lengths to deny they are racist or biased. These well-founded suspicions may make Black people wary of whites who wish to befriend them.

Racial identity appears to be related to how Black people respond to racism (Demo & Hughes, 1990), as well as to racist attitudes among whites (Pope-Davis & Ottavi, 1994). Racial identity refers to an individual's awareness of his or her membership in a racial group and the personal, social, and political consequences of that membership. Blacks with a higher level of racial identity are more likely to actively confront or to reject white racist attitudes about Blacks (Demo & Hughes, 1990). Whites with high racial identity are less racist toward Black people (Pope-Davis & Ottavi, 1994). It is reasonable to speculate that racial identity may be connected to people's motivation to form cross-race friendships or to the quality of those relationships, as well. For instance, people with higher racial identity may be more knowledgeable about how race is likely to affect the friendship and may value cultural differences more. Conversely, having cross-race friendships may facilitate the development of racial identity by making the friends more aware of racial prejudice and discrimination.

Black racial identity has been described by Cross (1978, 1991) as having five stages: pre-encounter, encounter, immersion-emersion, internalization, and internalization-commitment. At the first stage, pre-encounter, the Black person adheres to many of the beliefs of the dominant white culture, including the notion that "white is right." The individual seeks to assimilate and be accepted by whites and may distance herself from other Blacks. Thus, cross-race friendships may be more common among individuals at this stage than others. The encounter phase is typically precipitated by an event that forces the individual to acknowledge the impact of racism on one's life. For example, the Black woman may come to realize that many whites will not view her as an equal. This is likely to have an adverse effect on cross-race friendships. The immersion-emersion stage is represented by the joint desire to embrace one's racial origins and to actively avoid association with white symbols. At this stage, same-race friendships are likely to be highly preferred over cross-race ones. At the fourth stage, internalization, pro-Black attitudes become less defensive, and the individual may be willing to establish carefully selected cross-race friendships with whites who are respectful and appreciative of the Black person's racial identity. The fifth stage, internalization-commitment, is similar to the fourth stage, except that the person translates her or his personal sense of being Black into a sustained plan to address the concerns of Black people as a group.

According to Helms (1990), white racial identity has five levels: contact, disintegration, reintegration, pesudo-independence, and autonomy. Individuals in the contact stage are unaware of their white identity and ignore the race of others, acting as if they are color-blind. They may avoid Black people as friends, or if they befriend them, it is typically to satisfy curiosity. Choosing to have Black friends moves the white person into the disintegration stage where the individual's whiteness becomes more salient to her or him. Conflict over one's internal standards and societal norms about interracial interactions occur. Overidentification with Blacks may result; however, Blacks may reject whites who overidentify with them. Alternatively, the person may retreat into white society to avoid the internal conflicts. At the next phase, reintegration, stereotypical attitudes of fear and anger toward Blacks are common as the white person tries to come to terms with being white, as well as having been rejected by Black people. Blacks may be avoided at this phase. With acceptance of being white, the stage of pseudo-independence is reached. Relations with a few Blacks are likely to occur, as the white person attempts to deal with race issues on an intellectual level. As interactions with Blacks increase, the person is likely to move to the autonomy stage. Here, a positive white identity is internalized and cross-cultural interactions are sought out as opportunities for growth. Racial differences and similarities are appreciated.

In summary, many white people hold negative attitudes toward Blacks that are likely to inhibit cross-race friendships. Black people, in turn, may not be very motivated to establish friendships with whites who do not regard them as peers or appreciate their culture. However, an individual's level of racial identity appears to provide insight into who chooses cross-race friendships, how successful the friendships are likely to be, and how they may be facilitated.

CROSS-RACE FRIENDSHIP

The goals of this lecture are to illustrate how racism and racial identity were expressed in student essays written about cross-race friendships and to discuss obstacles to cross-race friendship and how they might be overcome. Students first were required to read an essay by Minnie Bruce Pratt (1991, p. 19), in which she explained how she was taught by her family "who to keep in and who to keep out" as friends. The essay describes specifically how this message was communicated concerning race. For example, Pratt was taught to be cordial to Blacks but never to invite them into the house. Students were then asked to write a three-page essay exploring how race affected "who to keep in and who to keep out" as friends in their own lives. They were asked to focus specifically on Black-white friendships, indicating how interested they were in having a same-sex friend of the other race, how their family had influenced their attitudes, what would motivate them to pursue a cross-race friendship, what problems might arise in the friendship due to race, and how many close cross-race friendships they currently had.

I then classified each student's essay using the stage models of racial identity presented earlier. The following examples, taken from the essays, illustrate how cross-race friendships were affected by racial identity.[1] The discussion below is based on responses made by 10 Black and 43 white women students between the ages of 18 and 51 years who took psychology of women courses during 1994.[2]

Black Women's Responses

Essays from three of the Black women suggested they were at the first stage of Black racial identity, pre-encounter. Two characteristics were evident. First, the three were quite assimilated into white culture and tended to value it over Black culture. Second, they appeared to have little conscious awareness of racism. These attitudes appeared to be associated with a desire for cross-race friendships. For example, one 21-year-old woman of mixed African and Mexican American heritage, had only white friends. She attributed this to attending white schools as well as to rejection from Blacks.

> Nothing would inhibit me from pursuing a friendship with someone white because I've been around white people all my life. The schools I attended were predominantly white, so this also contributed to having all white friends. . . . It seems I'm more accepted by the white race. . . . Most black people, I've noticed, find something wrong as soon as they see me. For example, the first time I walked through the doors of M—High School, all the black girls decided right then they didn't like me. Their reason was that I didn't look black enough and I talked like a "white person."

[1]This approach could be improved either by presenting the models of racial identity in class and having students classify their own essay or by having students take a racial-identity measure, write an essay, and discuss the relationship between the two.

[2]Essays from 15 white and 6 Black men were not included.

Although her identification with white people showed some signs of being challenged, she still seemed predominantly to share a white frame of reference:

> In my whole 21 years, a problem never came up until recently. Most of my white friends automatically assume that just because a black man has a beeper, drives a nice car, or has nice clothes, he must be a drug dealer. They fail to realize he may have a beeper because it may be part of his profession (doctor, maintenance man).

Another 30-year-old Black woman at the pre-encounter stage placed a greater value on having friendships with white women than Black; the woman currently had no close friends of any race, but she preferred a cross-race one to a same-race one. The woman contended that "more damage can be done in same-race friendships than in a cross-race one [because] there is a tendency for one person to be jealous of the other one if she is prettier and more confident of herself . . . or if you are independent or have a spouse or boyfriend and the other person doesn't."

Five Black women were classified as being at the encounter stage because they recounted a significant social or personal event that had made them aware of racism and racial differences. Sometimes the event was due to an encounter with white racism; at other times, contact with the Black community forced the women to reconsider their views. These attitudes appeared to be related to a lack of interest in cross-race friendships. For example, patterns of racial segregation were an important factor in at least two of the women's lives. A 19-year-old woman, described how patterns of segregation had shaped her choice of friends.

> As a young African-American child, I was never given the option to let certain people in or out of my life. Economic segregation decided for me. It decided that I was going to only let my own people into my life. It made me realize at an early age that friends like myself were easy to obtain and very comfortable to have. [Then] we moved to a desegregated neighborhood. . . . Many of the whites in the neighborhood were those who could not afford to make the suburban exodus [away from blacks]. Our next door neighbors were a very nice white family, except for the father. My sister and I became very close to the children . . . As we grew older, things changed. . . . The father was very racist and he would do things to make me realize that cross-race friendships were going to be difficult to maintain and rare in my life.

Another 22-year-old Black woman indicated:

> It is quite difficult to make friends outside of my race. The students here are very antisocial and do not seem interested in talking to someone outside of their race. . . . Where I live also inhibits me from pursuing a cross-race friendship. I live in the city in a mostly African-American neighborhood where the crime rate is high. These two things usually keep White people away. If I make a cross-race friend, the person's family usually interferes or disapproves of them coming over to visit me or go out with me.

One 29-year-old Black woman described how her attitudes changed as a result of being in first a white reference group, then a Black one:

> I was accepted into the cliques that existed in my private predominantly white elementary school. I felt comfortable being one of the very few black children there. [Then] after attending a predominantly black public school, I saw hostilities that I had not seen or had not noticed before between whites and blacks. . . . My white friends from my previous school would call my mom to ask if I could sleep over at their homes and I would immediately whisper to my mom, "Does her mom know that I am black?" I had preconceived notions that her mom would not want me to sleep over if she knew that I was black. . . . I became unable to relate to my white friends as I had done before. Unconsciously, I was accepting my black peers as my exclusive circle of friends.

At the encounter stage, an awareness of cultural differences in forms of entertainment also posed a problem in cross-race friendships, particularly if the Black woman was not willing to assimilate, that is, to adopt white norms of speech and behavior. As one woman stated:

> I am very limited in the amount of time I have to spend cultivating relationships. There are no white people in the places that I enjoy going for recreation such as rollerskating, softball games, and get-togethers with family and friends. . . . White people I know seem to like golfing, tennis, skiing, surfing, bowling, iceskating, and soccer. . . . So, the likelihood of my developing a close relationship with a white person would be dependent upon the amount of effort I put into going outside my boundaries and into an environment which includes whites.

The experiences described above suggest that Black women at the encounter stage of racial identity may not be highly motivated to establish cross-race friendships, although they are aware that cross-race relations could transform racial stereotypes. Said one, "I realize that cross-race friendships are the key to ending racism, or at least making the world a better place to live in. They help dispel the stereotypes that foster racism. So I believe I should change my attitude [of indifference] and try to make a difference."

None of the Black women respondents were classified as being at the immersion-emersion stage. However, extrapolating from the attitudes likely to be expressed at this stage, cross-race friendships would be unlikely. This stage is characterized by a glorification of Black culture and denigration of white culture. The desire to explore Black history with the support of Black peers typically is strong. However, a new positive sense of self is likely to result from this exploration, and white-focused anger also usually dissipates as the person moves to the next stage of racial identity.

Emergence from the immersion-emersion stage marks the beginning of the internalization stage. Two Black women students expressed characteristics congruent with this stage, including a strong sense of Black pride, an inner security about their Black identity, and a tolerance toward other races based on their common humanity. These attitudes appeared to be associated with a desire to establish cross-race friendships with carefully selected white women. For example, a 41-year-old Black woman described her personal development as follows:

> Growing up, the only Caucasians that I remembered coming into my neighborhood were the bill collectors and the police. The bill collectors came to collect and then were gone. The police came under the guise of law enforcement. I remember some of the Caucasian officers shoving, kicking, and hitting several Black men. . . . It was clear to me that the Caucasian officers were the aggressors, since the Black men were handcuffed and the Black officers stood around without saying a word or stepping in to stop their fellow officers' aggression. Seeing the brutality of those police officers solidified an existing uneasiness of the Caucasian people. I believe this is the "why" I used to avoid building friendships with other races.

Her opinion of White people did not change until she was in her thirties. She met a young white woman who was the friend of some of her Black friends. She did not regard the woman as trustworthy because she wasn't Black and she was living with a Black man. Her opinion changed drastically one day, however, when the younger woman asked for her help and confided about her childhood sexual abuse and current marital problems. She said, "I sat and listened to B—with amazement and disbelief . . . surprised that she trusted me enough to talk openly about her pain . . . and disbelieving that a Caucasian woman could experience any of the things B—had just described to me, especially after seeing the happy-all-the-time June Cleaver depictions on television." Although still wary of whites, this personal experience made the woman more willing to respond to those whites who approached her with personal sincerity.

The second Black woman at this stage was 44 years of age. She expressed a strong sense of internal security about her identity.

> At this stage of my life, I don't feel the need to prove anything to anyone. I have broken through enough color barriers and am well aware of my abilities and attributes. If the intended friend is receptive to change, pliable, and willing to ignore possible long-held stereotypes, prejudices, and discriminatory practices, I am more than willing to educate, befriend, evolve, and grow with them.

A current long-standing friendship she had with a white woman met this description. Thus, attitudes common to the internalization stage of Black racial identity appear to facilitate the formation of carefully chosen cross-race friendships.

No Black women were identified as being at the internalization-commitment stage because none expressed an overt commitment toward advancing the cause of Black people as a group. However, in terms of feelings about oneself and others, this stage is quite similar to the internalization stage.

In sum, the Black women at the pre-encounter stage had much less understanding than those at other stages about how race and racism had affected their lives; thus, they desired cross-race friendships more. As Black women become more racially aware, as in the encounter and immersion-emersion stages, conflict in the friendships could be expected to occur, with few, if any, surviving. At the last two stages, internalization and internalization-commitment, Black women once again might become open to cross-race friendships. Those friends are likely to be carefully chosen, with a preference being shown for white women who have a highly developed racial identity themselves and who show appreciation for racial diversity.

White Women's Responses

Most of the white women ($N = 29$) were classified as being at the first stage of white racial awareness, contact. They tended to be unaware of their own racial identity and were inclined to assert they were color-blind in friendship. However, they also were likely to have very strong stereotypes that provided the context for comments like, "I could be friends with someone who didn't seem Black." These are some typical comments from students at this stage: "Friendships will come easily between two people who are open and honest and nice to one another no matter what race they happen to be." "What's race got to do with it? I have always believed that a person should not be judged by the color of her skin." "No one can ever have enough friends no matter what the race." "I am willing to befriend anyone who is nice to me." Although women at this stage professed that race was not a factor in their friendships, only four had a cross-race friend.

The contradictory beliefs about race that white women at the contact stage held appeared to be partly responsible for their lack of cross-race friends. For example, one 22-year-old woman asserted, "I do not think of potential friends as being Black or White." However, her fears about such relationships were revealed in a later statement: "There could be quite a few problems with having a cross-race friend . . . you could possibly be considered an outcast . . . society could look down on you." Many contradictory beliefs originated in family messages. Some participants described their families as prejudiced but minimized its severity and its influence on them. A 31-year-old woman's story illustrates this point.

> I used to go to bake sales with my mother when I was six. The black people would bring in beautiful pies and cakes, but after they left the church, people threw all of the desserts in the trash. My grandmother told me they were dirty people. . . . My mother also told me that my brother and I were not allowed to walk home from school with a Black boy we knew because the neighbors were complaining. Everyone had to stay on their own side of the tracks.

These early experiences were not seen as being connected to her current views, however. She claimed, "I have never really given much thought to having a friend of another race. I also don't have any."

The contradictory views held by participants contributed to their confusion. An 18-year-old woman who had no cross-race friendships explained:

> While it was unintentional on my parents' part, I grew up with slightly prejudiced views against African-Americans. I listened to my father describe the people he worked with. . . . Not until years later did I realize that my father wasn't prejudiced toward blacks, but that he just worked with incompetent people. He informed me there were just as many white people that were incapable of doing the job . . . it was not racial prejudice. . . . I am not prejudiced . . . [but] problems could arise in cross-race friendships [because] some whites are offended when the "master race" associates with inferior individuals. . . . [However] my personal view is that skin color doesn't matter.

White women at the contact stage also tended to be naive regarding the impact of race and racism on themselves and others. One example of naivete was the extent to which white women expected Black women to assimilate into white culture. "I pursue friendships when I have something in common with the other person. If I met a Black woman who I enjoyed being with . . . I wouldn't hesitate to become friends . . . [if] each of us had the same set of values and same lifestyle." This woman currently had no cross-race friends and did not expect to have any "because I can't think of any Black people who have the same values and lifestyle as I do. . . . It's not because they're different from me, but because of their values."

Other examples of naivete and stereotyping among the white women at the contact stage concerned their intolerance toward Blacks who spoke of discrimination or who held whites responsible for racism. "A major thing that would inhibit me from being friends with a Black woman would be [if] she blamed whites for their oppression and stereotyped us as a prejudiced, materialistic race," one woman commented indignantly. Likewise, a 24-year-old woman remarked, "Last semester I had a class with a black woman about my age who said that the whole campus was racist. I asked her how she could make such a broad statement. . . . I was offended by her comment. . . . It was evident that I would not be pursuing a friendship with her." White women also tended to side with other white people when the issue of race came up. For example, one woman described how her friendship with a Black woman ended.

> My black friend became very disturbed with [the way] our supervisor [had handled a racial situation] and told him that he was racist—that if it had been her in the situation, he would've taken action against her. Knowing my supervisor as well as I did, I knew he was not racist and that he treated everyone equally . . . this broke up our friendship.

Only three of the white women openly admitted to having negative attitudes about Black people. One, a 19-year-old woman, said:

> I am not particularly interested in having a friend of another race. If they lived in an entirely black neighborhood, I would be uncomfortable visiting their home. . . . I am more likely to pursue a friendship with those African-Americans who display ambition in business and who try to speak in a well-modulated voice. You might say I [would be willing to be] friends with blacks whom other blacks would refer to as "Uncle Toms," those blacks who show the traits of my white friends. . . . My friends have told me I am a racist and I suppose that I may seem that way to some.

In general, with the exception of the three women who admitted to being overtly prejudiced, the white women at the contact stage of racial identity had given little thought to being white and appeared to have minimal understanding of the effects of racism. As a result, they had not consciously considered what role race played in choosing or maintaining friendships until they did the assignment. Most claimed they would be open to such a friendship, if approached, but they indicated that they would not take the initiative themselves. Perhaps not surprisingly, few women at this stage had cross-race friends.

The other 16 white women completing the assignment were classified as being at the disintegration stage. They were becoming more aware of their own race, as well as of the effect of racism on Blacks. This greater awareness appeared to facilitate—or perhaps result from—cross-race friendships; 8 women at the disintegration stage had a close friendship with a Black woman.

Three themes congruent with the disintegration stage were expressed in the essays. First, most of the white women had experienced an event that forced them to examine or assert their personal values about race issues. For one young woman, being assigned a Black college roommate who was from the Chicago projects was the impetus for her to face her prejudices. Another woman noticed her own covert stereotyping and racism when she defended to her family a friendship she had with a Black woman. "I responded by saying, 'She's different. She's very educated.'" Others struggled with having received one message from parents to "love thy neighbor" and treat all people equally and an opposite message when the families deliberately fled from racially mixed neighborhoods and schools.

Challenges to or insights about parents' messages seemed to promote racial identity. For example, one 21-year-old white woman had serious arguments with her father about race.

> My father thinks that other races are the reason this country is in such bad shape. He was an active member of the KKK for a short period of time. . . . Most of his animosity was directed toward blacks. He tried to drill into my head that blacks were bad. . . . But I just knew my father was wrong . . . [often] I argued with him about it. . . . I've just never had that prejudice in me.

For a 28-year-old woman, recognizing the similarities between her mother's and her own behavior toward Black people provided the impetus for conflict.

> My grade school was considered progressive. It was a mixture of children of university faculty and children from, as my mother euphemistically said, "the other side of town" (black children). While I never heard or saw my mother say anything overtly racist—indeed, she proclaimed that we were getting a "better education" because we were "exposed to different people"— she was always very condescending toward the mothers of the black girls, taking particular care to explain in a simple way how to fill out the forms to award [Girl Scout] badges. She also made a point of telling me how fortunate I was to "have these experiences." Now, looking back, I realize she was drawing the line between "them" and "us."
>
> I also see that in my daily interactions I am still very aware of the line drawn in part by my mother. . . . I am careful with people of other races, take more time to be warm and helpful. . . . now that I examine those expressions, I'm afraid they are a bit too close to the attitude my mother used to take.

Guilt and depression, a second characteristic of the disintegration stage, also were common. For several of the participants, completing the assignment itself was a catalyst for internal reflection and conflict. One 42-year-old woman wrote:

> Why, now, do I feel uncomfortable when I read the questions in this exercise? I think that I try very hard to be open-minded, unprejudiced, nonjudgmental, and I feel disappointed in myself when I am brought face-to-face with my shortcomings in this area. The reality is that intellectually I see similarities between races more than differences, but on a gut level my fear of the differences outweigh rationality.

Similarly, a 35-year-old woman expressed guilt about her failure to continue friendships with Black women from work outside the work setting. Even though she had been invited to parties and dances, she had never attended, citing safety as a factor. She pondered whether this was an honest reason or "an excuse not to take the risk to really get to know those who are different."

Third, a number of white women at the disintegration stage mentioned an aspect of the self or an experience that made them more empathetic to people of other races. One 21-year-old woman thought that prejudice directed at her because she was overweight had made her reluctant to judge others. Another 22-year-old became more racially aware when she took a Black friend to a party aboard a boat in an affluent white community. The boat owner, a close white male friend of hers, made comments about how much his property value was being lowered by having someone Black on the boat. She chose to drop the white man as her friend. An entire family's racial identity was expanded by empathy for gay issues, according to a 34-year-old woman.

The summer of my freshman year, my older brother announced that he was gay. Mike's lover was a black man. . . . That year I discovered how cruel prejudice and fear could be. . . . [There were] nasty phone calls from neighbors. . . . I heard the hushed voices of my parents late into the night . . . [and] was surprised by the cruelty of [his peers]. . . . I often felt his pain . . . [then] my brother died of AIDS and I discovered another world of untouchables. . . . In the later years, Mike's partner became a member of our family. . . . We mourned together. . . . My father said, "People realize how little differences in color and lifestyles matter when they gotta rally together to survive," when we gathered for dinner a few months after Mike's death. His words were profound. As a family, we have come a long way in recognizing our prejudices.

Thus, attitudes expressed by white women at the disintegration stage appeared to have a positive effect on cross-race friendship. Alternatively, close personal contact with Black women might have provided the catalyst for developing a higher level of racial identity among white women.

None of the white women students were classified as being at the reintegration, pseudo-independence, or autonomy stage of white racial identity. However, it is possible to speculate how racial identity and cross-race friendships might interact by extrapolating from attitudes likely to be expressed at each stage. At the reintegration stage, the guilt and anxiety associated with the previous stage may be redirected as fear and anger toward Blacks, who are now blamed for the white woman's feelings of discomfort concerning race. Avoidance of Blacks may occur, reducing the odds of forming cross-race friendships. At the fourth, or pseudo-independence stage, the individual comes to terms with being white to some extent and is able to identify ways in which she and other whites benefit from racism. However, she may also subtly disavow that she is white. An effort will usually be made to seek out Black people at this stage, possibly leading to cross-race friendships. At the last stage, autonomy, the white woman has internalized a sense of oneself as white, along with an awareness of and appreciation for people of other races. The person might engage in antiracist work and seek to establish cross-race friendships with Black women who also have a high level of racial identity.

In sum, the white women at the first stage of racial awareness, contact, exhibited less knowledge about racism and their own identity; both appeared to have a negative effect on cross-race friendships. White women at stage 2, disintegration, had experienced incidents that forced them to become aware of their whiteness and to examine their cultural values; more cross-race friendships occurred at this stage. The fact that no white women were found at the higher levels of racial identity suggests that white women in general are underdeveloped in terms of thinking about themselves as racial beings. It is reasonable to speculate that this adversely affects the development of cross-race friendships. Conversely, it suggests that educating white women about race issues and enhancing the development of their racial identity might promote friendships between Black and white women.

*P*ROMOTING CHANGE

Is it possible for Black and white women to be friends? The analysis of racism, racial identity, and cross-race friendship presented here suggests that mutually satisfying and fully reciprocal cross-race friendships are rare. Moreover, the desire and ability to establish them may depend not only on the individual women's racial identity but the match between the two. If friendships do happen to be established across the color line, some typical conflicts are likely to occur. A racially unaware white woman's insensitivity toward racism or unconsciously prejudiced remarks may offend the Black woman. The Black woman who is becoming racially aware may start reevaluating her relationship with her white women friends. Or, the reaction of the respective white or Black family or community to the friendship may be hostile. Thus, it appears that Black and white women can indeed be friends, but only if the right combination of people and circumstances is present. Otherwise, as one Black woman asserted, the friendships will be held together "by a very weak glue."

The results presented here suggest that enhancing women's awareness of their racial identity might increase the likelihood that cross-race friendships will survive. Assignments such as the one described here in conjunction with other experiential exercises (Katz, 1989) appear to promote greater racial awareness and serve as a catalyst for change. For example, one of the white women who participated in the exercise described here had been extremely upset during a discussion of white privilege. She argued that she treated everyone fairly and that *she* did not benefit from institutional racism. However, an event occurred during the semester that forced her to challenge her assumption. In her friendship essay, she had described an incident at work where the cook, a Black male coworker, had cursed her, mentioning her race. She was shocked at what she labeled "reverse racism" and reported the incident to the white owner of the restaurant. Her view of the situation had changed drastically a few days later, when she presented me with a supplement to the essay. The cook had apologized to her. She learned that he had been forced to do so by the owner who angrily told him, "You picked the wrong white girl to mess with." The event caused her perception of the situation to shift. She wrote:

> I felt very confused and upset about this. It made me realize that racism really is prejudice + institutional power. The cook may have been prejudiced against me or even angry with all whites. However, I realized that he couldn't have been racist even if he wanted to. He was "put in his place" and made to apologize, not because of our argument, but because he is black and I am white. It was no longer "our" argument. It had become bigger than that and I began to feel like the one to blame. I felt like something had been turned around and I was on the wrong side.

How can Black and white women become friends? From the information presented here, it appears that cross-race friendships will be enhanced when both Black and white women are at the highest levels of racial identity. Although more investigation is necessary to establish empirically that racial identity and friendship are connected, case studies conducted by Hall and Rose (in press) provide some support for this view. We interviewed a small group of Black and white women who were at a high level of racial identity about their cross-race friendships. Several themes were expressed consistently. First, the Black women were quite reserved about approaching white women as friends owing to previous negative experiences with whites. As a result, the white woman usually has to initiate the friendship. Second, the cross-race friends had to work to establish trust around racial matters specifically. Some ways this was accomplished were by socializing together in each other's homes, by the white women educating themselves about race, and by both becoming allies against racism, including taking public and private stands against racism. The rewards of cross-race friendships cited by the women were plentiful, particularly in terms of the insight they provided into another culture. Most remarked that their friendships were well worth the extra effort required to form and maintain them; in fact, struggling to bridge the race gap often made them stronger than same-race friendships. In terms of what blueprint to follow to establish a cross-race friendship, one Black woman in the psychology of women course who was at the internalization stage offered a description of what type of connection would perhaps yield the most durable tie.

> A motivation that would prompt me to establish a cross-race friendship would be an inquisitive Caucasian who honestly sought answers to age-old racial questions which may have troubled her for years. If the initial approach came from a genuine desire to develop a viable friendship, to promote a oneness of the human race, and destroy the racial barriers, and if by doing so, a mutual learning experience occurred, I would be motivated to let down my hair and "let in" this individual. Honesty is an important component. . . . I would further be motivated if I could be assured of a realistic, sincere interaction with no foolish mind games or power struggles. I would like to understand the blanket hatred deeply rooted in many Caucasians and be given the opportunity to explain my own deeply embedded anger. If we could come to grips with our inner feelings, bring them to the surface, face and deal with them intelligently, then work toward solving our problems, then we could begin to develop a friendship. . . . There are benefits to having cross-race friendships. . . . You may share ideas, compare lifestyles, negate the bad, build on the good, break down/shatter barriers, and possibly change the world.

In summary, understanding how cross-race friendships develop and interact with racial identity provides insight into the psychology of women by focusing on important variations in social behavior *among* women. It also addresses how bonds between women can be built across potentially divisive issues such as race.

REFERENCES

CARTER, R. T., WHITE, T. J., & SEDLACEK, W. E. (1987). White student attitudes toward Blacks: Implications for Black student recruitment and retention. *Journal of Behavioral and Social Sciences, 33*, 165–175.

CLARK, M. L., & AYERS, M. (1992). Friendship similarity during early adolescence: Gender and racial patterns. *Journal of Psychology, 126*(4), 393–405.

CROSS, W. E. (1978). The Cross and Thomas models of psychological nigrescence. *Journal of Black Psychology, 5*(1), 13–19.

CROSS, W. E., Jr. (1991). *Shades of Black: Diversity in African-American identity.* Philadelphia: Temple University.

DEMO, D. H., & HUGHES, M. (1990). Socialization and racial identity among Black Americans. *Social Psychology Quarterly, 53*(4), 364–374.

DUCK, S. (1991). *Understanding relationships.* New York: Guilford.

HALL, R. L., & ROSE, S. (in press). Friendships between African-American and white lesbians. In J. Weinstock & E. Rothblum (Eds.), *Lesbians and friendship.* New York: Routledge.

HELMS, J. (Ed.). (1990). *Black and white racial identity: Theory, research, and practice.* Westport, CT: Greenwood.

KATZ, J. H. (1989). *White awareness: Handbook for anti-racism training.* Norman, OK: University of Oklahoma.

MALLON, G. L. (1991). Racism: The white problem. In G. L. Mallon (Ed.), *Resisting racism: An action guide* (pp. 115–118). San Francisco: National Association of Black and White Men Together.

POPE-DAVIS, D. B., & OTTAVI, T. M. (1994). The relationship between racism and racial identity among white Americans: A replication and extension. *Journal of Counseling & Development, 72*, 293–297.

PRATT, M. B. (1991). *Rebellion: Essays 1980–1991.* Ithaca, NY: Firebrand.

SUE, D. W. (1990). Culture-specific strategies in counseling: A conceptual framework. *Professional Psychology, 21*(6), 424–433.

WEITZ, R., & GORDON, L. (1993). Images of Black women among Anglo college students. *Sex Roles, 28*(1/2), 19–34.

SUGGESTED READINGS

KATZ, J. H. (1989). *White awareness: Handbook for anti-racism training.* Norman, OK: University of Oklahoma.

NELSON, J. (1993). *Volunteer slavery.* New York: Penguin.

PRATT, M. (1991). Rebellion. In M. B. Pratt (Ed.), *Rebellion: Essays 1980–1991.* (pp. 9–26). Ithaca, NY: Firebrand.

TATUM, B. D. (1992). Talking about race, learning about racism: The application of racial identity development theory in the classroom. *Harvard Educational Review, 62*, 1–24.

*C*ARLA GOLDEN *is Associate Professor of Psychology at Ithaca College. Dr. Golden has taught courses on the psychology of women and gender since 1977 at Ithaca, Smith College, and the University of Pittsburgh's Semester at Sea Program. She has published and lectured widely on feminist psychoanalytic theories and on the development of women's sexuality.*

16

Relational Theories of White Women's Development

❖

*I*n the past twenty years, feminist psychologists have introduced a widely acknowledged but controversial set of theories regarding white women's psychological development. These "relational theories," as they have come to be
called, are concerned with how females become gendered into girls and women,
more specifically how they develop distinctly gendered personality styles. This
view that there are gender-differentiated paths of personality development is controversial within the field of psychology and no less debatable among feminist
psychologists.

Although laypeople may believe that there exist gender differences in
women's and men's personalities, there are many psychologists who reject the notion of personality as a stable and enduring collection of traits that characterize a
person. They would argue that rather than stable traits "inside" a person, it is
those things "outside" the person (for example, pervasive expectations and attitudes about people's behavior that are deeply encoded in our social institutions)
that significantly influence how we act in the world. In their view, we must look
more carefully at the situations in which people find themselves and at the interactions between people if we want to better understand why women and men behave differently or seem to have gender-differentiated personalities. As Janis Bohan (1993) explains,

> Gender is not a trait inherent in individuals; rather, qualities that are usually seen as
> sex related are in fact contextually determined. Gender is revealed as simply the term

given to a set of behavior-environment interactions that we have come to agree characterize members of one sex. (pp. 13–14)

Similarly, Rachel Hare-Mustin and Jeanne Maracek (1990) assert that "gender is not a property of individuals but a socially prescribed relationship, a process, and a social construction" (p. 54).

The views of Bohan, Hare-Mustin, and Maracek are an expression of the social-constructionist perspective on gender. A more elaborated discussion of this perspective can be found in most standard textbooks. The important point here is to understand that according to social-construction theory, gender is not something that one *has,* nor is it something that exists *inside* the person—rather gender is something one *does,* which is to say that it is socially constructed behavior based upon culturally shared meanings. Given this position, social constructionists do not see great value in discussing gender differences in personality.

Relational theorists present an alternative view of gender. They do believe that people in some sense "have" gender and that one form in which it gets expressed is in personality. They argue that as a result of patriarchy and different childhood socialization experiences, girls and boys develop into women and men with gender-differentiated personalities. This occurs through a process whereby the child internalizes the shared meanings and values of the larger culture into a core self-structure referred to as personality. Although personality formation can and does occur in ways unique to each individual, there are also believed to be similarities based on shared positions (for example, gender) within society.

As defined by the DSM-IV, personality traits are "enduring patterns of perceiving, relating to, and thinking about the environment and oneself that are exhibited in a wide range of important social and personal contexts" (American Psychiatric Association, 1994, p. 630). Whereas this definition does not specify cultural and historical contributants to the development of personality traits, relational theorists have done so. Nancy Chodorow (1978), for example, situates her analysis of personality development in the context of Western industrial capitalism and the white middle-class nuclear family, though many people who make use of her theory often overlook this point (Hare-Mustin & Maracek, 1990). The important issue here is that relational theorists are interested in how what is "outside" in society (for example, values, attitudes, and shared meanings of gender derived from culture, history, and language) gets "inside," and they name what is inside "personality."

Relational theorists are basically personality theorists who are less interested in specific quantifiable behaviors than they are in the underlying psychological substrate (that is, personality) that shapes specific behaviors and feelings and is responsible for discernable patterns in people's styles of responding to and coping with relationships and life events. When these theorists write about an individual's personality, their formal conceptualization is in terms of "ego structure" or more informally, the sense of self that informs how people perceive, think about, and relate to their environment. Thus, references to a person's "mode of relating" or "way of being" are really references to personality. Whereas social constructionists wish to further explore what is outside rather than inside the individual, relational theorists focus on the latter. In the view of relational theorists, many people do experience a sense of self that feels "coherent, continuous over time and relatively stable and boundaried" (Brown, 1994, p. 390) as well as gendered. For this reason, they argue that personality and the gendered self are legitimate subjects of study.

A wide variety of different psychological theorists have described women's personality, or sense of self, as fundamentally relational, meaning that relationships are central to women's self-definition (Belenky, Clinchy, Goldberger, & Tarule, 1986; Chodorow, 1978; Contratto, 1986; Eichenbaum & Orbach, 1983, 1984; Flax, 1978; Gilligan, 1982, 1991; Jordan, Kaplan, Miller, Stiver, & Surrey, 1991; Lerner, 1988; Miller, 1976; Westkott, 1986). In describing women as relational, these theorists suggest that skills essential to establishing and maintaining relationships are more highly developed in women and more prominent in their psychology, including the capacities for empathy, sensitivity, nurturance, and caring. From different vantage points (psychology, sociology, psychoanalysis) and using different terminology, each of these theorists has described how women's lives are organized around seeking intimacy and maintaining relationships, although they differ on the degree to which they see this relational orientation as healthy or in conflict with the expression of autonomous strivings.

Before considering their theories in more detail, we must ask just what "women" are we talking about here? To be more accurate, what these relational theories describe is that *some* women have a more relational way of being and *some* men have a more autonomous way of being in the world. I note *some* women and men, because these theories are almost certainly not generalizable to all women and men; rather they are likely to be most applicable to the kinds of people studied by the theorists who produced the theories. All of the theorists reviewed in this chapter are white, and they themselves are either clinicians or academicians who work with largely white, heterosexual women from a range of social class backgrounds, presumably mostly middle-class. The people upon whom the theories are based have been observed and studied in either educational or psychotherapeutic settings, including public and private schools, adult education programs, private psychotherapy practices, university counseling centers, and women's center groups.

These theories have been widely criticized for their lack of applicability to women of color (Spellman, 1988), but there has also been significant discussion of the ways in which the theories must be broadened so as to be more inclusive (Contratto, 1994) as well as some attempt to apply them to ethnic minority populations (Segura & Pierce, 1993; see also Castañeda, this volume). Still, one might question whether these theories are even generalizable to all white middle-class women or only to those who seek psychotherapy. Insofar as the women described by these theorists are dealing with everyday "problems in living," one could argue that they are not significantly different from middle-class white women who do not seek psychotherapy. For example, many of the young, white, middle-class women and men I have been teaching for 15 years recognize themselves in these theories, and so do some students, both white and of color, who come from working-class families. Similarly, many psychologists find that the descriptions resonate significantly with their own experience from either clinical practice or academic life (Tavris, 1994). Although there are certainly points of contention with particulars of the theory, I have been impressed by how these descriptions of difference in gendered personality styles seem to "resonate" or "click" with the experience of people who are exposed to this work.

Clearly, there is far more that must be done in developing theory that is relevant to, and inclusive of, women of diverse cultural groups. However, because a theory has limited generalizability doesn't mean we need to discard it and aim for the one theory that speaks to all women's experience. It is unlikely that there will be a universal psychology that is applicable to all women, and we must not claim that relational theory as it has been proposed is a universal one. Rather, it may be useful in describing and explaining the psychology of *some* women, and it is this qualification that must be kept in mind. To facilitate this, I will name the women described by these theories as white, though the theorists under consideration did not do so.

Jean Baker Miller (1976) was among the first to address white women's relational orientation when she described women as closer to their emotions, more willing to acknowledge their vulnerabilities, more interpersonally oriented, and more concerned about other people than white men are. Such characteristics have often been viewed as indicative of women's weakness, but Miller considered them to be strengths, representative of a more advanced and healthier way of living. Miller expressed concerns that theories of human development were really theories of men's development and that such male models did not even address, let alone explain, what she considered to be most prominent in women's psychology. In her view, the central feature of white women's psychology was the motivation to give to others; from years of clinical experience she was impressed by women's concern with whether they had given enough, in contrast to men who seemed much more concerned with whether they had done enough.[1]

Nancy Chodorow (1978, 1989), drawing on a particular version of psychoanalysis known as object relations theory, wrote more formally about ego development. She noted that traditional psychoanalytic theories defined development as a process of becoming increasingly separate,

---

[1]Black feminist theorists have also noted that Black women are expected to take care of and nurture those around them, often at the expense of tending to their own needs (Collins, 1990; hooks, 1993).

or "individuated," from others. The writings of Freud and Erikson, among others, made it clear that achieving psychological maturity meant becoming separate, independent, and autonomous. Chodorow agreed that this was one important outcome of development, but that another equally important aspect was the development of relational skills. Her work focused attention on what she called the relational ego (or more informally, the sense of self-in-connection) as it exists in (or out of) balance with the autonomous ego (or the sense of self-in-separation). She argued that both aspects of ego development were crucial for mental health, with the autonomous ego laying the foundation for healthy functioning as a separate, individuated adult, and the relational ego allowing for healthy involvement in intimate social relationships.

Chodorow's writing not only highlighted the significance of the relational ego and put it on a par with the autonomous ego; she also introduced gender into the equation. She argued that in white women, the relational ego was more highly developed than the autonomous ego, whereas in white men the reverse situation could be observed. In other words, Chodorow argued that some girls have a greater sense of self-in-connection than of self-in-separation, meaning not only that they define themselves in terms of their relationships and feel more comfortable in connection with others, but also that they actually have a greater need, as well as more highly developed capacities, for intimacy. Relational needs and capacities refer to all those things associated with being emotionally close to other people such as talking about and sharing feelings, experiencing empathy, sensitivity, nurturance, and caring for others. But along with greater relational needs and capacities, Chodorow described a less well-established autonomous ego, or sense of self-in-separation, reflected in the phenomenon of girls and women finding it easier to think in terms of "we" than "I." She claimed that white women often were characterized by a diminished capacity to assert their needs and desires.

Chodorow further contended that white women experience their closest emotional ties to other women, and she referred to this as women's homoemotionality. Friendship research consistently reveals that white women are generally more self-disclosing than white men within their friendships, and that when men do engage in intimate personal talk with a friend, it is most likely to be with a girlfriend or a close woman friend. Chodorow gives the term "heterosexual asymmetry" to this situation—meaning that heterosexual white women often experience a split between the person(s) who best meet their emotional needs and their sexual needs. Although they may turn to men for sexual relationships, their primary emotional relationships (the ones in which they extensively share their deepest feelings) are with women. For heterosexual white men, there is typically no similar split; these men often seek (and find) women who can meet their needs for both sexual and emotional closeness.

Jane Flax (1978) describes white women as having the capacity for great intimacy and depth in their friendships with other women. She depicts these relationships as having enormous emotional power and intensity, which also means that there is tremendous power to hurt and damage their women friends. Flax's descriptions of women's personalities draw heavily on the concepts of the autonomous and relational ego, and in agreement with Chodorow, she describes women as having difficulty with the expression of autonomy in adulthood. Her critical insight about friendships between white women is that the friends are seeking, but not finding, the simultaneous experience of feeling close and connected while also feeling supported for autonomy. She argues that typically women achieve one at the expense of the other, which is to say that relationships are intimate and supportive as long as there is no clear expression of difference, and that in order to maintain their closeness they must diminish or give up their autonomous strivings.

Luise Eichenbaum and Susie Orbach (1983, 1984, 1987) elaborate on the conflicted expression of white women's relational and autonomous strivings. They describe white women as having tremendous sensitivity to the needs of others, to the point where their concern for others significantly overshadows attention to their own needs. They claim that girls learn early to develop "emotional antennae" and internalize the message, conveyed both consciously and unconsciously, within and outside the family, to take care of others at the expense of themselves. Thus, girls' relational skills are viewed by Eichenbaum and Orbach as more reflective of a "compulsive concern for others" and an inability to act on one's own needs. Included among one's own needs would be such things as taking initiative, acting independently (for what they might want, rather than for what someone else might need), and generally showing self-concern. Having learned that their own needs are problematic, white girls' capacity to act on them will be inhibited and undeveloped. Eichenbaum and Orbach describe many women who as adults have great difficulty in clearly articulating what they want and need.

Carol Gilligan and her colleagues (1991) describe a similar phenomenon as it is expressed among some white girls as they make the transition to adolescence. In what Gilligan characterizes as the "central paradox of women's psychology" (1991, p. 26), she reports that many girls take themselves out of relationships for the sake of maintaining relationships. She portrays some girls as managing to stay in relationships only by becoming disconnected from their own thoughts and feelings. In a process she refers to as "psychological resistance," Gilligan describes how white girls end up silencing themselves for fear that if they expressed how they really thought and felt it would be dangerous to their relationships. But in so doing, they are in danger of losing touch with what they actually think and feel. In an important statement of the relative significance of relational and autonomous strivings, Gilligan and her colleagues define psychological health as staying in relationship with the self as well as with other people. They consider it as much a relational crisis when one becomes disconnected from one's own thoughts and feelings as when one becomes disconnected from other people.

The imbalance between relational and autonomous strivings has been identified as a consistent and pervasive problem for white women. First described by Miller in the mid-1970s, it has been discussed in similar terms by Chodorow, Flax, Eichenbaum and Orbach, and Gilligan as well as by most other feminist personality theorists who have concerned themselves with white women's psychology. Harriet Lerner (1988) has written about what she terms women's "de-selfing" behavior; Dana Jack (1991) talks about the "silencing of the self"; Marcia Westkott (1986) has written about "compliant relatedness." In the most stark rendering of this conflict, Jessica Benjamin (1988) devoted considerable attention to what she called "the problem of desire" and put it most bluntly when she wrote "to be a woman is to be unable to say, 'I want that'" (p. 88).

What feminist personality theorists have identified is that the maintenance of relationships is of such primary importance to white women that they often mute their own feelings and desires so as to avoid any disharmony or disconnection that might be caused by voicing them. A lifetime of engaging in such silencing can mean that these women often have a very hard time knowing what it is they want and need. What relational theories have depicted is a portrait of white women who are very adept at attending to the feelings of others, and in working to maintain relationships, but who at the same time have difficulty in experiencing a strong sense of self, autonomy, agency, power, or more simply, in knowing what they want and being able to pursue it without ambivalence or guilt. It is worth pointing out that it is not only in relation to men that white women are said to have a hard time expressing their own wants and needs. Each of these theorists suggests that this can be a significant problem in women's relationships with one another; Eichenbaum and Orbach (1987) actually argue that there is more room for difference and disagreement in heterosexual relationships than in women's friendships, and Chodorow (1989) asserts that there is greater distance and rationality in women's relations with men as contrasted with other women.

Although there is strong agreement on this point of white women's relational orientation having a stifling effect on their strivings for autonomy, there is not consensus among feminist psychologists. Jordan, Kaplan, Miller, Stiver, and Surrey (also known as the Stone Center theorists) reject the notion that women have a "weaker" sense of separate self because they reject the notion that there is such a thing as a separate sense of self at all.[2] Once certain feminist theorists had drawn

[2] The Stone Center for Developmental Services and Studies of Wellesley College was made possible by a grant to the college by Robert and Grace Stone, parents of a Wellesley graduate. It was dedicated in the fall of 1981, with Jean Baker Miller as its first director. As indicated by its name, the center has a dual focus on research and the provision of psychological services. The research focus is on the psychological development of people of all ages, and the counseling division involves the training of clinicians as well as direct services to clients. Since 1978, a group of psychologists affiliated with the Stone Center began meeting bimonthly to discuss women's psychological development from a feminist perspective. The core group consists of Judith Jordan, Alexandra Kaplan, Jean Baker Miller, Irene Stiver, and Janet Surrey; they have come to be referred to collectively as the Stone Center theorists.

attention to the relational ego (remember, it had previously been ignored or downplayed), the stage was set for other theorists to come along and argue that there is *only* a relational ego, or in their terms, a "self-in-relation." Theorists from the Stone Center have proposed what they call a "self-in-relation" model of female development.[3] They describe development as an entirely relational process, in which psychological maturity is marked by increasing levels of relatedness to others rather than separateness from others. Whereas Chodorow and the other relational theorists reviewed here posited a dual track of ego development (with maturity signified by relationality *and* autonomy), the Stone Center perspective is distinctive in arguing that growth for women occurs *only* in the context of relationships. They reject the notion that a sense of separateness is important to a child's sense of self. In their view, the self is defined not by its separateness but only by its capacity for connection to others.

Crucial to understanding the model of psychological development offered by the Stone Center theorists is the concept of mutuality in relationships. Most psychologists acknowledge that being loved, cared for, and understood are crucial to psychological well-being, but the Stone Center theorists emphasize the reciprocal nature of these needs. They argue that to understand, care for, and attend to the needs of *others* is as much a human motivation as the more obvious need to receive emotional supplies from others. Thus, they posit a motivation to "take care of relationships" along with the observation that in women this motivation is most developed and clearly expressed (what happens to this motivation in boys and men is an issue to which I shall return). They find that girls and women are quite literally *motivated* to understand the other, to give love and attention to the other as well as to have these behaviors reciprocated. Almost as if in response to Freud's perplexed query, Miller (1991) emphasizes that what (white) women really want is

> to be in relationships with others, and again, to really comprehend the other; wanting to understand the other's feelings; wanting to contribute to the other; wanting the nature of the relationship to be one in which the other person(s) is engaged in this way. (p. 22)

Central to the Stone Center claim that white women and girls need to take care of others is that they feel better about themselves when they are in relationship; their self-esteem is strengthened when they feel more related and are more able to take care of the other. Miller (1991) notes that "to feel more related to another person means to feel one's self enhanced" (p. 15), and that "the girl's sense of self-esteem is based in feeling that she

---

[3]It was Nancy Chodorow who first coined the term "self-in-relationship," though oddly, this is never acknowledged in the Stone Center writings.

is part of relationships and taking care of those relationships" (p. 16). Although the Stone Center theorists offer case examples of white women who give more to heterosexual relationships than they receive in return (a situation they refer to as a "failure in mutuality"), they do not adequately address the oppressive consequences of women's motivation to take care of others in a patriarchal culture where men are not motivated to reciprocate.

Nonetheless, their description of gender differences in personality is entirely consistent with those of the other relational theorists in asserting that white women's sense of self is more relational, and white men's is more autonomous. Self-in-relation theory identifies women as more invested in connection and acting in the world with a sense of "we-ness"; men are described as placing a much greater value on separateness and as being better able to shut off feelings and relationships from other realms of life, such as work. The Stone Center writings contain no ambiguity on the issue of difference: they assert that "most women have a greater ability for relatedness, emotional closeness, and emotional flexibility" than men, and that the capacity for empathy (defined as "the ability to experience, comprehend, and respond to the inner state of another person") is "consistently found to be more developed in women" (Surrey, 1991, pp. 53–54). The Stone Center theorists are in significant agreement with other feminist accounts in their observation that these differences create difficulties in heterosexual relationships, in contrast to the greater depth of emotional connectedness (or mutuality) that is common in women's relationships with other women (Jordan, 1991).

Thus far, I have reviewed different relational theorists' *descriptions* of gendered personality styles; each theorist also offers an *explanation* of their development. While the particular details differ, there are some important commonalities. Chodorow, Flax, Eichenbaum and Orbach, and the Stone Center theorists all draw explicitly on psychoanalytic theory and focus significant attention on the fact that it is almost always women, and rarely men, who are the primary caretakers of infants and young children. They consider how the mother's gender consciously and unconsciously affects her relationship with her infant and argue that gender does make a significant difference in personality development.

Each theorist starts with the basic premise that mothers, as women, feel more identified with their daughters than with their sons. This greater sense of sameness and identification is said to facilitate development of the daughter's relational skills and hamper the development of her autonomy. These theorists do not claim that mothers love their daughters more than their sons, only that at an unconscious level they feel more identified with, and hence similar to, their daughters. In relating to a primary parent who feels this way, it will be harder for the daughter to feel separate and differentiated (that is, autonomous). In contrast, mothers are said to experience their infant sons as "other," which makes it easier for boys to develop a sense of autonomy. This account was first presented by

Chodorow (1978) and has been further elaborated or modified by other theorists.

There are noteworthy variations on how the mother-daughter and mother-son relationships are depicted. Flax, and Eichenbaum and Orbach suggest that mothers react with greater ambivalence to the needs of their infant daughters than their sons, both because their daughters' needs remind them of their own unmet needs and because in a patriarchal society women are supposed to serve the needs of males. The consequence, they argue, is that mothers are more emotionally available to sons. In contrast, the Stone Center theorists argue that because the mother is more identified with the daughter, there is heightened empathic interaction and interdependency between the two from the very beginning and that girls get more practice in relating emotionally starting in infancy. The Stone Center theorists view the mother-son relationship as more cognitive and less affective, one in which the boy has fewer opportunities to practice mutuality in relationships. As a result, they posit that being close to and emotional with others feels threatening and scary to boys. They argue that boys need to feel separate and that this creates a "basic relational stance of disconnection and disidentification" (Surrey, 1991, p. 56).

The writings from the Stone Center merely state that boys need to feel separate; Chodorow's work details why. She argues that given a culture where women are the primary caretakers of infants, boys experience their earliest, core identification with a woman (as do girls). In the framework of psychoanalytic theory, such an identification is unconscious and precedes language; it constitutes a deeply rooted sense of self as "like mother." This earliest, unconscious sense of self presents problems for the boy as he grows older in a patriarchal culture where he will be expected to disidentify with his mother because she is a woman; to be a man in this culture is to be other than woman (see Bem, this volume). Thus, in the years of early childhood when boys are consolidating their masculine gender identity, they will feel a pressure, both conscious and unconscious, to repress this identification with the mother. Chodorow argues that in becoming gendered, boys disidentify with their mothers, and by extension with all women. This disidentification involves repression of that part of the ego or self (the relational ego) that was involved with her.

As explained at the beginning of this chapter, the theorists reviewed here are interested in personality or, more formally, ego structure. Despite variations in the particular details of their accounts, they all agree that as a function of being exclusively mothered (rather than parented by both women and men), what is built into feminine personality structure is a strong relational ego, with both the capacity and need for intimacy, and a relatively less developed autonomous ego. What is built into masculine personality structure is the reverse—a more firmly established autonomous ego, and relational needs and capacities that have been systematically repressed.[4] This is not an essentialist argument; these theorists do not maintain that women are *naturally* more relational, but rather that it is the *conditions* of child rearing (which could be changed) that contribute to gender-differentiated personality styles.

It should be noted that the emphasis in these theories on the mother's sense of sameness with her daughter and difference from her son fails to take into account those situations where because of temperament or physical appearance, a mother may in fact identify more with a son than a daughter. It may be wholly inapplicable to mothers of color for whom sense of sameness or difference in relation to children may be based more on ethnicity and color than gender. For example, it is possible that a black mother in a white-dominated culture would feel a greater sense of sameness to her child (male *or* female) based on their shared color than on their shared gender (Boyd-Franklin, 1989).

One might also wonder how these theories view the father's role in development. None of the theorists under consideration here gives much attention to fathers; this is partly in response to the lack of attention given to the mother-daughter relationship in earlier psychoanalytic literature. Other relational theorists whose work is not reviewed here (due to space limitations) give substantive attention to the role of the father in personality development (Benjamin, 1988; Contratto, 1986; Stiver, 1991; Westkott, 1986, 1990).

This necessarily brief overview of relational theory is designed to elaborate on the claim that some women have a relational way of being, while some men have a more autonomous style. It is also intended to present an alternative to the prevailing view put forth in most psychology of women courses—that personality differences between women and men are either nonexistent or so small, inconsistent, and unstable as to be unworthy of sustained attention. Academic feminist psychologists tend to be minimizers of gender difference (Hare-Mustin & Maracek, 1990; Kitzinger, 1994), but students should be aware that there are feminist psychologists who take a different view. The relational perspective described here is not based on laboratory studies of strangers who interact briefly under artificial circumstances, but on qualitative and clinical sources of data—mostly white women and men's own descriptions of their experience. Thus, it should not be surprising that claims of gender difference made by relational theorists are discrepant with those made in standard psychology of women texts (Lott, 1994; Unger & Crawford, 1992) as well as in other lectures in this collection (see Eagly or Geer & Shields).

---

[4]Gilligan and her colleagues (Gilligan, Rogers, & Tolman, 1991) provide a somewhat different account of women's muted strivings for autonomy, one that looks less at the mother-daughter relationship than at cultural pressures on girls. Although it is possible to read their account as a theory of differential gender socialization, one can find in their discussion the same emphasis on the underlying issues of connection and separation, intimacy and autonomy that characterize the other theories.

This brief introduction will leave you with many more questions than answers, and, I hope, with a curiosity to read more. Having introduced a new body of theory, I would like to end by raising the question of how we use theories and how we evaluate them. Among academic psychologists the worth of a theory is often measured by how well it generates testable hypotheses. But teaching is a different practice than doing research; as a teacher I use theories to provoke thought. If the presentation of theory can stimulate students to think more about their own and other people's lives as well as the world in which they live, and to want to read and know more, then I view that theory as useful to me in my teaching. It is for that reason that I find these relational theories both interesting and important. My goal is not to identify the one truth or one theory that completely explains why women and men are the way they are, but to talk about ideas that might help us to better understand who we are, why we are that "way," and how we can collectively work toward social change and justice for all people.

I have found that relational theories provoke much interest, discussion, and debate in my classroom. Many students find that the descriptions of women and men ring true to their experience; some do not. Other students find pieces of different theories that they can use in understanding their own motivations and what they need in relationships. Some have found that these theories inform their ideas about how they would like to rear their own children and what kinds of capacities they wish to encourage in their daughters and sons. Some find a new understanding of the importance of equal parenting; others find a different appreciation for the health and value of lesbian relationships. Some students of color see themselves in these theories; some white students do not. Some men regretfully acknowledge that they have less developed relational skills than many women they know; others find that these theories explain some men they know but not themselves. There are multiple reactions one can have to this material; you may find the narrow focus on gender (to the exclusion of ethnicity and class) to be problematic and/or you may find the descriptions of gendered personality ring true to your experience. You might decide that explanations based on what is inside (like personality) are less compelling than social-constructionist accounts of what is outside. Or you might see how these relational theories attempt to account, however inadequately at this time, for how what is outside gets inside the psyche. What is most important to this teacher is that you think critically about it, read more, talk about the issues these theories raise, and then engage in social action that will change the world!

REFERENCES

AMERICAN PSYCHIATRIC ASSOCIATION. (1994). *Diagnostic and statistical manual of mental disorders* (4th ed.). Washington, DC: Author.

BELENKY, M., CLINCHY, B., GOLDBERGER, N., & TARULE, J. (1986). *Women's ways of knowing: The development of self, voice, and mind.* New York: Basic Books.

BENJAMIN, J. (1988). *The bonds of love: Psychoanalysis, feminism, and the problem of domination.* New York: Pantheon Books.

BOHAN, J. (1993). Regarding gender: Essentialism, constructionism, and feminist psychology. *Psychology of Women Quarterly, 17,* 5–21.

BOYD-FRANKLIN, N. (1989). *Black families in therapy: A multi-systems approach.* New York: Guilford Press.

BROWN, L. M. (1994). Standing in the crossfire: A response to Tavris, Gremmen, Lykes, Davis, and Contratto. *Feminism & Psychology, 4,* 382–394.

CHODOROW, N. (1978). *The reproduction of mothering: Psychoanalysis and the sociology of gender.* Berkeley: University of California Press.

CHODOROW, N. (1989). *Feminism and psychoanalytic theory.* New Haven: Yale University Press.

COLLINS, P. H. (1990). *Black feminist thought: Knowledge, consciousness, and the politics of empowerment.* Boston: Unwin Hyman.

CONTRATTO, S. (1986). Father's presence in women's psychological development. In J. Rabow, G. Platt, & M. Goldman (Eds.), *Advances in psychoanalytic sociology* (pp. 138–157). Malabar, FL: Krieger.

CONTRATTO, S. (1994). A too hasty marriage: Gilligan's developmental theory and its application to feminist clinical practice. *Feminism & Psychology, 4,* 367–377.

EICHENBAUM, L., & ORBACH, S. (1983). *Understanding women: A feminist psychoanalytic approach.* New York: Basic Books.

EICHENBAUM, L., & ORBACH, S. (1984). *What do women want: Exploding the myth of dependency.* New York: Berkeley Books.

EICHENBAUM, L., & ORBACH, S. (1987). *Between women: Love, envy, and competition in women's friendships.* London: Penguin Books.

FLAX, J. (1978). The conflict between nurturance and autonomy in mother-daughter relationships and within feminism. *Feminist Studies, 4,* 171–189.

GILLIGAN, C. (1982). *In a different voice: Psychological theory and women's development.* Cambridge, MA: Harvard University Press.

GILLIGAN, C. (1991). Women's psychological development: Implications for psychotherapy. In C. Gilligan, A. Rogers, & D. Tolman (Eds.), *Women, girls, and psychotherapy: Reframing resistance* (pp. 5–32). Binghamton, NY: Harrington Park Press.

GILLIGAN, C., ROGERS, A., & TOLMAN, D. (1991). *Women, girls, and psychotherapy: Reframing resistance.* Binghamton, NY: Harrington Park Press.

HARE-MUSTIN, R., & MARACEK, J. (1990). Gender and the meaning of difference: Postmodernism and psychology. In R. Hare-Mustin & J. Maracek (Eds.), *Making a difference: Psychology and the construction of gender* (pp. 22–64). New Haven: Yale University Press.

HOOKS, B. (1993). *Sisters of the yam: Black women and self-recovery.* Boston: South End Press.

JACK, D. (1991). *Silencing the self: Women and depression.* Cambridge, MA: Harvard University Press.

JORDAN, J. (1991). The meaning of mutuality. In J. Jordan, A. Kaplan, J. B. Miller, I. Stiver, & J. Surrey (Eds.), *Women's growth in connection: Writings from the Stone Center* (pp. 81–96). New York: Guilford Press.

JORDAN, J., KAPLAN, A., MILLER, J. B., STIVER, I., & SURREY, J. (1991). *Women's growth in connection: Writings from the Stone Center.* New York: Guilford Press.

KITZINGER, C. (1994). Editor's introduction—Sex differences: Feminist perspectives. *Feminism & Psychology, 4,* 501–506.

LERNER, H. (1988). *Women in therapy.* New York: Harper & Row.

LOTT, B. (1994). *Women's lives: Themes and variations in gender learning.* Pacific Grove, CA: Brooks/Cole Publishing Company.

MILLER, J. B. (1976). *Toward a new psychology of women.* Boston: Beacon Press.

MILLER, J. B. (1991). The development of women's sense of self. In J. Jordan, A. Kaplan, J. B. Miller, I. Stiver, & J. Surrey (Eds.), *Women's growth in connection: Writings from the Stone Center* (pp. 11–26). New York: Guilford Press.

SEGURA, D., & PIERCE, J. (1993). Chicano/a family structure and gender personality: Chodorow, familism, and psychoanalytic sociology revisited. *Signs: Journal of Women in Culture and Society, 19,* 62–91.

SPELLMAN, E. (1988). *Inessential woman: Problems of exclusion in feminist thought.* Boston: Beacon Press.

STIVER, I. (1991). Beyond the Oedipus complex: Mothers and daughters. In J. Jordan, A. Kaplan, J. B. Miller, I. Stiver, & J. Surrey (Eds.), *Women's growth in connection: Writings from the Stone Center* (pp. 97–121). New York: Guilford Press.

SURREY, J. (1991). The "self-in-relation": A theory of women's development. In J. Jordan, A. Kaplan, J. B. Miller, I. Stiver, & J. Surrey (Eds.), *Women's growth in connection: Writings from the Stone Center* (pp. 51–66). New York: Guilford Press.

TAVRIS, C. (1994). Reply to Brown and Gilligan. *Feminism & Psychology, 4,* 350–352.

UNGER, R., & CRAWFORD, M. (1992). *Women and gender: A feminist psychology.* New York: McGraw-Hill.

WESTKOTT, M. (1986). *The feminist legacy of Karen Horney.* New Haven: Yale University Press.

WESTKOTT, M. (1990, Fall). On the new psychology of women: A cautionary view. *Feminist Issues,* pp. 3–18.

SUGGESTED READINGS

CHODOROW, N. (1989). *Feminism and psychoanalytic theory.* New Haven: Yale University Press.

EICHENBAUM, L., & ORBACH, S. (1987). *Between women: Love, envy, and competition in women's friendships.* London: Penguin Books.

JORDAN, J., KAPLAN, A., MILLER, J. B., STIVER, I., & SURREY, J. (1991). *Women's growth in connection: Writings from the Stone Center.* New York: Guilford Press.

*N*ANCY P. GENERO *is Assistant Professor of Psychology at Wellesley College, where she teaches courses on cultural psychology and social identity with an emphasis on gender, race, and ethnicity. Dr. Genero is also a Senior Research Scholar at the Stone Center for Developmental Services and Studies, where since 1988 she has directed the program on the prevention of depression in mothers of young children.*

17

The Mothers' Project:

Affirming Realities through Peer Support

❖

T hink about a day in the life of a mother with a young child. Do words like hectic, rushed, frenzied, exhausting, or frustrating come to mind? Chances are fairly good that at least one of these descriptors would apply. Today most people recognize that being a mother is as challenging as it is rewarding. For example, the challenges of motherhood are often depicted in popular parenting and self-help magazines. Given the potential for stress among mothers of young children, it is not unusual to find articles with titles like "Stop the World So I Can Get Off for a While" (Olson & Banyard, 1993). In addition, the number of scholarly articles on motherhood has soared over the past decade. Topics such as coping with parenting hassles, postpartum depression, and maternal self-esteem have received a great deal of attention. The findings of studies appear to support what we intuitively know about motherhood: It is a profoundly complex social role that is laden with stereotypes and misconceptions. A perceptive mother of a young daughter observed, "Motherhood remains a kind of foreign country that the inexperienced know only through Gerber advertisements" (Pywell, 1994, p. 3). To comprehend more fully the meaning of this statement, it is necessary to consider the relationship between culture and motherhood.

This research is supported by grant MCJ-250608-01 to the author from the Maternal and Child Health Program (Title V, Social Security Act), Health Resources and Services Administration, Department of Health and Human Services and by the Stone Center for Developmental Services and Studies at Wellesley College. I'm indebted to my colleagues Jean Baker Miller, Lauren Heim Goldstein, Dea Angiolillo, Janet Surrey, Roberta Unger, and Larry Baldwin for their collaborative support of the Mothers' Project. Many thanks to the Wellesley student research assistants and to Robin Akert and Sarah Jane Penn for their review of an earlier draft of this paper. And, above all, I would like to express my appreciation to the study participants and staff of the Mothers' Project for their commitment and invaluable insights.

Much of what we know about motherhood comes from a mixture of cultural beliefs and personal observations. In general, cultural beliefs reflect shared understandings about social values, normative behaviors, and customs. Unfortunately, shared understandings are shaped by biased assumptions and stereotypic generalizations. We assume, for example, that all women desire to be mothers and that most mothers of young children have a supportive social network, which consists of a spouse, family members, and friends. Evidence to the contrary violates our idealized views of women, motherhood, and family life. Moreover, even if we tried to resist cultural stereotypes and relied on personal observations, our understanding of what it means to be a mother would still be relatively biased. Research tells us that personal observations lead to distorted thinking because information about others is often limited and unreliable. When judging others' behaviors, for example, we typically do not know whether a person's behavior is consistent from one situation to the next. For instance, the way a mother disciplines her 2-year-old child on a crowded city street is likely to be very different from the way she disciplines the child on a lone stretch of beach. An accurate assessment of mothers' disciplinary practices would require a considerable amount of cross-situational information about a great number of women.

What may be most problematic, however, is that there is no clear consensus about the cultural meanings and practices of motherhood. In fact, cultural messages about motherhood tend to be both contradictory and devaluing. The classic example is the importance that our society attaches to caring for children while providing little recognition for women's childcare efforts. In expressing her personal sense of frustration, one mother commented, "dropping into a ghetto of women whose labor was celebrated by Hallmark but forgotten by the GNP [gross national product], almost did me in" (Pywell, personal communication, January 5, 1995). Jacobs (1993) has suggested that such mixed messages are ubiquitous in our culture and place women in untenable positions.

In addition, our prototypic images of motherhood continue to change. Three decades ago, the cultural standard of motherhood bore a striking resemblance to "Donna Reed." Many of us marveled at the way in which this full-time mother and housewife maintained her composure and always managed to keep her two children and physician husband happy. Life was nearly perfect in Donna Reed's television family, and viewers willingly aspired to emulate such perfection. Given contemporary society's ambivalence about motherhood, a suitable prototype for the 1990s and beyond has not yet emerged. We know that although "Donna" is out, "Roseanne" is not quite in. In addition, contemporary role models (for example, the career woman who can do it all and balance her parenting obligations without a hitch) smack more of Madison Avenue hype than reality. So, how do mothers learn about themselves and women like them?

The psychological literature is replete with references to the importance of empathic feedback in cases where individuals lack validation and feel marginalized. In particular, the social support literature suggests that people benefit from interacting with others facing similar situations. Mutual support helps individuals to validate their feelings and provides them with opportunities to explore alternative coping strategies and solutions to problems at the individual and community level. As such, peer support takes on added significance for mothers of young children. In this lecture we will explore the ways in which narrow cultural views of motherhood marginalize the diverse realities of women. Furthermore, we will examine the underlying rationale and potential psychological benefits of the Mothers' Project, a peer support intervention for mothers of young children.

WOMEN AS CARETAKERS

Perhaps the single most universal characteristic of motherhood is that of *caretaker*. Women have traditionally cared for their children and have sought out the support of other women—mothers, sisters, relatives, and neighbors—to assist them in performing this role. Although men have assumed more parenting responsibilities in recent years and the number of mothers of young children in the work force is unprecedented in U.S. history, women continue to be the primary and often sole caretakers of the overwhelming majority of children in our society. The conflicting demands of parenting and work roles have brought the provision of day care and the equitable distribution of parenting responsibilities under greater scrutiny. However, the resolution of these issues remains largely in the hands of individual families rather than being part of the national agenda. As a result, whatever real gains have been made along these lines have not come under public view, and the shared perception of mothers as the primary caretakers of children remains relatively intact.

The idea that mothers are singularly responsible for the day-to-day care of their children is so deeply ingrained in our culture that attempts to deviate from this norm have resulted in litigation. In a recent court case in Michigan, a young unmarried mother planning to attend a university was sued by her daughter's father because the child would be placed in the university's day care program for 35 hours a week. A lower court granted the father custody of the child, despite the fact that the parents had never been married and the child had always been cared for by the mother. The case is now being appealed. Not surprisingly, the father plans to have his mother care for his child should he be awarded permanent custody. This dramatic example illustrates that as women struggle to redefine the practices of motherhood, they risk being stigmatized as irresponsible, selfish, and uncaring, and, in extreme cases, they face the loss of custody.

As mothers seek to accommodate the realities of their changing lifestyles, values, and problems, they continue to come up against the narrow lens through which society views them. Being a "good mother" is synonymous with the care of children. This cultural ideal excludes the different paths that women have chosen to become mothers and the obstacles that they face on a daily basis to maintain their status as mothers. By deemphasizing the diverse experiences of mothers in favor of a cultural ideal, women's abilities to understand and legitimize their own experiences as mothers are diminished.

If we take a closer look at who mothers are, we find a great deal of diversity. For example, some mothers are married, others are single or divorced; some mothers are employed full- or part-time, others do not work outside of the home; some mothers are heterosexual, others are lesbian or bisexual; some mothers are adolescents, others are middle-aged; some mothers are homeless, others are renters or home owners; and finally, some mothers live in extended family situations or single-parent families, others live in "nuclear" two-parent households. Some are able-bodied; others are disabled. There are biological mothers, adoptive mothers, and those who become mothers by technological means. Moreover, differences in income and education (Belle, 1990), immigration status (Vega, Kolody, & Valle, 1986), and race and ethnicity (Cannon, Higginbotham, & Guy, 1989) have a large impact on mothers' lives and their psychological well-being. For example, low-income mothers of young children are at greater risk for negative psychological outcomes than are their middle-class counterparts (Hall, Williams, & Greenberg, 1985). Although women's realities vary considerably, the social lens through which we view motherhood does not yet adequately reflect this diversity. Perhaps this lack of recognition reflects our biases regarding who should and should not be a mother. It also suggests that stereotypes are hard at work, limiting our perception to the cultural ideal.

The invisibility of mothers' experiences also makes the rest of us highly susceptible to arguments about what they should and should not do. For example, when the fictitious character Murphy Brown decided to have a child out of wedlock, the former vice president of the United States, Dan Quayle, responded by launching an inflammatory, nationally televised campaign about traditional American family values. The message was that having children out of wedlock is an act of moral turpitude and detrimental to the child's welfare and the country as a whole. Very few studies have actually documented the consequences of out-of-wedlock births with the exception of low-income and adolescent mothers, so it is very difficult to say how single motherhood has affected women, children, or society as a whole. Within this context of fear and ambivalence, the prevailing cultural view of motherhood remains largely disconnected from women's actual experiences as mothers (Phoenix, Woollett, & Lloyd, 1991).

TOWARD THE AFFIRMATION OF MOTHERHOOD

Where does all of this leave women who are raising young children? Clinicians and researchers have argued that without adequate emotional and material supports, caring for young children can drain necessary physical and psychological resources and increase the risk of depressive symptoms (Hall, 1990; Weissman & Klerman, 1987). Moreover, mixed cultural messages and the lack of validation for the diversity of motherhood can leave women feeling confused and depressed (McCartney & Phillips, 1988). The question is, How do we begin to formulate ways to support and affirm the realities of mothers of young children to promote positive psychological outcomes?

Studies of social support in diverse community samples of women with children under the age of 6 have suggested that having others in whom one can confide is particularly important in reducing the risk of depression (Brown & Harris, 1978). The idea that women prefer giving and receiving support through confiding relationships has been empirically established (Heller & Lakey, 1985). Confiding relationships may have added significance for mothers of young children for a number of different reasons. First, the potential for stress during the early parenting years may result in an increased need to normalize feelings of anger, confusion, inadequacy, shame, and vulnerability. In the presence of confiding relationships, the validation of these feelings may become a source of psychological growth and empowerment. On the other hand, in the absence of such relationships, these feelings could lead to a diminished capacity to cope and a lowering of self-esteem.

In addition, as a process of normative adult development, motherhood involves a series of complex psychological changes. It is a major life transition that invariably transforms one's sense of identity and personal attitudes. For example, the busy senior executive who is also now the mother of a 3-year-old, is not only grappling with managing her many obligations, she is also trying to understand how being a mother has fundamentally changed her. Beliefs she might have had growing up about how one should care for a child may change when she is confronted with long working hours and extensive business trips. How will she cope?

Modifying views about one's self-concept and attitudes takes place within a context of relationships. Early theorists used the metaphor "the looking-glass self" to call attention to the importance of others in shaping a person's identity (Cooley, 1902). We often learn about aspects of our identity through conversations and shared activities with others. In addition, others' attitudes may affirm or challenge our views about important personal and social issues. Thus, in addition to normalizing intense feelings, confidants may provide a reasonably safe and feasible way to explore new personal identities and examine our views.

As mothers of young children experience changing identities, attitudes, and needs, they may also seek to renegotiate relationships with spouses, family, friends, and coworkers. Particularly problematic are spouses with negative attitudes toward childcare, friends with whom they no longer have much in common, and coworkers who resent mothers' often unpredictable work schedules. In addition, mothers may also find it necessary to sever old ties and integrate new relationships into their lives (Antonucci & Mikus, 1988). In the presence of confidante support, the negative impact of these relationship shifts and disruptions can be normalized to reduce feelings of guilt, alienation, and isolation.

When one considers the magnitude of the demands and developmental tasks associated with motherhood, the need for confiding support raises a number of other issues. In this case, who are the best providers of confiding support for mothers of young children, and typically, how accessible are such people? Research on maternal satisfaction and confiding support has suggested that women with children between the ages of 1 and 6 seek friendships with women in similar situations (that is, peer support) to share their understandings about motherhood (Crnic & Greenberg, 1990). In exploring the significance of friendships between mothers, Pywell (1994) describes the experiences of a close friend:

> When I tried to talk about how crazy I get around discipline problems my single friend sat back and said, "There's something really wrong with that. I think you should get professional help." I thought, God, maybe I'm a much worse mother than I thought! . . . Finally I forced myself to talk about the same tensions between my daughter and me with a women I respect who has two children. She laughed. She made a couple of suggestions. But more important, she knew what it meant to have a complicated, contradictory, powerful emotional response to your kid. She didn't treat it like pathology. (p. 4)

Unfortunately, many mothers of young children have limited access to confiding peer relationships outside of their own families. To some extent, the demands of motherhood account for their inability to establish quality relationships with their peers. If women do have friends, these relationships can take valuable time away from their children. With little time to socialize and with few structured ways within communities to bring women together, mothers of young children can find themselves dependent on family members for all of their support needs. In cases where there are few opportunities for meaningful peer interactions, the susceptibility to depression can increase.

THE DYNAMICS OF PEER SUPPORT

Keeping in mind that confiding peer support among mothers of young children is particularly important in reducing the risk of depression, my colleagues and I embarked on a social intervention program to increase mothers' access to peers. As part of our research, we established the Mothers' Project—a peer support program for mothers with children ages 1 through 6. The intervention was designed to affirm mothers' realities, promote a sense of community, and reduce the risk of depressive symptoms. Social support theorists and others have suggested that interventions with a focus on enlarging people's community networks can be especially beneficial to those who may be socially isolated or marginalized and to those whose networks may not provide adequate access to specific types of support (Gottlieb, 1981). The Mothers' Project acknowledged the difficulties mothers experience in developing and maintaining confiding peer relationships, and it facilitated meaningful contact with a peer group over a six-month period.

Although the intervention is based on social support research findings, its conceptual basis is rooted in a gender-specific framework that acknowledges the centrality of relationships in women's lives (Belenky, Clinchy, Goldberger, & Tarule, 1986; Gilligan, 1982; Miller, 1976). According to this theoretical perspective, women's life activities are relational, that is, embedded within a context of relationships (Miller, 1988). As a consequence, women derive knowledge about themselves and develop their psychological capacities in connection with rather than separation from others (Jordan, Kaplan, Miller, Stiver, & Surrey, 1991). A relational perspective of the psychology of women suggests that coping with developmental transitions occurs through mutual participation in relationships. The term "mutuality" refers to the bidirectional movement of feelings, thoughts, and activity between persons (Genero, Miller, Surrey, & Baldwin, 1992). Jordan (1986) has suggested that mutual participation in relationships involves "openness to influence, emotional availability, and a constantly changing pattern of responding to and affecting the other's state" (p. 1). In part, this participatory process also involves the co-construction of meaning between individuals. As Duck (1994) has suggested, relationships provide the means through which we continually interpret, organize, transform, and assimilate each other's experiences.

In describing the benefits associated with mutuality, Miller (1988) pointed out at least five positive outcomes. Both individuals in a relationship acquire an increased knowledge of self and the other, gain a greater sense of self-worth and validation, experience an increased sense of vitality, feel more able to take action, and may ultimately desire connection with others. As a direct consequence, mutual participation promotes the growth of individuals as well as the relationship. Miller (1988) has referred to the salutary effects of this interactive process as "mutual psychological development." The impact of cultural influences on mutuality and resiliency are currently being explored (Genero, in press). Adverse psychological outcomes such as depression can be traced to processes that weaken, subvert, and violate one's ability to form and sustain mutual relationships (Jack, 1987; Stiver & Miller, 1988).

By explicitly integrating the concept of mutual psychological development into the Mothers' Project, we went into the field with specific assumptions and ideas about peer relationships. As Stein (1991) has noted, "psychologists working at the dyadic level must be particularly aware of the premises upon which they base their intervention and its evaluation" (p. 95). Specifically, the Mothers' Project is based on the following two assumptions. The first is that confiding peer support will provide mothers of young children with a unique validation experience, one that will affirm their diverse realities. The second assumption is that mutual interchanges between peers will promote psychological functioning and growth. By so doing, the risks associated with depression will be minimized. Building on these premises, we identified four major relational elements: mutual validation, empathy, supportive engagement, and expressiveness. Validation involves the sharing of daily experiences and the normalization of intense feelings. Empathy refers to the shared flow of thoughts and feelings between individuals. Supportive engagement is the focusing on one another in a meaningful way. Finally, the term "expressiveness" emphasizes the interactive and confiding nature of peer support (Lin, 1986).

IMPLEMENTATION OF THE MOTHERS' PROJECT

The level of awareness, enthusiasm, and care with which we entered the field did not minimize the number of difficult research and program implementation issues we had to address. Problems such as creating a program that participants would not find burdensome or exclusionary, matching the peer dyads, and retaining study participants over the six-month study period were formidable indeed. The logistics of promoting the relationship between the program partners without excessive staff interference were particularly challenging. In our study, program partners were assigned on the basis of geographical proximity and maternal age to increase accessibility and similarity. As in other peer support interventions, telephone calls were the primary mode of contact. The dyads were asked to "check in" with each other two to three times per week. Pairs were free to decide between themselves how and when contact would be made.

In addition to phone contact, peer dyads were expected to attend seven structured dyad meetings, which were conducted by trained staff facilitators. These structured meetings provided partners with opportunities for in-person contact. At each meeting, facilitators provided information and guidance to participants about issues of establishing, maintaining, and negotiating differences in their peer dyads. Program partner exercises emphasized the following three major points: (1) frequent peer contact is valuable; (2) relationships develop uniquely—"there is no right way"; and (3) dyads are not expected to "solve" each others' problems. Thus, the overall goals of the structured meetings were to increase pair interactions, validate women's relational capacities, recognize the difficulties and demands of motherhood, instill confidence in participants to create peer relationships, and reduce anxiety about participating in the study. Meetings were also designed to provide informal contact between dyads. Mothers usually sat in small groups of four, which allowed for animated discussions.

The value of the Mother's Project was not limited to promoting peer relationships between mothers. It also provided an opportunity to collect research data on the psychological well-being of a large number of program participants. Through these data, we sought to evaluate systematically the effectiveness of the intervention program. To achieve our research goals, we collected both quantitative and qualitative data over the six-month period. Questionnaires elicited general information about participants' social support networks, self-esteem, mastery, interpersonal functioning, maternal satisfaction, depression, and self-report physical health status. Telephone interviews were utilized to gather data about the mothers' experiences with their peers, and in particular, the process of relationship development and frequency and duration of contact.

After four months of participation in the program, the mutual quality of the peer dyads was assessed using the Mutual Psychological Development Questionnaire (Genero et al., 1992). The questionnaire is structured to encourage respondents' perspective-taking: that is, to contemplate what she and the other person in the relationship might do during a meaningful conversation in response to a set of 22 items. Sample items include "pick up on my feelings," "be receptive," and "feel like we're getting nowhere." In a previous study (Genero, et al., 1992), we found that adequacy of social support, relationship satisfaction, and relationship cohesion were significantly predictive of mutuality. We also found that mutuality is negatively correlated with depressive symptoms in women.

L*EARNING FROM MOTHERS OF YOUNG CHILDREN*

The following data were generated from a sample of 55 predominantly middle-class women who participated in the peer support intervention. The mean age of respondents was 31 years (SD = 4.74); 73 percent were married, 11 percent had never been married, and 16 percent were either separated or divorced. The racial and ethnic composition of the sample was white (73 percent), African American (9 percent), Latina (14 percent), and "other" (2 percent). A majority of the women had a college education (58 percent), and most had only one child (56 percent). A majority were also employed outside of the home (78 percent).

TABLE 1

Most Frequent Topics of Conversation ($N = 55$)

Topics	Women endorsing topic (%)
Children	88
Day-to-day routines	73
Work	68
Parenting demands	63
Spouse/boyfriend	50
Health	50
Recreational activities	41
Friends	38
Other relatives	36
Money	29

In keeping with previous research, we found that a relatively high percentage of program partners reported talking most often about their children, daily routines, work, and parenting demands (see Table 1).

Using an adjective checklist, respondents also reported on the positive and negative qualities of their conversations. A significant number found their conversations to be friendly, relaxed, and supportive, and less frequently some women reported that their conversations were rushed and superficial (see Table 2).

The exit interviews, which were conducted at the end of the study, provided participants with an opportunity to express their thoughts and feelings about the peer experience. These qualitative data provided an understanding of the challenges and benefits of the intervention from the perspective of the participant. With regard to the challenges, women most often noted that it was difficult to bridge lifestyle differences and time constraints. As one respondent noted, "Some pairs didn't click. I might have wanted to continue a relationship with someone I liked better." It was also not uncommon for women to speak of incompatibility owing to differences in the ages and sex of their children. In one woman's words, "Our children's ages were off, so it was a little difficult."

However, a considerable number of respondents were surprised to find that they could transcend differences with their program partner. The following comments are illustrative:

"She was very different—someone I might not otherwise have met. It was refreshing."

"There are things you can talk about with someone with whom you have no history."

"Nice to have someone to talk to a couple of times a week to touch base who is not regularly in your life."

TABLE 2

Frequency of Positive and Negative Qualities of Conversation ($N = 55$)

Qualities	Women endorsing quality (%)
Positive	
Friendly	73
Relaxed	71
Supportive	63
Enjoyable	61
Attentive	59
Open	52
Easy-going	50
Negative	
Rushed	18
Superficial	13
Impersonal	9
Strained	9
Uptight	5
Judgmental	5
Difficult	5
Boring	5

"I like meeting her and her family and learning about her culture, which was different from mine."

We were particularly interested in exploring the ways in which program partners provided validation and affirmed their realities. The following statements reflect these processes and mutual quality of their interchanges:

"I could talk about my kids and family, and it was OK—it's what our lives are all about. I didn't worry if I was boring."

"Someone to bounce my ideas off. Specifically ideas about child rearing and things that are more intimate and harder to discuss."

"When you have kids and are home alone, you think you're the only one feeling overwhelmed, alone, and upset. Now I don't feel guilty. I'm not the only one."

"Feel validated as 'me' and not just someone's 'mom.'"

"Felt just as good to listen to my partner as to vent my own frustrations; helped to hear someone else speak about the things I was struggling with."

Although these statements suggest that participants derived some benefits from the program, analyses of the impact of the intervention remain preliminary. As we continue to sift through the data, we will explore the role of mutuality in determining psychological outcomes. For example, we are interested in knowing whether women who rated their peer experience as being highly mutual had significantly lower depression scores at posttest than women with lower mutuality scores. In addition, the follow-up data will enable us to answer the question of whether peers who perceived their relationship as mutual during the intervention continued their contact voluntarily beyond the six-month study period.

Ultimately, the success of intervention programs for mothers of young children resides in our ability to comprehend the realities of motherhood. Everyday parenting experiences, developmental issues, relationship concerns, and demographic factors must be understood against a backdrop of cultural beliefs and values that are relatively out of tune with many women's lives. Moreover, women's knowledge about relationships and the significance of mutual psychological development must be integrated into social support programs that are designed to meet their needs. As we continue to learn more about the risks associated with depression in mothers of young children, it is clear that a focus on the mutual and interactive nature of adaptation is essential. The psychological benefits of women talking to women about who they are and what they do remains largely understudied. The task of future researchers is to continue to explore the diverse ways in which women make sense of their experiences as mothers, and how they utilize these meanings to reap the rewards of motherhood that rightfully belong to them.

REFERENCES

Antonucci, T. C., & Mikus, K. (1988). The power of parenthood: Personality and attitudinal changes during the transition to parenthood. In G. Y. Michaels & W. A. Goldberg (Eds.), *The transition to parenthood: Current theory and research* (pp. 62–84). Cambridge, England: Cambridge University Press.

Belenky, M. F., Clinchy, B. M., Goldberger, N. R., & Tarule, J. M. (1986). *Women's ways of knowing: The development of self, voice, and mind.* New York: Basic Books.

Belle, D. (1990). Poverty and women's health. *American Psychologist, 45,* 385–389.

Brown, G. W., & Harris, T. O. (1978). *Social origins of depression.* London: Tavistock Publications.

Cannon, L. W., Higginbotham, E., & Guy, R. F. (1989). *Depression among women: Exploring the effects of race, class, and gender.* Memphis, TN: Center for Research on Women, Memphis State University.

Cooley, C. H. (1902). *Human nature and the social order.* New York: Scribner.

Crnic, K. A., & Greenberg, M. T. (1990). Minor parenting stresses with young children. *Child Development, 54,* 1628–1637.

Duck, S. (1994). *Meaningful relationships: Talking, sense, and relating.* Newbury Park, CA: Sage.

GENERO, N. P. (in press). Culture, resiliency, and mutual psychological development. In H. I. McCubbin, E. A. Thompson, A. I. Thompson, & J. E. Fromer (Eds.), *Resiliency in ethnic minority families: Vol. 1. Native and immigrant American families.* Madison: University of Wisconsin System.

GENERO, N. P., MILLER, J. B., SURREY, J., & BALDWIN, L. M. (1992). Measuring perceived mutuality in close relationships: Validation of the mutual psychological development questionnaire. *Journal of Family Psychology, 6,* 36–48.

GILLIGAN, C. (1982). *In a different voice: Psychological theory and women's development.* Cambridge, MA: Harvard University Press.

GOTTLIEB, B. H. (1981). *Social networks and social support.* Beverly Hills, CA: Sage.

HALL, L. A. (1990). Prevalence and correlates of depressive symptoms in mothers of young children. *Public Health Nursing, 7,* 71–79.

HALL, L. A., WILLIAMS, C. A., & GREENBERG, R. S. (1985). Supports, stressors, and depressive symptoms in low-income mothers of young children. *American Journal of Public Health, 75,* 518–522.

HELLER, K., & LAKEY, B. (1985). Perceived support and social interaction among friends and confidants. In I. G. Sarason & B. R. Sarason (Eds.), *Social support: Theory, research and applications* (pp. 287–300). Dordrecht, the Netherlands: Martinus Nijoff.

JACK, D. (1987). Self-in-relation theory. In R. Formanek & A. Gurian (Eds.), *Women and depression: A lifespan perspective* (pp. 41–45). New York: Springer.

JACOBS, R. H. (1993). *Be an outrageous older woman.* Manchester, CT: Knowledge, Ideas & Trends, Inc.

JORDAN, J. (1986). *The meaning of mutuality.* Work in Progress, No. 23. Wellesley, MA: Stone Center, Wellesley College.

JORDAN, J., KAPLAN, A. G., MILLER, J. B., STIVER, I. P., & SURREY, J. L. (1991). *Women's growth in connection: Writings from the Stone Center.* New York: Guilford Press.

LIN, N. (1986). Conceptualizing social support. In N. Lin, A. Dean, & W. Ensel (Eds.), *Social support, life events and depression* (pp. 17–29). Orlando, FL: Academic Press.

MCCARTNEY, K., & PHILLIPS, D. (1988). Motherhood and child care. In B. Birns & D. F. Hay (Eds.), *The different faces of motherhood* (pp. 157–179). New York: Plenum Press.

MILLER, J. B. (1976). *Toward a new psychology of women.* Boston: Beacon Press.

MILLER, J. B. (1988). *Connections, disconnections, and violations.* Work in Progress, No. 33. Wellesley, MA: Stone Center, Wellesley College.

OLSON, S. L., & BANYARD, V. (1993). "Stop the world so I can get off for a while": Sources of daily stress in the lives of low-income single mothers of young children. *Family Relations, 42,* 50–56.

PHOENIX, A., WOOLLETT, A., & LLOYD, E. (1991). *Motherhood: Meanings, practices, and ideologies.* London: Sage.

PYWELL, S. (1994). Friendship after kids. Manuscript under review.

STEIN, C. H. (1991). Peer support telephone dyads for elderly women: The wrong intervention or the wrong research? *American Journal of Community Psychology, 19,* 91–98.

STIVER, I. P., & MILLER, J. B. (1988). *From depression to sadness in women's psychotherapy.* Work in Progress, No. 36. Wellesley, MA: Stone Center, Wellesley College.

VEGA, W. A., KOLODY, B., & VALLE, J. R. (1986). The relationship of marital status, confidant support, and depression among Mexican immigrant women. *Journal of Marriage and the Family, 48,* 597–605.

WEISSMAN, M. M., & KLERMAN, G. (1987). Gender and depression. In R. Formanek & A. Gurian (Eds.), *Women and depression: A lifespan perspective* (pp. 3–15). New York: Springer.

SUGGESTED READINGS

BELLE, D. (1982). *Lives in stress: Women and depression.* Beverly Hills, CA: Sage.

COWAN, C. P., & COWAN, P. A. (1992). *When partners become parents.* New York: Basic Books.

HOBFOLL, S. E. (1986). *Stress, social support, and women.* New York: Harper & Row.

JORDAN, J. V., KAPLAN, A. G., MILLER, J. B., STIVER, I. P., & SURREY, J. L. (1991). *Women's growth in connection: Writings from the Stone Center.* New York: Guilford.

NANCY FELIPE RUSSO *is Professor of Psychology and Women's Studies at Arizona State University. Dr. Russo has taught the psychology of women since 1971. She served as President of the American Psychological Association's Division (35) on the Psychology of Women in 1989 and is the current editor of the journal* **Psychology of Women Quarterly**.

18

Understanding Emotional Responses after Abortion

❖

*D*o you know at least one person who has had an abortion? Most people do. This is not surprising given that about 1.5 million legal abortions are performed every year in the United States. Throughout history, abortion has been used by women of diverse class and ethnic backgrounds to time, space, and limit their childbearing. Nonetheless, women's access to abortion continues to be controversial. There are profound disagreements about religious, moral, and ethical issues related to abortion, disagreements that fuel intense public debates over laws and policies aimed at restricting women's access to this medical procedure. Although I will not focus on these moral and philosophical issues here, it is important to remember that our discussion of abortion takes place in a highly charged political context (see Butler & Walbert, 1992).

These debates are not confined to religious, moral, and ethical issues alone. Perhaps you have come across some variation of the argument that access to abortion should be restricted because abortion creates psychological problems for women. This argument is shaping state legislation. In an attempt to discourage women from choosing to terminate their pregnancies, laws have been passed in many states that force doctors to tell abortion patients that as a result of having an abortion, they may experience a variety of negative psychological symptoms, including guilt, anxiety, and depression—a "postabortion syndrome."

There is no scientific basis for such a syndrome. The argument that abortion is "legal, but not safe for your mental health" was developed after the political forces that opposed abortion were unable to make a case for the negative impact of abortion on physical health. Given that the risks of abortion are lower than the risks associated with childbirth, it's difficult to argue that a pregnant woman should choose childbirth over abortion out of concern for her physical health. How many of you have ever had a shot of penicillin? Your risk of death from that shot is higher than a woman's risk of death from having a first-trimester abortion.

But what about women's risk for *psychological* problems after abortion? Science cannot resolve moral issues—those depend on values—but it can answer testable questions about how people think, feel, and behave. Unlike many of the moral and ethical questions posed in abortion debates, the question of whether or not the experience of abortion is traumatic for women's mental health *is* testable by scientific methods. I will describe findings in the scientific literature related to women's postabortion emotional responses and the factors that shape those responses. At the end of this lecture, you should have a clearer understanding of the nature of the research findings and how they suggest that the argument itself may be undermining the mental health of women.

PSYCHOLOGICAL RESEARCH ON POSTABORTION EMOTIONAL RESPONSES

Whatever our opinion about the morality of abortion, psychologists have an ethical obligation to speak out when psychological findings are misrepresented, as currently happens all too often in abortion debates. Put most simply, contrary to the concerted efforts to convince the public of the existence of widespread and severe postabortion trauma, *there is no scientific evidence for the existence of such trauma, even though abortion occurs in a highly stressful context, that of unwanted pregnancy.* Although any individual piece of research may have specific flaws, the overwhelming body of scientific evidence, which is based on diverse samples, methods, and measurements, is consistent: For the majority of women, freely chosen legal abortion is not found to have severe or lasting negative psychological effects, especially when the abortion was conducted during the first trimester of pregnancy (Adler et al., 1990, 1992; Schwartz, 1986; Russo, 1992).

Does this mean that women are always "mentally healthy" after experiencing an abortion? No. Women's postabortion psychological responses vary. But the most important factor to consider in understanding them is psychological status *before* becoming pregnant. Pregnancy (wanted or unwanted) is a stressful life event, and it can exacerbate problems for women with histories of mental disorder (Schwartz, 1986). Psychological problems during and after pregnancy most often occur in women who have a history of psychological disorders, regardless of how the pregnancy is resolved (Hamilton, Parry, & Blumenthal, 1988).

Psychological health before becoming pregnant is not the only factor shaping postabortion responses. Other factors that predict women's mental health after abortion include the quality of her health care, the pregnancy's meaning to the woman, her comfort with her decision-making process, difficulty in deciding to have an abortion, termination of a pregnancy that was originally wanted, abortion in the second trimester of pregnancy, feeling coerced to have the abortion, not expecting to cope well with the abortion, and limited or no social support for the abortion decision (Adler et al., 1990, 1992).

But arguing that abortion is a risky option for a pregnant woman has little meaning without comparing that risk to her alternatives: having the child and keeping it or having the child and relinquishing it for adoption. The destructive impact of unwanted childbearing on the woman, her family, and society, is well documented (Dytrych, Matejcek, & Schuller, 1988; Russo, 1992). Little is known about the psychological effects of adoption. What is known suggests that it can involve substantial distress, and the predictors of that distress appear to be *similar* to those that predict distress after abortion. In studies that have compared psychological responses following abortion and term birth, the few differences found showed the positive effects to be associated with choice of abortion (Athanasiou, Oppel, Michaelson, Unger, & Yager, 1973; Russo & Zierk, 1992; Zabin, Hirsch, & Emerson, 1989).

For example, a nationwide study in Denmark examined the medical records of all women under 50 years of age—more than 1 million women. The researchers compared the rates of first admissions to psychiatric hospitals for women three months after birth and three months after having an abortion. They found that the rate of psychiatric hospitalization after abortion was about the same as that for giving birth—about 12 per 10,000 abortions or deliveries (David, 1985).

Similarly, a study in England found that risk for psychosis after pregnancy ending in birth did not differ statistically from such risk for women after having an abortion—the rates were 0.3 per 1,000 abortions and 1.7 per 1,000 deliveries, respectively (Brewer, 1977).

So, risk for severe psychological disorder after abortion is generally low and comparable to that of giving birth. But what about psychological distress that is severe enough to require treatment but not so severe that hospitalization is required? A number of studies in the United States have used psychological tests to assess various symptoms of psychopathology. Such studies report that levels of psychological distress after abortion are typically low, averaging below the clinical cutoff scores that signal the presence of a clinical disorder. For example, psychologist Brenda Major and her colleagues (1985), found that abortion patients averaged scores of 4.17 on the short form of the Beck Depression Inventory immediately after the abortion, and 1.97 three weeks later. Scores below 5 on that scale are considered *nondepressed.*

So how do we explain the fact that there are many women who are depressed or anxious and who have had abortions? First, it should be kept in mind that at any particular moment in time a certain percentage of women in the U.S. population have psychological problems whether or not they have an abortion. In addition, we must remember that abortion occurs in the context of an unwanted pregnancy—a stressful and negative life event. A woman's responses after resolving her pregnancy reflect the coping resources—physical, psychological, social, and financial—she has for dealing with such negative events (Adler et al., 1990, 1992).

Research that I conducted with my student Kristin Zierk confirmed that access to coping resources, not the experience of abortion, explains variation in women's postabortion emotional responses. Our study, which examined women's self-esteem as a measure of their well-being, was based on a national sample of 5,295 women aged 14 to 24 in 1979 who were interviewed annually for eight years (1979–1987). Our findings were incompatible with the assertion of the existence of severe and widespread negative effects of abortion. In fact, women who had one abortion had higher self-esteem than women who did not!

To understand the effects of abortion and childbearing in context, we examined the 1987 self-esteem of women who had no abortions before 1980, using multivariate statistical analyses to control for the effects of previous levels of self-esteem (measured in 1980), coping resources (education, employment, income, presence of spouse), abortion, and childbearing. What happened when previous levels of self-esteem, coping resources, childbearing, and abortion variables were all controlled? Well, the most important predictor of well-being in 1987 was well-being in 1980—that is, well-being *before* any abortions occurred. In addition, being employed, having a higher income, having more years of education, and bearing fewer children all continued to have significant and independent relationships to increased well-being. Abortion did not make a difference. Neither did marriage, but that's a story that will have to wait until happy and unhappy marriages can be identified (Russo & Zierk, 1992). By the way, I analyzed the data separately for Black women and white women and found the pattern of results to be similar for both groups.

Contrary to the stereotypes of abortion patients as seeking to avoid childbearing responsibilities and to have carefree lifestyles, we found that one out of three of the women who had had abortions had more than two children. Women having abortions had larger family sizes and were more likely to have unwanted children than other women. We concluded that abortion becomes linked to women's well-being through its role in reducing stress by reducing family size and increasing women's access to resources (i.e., ability to become employed, attain more education, and earn a higher income). When it comes down to comparing a pregnant woman's options—having an abortion or bearing and raising a child—the latter appears to be the more hazardous alternative as far as mental health is concerned (unfortunately, there is little evidence on the experience of relinquishing one's child for adoption).

What about the argument that women may not be distressed after having an abortion but in the long run they will suffer a delayed posttraumatic stress reaction? Evidence that examines the quality of emotional responses after resolving an unwanted pregnancy is incompatible with such a diagnosis.

Let's examine research on the *combination* of types of emotional responses a women has after having an abortion. Most women show a combination of positive and negative postabortion responses. However, positive emotions (relief and happiness) are more often experienced and experienced more strongly than negative emotions (shame, fear of disapproval, guilt, regret, anxiety, and depression). This is true both immediately after the abortion as well as in the months following (Adler, 1975; Lazarus, 1985; Osofsky & Osofsky, 1972).

For example, Nancy Adler (1975) studied positive and negative emotions expressed by women over two to three months following an abortion. Women rated how much they felt each emotion from 1 ("not at all") to 4 ("to a considerable degree"). Positive emotions were felt most intensely, averaging 3.96 on the 4-point scale. Ratings of negative responses clustered into two groups—internally based and socially based emotions—and ranged from an average of 2.26 for the emotions that were internally based (anger, anxiety, depression, doubt, and regret) to 1.81 for socially based emotions (fear of disapproval, guilt, and shame). In other words, most women have ambivalent feelings after having an abortion, but they are mostly satisfied, relieved, and happy. Focusing on negative feelings and building a portrait of negative emotional outcomes for abortion patients is a gross distortion of the reality of the experience for most women.

Research on the *timing* of the emotional responses also brings the reality of a "postabortion syndrome" in question. While reviewing the findings, keep in mind that studies of other life stressors suggest that women who show no evidence of severe negative responses after a stressful event are unlikely to subsequently develop significant psychological problems in conjunction with that event (Wortman & Silver, 1989).

Several studies have found that women's anxiety and depression levels are highest *before* their abortion, drop immediately afterward, and continue dropping for several weeks until they are lower than they were *before* the abortion (Cohen & Roth, 1984; Major, Mueller, & Hildebrandt, 1985; Zabin, Hirsch, & Emerson, 1989). This is not the pattern found in response to traumatic events and is inconsistent with the idea that abortion is a primary source of psychic trauma. On the contrary, this pattern suggests that *it is the unwanted pregnancy that is the primary source of distress for abortion patients.*

Nonetheless, some people argue that a time period of a few months is too short for postabortion distress to emerge—given more time, postabortion syndrome will develop, just as posttraumatic stress syndrome identified in Vietnam veterans and rape victims has been found to develop over time. (*Note:* This argument does ignore the fact that Vietnam veterans and rape victims do not report being relieved and happy immediately after their traumatic experiences.) Most studies of abortion patients have focused on early responses, with two years being the longest period of direct follow up (Adler et al., 1990, 1992). However, recall that Kristin Zierk and I (1992) examined the well-being of women who were followed over eight years. Time since abortion was not related to well-being over that eight-year time period, even when the sample was split and women who had abortions more than seven years previously were examined.

Finally, ask yourself, What exactly does it mean to say that the abortion experience *per se* is the "cause" of negative postabortion psychological responses. What about research that suggests that a woman's postabortion emotional problems can lie more in her situation than in her personal attributes? Recall that in the study by Nancy Adler (1975) described above, negative emotions after abortion clustered into two categories: internally based and socially based. These emotions were found to stem from different things. Internally based negative emotions were found to be related to the personal meaning of the pregnancy for the woman, whereas socially based negative emotions were related to the woman's social environment. For example, when age was controlled, unmarried women experienced socially based negative emotions more strongly than married women. Women who attended church more frequently were also more likely to express stronger socially based negative emotions. These findings point to factors *other* than the abortion experience *per se* as determinants of postabortion emotional status and remind us that it is possible to make the experience of abortion a traumatic event by ostracizing women and making them feel guilt and shame.

THE HARM OF CONSTRUCTING POSTABORTION SYNDROME

So what if anti-abortion activists try to deter women from seeking abortion by defining women's psychological responses after having an abortion as a mental disorder? You might argue that if fear of death, severe legal penalties, and unsafe conditions have not deterred women from seeking abortion around the world, psychological problems in some distant postabortion future are probably not going to be much of a deterrent.

One problem is that the argument can itself create psychological problems for women. True, legal abortion experience *per se* is not an important risk factor for severe psychopathology in women. But, as you have learned, some women are at higher risk for negative postabortion emotional responses, particularly if they have a history of psychological disorder. *It is possible to undermine their coping mechanisms and damage their mental health.* Experimental work has demonstrated that belief in one's ability to cope after the abortion is *causally* linked to postabortion emotional responses (Mueller & Major, 1989). The inaccurate portrayal of abortion as having widespread severe negative psychological effects could subvert women's mental health by undermining the positive coping expectancies that are associated with beneficial mental health outcomes after abortion. Social ostracism and harassment of women seeking abortion could also have harmful mental health effects, through inducing negative socially based emotions, undermining social support, and encouraging unwanted childbearing.

It is important to recognize that people do continually reconstruct and reinterpret past events in the light of subsequent experiences. Under stressful and tragic circumstances ideas of punishment and retribution surface, even among people who do not consider themselves especially religious. As Jeanne Lemkau (1988) has observed, under stressful conditions such as infertility, infant death, or catastrophic illness, which are associated with depressed mood and cognitive distortions, it is possible for a woman to make highly idiosyncratic causal connections to an earlier abortion as well as other events in her life history.

Such connections and their associated feelings need to be explored in therapy without prejudging their underlying causality. All people can experience sadness or depressed mood at times. But if a woman is severely anxious or depressed or has other symptoms of psychological distress it is important that she see a qualified, licensed mental health professional (Lemkau, 1988).

Because of their psychological, social, and environmental circumstances, women are at higher risk for depression than men (McGrath, Keita, Strickland, & Russo, 1990). One of the many factors that contributes to that higher risk is women's tendency to ruminate about things that bother them rather than to take instrumental action (Nolen-Hoeksema, 1990). Self-help groups have many useful benefits. However, when a woman is clinically depressed, merely talking to others who are sympathetic may only serve to perpetuate her depression, particularly if they are self-help groups that prejudge the woman's problems. It is thus possible for support groups that are not monitored by a qualified professional to contribute to prolonging clinical depression. Given that a history of mental disorder and expectancies for coping are associated with emotional problems after an abortion, focusing on the abortion itself rather than exploring the problems that preceded the pregnancy could impede the therapeutic process.

In this context, consider the words of Anne Speckhard, the person whose Ph.D. dissertation in sociology has been the foundation for constructing the myth of postabortion syndrome. She describes how prolife groups program negative postabortion responses:

> In these social systems [prolife and fundamentalist religious groups] subjects found members who allowed them to freely discuss their feelings of grief, guilt, loneliness, anger, and despair. . . . Members of these systems were not averse to discussing the details of the abortion experience with particular

reference to concern over pain that the fetus may have experienced and damage that may have occurred to the subjects' reproductive organs. (pp. 139–140)

Speckhard herself points out that as a result of their interactions with prolife groups, the women in this sample increasingly came to view abortion as the taking of a life.

They became increasingly angry about the way abortion had been explained to them. . . . Many learned a great deal from pro-life groups about fetal development which initially increased their guilt, grief, and anger. (pp. 140–41)

It is clear that these women were highly distressed. Some even had hallucinations. A disproportionate number had very late abortions. How these women would have felt had they been to a qualified and understanding mental health professional is unknown. What we can say is that neither their characteristics nor their experience are typical of the majority of abortion patients. (Ironically, many apparently even had abortions when abortion was illegal.)

In discussing the mental health risks of abortion and its alternatives, we must remember that even if a woman comes to accept and love a child who is born after an unplanned and unwanted pregnancy, *the importance of women's ability to space and limit the number of their children for physical and mental health should not be underestimated.* I don't have the space to summarize this literature—Jody Horn and I have summarized it elsewhere (Russo & Horn, 1994). But I want to make two points: one about childbirth intervals and one about family size.

We do not sufficiently appreciate how important spacing children is for the physical and mental health of a woman and her family. Small childbirth intervals are associated with many negative health outcomes. It is estimated that avoiding birth intervals of less than two years would reduce the risk of low birth weight and neonatal death from *5 to 10 percent* below its current level (Miller, 1991). Close child-spacing intervals are also *predictive* of child abuse (Altemeier, O'Connor, Vietze, Sandler, & Sherrod, 1984; Zuravin, 1987, 1988).

Abortion's role in reducing stress from potentially close child spacing is also not sufficiently appreciated. Yet research that my students and I have conducted has shown that its role is substantial. Consider: In 1987, nearly half of abortion patients were already mothers. Nearly one in four of those mothers who sought an abortion had a child under 2 years of age (Russo, Horn, & Schwartz, 1992). Among such mothers 20 years of age or older, more than one out of five had a child under 2 years of age; among teenage mothers seeking abortion that year, the figure was two out of three. Abortion's role in limiting family size was also apparent. More than half of mothers seeking abortion had two or more children. These mothers obviously had multiple sources of stress in their lives. Unfortunately, the stressors were not matched by high levels of coping resources: 71 percent of these mothers were unmarried, and 39 percent had family incomes below the poverty line (Russo, Horn, & Tromp, 1993).

By the way, have you ever heard the claim that the increase in reports of child abuse after *Roe vs. Wade* is evidence that abortion contributes to child abuse? Be aware that the child abuse reporting system was not even *instituted* until after *Roe vs. Wade,* so such comparisons are inappropriate. In reality, two of the strongest predictors of future child abuse are (1) having two or more children under age 5 and (2) less than a 12-month space between infants. Others include low self-image, unemployment, crowding, and large family size (Altemeier et al., 1984; Murphy, Orkow, & Nicola, 1985; Russo, 1992; Zuravin, 1987, 1988).

Why is it important to enable families to control their size? One does not have to have concerns about population issues to recognize the value of enabling women to control their childbearing. Larger family size is associated with social, educational, and economic disadvantages, including child abuse, antisocial behavior, delinquency, and criminality. Intelligence and academic achievement of children is inversely correlated with family size, and these effects seem to hold even when social class is controlled (Russo, 1992). Larger family size has been associated with feelings of powerlessness among women, a factor known to contribute to depression (McGrath, Keita, Strickland, & Russo, 1990). The association between female powerlessness and family size remains after controlling for use of contraception, age, education, husband's occupation, and family income (Morris & Sison, 1974). Family size is also negatively associated with women's self-esteem, even if education, income, and previous level of self-esteem (before having children) are controlled (Russo & Zierk, 1992).

A final comment: A point that is often left out of discussions of the mental health implications of restrictive abortion policies is consideration of the psychological effects of a woman's death from abortion on her family. The risk of death from a legal abortion may be less than that of a penicillin shot, but should abortion become illegal, the situation would change. Although I could find no empirical work on the subject, the reports of relatives of women who have died from abortions suggest that the event has long-lasting impact (Friedl, 1991).

> My earliest recollection is of my father standing at the head of [the dining room] table. I must have been four years old; my sister was two. . . . I can still see him [my father] standing there, and a woman with her dress on the floor. . . . That was my mother's death scene. . . . (p. 35)

> What makes me angriest about what happened to me is that everybody ignores the orphans. They don't even try to figure out how many children are orphaned by abortion, neither side, pro-life or pro-choice, not even a wild guess. (p. 38)

> When we get into it now . . . something will hit me and I get so emotional. I can't believe how strongly I feel. . . . It just tears me up. It never ceases to

amaze me that, when you talk about certain aspects of it, bang! It hits me. I'm not able to control it. But I'm sixty-six and a retired marine . . . I don't have to control anymore. (p. 39)

CONCLUSION AND IMPLICATIONS

In conclusion, bearing and raising a child is a private and personal decision considered by our society to require a deep, long-lasting commitment. When a child is unwanted, there are well-documented severe and negative health, social, and economic consequences for the child, the mother, her family, and society.

In contrast, having a legal abortion appears to be a relatively benign experience, particularly if it occurs in the first trimester. Postabortion syndrome is currently a myth—but it is a destructive myth that has the potential to become a reality through aggressive efforts to shame, ostracize, and intimidate abortion doctors and patients and to brainwash women into attributing their emotional problems to abortion. Effective strategies for enhancing a woman's mental health include promoting her feelings of personal control and self-efficacy and increasing her actual control over her important life choices (Major et al., 1990). Understanding the mental health implications of abortion and its alternatives means recognizing that abortion currently plays a critical role in enabling women to space and limit their childbearing. Denying women access to that effective tool without providing a similarly effective alternative is not likely to be a successful strategy, but it may have far-reaching and profound consequences to women, their families, and society. Ironically, the burdens of unwanted childbearing and its consequences will fall most heavily on those people least likely to have access to effective contraception or a voice in the making of the laws and policies affecting their reproductive alternatives—that is, women who are poor, ethnic minority, single, or young (Forrest, 1987).

What do you see as policy implications of such findings? There are many. Under current conditions, the effects of public policies that restrict women's access to abortion will be profound, widespread, and destructive. Policymakers and the public must learn to understand the realities of women's lives and appreciate the meaning of unwanted pregnancy and abortion from the pregnant woman's viewpoint. Unless effective and acceptable alternatives to abortion are developed, women will seek abortions to terminate unwanted pregnancies, whether or not safe and legal abortions are available. Developing such alternatives is absolutely essential and is something most (but admittedly, not all) people agree with, whether they call themselves pro-life or pro-choice.

Whatever our moral views on abortion, I hope that we will put women's mental health above religious and political agendas. I call on all of us to work together to ensure that misinformation in the service of policy debates is not used to undermine women's mental health. I hope that we will also work to ensure that every woman who is having psychological problems can obtain help from a qualified mental health professional who supports her choices and does not prejudge the causes of her symptoms.

REFERENCES

ADLER, N. E. (1975). Emotional responses of women following therapeutic abortion. *American Journal of Orthopsychiatry, 45*(3), 446-454.

ADLER, N. E., DAVID, H. P., MAJOR, B., ROTH, S., RUSSO, N. F., & WYATT, G. (1990). Psychological responses after abortion. *Science, 248*, 41-44.

ADLER, N. E., DAVID, H. P., MAJOR, B., ROTH, S. H., RUSSO, N. F., & WYATT, G. E. (1992). Psychological factors in abortion: A review. *American Psychologist, 47*, 1194-1204.

ALTEMEIER, W. A., O'CONNOR, S., VIETZE, P., SANDLER, H., & SHERROD, K. (1984). Prediction of child abuse: A prospective study of feasibility. *Child Abuse and Neglect, 8*, 393-400.

ATHANASIOU, R., OPPEL, W., MICHAELSON, L., UNGER, T., & YAGER, M. (1973). Psychiatric sequelae to term birth and induced early and late abortion: A longitudinal study. *Family Planning Perspectives, 5*, 227-231.

BREWER, C. (1977). Incidence of post-abortion psychosis: A prospective study. *British Medical Journal, 1*, 476-477.

BUTLER, J. D., & WALBERT, D. F. (Eds.). (1992). *Abortion, medicine, and the law,* 4th ed. New York: Facts on File Publications.

COHEN, L., & ROTH, S. (1984). Coping with abortion. *Journal of Human Stress, 10*(3), 140-145.

DAVID, H. P. (1985). Post-abortion and post-partum psychiatric hospitalization. In R. Porter & M. O'Connor (Eds.). *Abortion: Medical progress and social implications* (pp. 150-161). Ciba Foundation Symposium No. 45. London: Pitman.

DYTRYCH, Z., MATEJCEK, Z., & SCHULLER, V. (1988). *Born unwanted: Developmental effects of denied abortion.* New York: Springer Publishing Company.

FORREST, J. D. (1987). Unintended pregnancy among American women. *Family Planning Perspectives, 19*(2), 76-77.

FRIEDL, J. (1991). Jim Friedl. In A. Bonavoglia (Ed.). *The choices we made: Twenty-five women and men speak out about abortion* (pp. 35-39). New York: Random House.

HAMILTON, J. A., PARRY, B., & BLUMENTHAL, S. J. (1988). The menstrual cycle in context: I. Affective syndromes associated with reproductive hormonal changes. *Journal of Clinical Psychology, 49*, 474-480.

LAZARUS, A. (1985). Psychiatric sequelae of legalized first trimester abortion. *Journal of Psychosomatic Obstetrics and Gynecology, 4*, 141-150.

LEMKAU, J. P. (1988). Emotional sequelae of abortion: Implications for clinical practice. *Psychology of Women Quarterly, 12*, 461-472.

MAJOR, B., MUELLER, P., & HILDEBRANDT, K. (1985). Attributions, expectations and coping with abortion. *Journal of Personality and Social Psychology, 48*(3), 585-599.

MAJOR, B., COZZARELLI, C., SCIACCHITANO, A. M., COOPER, M. L., TESTA, M., & MUELLER, P. M. (1990). Perceived social support, self-efficacy, and adjustment to abortion. *Journal of Personality and Social Psychology, 59,* 452-463.

MCGRATH, E., KEITA, G. P., STRICKLAND, B. R., & RUSSO, N. F. (Eds.) (1990). *Women and depression: Risk factors and treatment issues.* Washington, DC: American Psychological Association.

MILLER, J. E. (1991). Birth intervals and perinatal health: An investigation of three hypotheses. *Family Planning Perspectives, 23*(2), 62-70.

MORRIS, N. M., & SISON, B. S. (1974). Correlates of female powerlessness: Parity, methods of birth control, pregnancy. *Journal of Marriage and the Family, 36,* 708-712.

MUELLER, P., & MAJOR, B. (1989). Self-blame, self-efficacy, and adjustment after abortion. *Journal of Personality and Social Psychology, 57,* 1059-1068.

MURPHY, S., ORKOW, B., & NICOLA, R. (1985). Prediction of child abuse and neglect: A prospective study. *Child Abuse and Neglect, 9,* 225-235.

NOLEN-HOEKSEMA, S. (1990). *Sex differences in depression.* Palo Alto, CA: Stanford University Press.

OSOFSKY, J. D., & OSOFSKY, H. (1972). The psychological reaction of patients to legalized abortion. *American Journal of Orthopsychiatry, 42,* 48-60.

RUSSO, N. F. (1992). Psychological aspects of unwanted pregnancy and its resolution. In J. D. Butler & D. F. Walbert (Eds.), *Abortion, medicine, and the law,* 4th ed. New York: Facts on File Publications.

RUSSO, N. F., & HORN, J. (1994). Unwanted pregnancy and its resolution: Options, issues. In J. Freeman (Ed.), *Women: A feminist perspective,* 5th ed. (pp. 47-64). Mountain View, CA: Mayfield Publishing.

RUSSO, N. F., & ZIERK, K. L. (1992). Abortion, childbearing, and women's well-being. *Professional Psychology: Research and Practice, 23,* 269-280.

RUSSO, N. F., HORN, J., & SCHWARTZ, R. (1992). U. S. abortion in context: Selected characteristics and motivations of women seeking abortions. *Journal of Social Issues, 48,* 182-201.

RUSSO, N. F., HORN, J., & TROMP, S. (1993). Childspacing intervals and abortion among blacks and whites: A brief report. *Women & Health, 20*(3), 43-52.

SCHWARTZ, R. A. (1986). Abortion on request: The psychiatric implications. In J. D. Butler & D. F. Walbert (Eds.), *Abortion, medicine, and the law,* 3d ed. (pp. 323-340). New York: Facts on File.

SPECKHARD, A. C. (1985). *The psycho-social aspects of stress following an abortion.* Unpublished doctoral dissertation, University of Minnesota.

WORTMAN, C. B., & SILVER, R. C. (1989). The myths of coping with loss. *Journal of Consulting and Clinical Psychology, 57,* 349–357.

ZABIN, L., HIRSCH, M. B., & EMERSON, M. R. (1989). When urban adolescents choose abortion: Effects on education, psychological status, and subsequent pregnancy. *Family Planning Perspectives, 21*(6), 248-255.

ZURAVIN, S. J. (1987). Unplanned pregnancies, family planning programs, and child maltreatment. *Family Relations,* 135-139.

ZURAVIN, S. J. (1988). Fertility patterns: Their relationship to child physical abuse and child neglect. *Journal of Marriage and the Family, 50,* 983-993.

S*UGGESTED READINGS*

ADLER, N. E., DAVID, H. P., MAJOR, B., ROTH, S. H., RUSSO, N. F., & WYATT, G. E. (1992). Psychological factors in abortion: A review. *American Psychologist, 47,* 1194-1204.

BONAVOGLIA, A. (Ed.) (1991). *The choices we made: Twenty-five women and men speak out about abortion.* New York: Random House.

LEMKAU, J. P. (1988). Emotional sequelae of abortion: Implications for clinical practice. *Psychology of Women Quarterly, 12,* 461-472.

RUSSO, N. F. (1992). Psychological aspects of unwanted pregnancy and its resolution. In J. D. Butler & D. F. Walbert (Eds.), *Abortion, medicine, and the law,* 4th ed. New York: Facts on File Publications.

*A*GNES N. O'CONNELL *is Professor of Psychology and Director of Community Psychology Programs at Montclair State University. Dr. O'Connell
has taught courses on the psychology of women since 1972 at Montclair,
Rutgers University, and the City University of New York. She is best known for
her work on women in the history of psychology for which she has won several
awards.*

19

Women in Psychology as Role Models:

Lives and Careers in Context

❖

Women's integral and active participation in the conception and evolution of psychology provides us with a very rich legacy of role models of achievement. Tracing and illuminating this legacy through the lives and careers of some exemplars helps us to better understand the impact of context on women's struggle toward acknowledgment and equality, provides a new vision of women as major contributors and notable role models, and serves as an essential source of inspiration and empowerment.

REFLECTING AND SHAPING THE PROFESSIONAL AND SOCIETAL CONTEXTS

In analyzing women's lives and careers, we are confronted with the fact that history, knowledge, and meaning are human constructions. For more than 20 years, as I have worked to record, preserve, and interpret women's contributions in psychology, I have appreciated anew time after time how important institutions, social relations, and networks are in shaping the field and defining which activities

Thanks to the editors and reviewers of this book and to Mary Anne Hone and Ira Sugarman for their comments on an earlier version of this chapter.

have status and worth and which do not. These definitions in large measure are developed and maintained by those in control of the field.

Too often women have been obliged to create their lives within restrictive social, historical, and professional contexts. Despite these restrictions, many have defined their identities with resilience against formidable forces. Examination of the lives, careers, and contributions of women to the field of psychology reveals the links between women's status and roles in the larger social context and in psychology. The stereotyping, devaluation, and invisibility of women in the larger society have been reflected in psychology. In a very real sense, the opportunities for women were shaped by their social and historical contexts; nonetheless, women clearly were and are active agents, seizing the opportunities that are open to them and creating new opportunities where none existed (O'Connell, 1983, 1988; Russo & O'Connell, 1980).

A NEW VISION OF WOMEN IN PSYCHOLOGY

When we look carefully we discover that women have made significant contributions to the cornerstones of psychology since its inception. Through recognition of women's integral and active involvement in the origins and development of psychology, a new vision of women in society arises. This new vision illuminates women as important contributors and significant role models and celebrates their power.

Role models are needed to aid in the acculturation of women into professional roles—to aid in clarifying how to enter and live successfully in the world of achievement. Further, role models have the power to inspire us toward higher goals, and they serve as sources of strength and guidance. The professional advantages of same-sex role models in the lives of prominent women have been well documented, and these advantages can be realized by us all as we read about distinguished women.

Women's heritage in psychology is extensive and spans the many varied subdisciplines. Women have made important contributions to theoretical and applied areas of psychology, including cognitive, developmental, experimental, industrial and organizational, physiological, social, testing, and methodology, as well as to the institutions of psychology.

It is not widely known, for example, that among Sigmund Freud's inner circle were women who were integral and instrumental participants in the development and refinement of psychoanalysis. These women included among others Lou Andreas-Salome (1861–1937), Marie Bonapart (1882–1962), Ruth Mack Brunswick (1897–1946), Anna Freud (1895–1982), and Dorothy Burlingham (1891–1979). Early contributors to the development of psychoanalysis and psychotherapy include Helene Deutsch (1884–1982), Erika Fromm (b. 1910), Karen Horney (1885–1952), Hermine von Hug-Hellmuth (1871–1924), Melanie Klein (1882–1960), Margaret

Mahler (1897–1985), and Clara Thompson (1893–1958) (Freeman & Strean, 1987; Lerman, 1986; Roazen, 1975; Russo & O'Connell, 1992). How many of these contributors have you studied in your classes?

ROLE MODELS AS SOURCES OF INSPIRATION

One of my favorite early contributors to psychotherapy is Karen Horney (1885–1952). She is a role model of courage, resilience, and intelligence. Born and raised in Germany, she overcame her father's reluctance to finance her premedical education. When she promised that if he provided this support she would ask nothing more of him, he agreed. Horney entered medical school in 1906. She was "the only woman among six men who passed the preclinical examination in her class in 1908" (O'Connell, 1980, p. 83). While in medical training, she married Oskar Horney. Two years later, in 1911, she took her state medical examination while returning home every several hours to nurse her firstborn daughter. She earned her medical degree in 1915, the same year her third daughter was born (O'Connell, 1980; 1990).

As a young contemporary of Sigmund Freud, the professional context in which Horney functioned was overshadowed by his concepts. In the early decades of the twentieth century, Horney pioneered and developed a feminine psychology that provided a new way of thinking about women (O'Connell, 1990). She had the courage to develop perspectives that were opposed to Freud's theories and androcentric views. These enlightened perspectives are contained most fully in her comprehensive theory of personality and method of psychotherapy. In contrast to Freud who believed that "anatomy is destiny," she emphasized the influences of culture and interpersonal relationships on personality and behavior and the potential for lifelong growth.

In 1932 Horney, at midlife, left the recognition she had earned at the Berlin Psychoanalytic Institute and established herself once again in a new country. She accepted an invitation from Franz Alexander to become his assistant at the Chicago Institute of Psychoanalysis and later moved to the New York Psychoanalytic Institute and the New School for Social Research. The transition from Europe to the United States underscored for her the importance of culture on mental health and pathology. When her departure from Freudian concepts was negatively received by the New York Psychoanalytic Society, she resigned and in the same year, 1941, became one of the founders of the Association for the Advancement of Psychoanalysis and the American Institute for Psychoanalysis, a respected training institute.

Horney's insights and concepts have been incorporated by diverse theorists and practitioners, including those of humanist, cognitive, client-centered, self, and gestalt persuasions.

As we move from the first half of the twentieth century to the latter half, we find other noteworthy and inspiring exemplars of achievement. In its more than 100-year history the American Psychological Association, the premier professional organization for psychologists, has elected just eight women to its presidency. The first two, Mary Whiton Calkins in 1905 and Margaret Floy Washburn in 1921, were president in the early years of the association when the presidency was primarily ceremonial (Furumoto, 1990; Scarborough, 1990). Over the next 50 years, the position became more influential. No other woman served in this high office until Anne Anastasi, scientist, scholar, and teacher, became the third woman president in 1972.

In the 1970s and 1980s within the social and historical context of the resurgence of the women's movement and the illuminated awareness of women's talents and abilities, five women—Anne Anastasi, Leona Tyler (1973), Florence Denmark (1980), Janet Taylor Spence (1984), and Bonnie Strickland (1987)—achieved the APA's highest elected position. In the 1990s, the one hundred and fifth president and the eighth woman, Dorothy Cantor (1996), achieved this position.

Although there is no clear documentation that social and historical contexts influenced the outcomes of these elections, after a 50-year drought it is a plausible explanation and consistent with the tenor of the times. Anne Anastasi (1908–), the first woman to begin to rectify the long absence of women from this office, exemplifies life in a context of extraordinary abilities and perceptions. A recipient of the National Medal of Science, she has repeatedly distinguished herself in a career of some 60 years. Anastasi was named the most prominent living woman in psychology in a survey conducted by Gavin in 1987. She is a foremost authority on psychological testing, differential psychology, and environmental and experiential factors of psychological development. Her books are classics and used throughout the world (Sexton & Hogan, 1990).

Anastasi began to read at 3 years of age, graduated Barnard College at 19 years, and earned her doctorate in psychology at 21 years. Her father died when she was 1 year old; she grew up with her mother, uncle, and maternal grandmother, who served as her educator during much of her precollege years.

In her autobiography, Anastasi recalls that shortly after her marriage she was treated for cervical cancer (Anastasi, 1988). Although she made a rapid and permanent recovery, the treatment left her unable to bear children. She responded to this life-altering event as she had to other difficult situations earlier—by accepting it and then concentrating with vigor on her work. Her reasoned and productive responses to adversity and her extraordinary life and career are inspiring.

The women who have served as president of the American Psychological Association in the 1970s and 1980s described their diverse backgrounds, lifestyles, and contributions in their autobiographies (O'Connell & Russo, 1988). Lacking socioeconomic privilege, Leona Tyler, the fourth woman president, describes her family of origin as "on the verge of poverty" (Tyler, 1988, p. 45), and Bonnie Strickland, the seventh woman president, describes herself as a "kid from the south side of the steel mills in Birmingham and the river swamps of northwest Florida" (Strickland, 1988, p. 322). In contrast, Florence Denmark (Denmark, 1988) and Janet Taylor Spence (Spence, 1988), the fifth and sixth women presidents, came from more affluent socioeconomic backgrounds and parents who nurtured high achievement. Of the six contemporary presidents, two were single, three were married, one was a widow; two of the married presidents had children.

The scholarly contributions of these presidents ranged from counseling and psychotherapy to social psychology, personality, and health (Deaux, 1990; Nowicki, 1990; Paludi & Russo, 1990; Zilber & Osipow, 1990). Tyler made contributions to counseling psychology, the understanding of individual differences, and creative thinking; Denmark to research on leadership and status, gender roles and gender differences; Spence to the understanding of achievement and achievement motivation and the reconceptualization of masculinity, femininity, and gender roles; Strickland to psychotherapy, depression, women's health, and the assessment of children's locus of control; and Cantor to the practice of psychotherapy, advocacy, and leadership, and to professional women's issues.

SOCIAL POWER AND THE STATUS OF WOMEN

Although these presidents of the American Psychological Association achieved significant social power and status, we cannot determine with absolute certainty how they did so. In general, when we think about the sources of social power, we wonder whether this power comes from the society in which we live (in some societies to be of a particular sex, race, or ethnicity is to have power) or from specific persons, things, or situations (specific persons, things, or situations empower us), or from within ourselves (we are powerful or empower ourselves). The research is not clear on the relative importance of each of these sources but it is evident that women and members of certain races and ethnicities endure disproportionate discrimination and the withholding of power.

Have you ever heard of African American Psychologist Mamie Phipps Clark (1917–1983)? She made significant contributions to psychology and society through her work on racial identity and discrimination against those lacking in power. She pioneered the developmental studies on the negative self-image of Black children that helped remove barriers to equal education. The research she did with her husband, psychologist Kenneth Clark, was instrumental in the U.S. Supreme Court *Brown v. Board of Education of Topeka* decision that promoted school desegregation and moved the attainment of civil rights forward.

Mamie Phipps Clark, the elder of two children, grew up in Hot

Springs, Arkansas, with her physician father and her mother who assisted him. She attended Howard University in Washington, D.C., on an academic scholarship and graduated magna cum laude with a B.S. in psychology in 1938. In 1943, she received her doctorate in psychology from Columbia University (Clark, 1983; Guthrie, 1990).

In her autobiography, Clark describes the social and historical contexts and the discrimination she encountered in seeking employment after earning her doctorate.

> Following my graduation it soon became apparent to me that a black female with a Ph.D. in psychology was an unwanted anomaly in New York City in the early 1940s. . . . It was heartbreaking to learn that a number of white men and women with far less qualifications were hired at relatively high salaries. When I applied . . . I was rejected without explanation. (Clark, 1983, p. 271)

Her first employment experience is described by Clark as "humiliating and distasteful," but her husband and two small children provided "a strong support system" (Clark, 1983, p. 271).

Together with her husband and friends, she established the much needed Northside Center for Child Development in 1946; it was a guidance center offering psychiatric, psychological, and casework services to children and families in Harlem. Most of the children assigned to Classes for Children of Retarded Mental Development (CRDM) who came to the center for help were found through psychological testing to be above the intelligence level for placement in these classes (I.Q. 70). The placements by the school system were illegal, and the children were returned to normal classes. The Clarks were instrumental in counteracting racial discrimination in education on local and national levels.

In the 1940s and 1950s there was considerable racial prejudice and stigma associated with mental health services. The social power, status, and many achievements of Mamie Phipps Clark are indeed impressive.

In studying social power and ethnic discrimination we discover that in 1962 Martha Bernal (1931–) became the first Mexican American woman to earn her doctorate in psychology (Bernal, 1988). Bernal grew up in El Paso, Texas, where she remembers that "the use of the Spanish language by Mexican children was punished in Texas schools" (Bernal, 1988, p. 264). She writes that she learned immediately "that the dominant society disapproved of my language and heritage" (p. 264).

The contexts of society, family culture, and gender mingled to limit educational opportunities for her. Bernal was the middle daughter of three. Unlike her sisters, her interests and ambitions conflicted with the expectations for a woman in the Mexican American culture. She recalls that she had to "conduct battle with my father about going to college" (Bernal, 1988, pp. 265–266) and again about going to graduate school.

Bernal recollects that around 1979 she experienced an acculturation struggle trying to reconcile two conflicting cultures.

All those years since becoming a graduate student, I had become White in my world view and perspectives, equally as ethnocentric as my White colleagues. . . . I even belittled members of my own ethnic group, as well as those of other ethnic groups. . . . Although the revelation stunned me, I knew that, since I had lived in a strictly White world for many years . . . it would have been difficult to escape being exposed to and internalizing its perspectives about racial and ethnic minorities. (Bernal, 1988, p. 271)

Bernal's self-examination and insights provided a new direction for her work and, as recorded so forthrightly, provide us with courage and inspiration for self-knowledge and meaningful direction.

Bernal achieved social power and status despite substantial barriers. She served as president of the National Hispanic Psychological Association and made numerous contributions to psychology, including parent-training techniques for conduct-problem children, training materials to serve the mental health needs of minority groups, and extensive work on issues of ethnic identity.

Carolyn Robertson Payton (1925–) is another role model who experienced the withholding of social and professional power because of discrimination yet achieved power and status. Payton, the first woman to serve as director of the Peace Corps, tells us about her childhood.

I have always been conscious of my Blackness and of the lack of status assigned to me as a consequence. My cues were the unpaved streets and sidewalks in my segregated neighborhood, the paucity of street lights, my elementary school with outdoor toilets—The city zoo . . . swimming pool and skating rink . . . [were] off-limits to Blacks. . . . You can be sure that I grew up knowing that I was Black. (Payton, 1988, p. 230)

She continues to remember and seems to have gotten strength from an important lesson during her early school years.

I learned, as all children in public school, that I was an American and as such was guaranteed the pursuit of happiness, equality, and justice. I learned that lesson well and have continuously struggled to achieve these rights as a minority and as a woman. (Payton, 1988, p. 364)

Payton was a U.S. Presidential Peace Corps appointee and a leader in cross-cultural and ethnic minority psychology (Keita & Muldrow, 1990). Her achievements were made in a worldwide context and the status and social power she achieved were noteworthy.

Psychologists Mildred Mitchell (1903–1983) and Thelma Alper (1908–1988) also experienced discrimination, as women, at Harvard University (Alper, 1983; Mitchell, 1983). Mitchell, then a graduate student, was denied a key to Emerson Hall and recalls waiting in snow, sleet, rain, and even a blizzard for a man with a key to let her into the building where she was doing research. She also recalls being denied access to the Harvard libraries in the evening hours because she was a woman. As an instructor at Harvard Thelma Alper was permitted to teach courses but not to proctor an examination for her male students or be granted tenure. After earning her doctorate at Yale, Mitchell opened numerous psychology departments in applied settings and had the distinction of being the first clinical psychology Army examiner for the astronaut program. Alper achieved the status of professor at Wellesley College and advanced the field of psychology through experimental approaches to the study of ego strength and achievement motivation.

NONCONSCIOUS IDEOLOGIES

Social power and the status of women are intertwined with the nonconscious ideologies that shape our behaviors and that of others. These ideologies are so pervasive and so out of awareness that we dance to their beat without knowing whether we are moving singly or in unison.

Lillian Troll (1915–) and Martha Mednick (1929–) write in their autobiographies how acceptance of the prescription for woman's role defined them to themselves (Mednick, 1988; Troll, 1988). It was only after their respective marriages ended and the women's movement began to reemerge that they were able to fully understand the nonconscious quality of this definition. Troll writes of being jolted into "confronting all the feminist issues that later became familiar to many women" (Troll, 1988, p. 111). Mednick describes her early career and marriage years as "I will follow you anywhere and do whatever comes up" (Mednick, 1988, p. 253).

Troll was awarded her doctorate from the University of Chicago at age 52. Her many significant contributions to the understanding of adult development and aging are strong testimony to lifelong growth and development. Mednick's distinguished contributions include research on women, achievement, creativity, motivation, and personality.

It is clear that dissolution of the marriage bond is not a necessary prerequisite to illuminate nonconscious ideologies. Carolyn Wood Sherif (1922–1983) describes the power of nonconscious ideologies and societal prescriptions in her married life (Sherif, 1983). When her social-psychologist husband asked her to appear as coauthor on work they had done together (rather than being thanked in a footnote or preface), she declined and continued to do so for many years in keeping with the then-prevailing societal prescriptions regarding a wife's role. In retrospect, she wishes she had done otherwise. Sherif writes in her autobiography:

> I now believe that the world which viewed me as a wife who probably typed her husband's papers (which I did not) defined me to myself more than I realized. (Sherif, 1983, pp. 285–286)

Sherif credits the resurgence of the women's movement with her own awakening and recognition.

To me, the atmosphere created by the women's movement was like breathing fresh air after years of gasping for breath. If anyone believes that I credit it too much for changes in my own life, I have only this reply: I know I did not become a significantly better social psychologist between 1969 and 1972, but surely was treated as a better social psychologist. (Sherif, 1983, p. 280)

Definitions of a woman's role have evolved and changed with each generation but the presence and impact of nonconscious ideologies remain with us, and so does the need to illuminate and correct them.

*T*WO-CAREER FAMILIES

There is ample evidence that actual behavior by women has been much more varied than the societal prescriptions and nonconscious ideologies. Although the parameters have been changeable, women in two-career families have been with us through the ages.

Perhaps the most widely known woman psychologist in the context of a two-career family is Lillian Moller Gilbreth (1878–1972) recognized internationally for her contributions to industrial psychology and personnel management. She is known also as the subject of the book and movie *Cheaper by the Dozen*, which recounted her life as a wife and mother of 12 children (Kelly & Kelly, 1990). When her husband and professional partner died in 1924, after 20 years of marriage, Gilbreth had the sole responsibility for providing for her children's support. At first, discrimination against her as a woman was pervasive but eventually her accomplishments overcame bias, and she became known as the Mother of Scientific Management, the First Lady of Management, the World's Greatest Woman Engineer, and a founder of the International Academy of Management. Her practical innovations included energy-saving designs of kitchens and household appliances, the foot-pedal trash can, and shelves for the interior of refrigerator doors.

Whether married to other psychologists or to men in other fields, women role models in two-career families provide a kaleidoscope of exemplars.

*T*RANSHISTORIC AND TIME-SPECIFIC PROFILES

Let's now look at a study of 34 eminent women in psychology born between 1891 and 1936. In this study I was able to delineate similarities and differences, trends and patterns in lives and careers across time and contexts (O'Connell, 1988). I discovered that the variables related to distinction include birth order and demographics of family of origin;

educational institutions, financial support for graduate study, and years from baccalaureate to doctorate; marital status and marriage partners; strategies for coping with barriers; and the presence of mentors and colleagues. Although a transhistorical profile emerged, time-specific historical and social forces contributed to changes in this profile for educational institutions, marital patterns, and years between college degree and doctorate. As a wider range of degree-awarding universities, including state institutions, emerged, women whose families of origin were not privileged were able to obtain professional training. Although being born into an educated, professional, and/or wealthy family continued to be advantageous, achievement was accessible to women who were not from a family privileged in at least one of these ways. Earning the doctorate in a timely manner was most common, yet 21 percent took more than a decade to go from baccalaureate to doctorate. Lillian Troll took 30 years! Various lifestyles, marital, and parental patterns were represented in the study; 18 percent of the women never married, and marriage and parenthood were more likely to become part of the texture of life for career women born later than earlier.

Generally, the transhistoric profile portrayed a group of predominantly firstborn women who went from baccalaureate to doctorate in less time than others in the doctorate population; received financial support for graduate study; had an impressive list of mentors and colleagues and good professional and social networks; and married professional men. They were trailblazers; persisted in the face of professional and personal obstacles, discrimination, and other barriers; focused on the task at hand; and brought their considerable talents to bear to contribute ideas, approaches, and definitive work to psychology.

LESSONS LEARNED

Let's summarize some of the things we have learned. Role models in psychology have diverse parental backgrounds, socioeconomic classes, and ethnic affiliations; educational, career, and lifestyle patterns; specializations in psychology; paths to achievement; and social and historical contexts. Despite severe constraints and inhospitable contexts, a long list of distinguished women endured the struggles, challenges, and demands to make important contributions to psychology, society, and future generations. Their lives and careers contain lessons that are valuable for all of us—courage, commitment, consistency, persistence, a work ethic, goal directedness, flexibility, the importance of supportive relationships, the existence of myriad roads to achievement, and the influence of context. Cumulatively and separately, the lives and careers of role models in psychology inspire us to persevere—especially when we might choose to do otherwise.

We know that celebrating women as role models challenges basic assumptions about women and their status, social power, and contributions. Bridging the gap between these basic assumptions and the under-recognized realities is a formidable challenge. Illuminating the reality of women as role models serves to counteract the invisibility, misattribution, devaluation, trivialization, and peripheralization of women's contributions and perspectives and to magnify the new vision of women in psychology. This approach is a fundamental challenge to women's secondary status in society and essential to women's empowerment. Empowerment is advanced by the new vision of women and their illumination as role models. It is facilitated by full recognition of the extraordinary impact women have had on the evolution, development, and transformation of psychology, its subfields, and its organizations and by full recognition of the contributions of women in shifting the field's epistemological center and shaping intellectual history (O'Connell & Russo, 1980; 1983; 1988; 1990; 1991). Understanding the conviction, determination, collective action, struggles, and sacrifices of our role models inspires and motivates us to protect and build on their legacy as we endeavor to shape our lives and careers, psychology and society.

REFERENCES

ALPER, T. G. (1983). Thelma G. Alper, 1908–. In A. N. O'Connell & N. F. Russo (Eds.), *Models of achievement: Reflections of eminent women in psychology.* (Vol. 1, pp. 189–199). New York: Columbia University Press.

ANASTASI, A. (1988). Anne Anastasi, 1908–. In A. N. O'Connell & N. F. Russo (Eds.), *Models of achievement: Reflections of eminent women in psychology* (Vol. 2, pp. 57–66). Hillsdale, NJ: Erlbaum.

BERNAL, M. E. (1988). Martha E. Bernal, 1931–. In A. N. O'Connell & N. F. Russo (Eds.), *Models of achievement: Reflections of eminent women in psychology* (Vol. 2, pp. 261–276). Hillsdale, NJ: Erlbaum.

CLARK, M. P. (1983). Mamie Phipps Clark, 1917–. In A. N. O'Connell & N. F. Russo (Eds.), *Models of achievement: Reflections of eminent women in psychology.* (Vol. 1, pp. 267–277). New York: Columbia University Press.

DEAUX, K. (1990). Janet Taylor Spence (1923–). In A. N. O'Connell & N. F. Russo (Eds.), *Women in psychology: A bio-bibliographic sourcebook* (pp. 307-316). Westport, CT: Greenwood.

DENMARK, F. L. (1988). Florence L. Denmark, 1932–. In A. N. O'Connell & N. F. Russo (Eds.), *Models of achievement: Reflections of eminent women in psychology* (Vol. 2, pp. 279–293). Hillsdale, NJ: Erlbaum.

FREEMAN, L., & STREAN, H. S. (1987). *Freud & women.* New York: Continuum.

FURUMOTO, L. (1990). Mary Whiton Calkins (1863–1930). In A. N. O'Connell & N. F. Russo (Eds.), *Women in psychology: A bio-bibliographic sourcebook* (pp. 57–65). Westport, CT: Greenwood.

GAVIN, E. (1987). Prominent women in psychology, determined by ratings of distinguished peers. *Psychotherapy in Private Practice, 5,* 53–68.

GUTHRIE, R. V. (1990). Mamie Phipps Clark (1917–1983). In A. N. O'Connell & N. F. Russo (Eds.), *Women in psychology: A bio-bibliographic sourcebook* (pp. 66–74). Westport, CT: Greenwood.

KEITA, G. P., & MULDROW, T. (1990). Carolyn Robertson Payton (1925–). In A. N. O'Connell & N. F. Russo (Eds.), *Women in psychology: A bio-bibliographic sourcebook* (pp. 266–274). Westport, CT: Greenwood.

KELLY, R. M., & KELLY, V. P. (1990). Lillian Moller Gilbreth (1878–1972). In A. N. O'Connell & N. F. Russo (Eds.), *Women in psychology: A bio-bibliographic sourcebook* (pp. 117–124). Westport, CT: Greenwood.

LERMAN, H. (1986). *Women in therapy.* Northvale, NJ: Jason Aronson.

MEDNICK, M. T. (1988). Martha T. Mednick, 1929–. In A. N. O'Connell & N. F. Russo (Eds.), *Models of achievement: Reflections of eminent women in psychology* (Vol. 2, pp. 245–259). Hillsdale, NJ: Erlbaum.

MITCHELL, B. B. (1983). Mildred B. Mitchell, 1903–. In A. N. O'Connell & N. F. Russo (Eds.), *Models of achievement: Reflections of eminent women in psychology* (Vol. 1, pp. 121–139). New York: Columbia University Press.

NOWICKI, S., JR. (1990). Bonnie Ruth Strickland (1936–). In A. N. O'Connell & N. F. Russo (Eds.), *Women in psychology: A bio-bibliographic sourcebook* (pp. 317–326). Westport, CT: Greenwood.

O'CONNELL, A. N. (1980). Karen Horney: Theorist in psychoanalysis and feminine psychology. *Psychology of Women Quarterly, 5*(1), 81–93.

O'CONNELL, A. N. (1983). Synthesis: Profiles and patterns of achievement. In A. N. O'Connell & N. F. Russo, (Eds.), *Models of achievement: Reflections of eminent women in psychology* (pp. 297–326). New York: Columbia University Press.

O'CONNELL, A. N. (1988). Synthesis and resynthesis: Profiles and patterns of achievement. In A. N. O'Connell & N. F. Russo, (Eds.), *Models of achievement: Reflections of eminent women in psychology* (Vol. 2, pp. 317–366). Hillsdale, NJ: Erlbaum.

O'CONNELL, A. N. (1990). Karen Horney (1885–1952). In A. N. O'Connell & N. F. Russo (Eds.), *Women in psychology: A bio-bibliographic sourcebook* (pp. 184–196). Westport, CT: Greenwood.

O'CONNELL, A. N., & RUSSO, N. F. (Eds.). (1980). Eminent women in psychology. *Psychology of Women Quarterly, 5*(1).

O'CONNELL, A. N., & RUSSO, N. F. (Eds.). (1983). *Models of achievement: Reflections of eminent women in psychology* (Vol. 1). New York: Columbia University Press.

O'CONNELL, A. N., & RUSSO, N. F. (Eds.). (1988). *Models of achievement: Reflections of Eminent Women in Psychology* (Vol. 2). Hillsdale, NJ: Erlbaum.

O'CONNELL, A. N., & RUSSO, N. F. (Eds.). (1990). *Women in psychology: A bio-bibliographic sourcebook.* Westport, CT: Greenwood.

O'CONNELL, A. N., & RUSSO, N. F. (Eds.). (1991). Women's heritage in psychology: Origins, development, and future directions. [Special issue]. *Psychology of Women Quarterly, 15*(4).

PALUDI, M. A., & RUSSO, N. F. (1990). Florence L. Denmark (1931–). In A. N. O'Connell & N. F. Russo (Eds.), *Women in psychology: A bio-bibliographic sourcebook* (pp. 75–87). Westport, CT: Greenwood.

PAYTON, C. R. (1988). Carolyn Robertson Payton, 1925–. In A. N. O'Connell & N. F. Russo (Eds.), *Models of achievement: Reflections of eminent women in psychology* (Vol. 2, pp. 227–242). Hillsdale, NJ: Erlbaum.

ROAZEN, P. (1975). *Freud and his followers.* New York: Knopf.

Russo, N. F., & O'Connell, A. N. (1980). Models from our past: Psychology's fore-mothers. *Psychology of Women Quarterly, 5*(1), 11–54.

Russo, N. F., & O'Connell, A. N. (1992). Women in psychotherapy: Selected con-tributions. In D. Freedheim (Ed.), *The history of psychotherapy: A century of change* (pp. 493–527). Washington, DC: American Psychological Association.

Scarborough, E. (1990). Margaret Floy Washburn (1871-1939). In A. N. O'Connell & N. F. Russo (Eds.), *Women in psychology: A bio-bibliographic sourcebook* (pp. 342–349). Westport, CT: Greenwood.

Sexton, V. S., & Hogan, J. D. (1990). Anne Anastasi (1908). In A. N. O'Connell & N. F. Russo (Eds.), *Women in psychology: A bio-bibliographic sourcebook* (pp. 13–22). Westport, CT: Greenwood.

Sherif, C. W. (1983). Carolyn Wood Sherif, 1922–1982. In A. N. O'Connell & N. F. Russo (Eds.), *Models of achievement: Reflections of eminent women in psychology.* (Vol. 1, pp. 279–293). New York: Columbia University Press.

Spence, J. T. (1988). Janet Taylor Spence, 1923–. In A. N. O'Connell & N. F. Russo (Eds.), *Models of achievement: Reflections of eminent women in psychology* (Vol. 2, pp. 189–203). Hillsdale, NJ: Erlbaum.

Strickland, B. R. (1988). Bonnie R. Strickland, 1936–. In A. N. O'Connell & N. F. Russo (Eds.), *Models of achievement: Reflections of eminent women in psychology* (Vol. 2, pp. 295–313). Hillsdale, NJ: Erlbaum.

Troll, L. E. (1988). Lillian E. Troll, 1915–. In A. N. O'Connell & N. F. Russo (Eds.), *Models of achievement: Reflections of eminent women in psychology* (Vol. 2, pp. 103–117). Hillsdale, NJ: Erlbaum.

Tyler, L. E. (1988). Leona E. Tyler, 1906–. In A. N. O'Connell & N. F. Russo (Eds.), *Models of achievement: Reflections of eminent women in psychology* (Vol. 2, pp. 295–313). Hillsdale, NJ: Erlbaum.

Zilber, S. M., & Osipow, S. H. (1990). Leona E. Tyler (1906). In A. N. O'Connell & N. F. Russo (Eds.), *Women in psychology: A bio-bibliographic sourcebook* (pp. 335–341). Westport, CT: Greenwood.

SUGGESTED READINGS

O'Connell, A. N., & Russo, N. F. (Eds.). (1983). *Models of achievement: Reflections of eminent women in psychology* (Vol. 1). New York: Columbia University Press.

O'Connell, A. N., & Russo, N. F. (Eds.). (1988). *Models of achievement: Reflections of eminent women in psychology,* (Vol. 2). Hillsdale, NJ: Erlbaum.

O'Connell, A. N., & Russo, N. F. (Eds.). (1990). *Women in psychology: A bio-bibliographic sourcebook.* Westport, CT: Greenwood.

Scarborough, E., & Furumoto, L. (1987). *Untold lives: The first generation of Ameri-can women psychologists.* New York: Columbia University Press.

GERALDINE **BUTTS STAHLY** *is Associate Professor of Psychology at Califor-nia State University at San Bernardino, where she has been teaching psy-chology of women since 1980. Dr. Stahly has written and lectured widely on women's experiences of relationship violence. She frequently conducts training sessions on domestic violence for the police and judiciary and has testified as an expert witness in cases involving battered women.*

20

Battered Women: Why Don't They Just Leave?

❖

Violence against women is a problem of international proportions, and nowhere is a woman in greater danger than in her own home. The U.S. Bureau of Justice Statistics has estimated that 2.1 million women are beaten each year by their current or former partners (Langer & Innes, 1986), and battered women account for over one-third of the women murdered each year. More American women are injured by their partners than suffer injury due to muggings, rapes, and automobile accidents combined (O'Reilly, 1983).

The tragedy of violence extends beyond the physical and emotional injuries to the woman. Children of violent homes are at increased risk of both physical and emotional abuse. Even if the battering husband does not physically injure the children, they live in an environment of terror. Children of battered women who have never been physically abused show all the characteristics of battered children. As the director of a shelter in the late 1970s I observed the effects on children firsthand. Hardly a night went by without several children waking up screaming with night terrors. Children as young as 10 had high blood pressure and even ulcers. The damaging effects on the children's emotional and behavioral well-being was also clear. Little boys often hit their mothers to get attention, and one day several little girls hid in terror when a man came to repair the house.

Empirical studies have confirmed the serious effects of family violence on children that I observed in the shelter. Boys who have witnessed their fathers beating their mothers are 24 times more likely to commit sexual assault than are boys with nonviolent fathers; they are 74 percent more likely to commit violent crimes in general. Girls and boys who witness their mothers beaten are six times more likely to commit suicide, and the girls are more likely to engage in teenage prostitution (Jaffe, Wolfe, & Wilson, 1990). Ultimately the son may try to protect his mother from violence, and as a result 63 percent of males between the ages of 11 and 20 who are in jail for homicide are there for killing their mother's batterer. Tragically, these young men who went to prison for protecting their moms may well become batterers of their own intimate partners because sons who witness their mother's battery are three times more likely to become batterers than are sons of nonviolent fathers (Hotaling & Sugarman, 1986). In my work (Stahly, 1987), I have found what may be part of the attitudinal base of the intergenerational transmission of partner battering. Male college students who had witnessed their mothers being battered had the most negative attitudes toward women—and were significantly more antifeminist than males in general, even more so than males who reported being emotionally or physically abused by their mothers (Stahly, 1987). Clearly it's time to stop blaming the mothers for men's hatred of women! In the violent home the boy not only learns the behaviors of violence but also the misogynist attitudes that support and justify the abuse of women.

Given the tremendous toll of violence on the lives of women and their children, it is probably not surprising that the question people most often asked of battered women and their advocates is, Why does a battered woman stay? Over the course of the 18 years I have been working in the area of domestic violence—first as a shelter director beginning in 1977 and later as a social psychologist doing research—I have been asked this question hundreds of times. Sometimes the question is asked in a hostile and victim-blaming tone—as at a men's service club meeting where a member suggested to me that women who stay must like being battered. Sometimes the question is asked factually, in an attempt to understand and craft interventions, as it was by now Senator Barbara Mikulski when I testified before Congress in support of the first national domestic violence legislation in 1979 (a bill vetoed by Ronald Reagan as one of his early acts in office). Sometimes the question is asked in agony, as it was by a mother who called me in the middle of the night after her daughter had been murdered by her husband, despite the mother's best efforts to help her daughter leave and stay away.

However it is asked, it is a question worth answering. In this lecture we will explore some of the answers to this question from a number of different perspectives. Perhaps we can put to rest the question, Why does she stay? and begin to ask more clearly and forcefully the most appropriate question: Why should a woman and her children have to leave home in order to live in peace?

HISTORICAL PERSPECTIVE

A dog, a wife and a cherry tree, the more ye beat them the better they be.
ANONYMOUS

This old English rhyme of unknown origin captures the traditional attitude toward violence against women in the context of the patriarchal family. Historically, women have rarely had the option of leaving a battering
relationship. Under common law, the married woman and the children
she bore were the property of the man. He was obliged to control and discipline them, and violence was an accepted method to accomplish this
end. Evidence of a man's beating of his wife or children had no place in
any court of law and was accepted as a matter of privacy and due course
(Liss & Stahly, 1993). The home was the man's castle, and abuse of either
children or spouse was no one else's business (Aries, 1970).

There were some limits put on the man's exercise of his privilege of
violence against family members; under common law the "rule of
thumb"—a term we still use today to indicated a standard of behavior—
dictated that a man should not beat his wife or children with a stick
thicker than his thumb (Calvert, 1974). Needless to say, this standard did
little to insure the peaceful resolution of family disputes, and a battered
woman was left with little recourse but to endure her husband's violence.

The tolerant attitude toward a man's violence against his spouse continued for more than 100 years after the official demise of the rule of
thumb (Calvert, 1974). The criminal justice system continued, until very
recently, to view most of the violence against women in relationships as
matters of "privacy" and "civil disturbances" not appropriate for criminal
proceedings. Women who wanted to leave a violent relationship could expect little assistance from the police or the courts, and only recently have
shelters been available for battered women and their children.

RACE AND CLASS EXPLANATIONS OF FAMILY VIOLENCE

An early, and probably the most complete, statement of the sociology of
violence is the subculture-of-violence hypothesis (Wolfgang, 1958; Wolfgang & Ferracutti, 1967; Stahly, 1978). According to this theory, rather
than being deviant, a violent act may be a response to subcultural values,
attitudes, and rituals that define violent behavior as normative. Wolfgang
offered this subcultural explanation of violence after he conducted a
study in which he observed that most of the men convicted of homicide
in Philadelphia over several years in the 1950s were poor and minority
(Black and Puerto Rican in his sample). These men felt justified in their

violent responses as a defense against what they perceived as threats to their masculine identity—behavior by the victim that they considered demeaning, demasculinizing, or disrespectful. The notion that battering men were predominately poor and minority was based on observing only the men in jail. The bias of this sample reinforced existing stereotypes about violence and people of poverty and of color. As a result, domestic violence continued for nearly three more decades to be ignored as a problem of women of all classes and races.

The social perception that violence is "normative" only for certain stigmatized groups served to discourage women from leaving violent relationships. Women of poverty and color who experienced the "subculture of violence" often believed the violence was an inevitable part of male privilege. Several woman in the shelter told me that they had not left their batterer sooner because they feared "going out of the frying pan into the fire," or "the next man will just be the same." On the other hand, the associations of domestic violence with stigmatized groups left white and middle-class women often feeling shame and isolation because the violence against them was denied by the larger society. Because middle-class violence was not considered normative, the woman often thought the violence against her was highly unusual, and to acknowledge it would bring shame and a loss of social standing on her partner and herself.

Although poor people and people of color are more likely to be arrested and incarcerated for violent behavior, the notion that these groups are more prone to woman battering has probably never been true. An early survey of attitudes about interpersonal violence found no significant differences by race or class in acceptance of wife battering (Stark & McEvoy, 1970). A comparison of domestic violence calls between police precincts with different racial and socioeconomic demographics found no difference in the reported occurrence of violence, but poor and minority men were more likely to be arrested and incarcerated (Bard & Zacker, 1971). More recently, as arrests for partner battering have become mandatory in many jurisdictions, the bias toward arresting poor and minority men has been reduced. Arrested batterers now come from all races and income groups and include nationally known celebrities and politicians.

PSYCHOLOGICAL THEORIES AND VICTIM BLAME

Freud provided the earliest psychological theory of aggressive behavior; his explanations were intrapsychic and clinical (Freud, 1924/1974). Freud's theory of psychosexual development delineates gender differences in violence and suggests that sadism is an inevitable characteristic of normal male development and masochism of normal female development (Deutsch, 1945). Although the sadistic nature of males is rarely used to explain general male violence, the masochism of females became the defining feature of femininity and has been used extensively by psychiatry to blame women victims (Masson, 1984). According to the intrapsychic perspective, the battered woman stays in the violent relationship because of her unconscious need to be hurt and punished for her sexual feelings. This view of the battering relationship as rooted in female masochism is unfortunately not an anachronism—it is alive and well today. The continuing pathologizing of battered women by a significant number of mental health professionals is a form of victim blame, and it discourages serious analysis of the social forces that create violent men and trap battered women.

Another more recent intrapsychic explanation of family violence is found in family system theories. These theories suggest that all family members play roles in maintaining a status quo (homeostasis), even in violent and destructive families. The battered woman is seen as "equally" participating in the violence against her because of her intrapsychic needs (probably based on her own dysfunctional family experiences) and her secondary gains (she gets to be "right" when she "makes" the man hit her) (Lawson, 1989; Weitzman & Dreen, 1982). By attributing violence to the women's prior personality style and provocative behavior, family systems theorists diminish the responsibility of the perpetrator and perpetuate the victimization of women. Feminist psychologists have been highly critical of family systems theory. For example, Hansen (1993, p. 81) states, "Only when we recognize that battering is 'solely the responsibility of the man,' that 'no woman deserves to be beaten,' and that the social/political context has a direct impact on the maintenance of the behavior, is the family system likely to change."

A popular model that describes the alcoholic family takes the notion of "coresponsibility" even further and suggests that the partner plays a role in maintaining the dysfunctional family system by "enabling" the alcoholic behavior. This "enabling" individual (usually the woman) is seen as "codependent"—that is, facilitating the destructive behavior of the alcoholic to meet some intrapsychic needs of her own. This model of codependency has been extended to explain the behavior of a wide range of victims, including women who stay in violent relationships, although there appears to be no empirical data to support such a generalization (Cooley & Severson, 1993). The codependence model takes victim blame to the logical extreme of intrapsychic explanations of victimization; that is, the battered woman is "addicted" to violent relationships and therefore "finds" a man to abuse her. Like Freud's masochistic woman who "wants" to be beaten, the codependent woman "needs" the violent relationship to play out her internal script of "victim" or "rescuer."

Although the reversal of responsibility in violent families defies common sense and may seem ludicrous, such psychological theories of victim blame have real-world consequences. While conducting training for court mediators, I was told of a judge who routinely gave custody of children to the father in domestic-violence cases. The judge's bizarre rationale, apparently based on his cursory "understanding" of psychology, was that because battered women always sought violent relationships, it was better for the children to be with their own violent father than to be subjected to the violence of the men in their mother's future relationships! I wish I could say that no psychologist, even those who endorse the concepts of family systems theory or codependency, would make such an absurd judgment. Unfortunately, I have worked on several custody cases where a consulting psychologist has testified that the father's violent behavior was not significant and/or was "caused" by the mother's pathology.

FEMINIST THEORIES

Feminists come from a variety of theoretical backgrounds and may use parts of the traditional theories from sociology and psychology, but the aspect that best characterizes feminist analysis is the central position of gender and power as the fundamental issues in the explanation of violence within relationships (Bograd, 1990; Dobash & Dobash, 1979; Kurtz, 1989; Pagelow, 1984; Taubmand, 1986; Walker, 1989). Intimate relationships are based on a value structure that assumes an unequal distribution of power between the man and woman. The man is a member of the dominant class, and he has greater access to resources and social power (Bograd, 1984). Regardless of race, socioeconomic status, or the details of their personal relationship, the woman is devalued relative to the man. In a patriarchal society both partners learn that masculinity is superior. The masculine is defined by all that is "not feminine," and physically, cognitively, psychologically, and emotionally the male is normative. Patriarchal men share a sense of entitlement to respect and service from women based on the superiority of their sex alone. Feminist theorists view violence against women as, first and foremost, political acts of terrorism designed to maintain the privilege and power of men and the structure of patriarchy at whatever cost to women and children (Bograd, 1984; Brownmiller, 1975; Taubman, 1986; Yllo & Bograd, 1988).

To understand why women stay in abusive relationships, feminists note that social institutions, including most religions, the criminal justice system, and the mental health establishments, function within the rules and assumptions of patriarchy. These institutions, like marriage itself, generally support the right of men to dominate the women, ignore or trivialize violence against women, and blame the victims. The woman who is battered has traditionally been discouraged from leaving by a combination of social forces that ignore her plight and deny her resources (APA Task Force, 1975; California Judicial Council, 1991; Ullrich, 1986). Feminists stress the practical reasons why women stay in dangerous relationships, for example, economic disadvantage in the work place (women still earn 30 percent less than men), fear of men's threats of retaliation, and lack of protection afforded by the police.

The Three-Stage Cycle of Violence

The classic work of Lenore Walker (1979) gave the first detailed analysis of the psychosocial forces that may trap a woman in a battering relationship. Based on clinical observations and a detailed questionnaire filled out by hundreds of battered women, Dr. Walker concluded that the battering relationship was cyclic, with an escalating and reinforcing nature that both isolates and traps the woman. The three stages of the "cycle of violence" were identified as the tension-building phase, the acute episode, and the loving reconciliation.

During the tension-building phase, the woman becomes aware of the man's increasing tension, as he becomes edgy and lashes out in anger. The woman often reports feeling that she is "walking on eggshells." The man's demands and accusations may be exaggerated and unreasonable. One battered woman with whom I worked was accused of trying to sabotage an important business meeting by forgetting to pick up her husband's suit from the cleaners.

The man shatters the woman's self-esteem and self-confidence. He may criticize her appearance or call her stupid or incompetent. (The businessman I mentioned above told his wife that if she were his secretary, he would fire her!). As the woman tries to anticipate the man's needs and "keep a lid on" the situation, she is taking responsibility for making him feel better. When eventually the batterer explodes in violence despite her best effort, she usually feels partially responsible and looks for ways she could have "tried harder."

As the man's unreasonable demands and threats increase, the woman may withdraw emotionally and even physically. Or the woman may try even harder to please and placate the man, only to find that he explodes anyway. Other women may be accused of provoking the violence when they are finally "fed up" and "talk back," or even explode themselves at the men's excesses, giving the men a rationale for battering. Whether or not the woman knows what triggered the violence, she generally thinks she has failed and tries desperately to figure out what she could have done to prevent it.

The tension-building phase ends in an explosion of violence that is the second stage, the acute battering episode. The incident that sets off the man's violence is often trivial or unknown. Although people often ask the woman, "What did you do to make him so angry?" assuming that there must be some relationship between the offensiveness of the woman's behavior and the severity of the man's violence, I have rarely found this to be the case. On the contrary, the events that generally trigger violence are often mundane and even absurd. In one case I know of, a wealthy professional man broke his wife's jaw when he discovered the large palm plant in the foyer of their mansion was dry; in another case, when a construction worker's wife served him "sunny-side up" eggs that had broken and run into his toast, he threw the plate across the room and then cut her face with the broken glass. Some women even report that behavior that pleases their man one day may cue his rage on another, leaving them desperately confused and feeling very helpless. For example, a woman in the shelter had been accused by her husband of not being interested in sex; when she bought a sexy negligee and behaved romantically to please him, he accused her of being demanding and a "whore."

During the violent beating, the woman may try to defend herself. If she manages to scratch or kick the man, he will often claim later that she started the violence or that she is as violent as he is. Women may actually be arrested for defending themselves!

The period following the battering is the third stage, the loving reconciliation. This stage is one of great relief for the woman—the tension that has been building is finally released, and the beating is over. The woman may initially be very frightened or angry, she may cooperate with the police and seek shelter with friends or relatives (she may even go to a battered women's shelter if there is one in her area that's not full). However, within hours or days of the beating the loving reconciliation begins. The man is often sorry and frightened that this time he may lose the relationship. He begins an intense campaign to "win her back," showering the woman with apologies, gifts, and loving sentiments. The man's attention helps repair the woman's shattered sense of herself as competent and lovable. The couple may appear to be on a "second honeymoon." Lenore Walker calls this the "love bond" that is reinforced as the cycle of tension and pain is followed by closeness. The battered woman may believe that the way the man behaves during the loving reconciliation is her "real" partner—and he could be this way all the time if they could just solve this problem or that. If the man has been arrested and charged with battery, the woman may beg the district attorney to drop the charges against her husband. If the case goes forward, the woman may testify in the man's defense, sometimes even contradicting her statements to the police and perjuring herself.

Not all battered women defend their batterers out of love—they may also defend them out of fear. When the district attorney's office has a policy that allows women to drop the charges—and many still do—the criminal justice system is, in effect, making the woman responsible for the outcome of the case and putting her in a terribly dangerous dilemma. If she testifies, the batterer will blame her and retaliate; if she doesn't testify, the violence will continue and she will blame herself for not following through and be less likely to call for help in the future.

The loving reconciliation can also be isolating for the woman. Helpers or friends may be unwilling to overlook the seriousness of the violence; friends will often reject the couple, and helping professionals will be dismissed by them. When the violence recurs, the woman finds she has fewer places to turn for support. Her isolation increases and, over time, the reinforcing nature of the cycle of violence may lead to escalation, trapping the woman in an ever-more violent and abusive relationship (Stahly, 1980).

Learned Helplessness

Studies of animal behavior indicate that when an animal is repeatedly prevented from escaping punishment it will eventually stop trying to escape (Seligman & Maier, 1968). Most animals can learn in one trial to escape from the white to the black side of a cage to avoid electric shock. But once an animal has been repeatedly prevented from escaping, it "learns to be helpless." Once this learning occurs, it may take as many as 100 trials with the experimenter literally dragging the animal to the safe side of the cage before it will finally escape on its own. Studies of learned helplessness in animals have been used to explain the reactions of humans caught in chronically abusive situations (Seligman, 1975; Walker, 1977). The experience of battered women is certainly different than that of the trapped animals in the above studies. The woman is not just punished unconditionally, but is specially punished for behavior that asserts her independence from the batterer. Further, she is rewarded for behaviors that make it more difficult for her to leave, for example, for passivity, compliance, and dependence. However, some elements of the learned-helplessness model do seem to fit the violent relationship.

Early in the relationship, the woman often tries many different ways to stop the violence or escape. She changes the behavior the man criticizes, but in spite of her best efforts the beatings eventually come. She calls the police for help, only to find they do not respond. If the police do respond, their solution may be to tell the man to walk around the block to calm down, and when the police are gone, he returns to beat the woman again. The woman may turn to a clergyman and be told to be a better wife, or to pray, or to be more submissive. She may try to follow this advice, but the violence continues. The woman may turn to her doctor, who tells her she needs to relax; he may give her pills and she may become addicted to tranquilizers, but the violence still escalates. (I found that over 75 percent of the women entering Womenshelter in Long Beach, California, brought prescription tranquilizers or sleeping pills with them.) Other women may self-medicate, using alcohol or drugs to try to escape the tension and fear and reduce the pain.

If the woman leaves after a beating to stay with friends or relatives, the man follows her with threats or promises. She returns to him, often to find herself an unwelcome guest at that home the next time violence occurs. The list of experiences is nearly endless, but the result is the same. Eventually the woman may become so depressed and feel so helpless that even if alternatives to leave the situation are offered, it will be difficult for her to believe escape is possible and even more difficult for her to take action.

The Hostage Syndrome and Traumatic Bonding

Psychologists studying hostage situations have identified a pattern of behavior that emerges when individuals find their survival depends on placating a violent, hostile, unpredictable aggressor. After an initial period of shock and numbness, the hostages begin to communicate with the person threatening them. The abuse may be intermittent, interspersed with pleasant moments and even acts of consideration by the aggressor. A bond of sympathy, even friendship, may emerge.

Some psychologists consider the hostage's positive feelings toward the aggressor to be the result of a traumatic bond that appears to develop in chronic, intermittent abusive situations (Dutton & Painter, 1981). Even studies of animal behavior indicate that intermittent punishment and reward appear to strengthen the power of attachment. In studies of puppies' attachment to humans it has been found that a puppy that is intermittently punished and treated kindly shows 2 1/3 times greater orientation to humans than the consistently indulged puppy (Dutton & Painter, 1993). Similar findings appear in the study of attachment of infants to caregivers. Researchers have concluded, "the data show that inconsistent treatment (that is, maltreatment by, and affection from, the same source) yield an accentuation of attempts to gain proximity to the attachment object" (Rajecki, Lamb, & Obmascher, 1978, p. 425). Unlike puppies or infants, the battered woman's thinking as well as her feelings are distorted by the power the abuser has over her. Battered women who explain and defend their batterers' behaviors may be showing cognitive distortions created by the survival demands of their situations. They learn to survive by taking the point of view of the person who presents a threat to their survival. Battered women and battered children often love their abuser and try to survive by anticipating the abuser's needs and satisfying his wants, that is, by learning to think like the abuser.

The victims view themselves through the abuser's eyes, and find fault with themselves and excuses for the abusers. This strategy may reduce the abuser's anger and may have important survival value for the woman or child while they are under the abuser's control. However, the perspective of the batterer cannot be easily abandoned, even when the victim is safely away from the battering situation. Battered women may come to court to testify in defense of their abusers, and at the time of a divorce, battered children may actually ask to live with the abusive parent. Sometimes this behavior reflects cognitive distortion, and the victim really has taken the abuser's perspective. On the other hand, the woman and the child know they will have to deal with the abuser long after the court trial is over, and anticipating what the batterer would want them to say may be a way of trying to survive in the long run.

Effects on Self-Esteem

Because women have been reinforced for relationships more than for achievement, psychologists have found that women, more than men, depend on their primary love relationship for self-esteem and self-confidence. Many battered women adhere to traditional stereotypes of femininity and may consider their roles as wives and mothers central to their identity. The woman may believe it is her primary responsibility to make a happy home. When her partner beats her, it is "proof" that she has failed in this most important role. If she cannot please her man, she feels worthless and unlovable.

The battered woman is often socially isolated by her partner. He may restrict her activities and embarrass friends who visit until she is literally alone. She may get little feedback from people or activities outside her home. On the other hand, the battered woman's isolation may be more subtle. I worked with a very successful attorney who was also a battered woman. In court, the woman was a defense attorney who fought hard and successfully for her clients. At home at night, she was expected to prepare her husband's dinner, and if he was displeased with her cooking, her appearance, or even her conversation, she would be hit. No one in her public life could have guessed that this assertive woman would play such a traditional, subservient role at home. This woman reported that she felt competent and strong at work, but she believed that if she couldn't please her husband she was not really a successful woman. Like many battered women, she hid the violence against her in shame and embarrassment.

Whether the battered woman is literally imprisoned by her batterer or finds herself isolated from others by shame and silence, she gets little feedback from others. The batterer becomes the primary source of her information about her attractiveness, competence, and worth. As the battering and isolation continue, women report that it becomes harder and harder for them to remember "who I was" before the battering began. During the loving reconciliation, the man often rebuilds the woman's shattered self-esteem with his love and praise. It is not surprising that it is very difficult for her to leave him when he is meeting such a desperate need and easy for her to believe that somehow this time it is different and things will be better.

Passive and Dependent Behavior

As we have seen, the batterer is usually very jealous and controlling. The woman learns that to appear to be too independent or assertive will increase his anger and invite violence. The woman's passive and dependent behavior makes the man feel powerful and in control; it reassures him and sometimes postpones the violence. Thus, the passive-dependent behavior of the woman is adaptive, a survival strategy that is rewarded within the battering relationship. Unfortunately, such behavior helps to trap the woman in the relationship. Passivity and dependence increase her sense of helplessness and make it more difficult for her to gather the courage and resources she needs in order to leave.

Guilt and Shame

One aspect of the cognitive distortion we have discussed is the victims' belief that they can control the violence by changing their own behavior. The woman may accept the man's explanations for the violence as well as the common social attitude that "no man beats a good woman." The woman feels ashamed that she has failed to be "good enough." Accepting blame for her situation may actually be the woman's attempt to combat the sense of despair and helplessness she feels. She holds onto the hope that a change in her behavior will stop the violence.

Hope notwithstanding, nothing the woman does can ultimately control the man's violence. She may cook perfect meals, look like a Barbie doll, and agree with everything the man says, yet she will still be beaten. It is the abuser who is in control, not the victim. Ultimately the woman finds herself with a painful choice between guilt and despair. When she believes she has the power to control the violence, she escapes the feelings of total helplessness and despair. However, by accepting responsibility for the man's violence, she is also accepting the man's blame of her. The double bind can be devastating. If the woman realizes that she has no control over the violence, then she may not feel guilt, but her feelings of fear, despair, and powerlessness may be immobilizing, and she may find it difficult to act to protect herself or leave. On the other hand, if she feels responsible and believes she has some control, then the guilt keeps her in the relationship trying to change her behavior to stop the violence. Either way, she is trapped.

While working in the shelter, I found that battered women were very relieved to learn about the cycle of violence and the social-psychological theories of victim response. For the first time, many felt less isolated and "crazy"—their behavior in forgiving the man and staying in the relationship made sense to them, and they were not alone. Ironically, women may find that they can stay away once they stop blaming themselves for staying so long.

WHEN THE BATTERED WOMAN LEAVES

The U.S. Department of Justice included questions about domestic violence in the National Crime Survey for the first time in 1986. This scientific poll questions a stratified sample of more than 800,000 Americans and is the basis for the FBI's estimates of the frequency of crime in the country. When this huge sample of people were asked about crime in relationships, a phenomenal statistic emerged. The U.S. Department of Justice found that 70 percent of domestic violence happened *after* the women had left the relationship.

The battering man's need for power and control are increased when the woman leaves him, and the result is increased harassment and violence. When California enacted a law against stalking in the early 1990s— after a series of assaults on movie stars by berserk fans—the primary beneficiary became battered women because most stalkers turned out to be former husbands and boyfriends. Studies of partner homicide have also revealed that the time of a women's leaving is the most deadly, for both the woman and the man. Some critics of the feminist view of family violence have used homicide statistics to suggest that women are nearly as violent as men; the most recent findings suggest that over 40 percent of partner homicides are men killed by women (Hirschman, 1994; Sherven & Sniechowski, 1994). These critics overlook an important gender difference in partner homicide: Battered women kill defending themselves and trying to leave; battering men kill the women who are trying to leave or have succeeded in doing so.

Violence is not the only strategy the battering man uses to keep the woman from leaving or forcing her to return. In discussions in the literature of the reasons women stay in or return to violent relationships, the women's fears for their children's safety and well-being have been generally overlooked. Threats of child kidnapping, custody battles, or violence against the children are significant factors in keeping the women in violent relationships. I conducted a pilot study (Stahly, Oursler, & Takano, 1988) of 94 women in shelters who reported that their batterers had tried to keep them from leaving by threatening the children with physical harm (25 percent), kidnapping (25 percent), or legal actions for custody (35 percent). In this sample, 20 percent of the women reported returning to the batterer at least once because of his threats to hurt or take away the children.

In a larger survey of the problems battered women face when they leave the batterer, staff members from 37 shelters in California completed a survey to describe the experiences of their clients (Stahly, 1990). During a one-year period, these shelters reported serving 6,034 women and 8,550 children as resident clients and 14,637 women and 4,204 children as nonresident clients and providing hotline counseling to an additional 87,378 women. The shelter staff were asked to reconstruct from their case files and staff logs information regarding the problems their clients experienced with custody and visitation. Their reports were astonishing. Of more than 100,000 women with whom the shelter staff had contact, 34 percent had children threatened with kidnapping, and 11 percent of the batterers had actually kidnapped a child—a total of 10,687 kidnappings in California in one year! Most of these kidnappings were never reported to the police, and the father returned the children after hours or days, but the point was made. The women were on notice that if they did not return to their batterer or give him whatever he wanted, he would take the children and she might never see them again!

Fathers also used court action to intimidate and control the women, with 22,813 (23 percent) fathers threatening custody action and 7,168 fathers filing actions for sole custody. It is disturbing that the shelter staff reported that the batterers who had not directly abused their children actually won full custody less often (1,844) than fathers who were physically (2,997) or sexually abusive (2,262). This finding is consistent with the observation that mothers who report child abuse during custody proceedings are not only ignored but are sometimes seen as "vindictive" and are actually punished by the court (Chesler, 1986). Also disturbing is the tendency of courts to ignore violence and abuse in orders regarding visitation. In 25 percent (24,719) of the cases the batterer used court-ordered visitation as an occasion to continue verbal and emotional abuse, and in 10 percent (9,512) of cases the mother was physically abused during the father's visits.

When the father makes good his threat to dispute custody, he is surprisingly successful. Chesler (1986), in an extensive clinical and case history study of women's experiences with custody, found that "good-enough" mothers lost custodial challenges 70 percent of the time, often to fathers who were abusive of the woman and children. In a study of randomly selected court records, a colleague and I found that violent fathers were twice as likely as nonviolent fathers to dispute the mother's custody of the children (Suchanek & Stahly, 1991). The courts apparently did not consider the history of violence important, because the violent fathers won custody as often as the nonviolent fathers—or the mothers. The violent fathers were also more likely to want custody of sons than daughters, and they were more likely *not* to be paying court-ordered child support (a fact that seemed not to influence the judges' assessment of their parental fitness). The findings regarding custody disputes and woman battering seem to support the feminist analysis of battering men as motivated by power and control needs—and by misogyny.

CONCLUSION

We have discussed a number of explanations of why a battered woman stays in a violent relationship. Many different theories have been advanced to explain the women's behavior. This reinforces the notion that the problem of family violence could be solved by convincing the women to leave. Early on, feminists focused their energy on developing alternatives for battered women, including working to establish shelters and change the policies of the criminal justice system and social-welfare systems that discouraged a woman from leaving and staying away.

I found that at every speech I gave as a shelter director, someone would ask some variation of the question, Why doesn't she just leave? I would do my best as a social psychologist and a women's advocate to help the audience understand and sympathize. I often asked the question I posed earlier: Why should a woman and her children have to leave home to be safe? Then after working 10 years on the issue of battered women, something dramatic happened to my thinking about the issue of leaving. I read the National Crime Survey of the Department Justice cited above indicating that 70 percent of domestic violence crime happened after the woman left. I realized that asking, Why does she stay? was begging the question! The fallacy of victim blame informed the question: We assumed that leaving would end the violence, and therefore the woman was made culpable for staying.

Now we know the terrible truth. Leaving the relationship does not end the violence for thousands of battered women. Not only does the violence continue, it often escalates when the woman leaves. The feminist theory of battering as political—based on the man's power and control needs—is validated by the fact that the man is even more likely to assault and even kill the woman *after* she leaves. The reality of the battered woman's situation is not only that she is often trapped in the relationship, but even when she escapes that trap she is still prey to the violent, possessive man. It is important to understand the factors that discourage women from leaving, but the real dilemma is how to protect women who do find the courage and resources to leave.

In the final analysis, the best answer to the question, Why don't they just leave? is simply, They can't. Battered women don't stay because of love, or dependency, or even economics; too often they stay from the sheer terror that leaving will be even more dangerous than staying. We, as a society, will not effectively address the tragedy of family violence until we stop asking questions about the victim's character and behavior and demand instead that the abuser be held responsible.

REFERENCES

APA Task Force. (1975). Report of the task force on sex bias and sex role stereotyping in psychotherapeutic practice. *American Psychologist, 30,* 1169–1175.

Aries, P. (1970). *Centuries of childhood: A social history of family life.* New York: Knopf.

Bard, M., & Zacker, J. (1971). The prevention of family violence: Dilemmas of community intervention. *Journal of Marriage and the Family, 33,* 677–683.

Bograd, M. B. (1984). Family systems approaches to wife battering: A feminist critique. *American Journal of Orthopsychiatry, 54*(4), 558–568.

Bograd, M. B. (1990). Why we need gender to understand human violence. *Journal of Interpersonal Violence, 5*(1), 132–135.

Brownmiller, S. (1975). *Against our will: Men, women, and rape.* New York: Simon & Schuster.

CALIFORNIA JUDICIAL COUNCIL. (1991). *Gender bias in the courts.* Sacramento, CA: State of California.

CALVERT, R. (1974). Criminal and civil liability in husband-wife assaults. In S. Steimetz & M. Straus (Eds.), *Violence in the family* (pp. 88–90). New York: Harper & Row.

CHESLER, P. (1986). *Mothers on trial.* New York: McGraw-Hill.

COOLEY, C. S., & SEVERSON, K. (1993). Establishing feminist systemic criteria for viewing violence and alcoholism. In M. Hansen & M. Harway (Eds.), *Battering and family therapy: A feminist perspective* (pp. 217–225). Newbury Park, CA: Sage

DEUTSCH, H. (1945). *The psychology of women: A psychoanalytic interpretation, (Vol. 2).* New York: Grune & Stratton.

DOBASH, R. E., & DOBASH, R. P. (1979). *Violence against wives.* New York: Free Press.

DUTTON, D. G., & PAINTER, S. (1981). Traumatic bonding: The development of emotional attachments in battered women and other relationships of intermittent abuse. *Victimology: An International Journal, 1*(4), 139–155.

DUTTON, D. G., & PAINTER, S. (1993). Emotional attachments in abusive relationships: A test of traumatic bonding theory. *Violence and Victims, 8*(2), 105–120.

FREUD, S. (1925/1974). Some psychical consequences of the anatomical distinction between the sexes. In *The standard edition of the complete psychological works of Sigmund Freud* (Vol. 19). London: Hogarth Press and the Institute of Psycho-Analysis.

HANSEN, M. (1993). Feminism and family therapy: A review of feminist critiques of approaches to family violence. In M. Hansen & M. Harway (Eds.), *Battering and family therapy: A feminist perspective* (pp. 69–81). Newbury Park, CA: Sage.

HIRSHMAN, L. (1994, July 31). Scholars in the service of politics. *The Los Angeles Times,* p. M5.

HOTALING, G. T., & SUGARMAN, D. B. (1986). An analysis of risk markers in husband to wife violence: The current state of knowledge. *Violence and Victims, 1,* 101–124.

JAFFE, P. G., WOLFE, D. A., & WILSON, S. K. (1990). *Children of battered women: Issues in child development and intervention planning.* Newbury Park, CA: Sage.

KURTZ, L. (1989). Social science perspectives on wife abuse: Current debates and future directions. *Gender & Society, 3*(4), 489–505.

LANGER, P., & INNES, C. (1986, August). *Preventing violence against women.* Bureau of Justice Statistics Special Report. Washington, DC: U.S. Department of Justice, p. 3.

LAWSON, D. M. (1989). A family systems perspective on wife battering. *Journal of Mental Health Counseling, 11*(4), 359–374.

LISS, M. B., & STAHLY, G. B. (1993). Domestic violence and child custody. In M. Harway & M. Hansen (Eds.), *Battering and family therapy: A feminist perspective* (pp 175–187). Newbury Park, CA: Sage

MASSON, J. M. (1984, February). Freud and the seduction theory. *The Atlantic,* p. 12.

O'REILLY, J. (1983, September 5). Wife beating: Silent crime. *Time,* p. 30–32.

PAGELOW, M. D. (1984). *Family violence.* Westport, CT: Praeger.

RAJECKI, D. W., LAMB, M., & OBMASCHER, P. (1978). Toward a general theory of infantile attachment: A comparative review of aspects of the social bond. *Behavioral and Brain Sciences, 3,* 417–464.

SELIGMAN, M. E. (1975). *Helplessness: On depression, development and death.* San Francisco: Freeman.

SELIGMAN, M. E., & MAIER, S. F. (1968). Failure to escape traumatic shock. *Journal of Experimental Psychology, 78,* 340–343.

SHERVEN, J., & SNIECHOWSKI, J. (1994, June 21). Women are responsible too. *Los Angeles Times,* p. B7.

STAHLY, G. B. (1978). A review of select literature of spousal violence. *Victimology, 2* (3-4), 591–607.

STAHLY, G. B. (1980, August). *Psychosocial aspects of wife abuse: A theory of the spiralling effect of marital violence.* Paper presented at the meeting of the American Psychological Association, New York, NY.

STAHLY, G. B. (1987, March). *Roots of misogyny: Long-term effects of family violence on children's attitudes.* Paper presented at the meeting of the Association for Women in Psychology, Denver, CO.

STAHLY, G. B. (1990, April). *Battered women's problems with child custody.* Paper presented at the annual meeting of the Western Psychological Association, Los Angeles, CA.

STAHLY, G. B., OURSLER, A., & TAKANO, J. (1988, April). *Family violence and child custody: A survey of battered women's fears and experiences.* Paper presented at the annual meeting of the Western Psychological Association, San Francisco, CA.

STARK, R., & McEVOY, J. III. (1970, November). Middle-class violence. *Psychology Today,* pp. 30–31.

SUCHANEK, J., & STAHLY, G. B. (1991, April). *The relationship between domestic violence and paternal custody in divorce.* Paper presented at the meeting of the Western Psychological Association, San Francisco, CA.

TAUBMAN, S. (1986). Beyond bravado: Sex roles and the exploitive male. *Social Work, 31*(1), 12–18.

ULLRICH, V. H. (1986). Equal but not equal: A feminist perspective on family law. *Women's Studies International Forum, 9*(1), 41–48.

U.S. DEPARTMENT OF JUSTICE, BUREAU OF JUSTICE STATISTICS. (1986a). *Preventing domestic violence against women: Special report.* Washington, DC: U.S. Government Printing Office.

U.S. DEPARTMENT OF JUSTICE, BUREAU OF JUSTICE STATISTICS. (1986b). *National crime survey.* Washington, DC: U.S. Government Printing Office.

WALKER, L. E. A. (1977–1978). Battered women and learned helplessness. *Victimology, 2*(3/4), 525–534.

WALKER, L. E. A. (1979). *The battered woman.* New York: Springer.

WALKER, L. E. A. (1989). Psychology and violence against women. *American Psychologist, 44,* 695–702.

WEITZMAN, J., & DREEN, K. (1982). Wife beating: A view of the marital dyad. *Social Casework, 63,* 259–265.

WOLFGANG, M. E. (1958). *Patterns of criminal homicide.* Philadelphia: University of Pennsylvania Press.

WOLFGANG, M. E., & FERRACUTTI, F. (1967). *The subculture of violence: Towards an integrated theory of criminology.* New York: Tavistock Publications.

YLLO, K., & BOGRAD, M. (Eds.) (1988). *Feminist perspectives on wife abuse.* Newbury Park, CA: Sage.

SUGGESTED READINGS

HANSEN, M., & HARWAY, M. (Eds.). (1993). *Battering and family therapy: A feminist perspective.* Newbury Park, CA: Sage.

KOSS, M., GOODMAN, L., BROWNE, A., FITZGERALD, L., KEITA, G., & RUSSO, N. (1994). *No safe haven: Male violence against women at home, at work, and in the community.* Washington, DC: American Psychological Association.

WALKER, L. E. (1979). *The battered woman.* New York: Springer.

YLLO, K., & BOGRAD, M. (Eds.). (1988). *Feminist perspectives on wife abuse.* Newbury Park, CA: Sage.

PATRICIA **D. R**OZEE *is Associate Professor of Psychology and Women's Studies at California State University at Long Beach. Dr. Rozee has taught courses on the psychology of women since 1983 and has conducted research on a variety of women's issues. She is best known for her work on trauma, abuse, and psychosomatic blindness in Cambodian women immigrants.*

21

Freedom from Fear of Rape:

The Missing Link in Women's Freedom

❖

*A*set of collector prints called "The Four Freedoms" by the well-known artist Norman Rockwell was recently advertised in a popular magazine. Rockwell's four freedoms, as immortalized in these Americana prints, are freedom of speech, freedom from want, freedom of worship, and freedom from fear. The artist's message is that these are the freedoms Americans hold most dear. This lecture is concerned with the last of these—freedom from fear. For women in American society, freedom from fear, especially from fear of rape, is far from the present reality. Without freedom from fear, the other three freedoms are not possible. For how can you have freedom of speech and worship if you are afraid to leave your house? How can you have freedom from want if your economic opportunities are limited by fear of night work, bad neighborhoods, and aggressive coworkers? In fact, many writers have pointed out that the threat of sexual assault has essentially closed the door on women's freedom. As one therapist expresses it: "I have come to realize that fear is the last remaining enslaver of women" (Leland-Young & Nelson, 1987, p. 203). Women may fear a number of things—getting older, not being thin—but many theorists point out that the fear of rape unites all women (Koss et al., 1994, p. 157).

Feminist theorists Susan Brownmiller (1975) and Susan Griffin (1979), among others, have held that the fear of rape is universal among women. Susan Griffin expressed the feelings of many women when she wrote: "I have never been free of the fear of rape. From a very early age I, like most women, have thought of rape as part of my natural environment—something to be feared and prayed against like fire or lightning" (p. 3). "The fear of rape keeps women off the streets at night. Keeps women at home. Keeps women passive and modest for fear that they be thought provocative" (p. 21).

Both theorists and researchers have considered the fear of rape to be a means of social control, a way to keep women in their place: at home or under male protection. Several studies have shown that, indeed, fear of rape is quite prevalent among women, as are self-imposed restrictive behaviors intended primarily to avoid rape (Riger & Gordon, 1981; Warr, 1985).

In a study of fear of rape among urban women, Mark Warr (1985) found that rape is feared more than any other offense (including murder, assault, and robbery) among women under age 35. Two-thirds of the young women in his study were classified as fearful of rape. One-third of the entire sample reported the highest possible levels of fear (10 on a scale of 0 to 10). A high fear of rape is reported in my own surveys of both community and college women. On the item, "I am scared of rape" 46 percent of the women marked the highest possible agreement, 6 or 7 on a 7-point Likert scale. When asked to what extent they thought getting raped would be devastating to their lives, nearly half of the women marked the highest possible agreement levels (Rozee-Koker, Wynne, & Mizrahi, 1989). Think about your own fear of rape: How would you rate yourself on the above items?

Women who report high fear of rape describe it as "the hum that's always there" in women's lives (Rozee-Koker et al., 1989). They were also more likely to believe that there is a "core of fear" instilled early in little girls. These women saw the fear of rape as a major organizing principle of women's lives.

Women's fear of crime, especially rape, results in their use of more precautionary behaviors than men (Riger & Gordon, 1981; Rozee-Koker, 1987). Fear of rape is also the best predictor of the use of isolation behaviors, such as not leaving the house (Riger, Gordon & LeBailly (1982), and of assertive behaviors (Rozee-Koker, 1987; Rozee-Koker et al., 1989). Assertive behaviors include "street-savvy" tactics intended to reduce risks in dangerous situations, such as wearing shoes that allow one to run and being aware of whom one sits near on the bus, as well as physical self-defense tactics. Stephanie Riger and Margaret Gordon (1981) conducted in-person interviews with women and found that 41 percent used isolation tactics all or most of the time or fairly often, and 74 percent reported frequent use of street-savvy tactics.

Women's fears were most likely to result in avoidance of discretionary activities, those activities they enjoy most, such as visiting friends or going out for evening entertainment.

Although these are disheartening findings in terms of women's freedom, it occurred to me that the frequent use of active strategies or street savvy by about three-quarters of the women in Riger and Gordon's study could also be looked at in a more positive way. These women are not just sitting around being timid and fearful; they are actively engaged in manipulating a dangerous environment for their own protection. These women are not victims—most women take a great many actions to prevent victimization. Later I will discuss specific avoidance and prevention strategies used by women. But first, how does fear of rape develop among girls and women?

DEVELOPMENT OF FEAR OF RAPE

Studies that attempt to explain women's fear of rape have come to a number of conclusions. Women fear rape because women are the primary victims of rape and other forms of male sexual violence, women perceive a high likelihood of becoming victimized, women are socialized to be vulnerable to rape and to fear it, and the social and institutional systems reinforce fear of rape by placing blame on the victim. Through these mechanisms women come to fear rape and distrust other people, especially men. In fact some writers have asserted that the fear of rape is essentially the fear of men (Stanko, 1993).

Female Victimization and Assessment of Likelihood

Early studies repeatedly documented women's greater fear of crime, especially rape. Women report levels of fear three times higher than men's (Stanko, 1993). Women's apparently lower levels of crime victimization compared to men in crime victim surveys may lead people to believe that somehow women's fears are not objectively based. But recent authors have pointed out the "hidden" forms of victimization of women (Smith, 1988) and the fact that such victimization takes place in a pervasive atmosphere of sexual threat to women (Stanko, 1993). Crime victim surveys frequently do not ask about the forms of victimization most prevalent in women's lives. Women's assessment of the risk of rape is based on a background of other experiences of victimization, from harassment by men on the street and in the office, to obscene phone callers and flashers, to rape by trusted intimates (that is, date, acquaintance, incestuous, and marital rapes) and woman battering. Most women who are beaten and raped are not attacked by strangers but by trusted male intimates. A majority of women who are murdered are murdered by husbands or boyfriends (Barnett & LaViolette, 1993). Elizabeth Stanko (1993) puts this sense of sexual danger most succinctly:

> Women gather information about potential personal danger and violence throughout their lifetime (Stanko, 1990). Direct involvement with violence; the "but nothing happened" encounters; observations of other women's degradation; the impact of the media and cultural images of women; and

> shared knowledge of family, friends, peers, acquaintances and co-workers all contribute to assessments of risk and strategies for safety. (p. 159)

From these observations women assess their level of sexual vulnerability, and from this assessment comes their level of fear.

There is a strong relationship between experiences of sexual intrusion and fear of rape. Alina Holgate (1989) found that all the women in her sample had experienced fear-inducing sexual intrusions or harassment and that such intrusions were significantly related to reported fear of rape. Every woman had been honked at, whistled at, leered at, propositioned, and commented upon sexually. Nearly all the women (two-thirds or more) reported that they had been followed, physically restrained, pressured for sex, hassled by men in hotels, rubbed against, grabbed or fondled; they had received obscene phone calls, witnessed a flasher or masturbator, or been in a likely rape situation. The most fearful women were those who had been followed (71 percent) or been in a likely rape situation (62 percent). Other researchers (for example, Junger, 1987; Rozee-Koker et al., 1989) have also found that the more victimization experiences a woman has had, the more fearful she is.

Situational or environmental factors can also elicit fear of rape. Research indicates that the physical environment is one of the strongest factors in exacerbating fear of rape and enacting protective strategies among women (Riger & Gordon, 1984). The most fearful situation for the working women in my study was being harassed on the street by men (Rozee-Koker et al., 1989). Three-fourths of the women marked the highest possible fear response (6 or 7 on a 7-point scale) for this item. The strong, negative psychological effects of street harassment reported here belie the common myth among men that women enjoy such attentions and take them as compliments.

Among professional working women situational factors in the workplace, such as poor lighting, lack of security in parking areas, and sexual harassment contribute to women's fear of rape (Rozee-Koker et al., 1989). The most fearful work-related situations tend to be associated with working late or being in unfamiliar surroundings. Fears directly pertaining to professional travel were the fear of arriving late at night in a distant city, working in unfamiliar parts of town, and fear of travel in rural areas. Working overtime when no one else is around was also fear-inducing for many women. Other major fear-inducing situations were having to be in poorly lighted areas, being alone and having strangers pay unwanted attention to you, being around physically aggressive people, and having to use underground or isolated parking areas.

Women who perceive themselves as having a high likelihood of being raped report more fear of rape (Riger, 1981; Rozee-Koker, 1987). In addition to previous victimization experiences, another way that women assess the likelihood of rape concerns the way rape is represented in the mass media. Media depictions of women as the victims of all manner of brutal sex crimes heighten women's perception of the likelihood of rape. Recently, a number of television commercials sponsored by home security companies and cellular phone companies have capitalized on women's fear of rape in order to sell products. One particularly offensive ad depicts a woman who is stranded when her car breaks down at night on a deserted stretch of road. She looks fearfully over her shoulder when she sees a strange man pull up behind her and get out of his car to help. She is portrayed as weak, helpless, and badly in need of—you guessed it, a car phone! The National Rifle Association has also capitalized on women's increasing fears by offering their particular brand of solution—automatic weapons (Neuborne, 1994). And it has worked. Women are buying guns in unprecedented numbers despite a threefold increase in the risk of being killed or having someone in one's family killed when there is a gun in the house (Jones, 1994). Nearly 50,000 children were killed by firearms between 1979 and 1991; and every six hours a teenager commits suicide with a gun (Jones, 1994; see also *Ms.,* May/June 1994, for an excellent issue on women and guns).

The way in which the news media report rape leaves one with the impression that it happens all the time and that women have little or no chance of escaping a would-be rapist. This couldn't be further from the truth. In fact, most women *do* escape. The random-sample survey of households conducted by the National Crime Victim Survey (NCVS) for the Census Bureau found that there are four attempted rapes for every completed rape (a ratio of 4 to 1). But the press covers only one attempted rape for every thirteen completed rapes. This gives the false impression that there are far more completed rapes than attempted rapes, whereas the reverse is actually true (Riger & Gordon, 1989). Why is this important? Because an attempted rape is a rape where the victim fought back, escaped, and was *not raped*. Women are 4 times more likely to fight back and escape their would-be rapists than they are to be raped. Who would not be scared if they believe media reports that women are 13 times more likely to be raped than to escape rape? What a terrible disservice this kind of sensationalist reporting is to women! It exaggerates women's helplessness, increases fear of rape among women, and instills a lack of confidence in our ability to fight back.

One lesson that can be learned from the pervasive fear-inducing effects of media presentations of rape is that firsthand experience with rape is not needed to instill a fear of rape among women. In societies where rape is classified as rare, even the concept of rape as communicated through folk tales (for example, where a fictional person is punished by being raped) is effective in keeping women in their place and fearful (Rozee, 1993).

In addition, the racist portrayal by the media of rapists as disproportionately Black men, as well as the greater frequency of arrests of Black men due to inequities in the criminal justice system, lead white women to fear Black men in particular. In truth, most violent crimes are intraracial, occurring primarily between people of the same race and socioeconomic class (Amir, 1971; O'Brien, 1987). When one also considers that many unreported sexual assaults are within families (incestuous or marital rapes), the probability of being sexually assaulted by a person of the same race becomes even greater.

We can conclude then that women experience a wide variety of sexual intrusions throughout life as well as media images of women as ineffective at stopping such intrusions. Women's fear of rape is thus based on an accurate assessment of the risk of sexual intrusion coupled with a wide variety of prior victimization experiences and media reinforcement of the victim image of women.

Socialization of Fear

Many authors have pointed to the socialization practices of U.S. society and the tendency to encourage girls to be weak and passive and boys to be strong and aggressive. Many women are still raised to defer to men, to support men in their goals, and to expect men to take care of them and protect them. Girls are expected to be ladylike, timid, dependent, and quiet and never to embarrass anyone by making a scene. Many of these socialized traits are in direct opposition to being able to successfully defend oneself. They may also leave women with negative perceptions of their physical competence and a lack of physical strength and endurance. I have seen women at the gym lifting tiny 5-pound weights, one in each hand, and saying to the trainer, "I don't want to get big muscles." A friend told me recently that her former partner used to admonish her to stop working out so much because she was getting too muscular. Why are we socialized to believe that physical strength is a negative trait? Women's negative perceptions of physical competence may play a part in their levels of fear and precaution (Riger, 1981).

In addition there is a social expectation that women will, and should, have a man to protect them. Yet how can women feel safe in the company of men when most rapes are committed by male dates and acquaintances? Still, I have heard female students ask a male stranger (a fellow student) in the class to walk her to her car rather than risk walking with a female friend!

Fear of rape seems to develop early in life. The women in our sample remembered receiving parental warnings between the ages of 2 and 12 years old about avoiding strangers (Rozee-Koker et al., 1989). The nervousness of some parents about this issue is illustrated by the fact that the earlier a girl received warnings about such things as avoiding strangers, the more often she was warned to avoid them. Some parents encourage their young daughters to fight back if ever confronted by a threatening situation. In their book, *Stopping Rape: Successful Survival Strategies*, Pauline Bart and Patricia O'Brien (1985) report the results of in-depth interviews with 94 women volunteers from an urban community who were either raped or who had avoided rape. They found significant racial and ethnic differences in childhood socialization to fight back. A majority of Black women were advised by parents to fight back, whereas Jewish women were least likely of all groups to receive such parental advice. The authors note that although verbal skills are prized in traditional Jewish families, physical fighting is considered "un-Jewish." Discussion of rape was reportedly more common among Black families. The Black women in their study seemed to learn how to deal with violence in concrete ways rather than developing a somewhat abstract fear of rape. Black women who were accosted used more kinds of strategies than did other women, and even though they often faced weapons or multiple offenders, their strategies were more likely to fend off an attacker.

Bart and O'Brien also found differences between women who were raped and those who avoided rape on parental discipline, sports participation, and expectations for their future. Women who avoided rape were more likely to have played contact sports like football as children and to have maintained their participation in sports as an adult. Their greater physical strength, agility, and belief in their own physical competence may explain this finding. Rape avoiders were also more nontraditional in their ideas of how they would be as grown-ups. Whereas 40 percent of raped women looked forward to an adult life of domesticity, rape avoiders were more likely to mention jobs or careers. All children fight with their siblings, but parents of women who were raped were more likely to intervene in the fight and punish the children and less likely to advise daughters to fight back in quarrels. Women who avoided rape were more likely at an early age to have been encouraged to "fight it out" and stick up for themselves without help. Such parental attitudes seem to instill an early sense of both the right and the ability to fight for oneself.

It is interesting that 51 percent of rape avoiders in the Bart and O'Brien study said that fear of rape and/or the determination not to be raped was their main thought in the rape situation compared to only 7 percent of raped women. Women who were raped were more concerned about avoiding physical injury or death. They reasoned that if they went along with the rape they would reduce the chances of physical injury or death. Unfortunately, many of these women were physically injured anyway.

Contrary to popular belief, researchers have found that by physically resisting immediately, women reduce both the chances of being raped *and* the amount of injury to themselves (Bart, 1981, 1985; Kleck & Sayles, 1990; Queens Bench Foundation, 1975). These studies found that physical resistance by the woman was much more likely to result in avoiding rape than to result in injuries. However, it is important to note that not all women can avoid rape, even if they do fight back. But even among women who are raped, fighting back has the effect of facilitating psychological recovery. Perhaps women who fight back are more likely to believe that they did all they could to prevent the assault. Even if she does not fight back, it is important to remember that each woman makes the best decision she can under such circumstances; no woman should be blamed for being raped if she chooses *not* to defend herself.

Women receive warnings about various dangers throughout their lives. The warnings come from a number of sources including parents, boyfriends, friends, and, of course, the media. Martha Burt and Rhoda Estep (1981) describe the way in which such warnings communicate a sense of danger among women.

> If warnings reflect other people's expectations that someone needs protecting, the present data on warnings suggest that adult males are perceived as able to take care of themselves, while adult females and children of both sexes received warnings which assume they are in some danger. (p. 516)

Presumably, when one is instilled with a sense of danger it will arouse a measure of fear.

Societal and Institutional Factors

Joyce Williams (1984) cites public attitudes about rape as a source of the secondary victimization of women; she maintains that the pervasive atmosphere of victim blaming in our society adds to the trauma of a rape victim. Although both women and men engage in victim blaming, research finds consistent gender differences, with females less likely than males to blame the victim for her rape. On our campus a female student was raped at knife point on a Sunday afternoon while she worked on a project in the art studio. I heard students talking about the case. They asked, "What was she doing on campus alone?" "Why was she there on a Sunday?" "Didn't she scream—surely there were others somewhere around?" According to the just-world theory, people blame the victim because of their belief that the world is a just place where bad things only happen to bad people. By distancing themselves from the victim in this way, they can feel safer.

The social tendency to blame and restrict women while excusing men's behavior extends to so-called solutions to the social problem of violence against women. Golda Meir, the late prime minister of Israel, upon hearing that the Parliament was considering a curfew on women in order to stop violence against women called into question the androcentric (male-centered) assumptions inherent in such a solution. She pointed out that if you really want women to be safe on the streets, you need to put a curfew on *men!* Indeed some students at Brigham Young University (BYU), prompted by an on-campus attack of a female student proposed such a curfew. BYU admonished women not to walk alone on campus at night, thus effectively putting a curfew on women. Women students claimed that violence against women would stop immediately if men, not women, had such a curfew (Corbin, 1991). They hung flyers all over campus that said:

> Due to the increase in violence against women on BYU campus, a new curfew has been instated. Beginning on Wednesday, November 20, men will no longer be allowed to walk alone or in all-male groups from 10 PM until 6 AM. Those men who must travel on or through campus during curfew hours must be accompanied by two women in order to demonstrate that they are not threatening. Provisions have been made for men who need to be escorted home. (p. 6)

The action by the women on campus was itself empowering. By refusing to be restricted in their behavior they at least opened a dialogue among students about the inherent assumptions in such restrictions. The men seemed to understand restrictions of *their* rights; one male stated, "You can't curb our rights just to give someone else rights" (p. 6) Click!

Other ways in which social and institutional forces tend to engender fear of rape include the "revictimization" of rape victims by police, hospitals, and the courts. In fact, the criminal justice system, the state, and the individual men with whom women live have been termed "the collective male protection system" (Hanmer & Saunders, cited in Smith, 1988.) It is a male-controlled system that *regulates* violence against women in the guise of protecting women (Rozee, 1993). All women are taught to be dependent for protection on the very system that enables violence against women to go essentially unpunished.

To summarize, there are a number of ways in which the fear of rape is instilled in women, starting at an early age and continuing throughout adulthood. Socialization practices, personal experiences with male violence, media representations of women, and social and institutional supports for women's fear of rape insure that women will perceive a high likelihood of being raped and thus a heightened level of fear of rape.

Many women are beginning to challenge the institutions that keep them in fear. Rape crisis centers and hotlines are banding together with police, district attorneys, and hospital staff to form sexual assault response teams (SART), safe places for women to report rape and receive treatment for injuries. The processing of rape complaints has improved greatly in cities with SART teams. Many women's groups are pressuring legislators, government and university officials, and corporate leaders to make changes in the situations that create fear.

Many recent writers have focused on the role of men and male-controlled institutions in stopping rape (see Funk, 1993; Riger & Gordon, 1989; Warshaw, 1988). This is a positive step in the direction of curbing rape in our society. In the meantime, though, women must cope with the threat of rape every day of their lives. How do they cope with the fear that this engenders?

*C*OPING WITH FEAR

From childhood on, women develop certain coping mechanisms and behaviors to reduce fear. These may involve general coping style as well as orientation toward action solutions such as self-defense, home security, and so on. I will first discuss women's ways of coping with fear of rape. Later I will describe the tactics that women use to defend against rape and thus alleviate fear.

My survey of professional women (Rozee-Koker et al., 1989) indicates that women tend to cope cognitively with fear in one of three ways: by denial, flooding, or reasoning. Women who use *denial* as a primary mechanism are most likely fearful, but they have buried their fear as a method of defense against it. Their lives may actually revolve around the fear of rape, but their preventive mechanisms are so firmly in place that they have lost sight of the fact that they are even using such mechanisms. They will say such things as, "I don't worry about rape, I always carry a 357 Magnum with me." These women may see fear as a weakness and thus fight to control it by bravado (for example, carrying a gun) or rationalization ("It will never happen to me.").

Women who use *flooding* as their primary coping style are quick to acknowledge fear of rape, sometimes to an extreme degree. Such women are frequently overtly fearful, constantly vigilant, and incorporate a bewildering array of prevention and avoidance tactics into their lifestyles as a way of reducing fear.

Women who use *reasoning* as a coping style acknowledge fear but try to balance it with their needs for freedom. They may perform a kind of cost-benefit analysis, weighing the value of the behavior (for example, taking a new higher paying job) against the risks of such behavior (for example, having to work in a bad part of town).

Behaviorally, women may cope with fear of rape by taking some kind of personal, social, or political action related to the problem situation. Most women have a multitude of methods for easing fear. In my class on the psychology of women, I ask women to call out the daily precautions that they take while I write them all on the chalkboard. The number of individual precautions most women take every day is staggering. The men in my classes are usually astonished at the lists. One female student told me that while we were constructing this huge list of strategies, her boyfriend whispered to her, "You don't do all these things, do you?" She was as amazed by the question as he was by the answer, "Yes, of course I do." Men lead very different existences with regard to safety; they find it hard to believe that women live this way. You might take five minutes and jot down a list of the precautions you take every day. Share your list with a male friend.

Some common safety strategies are walking to the car with others when possible, holding keys between the fingers, carefully checking the back seat and under the car before getting in, always having both money and gasoline in the car when leaving the house, keeping doors and windows locked at home and in the car, always telling someone where they will be and when they expect to return. Half of the professional women in my study had taken self-defense classes, and over three-quarters had planned rape prevention strategies for themselves (Rozee-Koker et al., 1989).

Women who are fearful of rape or who perceive themselves as having a strong likelihood of being raped are more likely to take actions to prevent rape (Rozee-Koker et al., 1989). Of course, if and how women decide to take action must be determined by each woman based on her individual needs and skills (Rozee, Bateman, & Gilmore, 1992). Some women have made major job sacrifices in order to reduce fear and increase perceived safety. Over one-fourth of the women in my study reported refusing job opportunities in bad areas, over half reported making longer commutes to work in order to live in safer neighborhoods, and 20 percent had refused a job for reasons of personal safety (Rozee-Koker et al., 1989). Obviously, these strategies have costs: fewer opportunities and less time for job-related commitments because of long commutes.

No matter how you look at it, the fear of rape has profound effects on the freedoms experienced by most women. Clearly women are taking every precaution to protect themselves. One wonders about the psychological stress produced as a result of having to enact such a vast array of protective strategies. Because rape and its accompanying stigma affect women to a far greater extent than men, it is unlikely that many males must pay such extreme costs to protect themselves.

In addition, about half of the working women in my study saw fear of rape as a barrier to women's career development (Rozee-Koker et al., 1989). Nearly two-thirds of the women thought that women are denied equal access to occupational status because of their own or others' worries about their sexual safety. Jan Leland-Young and Joan Nelson (1987) had a particularly powerful way of expressing how fear of rape affects women's education and career development:

> No matter how many reforms were accomplished, if women were in danger and in fear of utilizing those reforms, they were useless. It seemed to me that our society, by ignoring and often condoning violence against women, had very successfully found a way to make women oppress and limit themselves. It was not necessary to forbid women to go to school or work. With the fear of rape, women would avoid certain jobs, locations, libraries, buildings, even cities. (Leland-Young & Nelson, 1987, p. 204)

Successful reductions of women's fear of rape will require a multifaceted approach. First, as Leland-Young and Nelson point out above, the internalization of fear and its concomitant self-enforced behavioral restrictions must be addressed. The socialization of girls' and boys' roles in the victim-victimizer scenario must be challenged. In addition, changes must be made to insure women's safety, such as improvement of physical environments, education of the public as well as members of the criminal justice system, enforcement of existing rape laws, and creation of new antirape policies.

Combatting fear of rape and empowering women require solutions aimed at *changing* the dangerous situations first (such as adding security in parking areas) rather than only focusing on helping women *adapt* to dangerous situations (as in learning to walk assertively). The physical environment is especially in need of attention by installing more and better lighting, more accessible and patrolled parking, escort service, and other measures designed to relieve women of the entire burden of self-protection. Next, educational programs need to be set up for men with regard to sexual harassment, sexually aggressive behavior, and sexual remarks and pictorial displays. Explicit enforcement of antisexual harassment policies are necessary. Institutions need to become more mindful of their role in preventing rape. After changes have been enacted in the *situational* factors that contribute to reduced perception of safety, the *empowerment* of women can be served by free or low-cost self-defense classes and rape prevention trainings. Prevention efforts must have a much greater focus on the prevention of date and acquaintance rape because it is estimated that they comprise the majority of sexual assaults. Education of women to potential hazards, as well as training in protective responses, can be helpful after situational causes of fear have been addressed (Rozee et al., 1992).

Expression of concern for and action toward women's safety is in itself empowering. Many actions that are not costly immediately increase the perception of a safer environment (for example, sexual harassment workshops) and thus reduce fear. Public policies and practices aimed at fear reduction and empowerment may give women a first step toward enjoying *all* of the four freedoms.

REFERENCES

AMIR, M. (1971). *Patterns in forcible rape.* Chicago: University of Chicago Press.

BARNETT, O. W., & LAVIOLETTE, A. D. (1993). *It could happen to anyone: Why battered women stay.* Newbury Park, CA: Sage.

BART, P. (1981). A study of women who both were raped and avoided rape. *Journal of Social Issues, 37,* 123–137.

BART, P. B., & O'BRIEN, P. (1985). *Stopping rape: Successful survival strategies.* New York: Pergamon Press.

BROWNMILLER, S. (1975). *Against our will: Men, women and rape.* New York: Simon & Schuster.

BURT, M. R., & ESTEP, R. E. (1981). Apprehension and fear: Learning a sense of sexual vulnerability. *Sex Roles, 7,* 511–522.

CORBIN, B. (1991, December). Women's group proposes curfew for men. *National NOW Times,* p. 6.

FUNK, R. E. (1993). *Stopping rape: A challenge for men.* Philadelphia: New Society Publishers.

GRIFFIN, S. (1979). *Rape: The power of consciousness.* San Francisco: Harper & Row.

HOLGATE, A. (1989). Sexual harassment as a determinant of women's fear of rape. *Australian Journal of Sex, Marriage and Family, 10,* 21–28.

JONES, A. (1994, May/June). Living with guns, playing with fire. *Ms. Magazine,* pp. 38–45.

JUNGER, M. (1987). Women's experiences of sexual harassment. *British Journal of Criminology, 27,* 358–383.

KLECK, G., & SAYLES, S. (1990). Rape and resistance. *Social Problems, 37,* 149–162.

KOSS, M. P., GOODMAN, L. A., BROWNE, A., FITZGERALD, L. F., KEITA, G. P., & RUSSO, N. G. (1994). United all women: The fear of rape. In *No safe haven: Male violence against women at home, at work, and in the community* (pp. 157–176). Washington, DC: American Psychological Association.

LELAND-YOUNG, J., & NELSON, J. (1987). Prevention of sexual assault through the resocialization of women: Unlearning victim behavior. *Women & Therapy, 6,* 203–210.

NEUBORNE, E. (1994, May/June). Cashing in on fear: The NRA targets women. *Ms. Magazine,* pp. 46–50.

O'BRIEN, R. M. (1987). The interracial nature of violent crimes: A reexamination. *American Journal of Sociology, 92,* 817–835.

QUEEN'S BENCH FOUNDATION. (1975). *Rape victimization study: Final report.* San Francisco: Queen's Bench Foundation.

RIGER, S. (1981). Reactions to crime: Impacts of crime on women. *Sage Criminal Justice System Annuals, 16,* 47–55.

RIGER, S., & GORDON, M. (1981). The fear of rape: A study in social control. *Journal of Social Issues, 37*(4), 71–94.

RIGER, S., & GORDON, M. (1984). The impact of crime on urban women. In A. Rickel, M. Gerrard, & I. Iscoe (Eds.), *The social and psychological problems of women* (pp. 139–156). Washington, DC: Hemisphere.

RIGER, S., & GORDON, M. (1989). *The female fear.* New York: Free Press.

RIGER, S., GORDON, M., & LEBAILLY, R. (1982). Coping with urban crime: Women's use of precautionary behaviors. *American Journal of Community Psychology, 10,* 369–386.

ROZEE, P. (1993). Forbidden or forgiven: Rape in cross-cultural perspective. *Psychology of Women Quarterly, 17,* 499–514.

ROZEE, P., BATEMAN, P., & GILMORE, T. (1992). The personal perspective of acquaintance rape prevention: A three-tier approach. In A. Parrot & L. Bechhofer (Eds.), *Acquaintance rape: The hidden crime* (pp. 337–354). New York: John Wiley.

ROZEE-KOKER, P. (1987, March). *Effects of self-efficacy, fear of rape and perceived risk on intention to take a self-defense class.* Paper presented at the meeting of the Midwest Society for Feminist Studies, Akron, OH.

ROZEE-KOKER, P., WYNNE, C., & MIZRAHI, K. (1989, April). *Workplace safety and fear of rape among professional women.* Paper presented at the meeting of the Western Psychological Association, Reno, NV.

SMITH, M. D. (1988). Women's fear of violent crime: An exploratory test of a feminist hypothesis. *Journal of Family Violence, 3,* 29–38.

STANKO, E. (1993). Ordinary fear: Women, violence, and personal safety. In P. Bart & E. Moran (Eds.), *Violence against women: The bloody footprints* (pp. 155–165). Newbury Park, CA: Sage.

WARR, M. (1985). Fear of rape among urban women. *Social Problems, 32*(3), 238–250.

WARSHAW, R. (1988). *I never called it rape: The MS. Report on recognizing, fighting and surviving date and acquaintance rape.* New York: Harper & Row.

WILLIAMS, J. E. (1984). Secondary victimization: Confronting public attitudes about rape. *Victimology: An International Journal, 9,* 66–81.

SUGGESTED READINGS

BART, P. B., & O'BRIEN, P. (1985). *Stopping rape: Successful survival strategies.* New York: Pergamon Press.

FUNK, R. E. (1993). *Stopping rape: A challenge for men.* Philadelphia: New Society Publishers.

RIGER, S., & GORDON, M. (1989). *The female fear.* New York: Free Press.

WARSHAW, R. (1988). *I never called it rape: The MS. Report on recognizing, fighting and surviving date and acquaintance rape.* New York: Harper & Row.

MICHELE **A.** **P**ALUDI is President of Paludi & Associates, Consultants in Sexual Harassment. Dr. Paludi has taught courses on the psychology of women and gender at Hunter College, Union College, and Kent State University. She has published extensively in such areas as sexual harassment, mentoring, women and achievement, and teaching the psychology of women.

22

Sexual Harassment in College and University Settings

❖

---

*T*rue or false?

- You have been sexually harassed only when you've been physically assaulted.
- Sexual harassment only affects a small number of persons.
- Sexual harassment is harmless and is similar to flirtation.
- Sexual harassers are pathological.
- Individuals who don't say no to the harasser must enjoy the harassment.
- There is nothing one can do about sexual harassment.

There is a classic experiment in social psychology that was conducted by Solomon Asch in 1952. The experiment concerns social influence—how people alter the thoughts, feelings, and behavior of other people. In short, it is an experiment in conformity, that is, when we change our behavior in order to adhere to social norms.

I would like to briefly summarize Asch's experiment for you. A participant enters a laboratory room with six people and is told that the experiment concerns visual discrimination. The task is simple. Individuals are shown two cards. On the first card a single line is drawn. On the second, three lines are drawn and numbered 1, 2, 3. One of the three lines on this second card is the same length as the line on the first card. Participants are instructed to call out—one at a time—which of the three lines is the same length as the line on the first card.

Unbeknown to one of the seven individuals—the real participant in the study—the remaining six are confederates of the researcher who have prearranged a number of incorrect responses. For example, five of these confederates say "1" when the correct answer is obviously "3." Confronted with five people responding with the objectively incorrect answer, the participant either conforms to the erroneous group judgment or not.

Asch reported that this experiment made individuals doubt their own judgment. Their discomfort was caused by the pressure to conform. Fully 75 percent of participants went along with the crowd rather than assert what they knew to be the right answer!

This study can help us to understand how victims of sexual harassment react when their perceptions of what happened are invalidated by those around them. The more victims seek validation for their view about the events that have occurred, the more hostile and rejecting their world becomes. They are seen as "rocking the boat" and may be called whistle-blowers. Like the participants in the Asch study, most victims of sexual harassment come to doubt what they see with their own eyes; they are encouraged to conform to their professors' or peers' erroneous perspectives. Because they have lower social status in the campus hierarchy, student victims are perceived as being more conformist and easier to push around.

Sexual harassment creates a setting for social influence—for students and faculty to try to alter victims' thoughts, feelings, and behaviors with respect to the victimization. I would like to discuss some ways this social influence occurs and how it relates to the definition, incidence, and reporting of sexual harassment; the psychological profiles of harassers; and the somatic, psychological, and education- and work-related reactions individuals have. I then want to readdress each of these issues by discussing what students and college administrators can and should do in order not to alter victims' perceptions but to change the campus' perspective of sexual harassment and victims of sexual harassment.

DEFINITION OF SEXUAL HARASSMENT

The definition of sexual harassment is one way to invalidate the concerns of victims. Many people believe that sexual harassment only involves physical assault; if one isn't assaulted, one hasn't been harassed. However, as victims of sexual harassment know, most sexual harassment is far more pervasive and less obvious than physical assault. Sexual harassment does not fall within the range of personal private relationships. It happens when a person with power abuses that power and uses it to intimidate, coerce, or humiliate someone because of their sex. It is a breach of trust that normally exists among members of a college or university setting. Sexual harassment creates confusion because the boundary between professional roles and personal relationships is blurred. The harasser introduces a sexual element into what should be a professional situation.

Sexual harassment is unwelcome behavior. It can be an action that occurs only once, or it may be repeated. In voluntary sexual relationships individuals can exercise freedom of choice in deciding whether to establish a close, intimate relationship. This freedom of choice is absent in sexual harassment. Thus, there does not have to be physical assault for an individual to be sexually harassed. Research has documented that most individuals who experience sexual harassment have never received any physical touch throughout the duration of the victimization (Fitzgerald, 1990).

According to the Equal Employment Opportunity Commission, sexual harassment is defined as "unwelcome sexual advances, requests for sexual favors, and other verbal or physical conduct of a sexual nature" when any one of the following criteria is met.

- Submission to such conduct is made either explicitly or implicitly a term or condition of the individual's employment or academic standing.
- Submission to or rejection of such conduct by an individual is used as the basis for employment or academic decisions affecting the individual.
- Such conduct has the purpose or effect of unreasonably interfering with an individual's work or learning, creating an intimidating, hostile, or offensive work or learning environment.

Sexual harassment can include:

- Using pornographic teaching material
- Staring, rubbing against breasts, leering
- Professor offering a student a good grade for being sexually cooperative
- Professor subtly threatening a student with some sort of punishment for not being sexually cooperative
- Sexual innuendos, comments, and remarks
- Assault
- Obscene gestures
- Suggestive, obscene, or insulting sounds

*I*NCIDENCE OF SEXUAL HARASSMENT ON CAMPUS

Another way victims of sexual harassment are encouraged to change their perception of the events is through a discussion of the incidence of sexual harassment. Frequently individuals are told that sexual harassment is a rare occurence or that the campus has never had a complaint filed against an individual for sexual harassment.

Although generalizations are difficult given the differing methodologies and samples used, the best estimate is that one out of every two women will be sexually harassed at some point during her academic or working life. This indicates that harassment is the most widespread of all forms of sexual victimization that have been studied (Paludi, 1990; Paludi & Barickman, 1991).

Billie Dzeich and Linda Weiner (1984) reported that 30 percent of undergraduate women experience one or more levels of sexual harassment from at least one of their professors during their four years of college. When definitions of sexual harassment include sexist remarks and other forms of "gender harassment," the incidence rate in undergraduate populations nears 90 percent. Jan Kottke and her colleagues (Adams, Kottke, & Padgitt, 1983) reported that 13 percent of the women students they surveyed said that they had avoided taking a class or working with certain professors because of the risk of being subjected to sexual advances. Furthermore, a 1983 study conducted at Harvard University indicated that 15 percent of the graduate students and 12 percent of the undergraduate students who had been harassed by their professors changed their major or educational program because of the harassment. Wilson and Kraus (1983) found that 9 percent of the female undergraduates in their study had been pinched, touched, or patted to the point of personal discomfort, and 17 percent of the women in the Adams et al. (1983) survey received verbal sexual advances, 14 percent received sexual invitations, 6 percent had been subjected to physical advances, and 2 percent received direct sexual bribes.

Nancy Bailey and Peggy Richards (1985) reported that of 246 women graduate students in their sample, 13 percent indicated that they had been sexually harassed, 21 percent had not enrolled in a course to avoid harassment, and 16 percent indicated that they had been directly assaulted. Meg Bond (1988) reported that 75 percent of the 229 women APA members who responded to her survey had experienced jokes with sexual themes during their graduate training, 69 percent were subjected to sexist comments demeaning to women, and 58 percent of the women reported experiencing sexist remarks about their clothing, body, or sexual activities.

Professors have considerable power over certain groups of students (Barickman, Paludi, & Rabinowitz, 1993), particularly

- Graduate students, whose future careers are often determined by their association with a particular faculty member
- Students in small colleges or small academic departments, where the number of faculty available to students is quite small
- Women of color, especially those with "token" status
- Women in male-populated fields, such as engineering
- Students who are economically disadvantaged and work part-time or full-time while attending classes

Victims of sexual harassment are typically not informed about the incidence of sexual harassment of women and men in general or of individuals on their campus. This information may not be readily shared with them. They thus may be more likely to reinterpret their experiences as not actually being sexual harassment.

FOCUS ON HARASSERS

A third way in which victims of sexual harassment are asked to change their perceptions of their experiences concerns focusing attention on the motives of the harasser. Most individuals believe that sexual harassers are pathological and abnormal and can easily be spotted. There is a common myth that there is a "typical" harasser who can be identified by his blatant and obvious mistreatment of many women; this is a serious oversimplification of a complex issue and contributes to the misunderstanding of sexual harassment. Harassers are found in all types of academic disciplines. Research suggests that there is no typical harasser.

Individuals who harass generally do not label their behavior as sexual harassment despite the fact that they do report that they frequently engage in behaviors that meet the legal definition of sexual harassment. They deny the inherent power differential between themselves and their students, for example.

John Pryor (1987) noted that sexual harassment bears a conceptual similarity to rape. He developed a series of hypothetical scenarios of situations that provided opportunities for sexual harassment—if the man so chose. Instructions asked men to imagine themselves in the roles of the men in the scenarios and to consider what they would do in each situation. They were further instructed to imagine that regardless of their chosen course of action, no negative consequences would result from their choices. Men's scores on the likelihood of engaging in sexual harassment were positively related to gender-role stereotyping and negatively related to feminist attitudes and the component of empathy that has to do with the ability to take the standpoint of the other.

These findings suggest that the man who is likely to initiate severe sexually harassing behavior appears to be one who emphasizes male social and sexual dominance and demonstrates insensitivity to other individuals' perspectives. In addition, men are less likely than women to define sexual harassment as including jokes, teasing remarks of a sexual nature, and unwanted suggestive looks or gestures. Men were also significantly more likely than women to agree with the following statements (Paludi, in preparation):

- Women often claim sexual harassment to protect their reputations.
- Many women claim sexual harassment if they have consented to sexual relations but have changed their minds afterward.
- Sexually experienced women are not really damaged by sexual harassment.
- It would do some women good to be sexually harassed.
- Women put themselves in situations in which they are likely to be sexually harassed because they have an unconscious wish to be harassed.
- In most cases when a woman is sexually harassed, she deserves it.

Bernice Lott (1993) has also found empirical support for sexual harassment being viewed as part of a larger and more general dimension of misogyny and hostility toward women. Kathryn Quina (1990) related common forms of sexual harassment in the workplace to characters in the comic strip *Beetle Bailey.*

> General Halftrack is the archetypic older gentleman whose dowdy wife starves him for affection. His secretary, Miss Buxley—who can't type—drives him wild with her sexy figure and short skirts. "Killer" (short for "lady killer"—a curiously violent name) is always whistling at "chicks" (who love it), accompanied by Beetle, who is equally aggressive but not as successful. Zero just stares at women's bodies. (p. 93)

Although we may laugh when reading the comic strip, played out on campuses these scenarios are not humorous. In some of my recent research on why men sexually harass women (Paludi, in preparation), I have focused not on men's attitudes toward women but on men's attitudes toward other men, competition, and power. Many of the men with whom I have discussed sexual harassment have stated that they often act out of extreme competitiveness and concern with ego or out of fear of losing their positions of power. They don't want to appear weak or less masculine in the eyes of other men, so they engage in "scoping" women (rating women's bodies from 1 to 10), pinching women, making implied or overt threats, or spying on women. Women are the game to impress other men. Similar to Peggy Sanday's (1990) findings concerning fraternity men's involvement in date rape, I am finding that when men are being encouraged to be obsessionally competitive and concerned with dominance, it is likely that they will eventually use violent means to achieve dominance. They are also likely to be verbally abusive and intimidating in their body language. Deindividuation is quite common among fraternity members who scope women as they walk by. These men stop evaluating their own behavior and adopt group norms and attitudes. Under these circumstances, group members behave more aggressively than they would as individuals.

The element of aggression that is so deeply embedded in the masculine gender role is clearly present in sexual harassment (Doyle & Paludi, 1992). For many men, aggression is one of the major ways of proving their masculinity, especially among those men who feel some sense of powerlessness in their lives. The male-as-dominant or male-as-aggressor is a theme so central to many men's self-concept that it literally carries over into their interpersonal communications, especially with women peers and students. Sexualizing a professional relationship may be the one area where the average man can still prove his masculinity when few other areas can be found for him to prove himself in control or dominant in a relationship. Thus, similar to what Diana Russell (1984) has stated with respect to men who rape, sexual harassment is not so much a deviant act as an overconforming act.

SEXUAL HARASSMENT: FLATTERY? FLIRTATION? ABUSE?

The final example I would like to use to illustrate how victims, especially women victims, are socially influenced with respect to sexual harassment concerns the denial of women's responses to sexual harassment along the domains of work, psychological, and somatic outcomes. Women may not label their experiences as sexual harassment even though the experiences meet the legal definition of this form of victimization. Consequently they may not label their stress-related responses as being caused by the sexual harassment. Their responses are attributed by classmates and faculty to other events in their life—biological or social. However, several reports have documented the high cost of sexual harassment to women.

Education and Work-Related Outcomes

Research has documented decreased morale, increased absenteeism, decreased work satisfaction, performance decrements, and damage to interpersonal relationships at school (Rabinowitz, 1990) in women who have been sexually harassed.

Psychological Outcomes

Harassment can be devastating to emotional health and lead to depression, helplessness, strong fear reactions, loss of control, life disruption, and decreased motivation (Quina, 1990; Rabinowitz, 1990). Furthermore, like victims of rape who go to court, sexual harassment victims may experience retaliation when they attempt to deal with the situation through institutional channels.

Physiological Outcomes

The following physical symptoms have been reported in the literature concerning academic sexual harassment: headaches, sleep disturbances, disordered eating, gastrointestinal disorders, nausea, weight loss or gain, and crying spells (Crull, 1982; Rabinowitz, 1990). Recently, researchers and clinicians have argued that victims of sexual harassment can exhibit a postabuse syndrome characterized by shock, emotional numbing, constriction of affect, flashbacks, and other signs of anxiety and depression. These responses are influenced by disappointment in the way others react and the stress of harassment-induced life changes such as moves, loss of income, and disrupted studying.

WHAT CAN BE DONE ABOUT SEXUAL HARASSMENT ON CAMPUS

I have outlined some of the ways individuals try to make victims of sexual harassment dismiss their own experiences. People do this primarily by relying on myths rather than facts about sexual harassment. Remember the true-false questions with which I began this chapter? Each of these statements were addressed earlier in this lecture. To summarize, we know from research that:

- Sexual harassment is far more pervasive and less obvious than physical assault.
- Sexual harassment is the most widespread of all forms of sexual victimization.
- Victims of sexual harassment, their families, and their coworkers report debilitating stress reactions affecting study performance and attitudes, psychological health, and physical health.
- Individuals who sexually harass others hold misogynist views of women and are likely to be repeat offenders.
- Victims of sexual harassment may fear retaliation if they confront their harasser.

I would like to turn to the final myth: "There is nothing one can do about sexual harassment." Specifically, I would like to address some ways students can ensure that their campus is free of sexual harassment and free of the fear of being retaliated against for speaking about sexual harassment experiences. My suggestions fall into three main areas: policies and procedures, research, and educational interventions.

Policies and Procedures

First, students can find out whether their campus has policies and effective procedures for dealing with sexual harassment. Students can also determine whether the policy includes the following information:

- Legal definition of sexual harassment
- Behavioral examples of sexual harassment
- Impact of sexual harassment on individuals and the campus
- Statement of individual's responsibility in filing complaint
- Statement of campus's responsibility in investigating complaint
- Statement of sanctions
- Statement of sanctions for retaliation
- Statement concerning false complaints
- Identification of individuals responsible for hearing complaints

Informal discussions with individuals responsible for enforcing the policy statement can be held to share concerns about the content of the policy statement. In addition, students can ask to see an annual report that lists the number of complaints of sexual harassment that were handled and the respective sanctions, if any, that were recommended and enforced.

Furthermore, students and faculty can begin discussing "consensual relationships" between faculty and students or staff and students, as has happened at the University of Virginia. Meryl Zacker and I (1989) found that few campuses have adopted a policy statement that includes information about consensual relationships. For example, the University of Iowa's policy on sexual harassment includes the following statement:

> Amorous relationships between faculty members and students occurring outside the instructional context may lead to difficulties. . . . A faculty member who fails to withdraw from participation in activities or decisions that may reward or penalize a student with whom the faculty member has or has had an amorous relationship will be deemed to have violated his or her ethical obligation to the student, to other students, to colleagues, and to the University.

Harvard University's policy on sexual harassment also includes a statement about consensual relationships:

> Amorous relationships that might be appropriate in other circumstances are always wrong when they occur between any teacher or officer of the University and any student for whom he or she has a professional responsibility. It is incumbent upon those with authority not to abuse, nor to seem to abuse, the power with which they are entrusted.

These policy statements address the fundamental issue in sexual harassment between faculty and students: the abuse of power because of the role as professor. As Sue Rosenberg Zalk and her colleagues have commented (Zalk, Paludi, & Dederick, 1991):

> The bottom line in the relationship between faculty member and student is POWER. The faculty member has it and the student does not. As intertwined as the faculty-student roles may be, and as much as one must exist for the other to exist, they are not equal collaborators. The student does not negotiate—indeed, has nothing to negotiate with. (pp. 101–102)

Research on Sexual Harassment

Second, students can ask to conduct or participate in research on gender roles and the psychology of victimization in general and sexual harassment specifically. There are several areas in academic sexual harassment that require psychological research. For example, research should include women from general populations as well as specific populations, e.g., victims who have filed law suits, and victims who have sought counseling regarding the sexual harassment. Within this framework, mediating and moderating variables such as age, perception of the meaning of the trauma, duration, response to the harassment, availability of resources to assist victims, and social support must be discussed in order to elucidate the conditions under which sexual harassment leads to the various somatic, physical, and career outcomes previously discussed.

In addition, we need studies that document lesbian women's experiences with sexual harassment. Maryka Biaggio (in preparation) has recently written that lesbian women may experience sexual harassment differently and may be exposed to some unique forms of sexual harassment. For lesbian women, sexual harassment may be experienced as an affront to her sexual orientation, and it may reinforce her sense of being an outsider.

Finally, sexual harassment has a radiating impact and can thus affect the learning experiences of all women and men in a classroom. This radiating impact must be considered in the development of policy statements as well as in future research on the effects of sexual harassment.

Educational Interventions

Students and other members of the campus community can monitor their verbal and nonverbal communication patterns. For example:

> When making general statements about women (or any other group), be sure that they are based on accurate information. Universal generalizations about any social group, such as "Women don't think geographically," are likely, at best, to represent uncritical oversimplifications of selected norms.

> Avoid "humor" or gratuitous remarks that demean or belittle people because of sex or sexual orientation, just as you would avoid remarks that demean or belittle people because of their race, religion, or physical characteristics.

> Respect the dignity of all individuals.

> Avoid using generic masculine terms to refer to people of both sexes. Although the effort to do this may involve some initial discomfort, it will result in more precise communication and understanding.

> When using illustrative examples, avoid stereotypes, such as making all authority figures men and all subordinates women.

In addition to more effective communication strategies, students can help to institute a Sexual Harassment Awareness Week in which issues related to definition, incidence, and explanatory models of sexual harassment are discussed. Some campuses (e.g., Nassau Community College) put on a play concerning the stress effects of sexual harassment and victims' responses to the threat of retaliation for speaking out against sexual harassment. Students on other campuses (e.g., Hunter College in New York City) facilitate discussion groups and show movies on sexual harassment, gender, and power in the classroom. Some campuses encourage sororities and fraternities to present programs on sexual harassment and date rape.

As a final example of an educational intervention strategy, students can start a peer educators group on campus. Students need to know that if they are sexually harassed, they will receive support. Peer educators can provide much needed support. They can

> Acknowledge students' courage by stating how difficult it is to label, report, and discuss sexual harassment.

> Encourage students to share their feelings and perceptions.

> Provide information to students about the incidence of academic sexual harassment. Also share with them the somatic and physical symptoms associated with sexual harassment.

> Assure students that they are not responsible for their victimization.

Work with students in their search for the meaning in their victimization; support them while they mourn their losses.

Provide a safe forum for students' expression of anger and resentment.

Work with students on ways to validate themselves so as to feel empowered.

In describing her experiences as an undergraduate student trying to establish policies and procedures against sexual harassment at her university, Lela Demby (1990) stated:

> If I had to choose one thing to leave you with . . . it would be the plea to listen to student input when formulating your own policies on dealing with sexual harassment and assault. We all want policies that are the most optimal and efficient, addressing the needs of the survivor and the community. We will tell you some of the most important things you need to know, because we've been there. We know. (p. 188)

As I close I would like to offer you a challenge: to consider sexual harassment from the victim's perspective and to learn from individuals who have experienced sexual harassment. Instead of considering the Asch experiment on conformity a "classic" and the behavior of the majority of participants in that study normative, it may well be worthwhile to value students' perceptions and experiences and to avoid social influence. Share your experiences with each other. Students' stories are important. They tell us many things we need to know.

REFERENCES

ADAMS, J., KOTTKE, J., & PADGITT, J. (1983). Sexual harassment of university students. *Journal of College Student Personnel, 24*, 484–490.

ASCH, S. (1952). *Social psychology.* Englewood Cliffs, NJ: Prentice-Hall.

BAILEY, N., & RICHARDS, P. (1985, August). *Tarnishing the ivory tower: Sexual harassment in graduate training programs.* Paper presented at the annual conference of the American Psychological Association, Los Angeles, CA.

BARICKMAN, R. B., PALUDI, M. A., & RABINOWITZ, V. C. (1993). Sexual harassment of students: Victims of the college experience. In E. Viano (Ed.), *Victimization: An international perspective* (pp. 153–165). New York: Springer.

BIAGGIO, M. (in preparation). Sexual harassment in the workplace: The lesbian experience and the role of homophobia. In M. Paludi (Ed.), *Working 9 to 5: Women, men, sex, and power.* Albany, NY: State University of New York Press.

BOND, M. (1988). Division 27 Sexual Harassment Survey: Definition, impact, and environmental context. *The Community Psychologist, 21*, 7–10.

CRULL, P. (1982). Stress effects of sexual harassment on the job: Implications for counseling. *American Journal of Orthopsychiatry, 52*, 539–544.

DEMBY, L. (1990). In her own voice. In M. Paludi (Ed.), *Ivory power: Sexual harassment on campus* (pp. 184–189). Albany, NY: State University of New York Press.

DOYLE, J., & PALUDI, M. A. (1992). *Sex and gender: The human experience.* Dubuque: W. C. Brown.

DZIECH, B., & WEINER, L. (1984). *The lecherous professor.* Boston: Beacon Press.

FITZGERALD, L. F. (1990). Sexual harassment: The definition and measurement of a construct. In M. A. Paludi (Ed.), *Ivory power: Sexual harassment on campus* (pp. 21–44). Albany, NY: State University of New York Press.

LOTT, B. (1993). Sexual harassment: Consequences and realities. *NEA Higher Education Journal, 8,* 89–103.

PALUDI, M. A. (Ed.). (1990). *Ivory power: Sexual harassment on campus.* Albany, NY: State University of New York Press.

PALUDI, M. A. (Ed.). (in preparation). *Working 9 to 5: Women, men, sex, and power.* Albany, NY: State University of New York Press.

PALUDI, M. A., & BARICKMAN, R. B. (1991). *Academic and workplace sexual harassment: A resource manual.* Albany, NY: State University of New York Press.

PRYOR, J. (1987). Sexual harassment proclivities in men. *Sex Roles, 17,* 269–290.

QUINA, K. (1990). The victimization of women. In M. Paludi (Ed.), *Ivory power: Sexual harassment on campus* (pp. 93–102). Albany, NY: State University of New York Press.

RABINOWITZ, V. (1990). Coping with sexual harassment. In M. Paludi (Ed.), *Ivory power: Sexual harassment on campus* (pp. 101–118). Albany, NY: State University of New York Press.

RUSSELL, D. (1984). *Sexual exploitation: Rape, child sexual abuse, and workplace harassment.* Beverly Hills, CA: Sage.

SANDAY, P. (1990). *Fraternity gang rape: Sex, brotherhood, and privilege on campus.* New York: New York University Press.

WILSON, K., & KRAUS, L. (1983). Sexual harassment in the university. *Journal of College Student Personnel, 24,* 219–224.

ZACKER, M., & PALUDI, M. A. (1989). *An analysis of sexual harassment policy statements.* Unpublished paper, Hunter College, City University of New York.

ZALK, S. R., PALUDI, M. A., & DEDERICH, J. (1991). Women students' assessment of consensual relationships with their professors: Ivory power reconsidered. In M. A. Paludi & R. B. Barickman (Eds.), *Academic and workplace sexual harassment: A resource manual* (pp. 99–114). Albany, NY: State University of New York Press.

*S*UGGESTED READINGS

AMERICAN ASSOCIATION OF UNIVERSITY WOMEN. (1993). *Hostile hallways: The AAUW survey on sexual harassment in America's schools.* Washington: Author.

PALUDI, M. A. (Ed.). (1990). *Ivory power: Sexual harassment on campus.* Albany, NY: State University of New York Press.

PALUDI, M. A., & BARICKMAN, R. B. (1991). *Academic and workplace sexual harassment: A manual of resources.* Albany, NY: State University of New York Press.

MAUREEN **C. M**CHUGH is Professor of Psychology and Director of Women's Studies at Indiana University of Pennsylvania. Dr. McHugh has taught psychology of women since 1974 in a variety of institutional settings to diverse student groups. She is a social psychologist, and her research is mainly in the areas of women and violence and women and achievement.

23

A $\mathcal{F}$eminist Approach to Agoraphobia:

Challenging Traditional Views of Women at Home

❖

What is free will if you can't walk down your own road, if the idea of going to the market makes you so nauseated you have to lie down? You would trade your soul for a cigarette, which unfortunately you can't have because you can't get to the store.
— Vonny, in Illumination Night *by Alice Hoffman, 1987*

AGORAPHOBIA "EXPLAINED"

Diagnostic Criteria

Agoraphobics are defined by fears of public places and by the fear of being away from home. Fears of going places such as crowded stores or restaurants are frequently reported. Agoraphobes often experience panic attacks when traveling, including driving and riding on public transportation. The agoraphobe may fear either closed-in spaces such as elevators or tunnels, or open

This lecture is dedicated to the memory of Marjorie Gelfond, feminist psychologist and researcher, whose work first challenged my thinking about agoraphobia. She died of breast cancer in 1992.

spaces such as fields and empty streets, or both. Going to strange and unfamiliar places and being alone when away from home are the two most common fears reported. The agoraphobe may avoid any situation in which an easy retreat to safe and familiar territory is not possible. Normal activities become increasingly restricted. Some agoraphobes are housebound; others may travel when escorted by a "safe person," often a specific companion.

Typically, the agoraphobic individual has experienced an attack in one or more public situations. The attack may have been medical in nature (e.g., asthma) but is more typically reported as panic. The panic attacks involve shortness of breath, heart palpitations, dizziness, nausea, weakness in the limbs, and the threat of bladder or bowel incontinence. These attacks are often accompanied by a sense of doom and a fear that one will die, become insane, faint, or otherwise lose control. Today the disorder is officially viewed as a subcategory of panic disorder; the agoraphobe is defined as an individual who has experienced an attack with four or more of the above symptoms and has increasingly restricted his or her activities as a result (American Psychiatric Association, 1994).

Agoraphobia is the most common of the phobias. Over 50 percent of the individuals who report phobic distress are diagnosed as agoraphobic. Moreover, clinicians have described agoraphobia as the most distressing, disabling, and all-consuming of the phobias (Goldstein, 1987; Sable, 1991). Agoraphobes represent about 5 percent of the population (Thorpe & Burns, 1983). Research has focused on white, middle-class populations, but some evidence indicates that there may be more agoraphobia in minority groups, and among the poor, than had been previously assumed (Michelson, 1987). Agoraphobic individuals are believed to exist across all classes and ethnic groups (Fleming & Faulk, 1989).

A Case Study

My grandmother was an agoraphobe. For the six years before she died she only left her apartment in downtown Pittsburgh on a handful of occasions. These occasions diminished in frequency so that for the last year of her life she was completely apartment-bound. On one occasion I coaxed her to ride the elevator of her high-rise apartment down 16 floors to the Muffin Burger on the ground floor. She raised her usual objections: She wasn't dressed right. She would have to "do" her hair. She might have an asthma attack. I don't know why, on that particular day, I was able to convince her when numerous other attempts failed.

I visited her in her apartment regularly. Usually I took a bus from another part of town where I was attending graduate school. I was one of her "suppliers." My mother and my aunts also helped to keep Grandma supplied with fresh milk, bread, and groceries. It was difficult for my mother, who did not drive. I had to make my visits during the day because that section of town with its adult bookstores and bars was not safe at night. On weekdays the streets were crowded and we couldn't park; on weekends the streets were deserted and scary. As a healthy and strong woman in her twenties, I was sometimes afraid in downtown Pittsburgh. Question: *Was my grandmother's fear of leaving her apartment an irrational one?*

My grandmother was moved to this downtown apartment by her children. After she became a widow, the house that she lived in for her adult life was sold, and living with my aunt had created conflict. So at the age of 73 she was moved into this "comfortable" urban high-rise. My mother and her siblings thought their mother would like living downtown because downtown was the only place she would go unescorted (by public transport) in her adult years. Like many women of her generation, she did not drive and had never been employed outside the home. I can only remember seeing my grandmother away from her home (at our house, for example) on a few occasions. Usually we visited her at her house. She lived on a steep hill. As a fat woman and an asthmatic she could not easily walk anywhere. Question: *When did her staying at home become a "condition"?*

Even looking back I can't say when her condition would qualify as agoraphobia, and at the time I didn't recognize the problem. But it did become more noticeable, and more inconvenient for others after she moved downtown. Question: *Did she feel trapped in her apartment? Did she yearn to travel, to visit us, to shop in the downtown department stores?*

My grandmother, like most agoraphobes, was never diagnosed as such. Yet in many ways her case is a classic one. She was a woman with a medical or physical condition; she was afraid she would experience an attack in public. She couldn't shop. The onset was related to role transition, to physical relocation, and to loss of autonomy.

I now have a better understanding of my grandmother's experience and that of many other women like her, which I would like to share with you. In this lecture I will briefly present the current treatment approaches to agoraphobia and the feminist critique of traditional theories and treatments. Several alternative feminist perspectives on why some women are afraid of the marketplace and public streets are presented.

Traditional Approaches

Behavioral and pharmaceutical approaches have replaced the original psychodynamic interpretations of agoraphobes (Fodor, 1992). Historically agoraphobia was attributed to fixation, regression, projection, or displacement of sexual and aggressive feelings (Sable, 1991). Agoraphobics were viewed as dependent personalities; the focus was on deep-seated individual psychopathology (Andrews, 1966; Deutsch, 1929; Weiss, 1964).

One current psychodynamic approach is to view agoraphobic individuals as experiencing anxious attachment (Bowlby, 1988; Sable, 1991). The concepts of attachment and separation may be used to guide therapy; the therapist provides a reliable attachment relationship from which the client explores present and past attachment and separation experiences (Sable, 1991).

Contemporary treatment of agoraphobia typically involves medication and behavioral therapy. Agoraphobes may be prescribed antianxiety or antidepressive medication. An underlying, usually unstated assumption of the medication approach is that something is wrong with the basic organism, for example, the brain, brain functions, or the endocrine system (Fodor, 1992). According to Fodor (1992), biologically based treatment and research has increased over the last few decades. The medication may be used alone or in combination with a behavioral approach.

Behaviorists view phobias as the result of the association (through classical conditioning) of anxiety with certain situations or stimuli. The avoidance of the feared situations or stimuli eliminates the anxiety and is reinforced physiologically and socially. Behavior therapy typically attempts to reduce the anxiety associated with the feared situation through systematic desensitization. The client is supported and reinforced through a series of approximations to the feared situation. For example, the agoraphobe may first be escorted to the store but not go in. This is followed by several trips in which she goes in and walks through increasing portions of the store quickly and without purchase. The desensitization is built up until she can shop alone under normal or even crowded conditions. In *Illumination Night* by Alice Hoffman (1987), the protagonist repeatedly drives up and down her driveway and then later drives to progressive points down a feared street.

Today many of the behavioral treatments include some attention to cognitive variables. The therapy explores the irrational nature of catastrophic thinking and other anxiety-provoking cognitions (Beck & Emery, 1985). The client is taught to combat such thinking or to substitute productive thinking. For example, Chambless and Goldstein (1980) outlined a comprehensive cognitive behavioral treatment package for agoraphobia. Although there has been research supporting exposure as an effective treatment (Barlow, 1988), there is also criticism regarding high dropout rates and recidivism (Gournay, 1989).

Fodor (1992) reports an in-house debate that occurred during the preparation of the DSM-IV. The debate was among the most influential researchers in the field over whether agoraphobic symptoms are triggered by cognitive-behavioral causes or result from defective biology. "For the most part, none of the principal researchers, in either of the camps, addresses women's issues or views sociocultural variables as crucial, even though agoraphobia and panic disorders occur primarily in females" (Fodor, 1992, p. 187).

Sex Linkage of Agoraphobia

Agoraphobia is by all accounts a sex-linked disorder. In the United States it is estimated that 75 percent (Myers, Weissman, & Tischler, 1984) to 95 percent (Marks & Herst, 1970; Eichenbaum & Orbach, 1983) of agoraphobes are women. Given these numbers, isn't it likely that the experience of agoraphobia has something to do with being a woman in our culture? Shouldn't the theories about the causes of agoraphobia and the intervention strategies employed to treat agoraphobes incorporate some form of gender analysis or sensitivity?

Yet authors of articles and books on agoraphobia rarely attempt to explain why most agoraphobes are women. The two most popular treatment approaches do not address the question of gender. Chemotherapy and pharmaceutical approaches are not explicitly gendered. (However, the feminist critique of the mental health industry has charged that there is a greater likelihood of treating women's mental health problems with drugs, especially drugs that interfere with motor and cognitive functioning.) Behavioral approaches that encourage exposure to the feared situation do not address any psychic or cultural causal factors including gender issues. Researchers have not even examined simplistic notions that a particular therapy may be more successful with one sex than the other.

Franks (1986) and Lott (1994), among others, identify agoraphobia as one of the several mental health problems that are more prevalent among women. Also identified are depression and eating disorders. Yet feminist therapists and researchers have not given agoraphobia the same attention that eating disorders, depression, and posttraumatic stress have received (Fodor, 1992).

The Feminist Perspective

A feminist perspective asks why more women than men would have each of these disorders. Feminists urge us to consider the sociopolitical context in which women experience mental disorders. A feminist perspective includes an analysis of how cultural gender roles and sexual inequality create stress for women or affect the ways in which women react to stress. A feminist approach considers the possibility that women's problems in general, and an individual woman's problem in particular, may be rooted in gender roles or gender inequalities.

Why have feminist researchers, theorists, and practitioners not more fully developed feminist analyses of agoraphobia as a sex-linked disorder? Feminists, like their nonfeminist counterparts, are subject to the fundamental attribution error, that is, a tendency to focus on the person as the primary causal agent. American feminist psychologists have been culturally and professionally trained to focus on the individual, and therapists are trained to intervene at the individual level. It may be hard not to see a client as a unique individual and not to focus on some aspect of his or her personality or family background as the "cause" of the disorder. However, this focus does not address the larger issue of why so many of the clients are women, and why these women experience symptoms and distress differently from men. Until we can answer the questions about the gendering of such disorders, we will not be able to completely understand the problems of the individual woman, and we will not be able to move to a more proactive, preventive approach to women's mental health. Thus, a consideration of the sex linkage of agoraphobia, and a feminist analysis of why most agoraphobes are women is part of a larger movement to place women's mental health problems in a cultural context and to develop a structural, societal, preventive approach to such problems. An understanding of agoraphobia (or any sex-linked disorder) may also lead to new insights into the female experience.

FEMINIST APPROACHES TO AGORAPHOBIA

"The disorder of agoraphobia is a quintessential women's issue" (Fodor, 1992, p. 189). Fodor's (1992) conclusion is based on the same observation made by Seidenberg and DeCrow (1983) that agoraphobia in women is related to the ways in which all women are socialized to relate to the world.

Examining Agoraphobia as a Cultural Construct

In many historical periods and cultures women were not allowed to or were discouraged from participating in the public spheres of society. Remaining at home or being afraid to enter public streets would not be considered pathological in such a context. For example, women who remain at home in Islamic cultures would not be considered agoraphobic. Thus, labeling the anxiety associated with participation in public spheres as "pathology" is related to the changing conception of what is appropriate behavior for women in our culture. The disorder agoraphobia was first named in 1871, at a point in Western society when women's roles were beginning to change (Fodor, 1992).

Gelfond (1991) argues that the assumption that the agoraphobe's fears are unrealistic or irrational needs to be closely examined. The phobic's anxiety is only unrealistic to the extent that the streets are objectively safe and that public places are comfortable for women. She suggests that many women who are not overtly phobic lead environmentally restricted lives.

In her own research, Gelfond (1991) compared agoraphobic women with two other groups: highly independent women and average women. (She recruited snowball samples and used an autonomy scale and the

Brief Symptom Inventory by Derogatis and Spencer, 1982, to determine the groups.) She reports that 55 percent of the average women scored at or near the clinical range for agoraphobia. The average women also resembled the agoraphobes in their negative attitudes toward traveling alone, limited way-finding skills, and infrequent use of cultural, social, and recreational activities. Similarly, Brown and Cash (1990) found avoidance behaviors to be common among a normal sample of college students, and one-fourth of the sample reported a history of panic. Meyer (1987) describes a group of women in the community who met the criteria for agoraphobia but who forced themselves to override their anxiety and continue to function. These women were less phobic and had fewer panic attacks than the matched agoraphobic controls.

This line of research questions traditional conceptions of agoraphobia as a distinct clinical entity and challenges traditional clinical research that fails to incorporate appropriate comparison or control groups. Both Gelfond (1991) and Fodor (1992) argue that agoraphobia might be more appropriately viewed as one end of a continuum; agoraphobes can be seen as sharing characteristics and behaviors with much of the female population. Gelfond (1991) questions whether the opposing end of the continuum would be fear of being at home (domiphobia) or being comfortable at home. In her research she employs highly independent women as a third point of comparison.

The Gendering of Public Spaces

Both Gelfond (1991) and Fodor (1992) suggest that public environments may not be safe or comfortable for women, especially for women who are unescorted. There are environments in U.S. society from which women are excluded or are strongly discouraged. Some examples are football games, military academies, coal mines, and Wall Street. Women who are anxious about going to a pool hall or who are afraid to run for U.S. Congress are not viewed as suffering from a disorder. Gelfond (1991) suggests that our understanding of agoraphobia, and our understanding of the female experience in general, would be assisted by viewing agoraphobia in relation to women's reluctance to enter public places unescorted.

I would like to illustrate Gelfond's (1991) point with a personal example. Although I am an independent woman who currently travels 100 miles a day to work at a university, I have a history of avoiding gas stations. I had an aversion to gas stations which I initially viewed as a personal idiosyncratic neurosis. But based on Gelfond's (1991) analysis, I reexamined my discomfort with gas stations. I never had a traumatic experience at a gas station, but I perceived them as distinctly male environments in which women were unwelcome and were likely to be ridiculed or exploited. This is especially true of certain stations and was more true in the past than now. So I deliberately began to purchase gas at more female-friendly stations, ones that were clean, well-lit, or had women pumping gas. This analysis was confirmed for me when a large gas company called me as part of a national market survey. They were interested in what influenced women (a growing share of the market) to frequent particular service stations. I now see the redesign of service stations to include convenience stores and to exclude mechanical services as a response to women's stated preferences for a clean environment and one in which they could simultaneously perform another (women's) task. This example suggests that a serious societal response to women's anxieties, including those of agoraphobes, would be to analyze and potentially redesign many of our public spaces to make them female-friendly. We should inquire into whether or not public environments do present real dangers for women and whether or not unescorted women are made to feel safe and welcome (Gelfond, 1991).

Women at Home

Gelfond (1991) suggests that our understanding of agoraphobia could be enhanced not only by an examination of the experience of public spaces but also by a consideration of the meaning of home to women in general and to agoraphobes in comparison. She suggests that home, and a sense of place in general, play a greater role in women's psychic lives than in men's. Women's homes may represent a significant aspect of their identity. For example, the home is a symbol for family, which is a significant aspect of most women's lives. In her study, highly independent women as well as phobic and average women stayed home when disturbed. "From this perspective, women's reluctance to leave home can be seen to result from the control, status, identity, and personal meaning embedded in the place and concept of home" (Gelfond, 1991, p 253).

As an interesting extension of this reasoning, Gelfond reports on her home visits. She describes the homes of the phobics as highly personalized, reflecting a "life compressed into a limited space" (Gelfond, 1991, p. 257). Agoraphobes were likely to be collectors, especially of dollhouses or miniatures, and their homes created a feeling of enclosure and separation from the outside world. In contrast, the homes of the average women were "pleasant, yet unremarkable," and the homes of the highly independent women were functional, "bereft of expressions of the self" (p. 257). Thus it appears that these women differed not only in their comfort with public environments but in their relationships to their homes as well.

Agoraphobia in Relation to Women's Roles

Today, women's roles often require them to leave home and frequent public spaces. Even the traditional role of homemaker includes public travel such as shopping and community involvement. An analysis of agorophobia might begin with what tasks or activities agoraphobic women avoid. In what context did they originally experience a panic attack?

Mary, a friend of mine, experienced a classic but mild form of agoraphobia. She was a suburban homemaker with two young children. She was not employed outside the home. She experienced a panic attack when taking her children to visit her in-laws. As a result of this attack, she was afraid to chauffeur her children to their many activities. This represented a problem for the family. When women cannot perform their traditional roles, when their anxieties inconvenience family members—that is, when they can no longer shop or chauffeur their children—then we design a label and an intervention for their fears. Mary was prescribed an antianxiety medication. Eventually she resumed more limited chauffeuring duties. Today she is employed as a school bus driver. There are two big differences between her original chauffeuring and being a school bus driver—autonomy and salary—that may be instructive in our consideration of the dynamics of agoraphobia. In my grandmother's case it was her aversion to shopping that was considered the most indicative of a problem, not her refusal to take a vacation, to be active in community organizations, or to attend sports or cultural events.

Seidenberg and De Crow (1983) offer a political analysis of agoraphobia. They suggest that the agoraphobic woman is "a living and acting metaphor, making a statement, registering a protest, effecting a sit-in strike" (p. 209). In their analysis, agoraphobia calls our attention to the limitations placed on women and to women's limited participation in the decisions of the world by exaggerating or caricaturing women's limited roles.

Growing Up Anxious

Franks (1986) remarks on the similarity between agoraphobic behavior and gender-role stereotypes. In our culture girls are socialized to express fear, whereas boys are encouraged to become independent and to fend for themselves. Women have traditionally been allowed to express fears and anxieties and to withdraw from feared activities in ways that men have not been.

Fodor (1974) also explored the relationship between societal expectations for women and the helplessness and dependency that is characteristic of agoraphobia. She argues that agoraphobia is an exaggeration of the female role. Agoraphobic women are viewed here as being oversocialized into the female role, receiving overdoses of feminization training to be fearful, emotional, avoidant, nonassertive, and nonadventuresome. Other theorists have adopted similar arguments that the gender-role training of women leads to their socialization into a prescribed role that promotes fearfulness (Brehoney, 1983; Wolfe, 1984). Chambless (1982) suggests that passively avoiding a feared situation rather than facing it may be more typical of women in our society.

Gelfond (1991) calls our attention to studies demonstrating that girls are more restricted and supervised and are given less encouragement to explore their environments (Block, 1978; Maccoby & Jacklin, 1974). Possibly as a result of these messages, girls and women have a less developed sense of direction than men and are less able to form cognitive maps (Bryant, 1982; Koslowski & Bryant, 1977; Saegert & Hart, 1978). In her study (Gelfond, 1991), the independent women were found to be more geographically competent than the agoraphobic and average women. She reports that the independent women in her study were given more opportunity as children to be alone, both indoors and outdoors, than were the phobic and average women. For example, they were more likely to have attended overnight camp and to have gone downtown unchaperoned.

Support for this gender-role training perspective is offered in the research of Chambless and Mason (1986), who compared female agoraphobics with normals. Although not more stereotypically feminine than normals, agoraphobes did have lower masculinity scores; that is, they were less instrumental, active, and assertive. Hafner and Minge (1989) also found agoraphobic women to be less autonomous than controls. Gelfond (1991) contends that this research should be extended. We should examine how women, agoraphobic and nonagoraphobic, have been socialized to adapt to private and public environments and how their behavior might vary as a function of their gender identity and training.

Agoraphobia runs in families. Most researchers in the area of agoraphobia agree that agoraphobics learn a dependent-avoidant pattern in childhood, and that their families promote dependency and mistrust of the outside world while inhibiting the desire to move away (Fodor, 1992). Parental overprotection has been observed (Andrews, 1966). Fodor (1992) reports that in her clinical experience agoraphobics are likely to have families that promote traditional values, including that the women's place is in the home. She observes that her clients come frequently from first-generation, working-class and middle-class Italian-American, Greek-American, Puerto-Rican, and Jewish families.

Agoraphobia and Marital Status

The onset of agoraphobia is typically between the ages of 18 and 35; the average age at onset is 28 years. Most female agoraphobes are young married women. The onset of agoraphobia is typically soon after their marriage. Chambless (1982) describes the typical agoraphobe as a woman who is a housewife but would prefer to be employed; she is probably anxious, depressed, unassertive, and low in self-esteem. In Gelfond's (1991) study, both the agoraphobes and the average women tended to be married and uneducated, whereas the highly independent women tended to be single and better-educated.

Fodor (1987) discussed agoraphobia in married women as stemming from a feeling of being trapped in marriage, a feeling of being dominated with no outlet for expression of assertiveness. She described agoraphobic women as wishing for and fearing autonomy. When threatened with loss of (her husband's) love, the agoraphobe suppresses assertive striving. The suppressed striving becomes temptation/sinful and results in increasing guilt. Agoraphobia assists the individual in avoiding autonomy, assertion, and conflict.

Alternatively, agoraphobia in married women can be viewed as a reaction to the change in living circumstances or locations (Beck & Emery, 1985). This is consistent with Marks's (1966) report that many cases surfaced in the relocation of families to new public housing. Moving to a new home means not only unfamiliar physical surroundings but often isolation from family and friends, especially for a newly married woman.

Beck and Emery (1985) present an illuminating discussion of the way in which the married individual develops agoraphobia. The agoraphobic individual is suppressed by another person on whom he depends for support. Domination by the spouse erodes his confidence in his ability to function independently. He wants to receive support from his partner, and yet be free and autonomous. The individual suppresses his expression of autonomy because it may alienate his spouse.

Notice that the use of the male pronoun in the above observations makes them nonsensical. The authors, Beck and Emery (1985), do not use the male generic; they employ the female pronouns even though their analysis is supposedly gender-neutral; that is, they do not address the question of why agoraphobes tend to be women. Yet their analysis about the effects of suppressed autonomy and domination within marriage (on women) is very revealing. Their analysis cannot be presented using the generic masculine pronouns because the logic of their analysis rests upon our understanding that *women* cannot remain autonomous in marriage. Their analysis specifically discusses the way in which the husband's domination reduces the agoraphobic wife's confidence and increases her dependence. Yet, the problem is located within the woman; the husband's domination is not challenged or seen as pathological.

The analysis of these authors, who are not feminists, gives credence to the feminist argument that traditional marital roles including male domination and female subordination are experienced by some women as "traps" and are the source of mental health problems for women (Chesler, 1972).

Agoraphobia and Marital Conflict

Goldstein and Chambless (1978) have observed that agoraphobia begins in a climate of interpersonal (usually marital) conflict. The onset of panic, although experienced by the agoraphobe as coming out of the blue, is subsequently revealed to be temporarily related to highly stressful and chronic interpersonal conflicts. Buglass and his colleagues (Buglass, Clarke, Henderson, Kreitman & Presley, 1977) observed that phobic wives tended to suppress their own views to avoid domestic conflict. However, apparently not all agoraphobic wives are able (or willing) to avoid all conflict. Domestic distress was reported by the agoraphobes as the one of the most prevalent precipitating factors for panic attacks (Weeks, 1973). In another study (Burns & Thorpe, 1977), domestic arguments and marital stress were reported as the situation that produced anxiety by 87 percent of the respondents. Chambless and Goldstein (1980) cite relationship disruption as a common antecedent to the onset of agoraphobia.

More recently, however, Arrindell (1987) reviewed the literature and research concerning the hypothesis that unhappy marriages are typical of agoraphobics. He concludes that unhappy marriages are not common in this population.

Agoraphobia is viewed by some (e.g., Vose, 1981) not as a reaction to conflict, but as creating marital stress and conflict. The spouse of the agoraphobe may complete all the outside household chores, may have to escort the agoraphobe to all events and activities, may be contacted repeatedly at work, and may experience limitations on his own social life.

Other reports in the literature suggest that marital distress and conflict occur in reaction to the patient's treatment and recovery. Unstable or unsatisfactory marriages get worse as the agoraphobe gets better. Marital disharmony increased in 60 percent of the couples studied during the course of treatment by Milton and Hafner (1979). Similarly, Hand and Lamontagne (1976) reported exacerbation of marital problems in 21 married couples after exposure therapy. Of the 14 couples who had reported marital problems prior to therapy, 6 experienced a "severe marital crisis" after therapy. Other research does not support this contention that improvement in the agoraphobic client results in marital disruption or spouse symptoms (e.g., Arrindell, Emmelkamp, & Sanderman, 1986; Cobb, Mathews, Childs-Clarke, & Blowers, 1984).

Marriages can and do break up once the agoraphobe has regained freedom of movement. For example, Goldstein (1973) presents a case in which the married female patient described her husband as a tyrant who constantly ridiculed her. When she needed emotional support he was likely to make fun of her or become explosively angry with her. After therapy, she acquired sufficient self-confidence to initiate separation and divorce, and her symptoms disappeared.

In other cases, marital conflict is significantly associated with relapse after treatment (Milton & Hafner, 1979; Lazarus, 1966). The partner may undermine the agoraphobe's recovery. Goldstein and Swift (1977) report three cases in which the patient's recovery was jeopardized by the spouse. Each of the patients had husbands who believed that control and authority over their wives was essential to their masculine image. In the first case the husband frankly stated that he could only be content with a completely submissive wife. The wife continued treatment and eventually divorced him. In a second case the husband, who had previously been labeled as hostile, was subsequently treated for depression as the wife improved. And in the third reported case, successful conjoint therapy convinced the husband that dominating and controlling his wife in an overbearing manner was not the best way to minimize the likelihood of her leaving him.

Hafner (1982) also presents some illuminating case studies of the effect of intervention on marital discord. These cases include instances of attempted suicide and acute behavior disturbance of the husband. Also described are threats of hospitalization, abnormal jealousy, interrogation of the client after she returned home, verbal abuse, and intense disagreements. A family systems therapist would note how successful treatment of the agoraphobe has in each case upset the family system. The cases represent different resolutions. Hafner (1982) presents the cases to underscore his position that we need a marital framework for understanding and treating married agoraphobes.

Agoraphobia and Violence

The first time I read through the case studies presented by Hafner (1982), I was upset by the images of agoraphobic women being dominated and intimidated "back" into illness by their husbands. I was also struck by the similarity between these descriptions of marital discord and a different set of cases with which I was familiar, those of battered women.

In particular, the jealousy, interrogation, and surveillance behaviors of the husbands are very similar to the spouse behaviors reported by battered women (e.g., Frieze & McHugh, 1993). Male batterers typically maintain control by limiting the wives' geographical and temporal mobility and by restricting her social interactions with her family and friends. In some cases the agoraphobic client reported feeling isolated. Often the onset is after physical relocation away from family and friends.

Social and physical isolation are also typical in a battering relationship. This similarity, combined with the researchers' report of psychological forms of intimidation such as attempted suicide and verbal abuse, convinced me that some of the marriages being described involved battering. The current evidence that many U.S. marriages involve physical violence suggests that some of the marriages of agoraphobes in treatment are probably violent; the fact that marital conflict is common in this population increases the likelihood of wife beating among these cases. Here is what one of my students recorded in her journal (used by permission):

> I personally feel that I was suffering from agoraphobia while involved in an abusive relationship. . . . Fear was an everyday, consistent, permanent emotion. . . . I was terrified that something would happen to harm my physical well-being. . . . I did not feel strong enough to defend myself against an act of

physical or sexual violence, and my partner always reminded me of that fact. . . . I never went anywhere alone. He would accompany me everyplace. . . .

Not only was I afraid of what act might be committed by a stranger, but also by my partner . . . you know you have to come home and be interrogated. . . . Eventually I wanted to avoid any conflict, and the obvious solution was to stop going out for any reason. . . .

Home is supposed to be a haven, a safe place. When all you feel there is hostility, your mind begins to play tricks on you. . . . You think everyone is going to hurt you. . . .

I also had little confidence in my own appearance. I heard very often how repulsive I was. . . . He criticized me for being unattractive, but if I wore makeup or curled my hair he insisted that I was trying to attract a new lover. . . .

When you feel sick, tired, and unattractive, you feel like you have nothing to offer anyone anymore.

The agoraphobic feelings experienced by this young woman made it difficult for her to leave her physically, sexually, and psychologically abusive boyfriend. When he began threatening to kill her she fled to a shelter for battered women and received counseling. If she had sought help first for the panic attacks she experienced, would the therapist have prescribed an antianxiety drug or systematically desensitized her to going out unescorted? Would those treatments endanger her safety?

A careful examination of the literature on agoraphobia has not yielded a single reference by any author to the possibility of woman battering (McHugh, 1989). Despite references to specific forms of psychological abuse (e.g., tyrannical, making fun of her, explosive anger, vigorous arguments), none of the authors have addressed the question of whether these marriages involve physical, sexual, or psychological abuse. Further, I have been unable to find any assessment or investigation of the incidence of violence in the marriages or families of origin of agoraphobes. However, Fodor (1992) reports incidents of panic disorder and an increase in fearfulness and anxiety that occurs following rape. Panic is also discussed as a feature of the posttraumatic stress disorder (Steketee & Foa, 1987). Fodor (1992) concludes that real-life experiences of trauma may contribute to the development of agoraphobia.

This analysis is distressing on several levels. It points to the need for better education of therapists so that questions about physical violence get asked. Current models, including the behavioral, psychoanalytic, medical, or family systems perspective, do not encourage the therapist to uncover family violence. Therapists who are not trained to deal with the answers are especially unlikely to ask questions about violence. Currently there is no suggestion in the literature that encourages the therapist or the researcher to consider or assess the possibility that violence has occurred or is occurring in the marriages of agoraphobes.

Are we obligated to assess or even capable of assessing for the presence of physical and psychological forms of battering? Can we accept the patients' or the spouses' reports that the marriage is good if there are clinical indications that battering may be occurring? The literature suggests that denial is characteristic of both agoraphobes (Goldstein, 1987; Goldstein & Chambless, 1978) and batterers (Gondolf, 1985; Saunders, 1984). Can we continue to ignore the possibility that violence is occurring, and can we identify those who are at risk for serious physical or psychological harm?

This suggestion also raises serious questions about the appropriateness of behavioral and drug therapies. Should we be treating the symptoms that the patient presents as problematic, or should we be addressing the distress, conflict, and unhappiness reported by these women? Hafner (1982) raises different questions about the ethics of treating agoraphobes. He questions whether the treatment should focus on symptom relief or on related problems such as marital conflict. Further, he raises the ethical questions of whether to treat an agoraphobic patient when there is a strong likelihood that successful treatment will lead to illness or disability in the spouse.

Several studies on agoraphobes indicate that the partner may be employed as a cotherapist (Mathews, Jannoun, & Gelder, 1979; Mathews, Teasdale, Munby, Johnston, & Shaw, 1977). Sable (1991) reviews the literature on including the spouse in treatment and concludes that the results are mixed. Emmelkamp (1982) challenges the dynamics and effectiveness of such an intervention. He contends that by using the partner as cotherapist, the dependent relationship between the patient and partner may inadvertently be reinforced. My suggestion that the marriages of some agoraphobes may involve physical or psychological intimidation adds an urgency to Emmelkamp's caution.

*C*ONCLUSIONS

Why doesn't she just leave? This is the question most often asked about battered women (McHugh, Frieze, & Brown, 1993), and it might also be asked about agoraphobic women. Elsewhere I have argued that this question places the responsibility for the solution to societal problems on the shoulders of individual women and absolves men, and society in general, of any culpability or responsibility (McHugh, 1993; McHugh et al., 1993).

Therapeutic practices that focus on the individual woman and make it possible for her to leave do not solve the underlying problems. The batterer goes on to beat another woman; the dominating husband continues to dominate the agoraphobe or dominates someone else. Anxiety and fearfulness are still engendered in girls and women. Public streets and other settings remain dangerous or inhospitable for women who must have a "safe" companion to escort them. It remains customary to isolate young married women from their family and friends. Women are expected to fulfill traditional roles. Individualistic approaches are thus viewed as ineffective and inefficient. A feminist analysis calls for structural or societal changes, such as Gelfond's (1991) call for a preventive approach to agoraphobia.

The feminist perspective encourages us to view agoraphobia (and other sex-linked disorders) not as individual pathology but in relation to women's experiences in general. The panic experienced by the agoraphobe is compared to the fearfulness experienced by most women in public settings. The phobic reaction of some women is compared to other women's responses to battering, domination, and marital conflict. Traditional clinical research methods that fail to include comparison or control groups are thus seen as flawed. Questions are raised concerning what are appropriate comparison groups (Gelfond, 1991).

The feminist analysis also offers insight into some novel practices that could be incorporated into traditional therapy approaches. Agoraphobic women may be deficient in map-reading and way-finding skills (Gelfond, 1991), which suggests that skill building in these areas could be part of the solution. Therapists and researchers may explore the meaning of home to agoraphobes or examine the fears that women have about specific public settings. I have argued that therapists need to question the agoraphobic client about her experiences of violence both within the home and outside of it.

Feminists have argued for a thorough examination of the sociological, historical, cultural, economic, political, and psychological factors that affect and limit women's choices. Women's experiences and problems are seen as occurring in a sociocultural context, as affected by gender socialization and as limited by gender roles. In contrast to contemporary treatment approaches, a feminist analysis of agoraphobia explores how these factors influence women to "stay home."

REFERENCES

AMERICAN PSYCHIATRIC ASSOCIATION. (1994). *Diagnostic and statistical manual of mental disorders* (4th ed.). Washington, DC: Author.

ANDREWS, J. D. (1966). Psychotherapy of phobias. *Psychological Bulletin, 66,* 455–480.

ARRINDELL, W. A. (1987). *Marital conflict and agoraphobia: Fact or fantasy?* Delft: Eburon.

ARRINDELL, W. A., EMMELKAMP, P. M. G., & SANDERMAN, R. (1986). Marital quality and general life adjustment in relation to treatment outcome in agoraphobia. *Advances in Behaviour Research and Therapy, 8*(3), 139–185.

BARLOW, D. H. (1988). *Anxiety and its disorders: The nature and treatment of anxiety and panic.* New York: Guilford.

BECK, A. T., & EMERY, G. (1985). *Anxiety disorders and phobias: A cognitive perspective.* New York: Basic Books.

BLOCK, J. (1978). Another look at sex differentiation in the socialization behaviors of mothers and fathers. In J. Sherman & F. Denmark (Eds.), *The psychology of women: Future directions of research.* New York: Psychological Dimensions.

BOWLBY, J. (1988). *A secure base.* New York: Basic Books.

BREHONEY, K. A. (1983). Women and agoraphobia: A case for the etiological significance of the feminine sex role stereotype. In V. Franks & E. D. Rothblum (Eds.), *The stereotyping of women: Its effects on mental health* (pp. 112–128). New York: Springer.

BROWN, T. A., & CASH, T. F. (1990). The phenomenon of nonclinical panic: Parameters of panic, fear, and avoidance. *Journal of Anxiety Disorders, 4*(1), 15–29.

BRYANT, K. (1982). Personality correlates of sense of direction and geographical orientation. *Journal of Personality and Social Psychology, 43,* 1318–1324.

BUGLASS, D., CLARKE, J., HENDERSON, A. S., KREITMAN, N., & PRESLEY, A. S. (1977). A study of agoraphobic housewives. *Psychological Medicine, 7,* 73–86.

BURNS, L. E., & THORPE, G. L. (1977). The epidemiology of fears and phobias. *Journal of International Medical Research, 5,* 1–7.

CHAMBLESS, D. (1982). Characteristics of agoraphobics. In D. L. Chambless & A. J. Goldstein (Eds.), *Agoraphobia: Multiple perspectives on theory and treatment* (pp. 1–18). New York: Wiley.

CHAMBLESS, D., & GOLDSTEIN, A. (1980). Anxieties: Agoraphobia and hysteria. In A. M. Brodsky & R. Hare-Mustin (Eds.), *Women and psychotherapy: An assessment of research and practice* (pp. 113–134). New York: Guilford Press.

CHAMBLESS, D. L., & MASON, J. (1986). Sex, sex role stereotyping and agoraphobia. *Behavior Research and Therapy, 24,* 231–235.

CHESLER, P. (1972). *Women and madness.* New York: Doubleday.

COBB, J. P., MATHEWS, A. M., CHILDS-CLARKE, A., & BLOWERS, C. M. (1984). The spouse as co-therapist in the treatment of agoraphobia. *British Journal of Psychiatry, 144,* 282–287.

DEROGATIS, L., & SPENCER, P. (1982). *Brief Symptom Inventory: Administration, scoring and procedures manual* (Vol. 1). Baltimore, MD: Clinical Psychometric Research.

DEUTSCH, H. (1929). The genesis of agoraphobia. *International Journal of Psychoanalysis, 10*(1), 51–69.

EICHENBAUM, L., & ORBACH, S. (1983). *Understanding women.* Harmondsworth: Penguin.

EMMELKAMP, P. M. G. (1982). In vivo treatment of agoraphobia. In D. L. Chambless & A. J. Goldstein (Eds.), *Agoraphobia: Multiple perspectives on theory and treatment* (pp. 43–76). New York: Wiley.

FLEMING, B., & FAULK, A. (1989). Discriminating factors in panic disorder with and without agoraphobia. *Journal of Anxiety Disorders, 3*(4), 209–219.

FODOR, I. G. (1974). The phobic syndrome in women: Implications for treatment. In V. Franks & V. Burtle (Eds.), *Women in therapy* (pp. 132–168). New York: Brunner/Mazel.

FODOR, I. G. (1987). Cognitive/behavior therapy for agoraphobic women: Towards utilizing psychodynamic understanding to address family beliefs systems and enhance behavior change. In M. Braude (Ed.), *Women, power, and therapy: Issues for women* (pp. 103–123). New York: Haworth Press.

FODOR, I. G. (1992). The agoraphobic syndrome: From anxiety neurosis to panic disorder. In L. Brown & M. Ballou (Eds.), *Personality and psychopathology: Feminist reappraisals* (pp. 177–205). New York: Guilford.

FRANKS, V. (1986). Sex role stereotyping and diagnosis of psychopathology. *Women and Therapy, Special Issue: The Dynamics of Feminist Therapy.* 5(2-3), 219–232.

FRIEZE, I. H., & MCHUGH, M. C. (1993). Power and influence strategies in violent and nonviolent marriages. *Psychology of Women Quarterly, 16,* 449–465.

GELFOND, M. (1991). Reconceptualizing agoraphobia: A case study of epistemological bias in clinical research. *Feminism & Psychology, 1*(2), 247–262.

GOLDSTEIN, A. J. (1973, September). *Learning theory insufficiency in understanding agoraphobia: A plea for empiricism.* Paper presented at the European Association for Behavior Therapy and Behavior Modification, Munich, Germany.

GOLDSTEIN, A. J. (1987). *Overcoming agoraphobia.* New York: Viking.

GOLDSTEIN, A. J., & CHAMBLESS, D. L. (1978). A reanalysis of agoraphobia. *Behavior Therapy, 9,* 47–59.

GOLDSTEIN, R. K., & SWIFT, K. (1977). Psychotherapy with phobic patients: The marriage relationship as the source of symptoms and focus of treatment. *American Journal of Psychotherapy, 31*(2), 285–292.

GONDOLF, E. (1985). *Men who batter: An integrated approach for stopping wife abuse.* Holmes Beach, FL: Learning Publications.

GOURNAY, K. (Ed.). (1989). Failures in behavioral treatment of agoraphobia. In K. Gournay (Ed.), *Agoraphobia: Current perspectives on theory and treatment* (pp. 120–139). New York: Routledge.

HAFNER, R. J. (1982). The marital context of the agoraphobic syndrome. In D. L. Chambless & A. J. Goldstein (Eds.), *Agoraphobia: Multiple perspectives on theory and treatment* (pp. 77–118). New York: Wiley.

HAFNER, R. J., & MINGE, P. J. (1989). Sex role stereotyping in women with agoraphobia and their husbands. *Sex Roles, 20,* 705–711.

HAND, I., & LAMONTAGNE, Y. (1976). The exacerbation of the interpersonal problems after rapid phobia removal. *Psychotherapy: Theory, Research, and Practice, 13,* 405–411.

HOFFMAN, A. (1987). *Illumination night.* New York: Fawcett Press.

KOSLOWSKI, L. T., & BRYANT, K. (1977). Sense of direction, spatial orientation, and cognitive maps. *Journal of Experimental Psychology: Human Perception and Performance, 3,* 590–598.

LAZARUS, A. (1966). Broad-spectrum behavior therapy and the treatment of agoraphobia. *Behavior Research and Therapy, 4,* 95–97.

LOTT, B. (1994). *Women's lives: Themes and variations.* Pacific Groves, CA: Brooks/Cole.

MACCOBY, E. E., & JACKLIN, C. N. (1974). *The psychology of sex differences.* Stanford, CA: Stanford University Press.

MARKS, I. M. (1966). *Fears and phobias.* London: Heinemann.

MARKS, I. M., & HERST, E. R. (1970). A survey of 1200 agoraphobics in Britain. *Social Psychiatry, 5,* 16–24.

MATHEWS, A. M., JANNOUN, L., & GELDER, M. (1979, September). *Self-help methods in agoraphobia.* Paper presented at the Ninth Conference of the European Association of Behavior Therapy and Behavior Modification, Paris, France.

MATHEWS, A. M., TEASDALE, J., MUNBY, M., JOHNSTON, D., & SHAW, P. (1977). A home-based treatment program for agoraphobia. *Behavior Therapy, 8,* 915–924.

MCHUGH, M. C. (1989, March). *Rethinking agoraphobia.* Paper presented at the meeting of the Association for Women in Psychology, Tempe, AZ.

McHugh, M. C. (1993). Studying battered women and batterers: Feminist perspectives on methodology. In M. Hansen & M. Harway (Eds.), *Battering and family therapy: A feminist perspective* (pp. 54-68). Newbury Park, CA: Sage.

McHugh, M. C., Frieze, I. H., & Browne, A. (1993). Research on battered women and their assailants. In F. Denmark & M. Paludi (Eds.), *Psychology of women: A handbook of issues and theories* (pp. 513–552). Westport, CT: Greenwood Press.

Meyer, R. (1987). *The relation of cognition and affect in agoraphobics with differing avoidance patterns.* Unpublished doctoral dissertation, New York University, New York, NY.

Michelson, L. (1987). Cognitive-behavioral assessment and treatment of agoraphobia. In L. Michelson & L. M. Ascher (Eds.), *Anxiety and stress disorders* (pp. 213–279). New York: Guilford Press.

Milton, F., & Hafner, R. J. (1979). The outcome of behavior therapy for agoraphobia in relation to marital adjustment. *Archives of General Psychiatry, 36,* 807–811.

Myers, J., Weissman, M., & Tischler, G. (1984). Six-month prevalence of psychiatric disorders in three communities. *Archives of General Psychiatry, 41,* 959–967.

Sable, P. (1991). Attachment, anxiety and agoraphobia. *Women & Therapy, 11*(2), 55–69.

Saegert, S., & Hart, R. (1978). The development of environmental competence in girls and boys. In M. Salter (Ed.), *Play: Anthropological perspectives* (pp. 157–175). West Point, NY: Leisure Press.

Saunders, D. G. (1984). Helping husbands who batter. *Social Casework, 65,* 347–353.

Seidenberg, R., & DeCrow, K. (1983). *Women who marry houses: Panic and protest in agoraphobia.* New York: McGraw-Hill.

Steketee, G., & Foa, E. B. (1987). Rape victims: Post-traumatic stress responses and their treatment. *Journal of Anxiety Disorders, 1,* 69–86.

Thorpe, G. L., & Burns, L. E. (1983). *The agoraphobic syndrome: Behavioral approaches to evaluation and treatment.* Chichester, England: Wiley.

Vose, R. H. (1981). *Agoraphobia.* London: Faber.

Weeks, C. (1973). A practical treatment of agoraphobia. *British Medical Journal, 2,* 469–471.

Weiss, E. (1964). *Agoraphobia in light of ego psychology.* New York: Grune & Stratton.

Wolfe, B. E. (1984). Gender ideology and phobias in women. In C. S. Wisdom (Ed.), *Sex roles and psychopathology* (pp. 51–72). New York: Plenum.

SUGGESTED READINGS

Brown, L., & Ballou, M. (Eds.). (1992). *Personality and psychopathology: Feminist reappraisals.* New York: Guilford.

Gelfond, M. (1991). Reconceptualizing agoraphobia: A case study of epistemological bias in clinical research. *Feminism & Psychology, 1*(2), 247–262.

Seidenberg, R., & DeCrow, K. (1983). *Women who marry houses: Panic and protest in agoraphobia.* New York: McGraw-Hill.

*J*UDITH WORELL is *Professor of Educational and Counseling Psychology at the University of Kentucky. Dr. Worell has been teaching courses on lifespan gender development and counseling women since 1975. She is currently studying feminist identity development and working on measures to assess outcomes of feminist therapy.*

24

Feminist Identity in a Gendered World

❖

*F*EMINISM AND THE CONSTRUCTION OF GENDER

When I say, as I frequently do, "I am a feminist," what do I mean? There are many answers to this question, and the answer perhaps will be different for me than for others. To explore this question, I consider the development of feminist beliefs and identity from several viewpoints: as an extension of cultural and personal expectations about women and men, as an outgrowth of the feminist movement, as a personal transformation, and as a fascinating topic of psychological research.

Contemporary feminism is not just about women and men. Feminists have moved from a position of reconstructing the relationships between women, men, and society to one of reconsidering what it means to be female or male from many different perspectives. As feminist researchers, we ask many questions. In what ways do we differ from one another physically, biologically, emotionally, or in our behavior? How is it that some of us are accorded more privileges than others? Why are the sources of social, economic, and political power centered within particular ethnic and gender groups? We use the term "gender" to refer to this complexity of meanings and outcomes that are associated in all societies with the identification of each person as female or male. Central to the identity of contemporary feminists is an awareness of the pervasiveness of gender polarization, or distinctive expectations for women and men.

We start our consideration of feminist identity with some discussion of what we mean by the term "feminist." I then proceed with a brief account of the feminist movement that places contemporary feminism within a historical context. From there, we launch directly into the concept of feminist identity development. From my own experiences of becoming a feminist, we take a look at what some of the research has to say about how women (and men) develop a self-identity as feminist.

CONCEPTIONS OF FEMINISM

How do people come to define themselves as feminist? How is it that some women are overheard to say, "I want equal pay for equal work, I want my spouse to share home and childcare responsibilities, and I want to select and succeed at any career I choose—*but* I am not a feminist?" There are probably many answers to this question. Claire Renzetti (1987) suggests that this attitude represents a new wave of feminist thought rather than a rejection of feminist ideals. The college women in her sample believed they should deal with sex discrimination individually rather than collectively as women. Part of the answer, then, may lie in our conceptions of feminism.

From Dictionary to Diversity

Webster's New World Dictionary (1978) defines feminism as (1) "the principle that women should have political, economic, and social rights equal to those of men" and (2) "the movement to win such rights for women." As earlier feminist movements became reorganized and revitalized in the late 1960s, conceptions of feminist principles and beliefs expanded in many directions. Individual writers proposed alternative theses for understanding the position of women in the social structure. Submovements of feminism appeared, each with its own proponents. These separate currents of feminism retained certain commonalities; the major themes of women's subordination and a commitment to improving the status of women remained intact across all feminist thought. Disagreements arose regarding the sources of women's oppression and the solutions to be endorsed (Jagger & Rothenberg, 1984). It became increasingly clear that there was not one feminism, but many. What are some of these diverse views?

The *liberal* viewpoint in feminist thought targets inequalities in legal, political, and educational arrangements. The solution has been to promote laws to redress inequities in opportunity for education and employment. In contrast, the *cultural* feminist seeks to empower women by celebrating the enduring qualities of women as caring, intimate, cooperative, and connected to others. Women's special qualities are valued and become the major source of power and liberation. From a *radical* feminist approach, however, women's oppression is rooted in patriarchy and the unequal allocation of power in society to men. The source of women's oppression lies in institutional male dominance and control of women's lives. The identification of patriarchy as a system of male privilege leads to solutions that go beyond "equal pay for equal work"; it targets the institutions of our society that support this privilege. Other groups of feminist women added their concerns; lesbian women, for example, identified discrimination based on their sexuality, and women of color addressed their concerns to the oppressive effects of racism. In reality, few contemporary feminists restrict their vision to one or the other of these views. As we shall see from the research data, most feminists create their individual identities from a selective melding of values and beliefs that match their experiences and their personal goals.

From divergences within feminist communities, it became clear that there are many feminisms, and many themes within feminist thought, each with its own variations. Feminists discovered that although we have joined a common parade, we do not all march to the same music.

The Women's Movement Speaks

Many of the themes and variations in feminist thought are illustrated in the chronology of the women's movement of the twentieth century. Early accomplishments toward defining and working toward feminist goals of equal opportunity are beautifully documented and detailed in the *Feminist Chronicles* (Carabillo, Meuli, & Csida, 1993). These authors review the major legal and organizational landmarks in the movement for women's rights. Table 1 illustrates some of the most important of these events.

Despite clear legislative advances in Congress for women, progress toward equality has been slow, and mechanisms for correcting inequities are cumbersome. I believe that national attention to the ratification of the equal rights amendment (ERA), played out on the stage of every state legislature, brought the issues of equity for women closer to home. It stimulated women throughout the United States to become involved, whether in support of or opposition to the legislation. The goal of the ERA—to erase all legislative barriers to women's equality—provoked women everywhere to consider what women might have to gain or lose and to develop their own conceptions of women's place in the social structure. Feminism, defined in terms of equal rights and foreshadowing the Webster's entry, had indeed taken hold in the psyche of most women (and some men) in the United States. The mainstream had discovered feminism.

Psychology Discovers Feminism

As new groups of women entered the arena, concepts of feminism expanded. In particular, women in psychology began to meet the challenge

TABLE 1

Landmark Events in the Twentieth-Century Women's Movement

1920	Passage of the 19th Amendment to the Constitution and the right of women to vote.
1961	Establishment of the Commission on the Status of Women, which lobbied for women's equality in employment and education.
1963	Passage of the Fair Labor Standards Act, which prohibited sex-based discrimination in employment and wages (equal pay for equal work, equal access to jobs).
1964	Passage of Title VII of the Civil Rights Act, extending civil rights to women as well as to racial minorities (equal access to education).
1965	Establishment of the Equal Employment Opportunities Commission (EEOC), charged with enforcing the provisions of Title VII of the Civil Rights Act (enabling women to bring charges against unlawful educational and employment practices).
1966	Establishment of the National Organization for Women, a lobby group for women's rights.
1969	Founding of the Association for Women in Psychology (AWP) to advocate for women in psychology.
1972	Passage of the equal rights amendment. The ERA was not ratified by enough states, so it died.
1973	Establishment of the Division of the Psychology of Women within the American Psychological Association.

of the *zeitgeist,* or the temper of the times, with publication of theory, critique, and research related to women and gender (see Broverman, Broverman, Clarkson, Rosenkranz, & Vogel, 1970; Sherman, 1971; Weisstein, 1968). In the process, they discovered that, not only in the legal sphere but in all arenas, women and their life stories were either invisible, misrepresented, or denigrated (Crawford & Marecek, 1989). Women began to publish articles that challenged and questioned the methods and outcomes of traditional science (Bem, 1974; Constantinople, 1973; Grady, 1981). Groups of women gathered to form political and professional associations that addressed women's issues in the public forum. These individuals and groups formulated conceptions of the feminist agenda that gradually evolved as new information and dialogue emerged. The first journal devoted to the psychology of women was established in 1975—*Psychology of Women Quarterly.* Promoting a set of clearly feminist editorial policies, this journal recently published its eighteenth volume with a special issue on feminist transformations of theory and research with women (Worell & Etaugh, 1994). Academia, and psychology, had discovered feminism.

Feminist Psychologists Speak Out

From its inception as a legitimate area of academic study, feminist psychologists have defined the field in diverse ways. To summarize some contemporary views, let me describe some of the results of a recent research project with female professors of psychology (Worell, Todd, & Crosby, in press; Crosby & Worell, 1992). The purpose of the project was to understand how these scholars defined feminism, how they developed as feminists, and how they sustained their feminist commitment over time. During 1992 and 1993, we trained two experienced interviewers to conduct 1- to 2-hour taped telephone interviews with a national sample of 77 feminist academic psychologists. How did we select these women to be sure that their responses would reflect the thinking of typical feminist psychology professors? We started with a group identified as feminist—Division 35 (Psychology of Women) of the American Psychological Association (APA)—and selected all those who were employed in academic settings. We further distributed our sample equally among women who taught at women's colleges, coeducational colleges, and universities. We then drew 35 random names (would you believe pulling slips of paper from a jar?) from each of the three groups to achieve a sample of 26 women in each group. Ninety-two percent of all those we contacted agreed to participate, a very impressive response rate!

One of the questions we asked early in the interview was, "When you say 'I am a feminist,' what do you mean?" We joined with two independent coders to organize the responses according to the similarity of their themes. From our analysis of the free responses of the 77 academic women in our sample (one was retired and was therefore excluded), we found four major themes that characterized their feminist identity.

1. *Gender is a social category.* Understands that gender has multiple meanings; views gender within the context of societal power dynamics; sees gender as a social construction.
2. *Women are disadvantaged.* Believes that women as a group experience discrimination; believes in empowerment of women toward equal status in society; wants to eliminate roles based on gender.
3. *Women are important.* Values and respects all women and connects to their legitimate concerns. Is pro-woman.
4. *Activism is required.* Advocates and promotes action toward social change to benefit all women.

Now, not all women in our sample spontaneously included these four themes in the unstructured interview. For example, one of our respondents answered in this manner:

> It's a commitment to thinking about the world in terms of how gender makes a difference. Particularly what it has meant for women, historically and currently. To work to change those unfair aspects of what it has meant for women and also for cultural minorities who've traditionally been discriminated against.

Here, we see the issues of gender, equity, and action tied into a coherent statement.

Although the factor of valuing women did not appear specifically in this respondent's definition, another respondent defined her pro-woman stance in this manner:

> [It means] looking at life and culture and psychology from the point of view of women's experience.

When we later sent our respondents a questionnaire containing a written checklist of feminist values and goals, all but one respondent endorsed items from all four factors. We concluded that, for this sample of academic psychologists, these four themes represent the substance of contemporary feminist beliefs. From the content of the themes, we see that their descriptions are grounded broadly in three components: cognitive (thinking, believing), affective (feeling, valuing), and behavioral (acting, doing). Clearly, these psychologists endorse a more holistic conception of feminism than does Webster's dictionary. They also conceive of feminism within a broader social context than did Renzetti's (1987) college women; in contrast to the "new wave" group, the academic feminists in our sample were concerned with more than equal opportunities for themselves. They were concerned with inequality in societal power structures with respect to women, they valued the experiences of all women, and they were willing to advocate for social change. You may be able to detect components of the three views of feminism we discussed above: liberal, cultural, and radical, in these contemporary definitions.

DEVELOPING A FEMINIST IDENTITY

Moving from the development of the feminist movement to personal definitions of feminism, we can see that for committed individuals, feminism represents a *socially embedded identity*. That is, one's concept of self with respect to certain aspects of one's thoughts, feelings, and behavior becomes merged and consistent with the goals and values of larger social units or reference groups with whom one identifies (Miller & Prentice, 1994). You probably have many social identities associated with different reference groups, such as being American, Latina, Republican, female, or feminist (Oyserman & Marcus, 1983; Tajfel & Turner, 1986). Each of these identities defines and encompasses a subset of your beliefs and actions, and each plays a part in constructing the streams of your life story.

The expanded concept of a "socially embedded identity" refers to an alliance with a reference group whose aims and goals are focused on service to others or on promoting justice. I see the identification with feminism as a socially embedded position to the extent that the well-being of the group (all women), rather than advantage to the self, is of concern. The question we ask here is, In the face of a general social structure that supports and rewards adherence to the status quo, how do some women (and some men) develop a feminist social identity? This feminist identity is one that rejects the status quo, resists the imposition of current social structures on the lives of women and men, calls for social roles that are free of gender bias, and advocates for action toward social change. We explore this question by examining recent models of feminist identity development.

Models of Feminist Identity Development

A format for conceptualizing the development of a feminist identity was proposed by Nancy Downing and Kristin Roush (1985). Their model, patterned after an earlier one by Cross (1980) on Black identity, "is based on the premise that women who live in contemporary society must first acknowledge, then struggle with and repeatedly work through, their feelings about the prejudice and discrimination they experience as women in order to achieve authentic and positive feminist identity" (p. 695). The five stages of feminist identity proceed from acceptance of the status quo and denial of discrimination to one of commitment to activism for social change.

The application of the Downing and Roush model to women of color is unclear. For many women of color, the struggle for identity as a woman is bound up in their dual experience of racism and sexism. Growing up as a woman of color in American society carries the double jeopardy of devalued minority status for both gender and ethnicity (Reid, 1988). Borrowing from Black women writers the concept of "womanist" identity as more relevant to women of color, a somewhat similar model for womanist identity development was recently proposed by Janet Helms and her associates (Ossana, Helms, & Leonard, 1992). One goal of this model was to encompass the experiences of minority women in a dominant majority culture. The womanist approach aims to account for a positive minority female self-concept rather than a specifically feminist identity. The desirable outcome of this four-stage model is internalization, in which the woman rejects external definitions of herself and develops "personally meaningful internal standards of womanhood" (p. 404). Within this model, women may or may not endorse feminism as a personal and political position, and the social-activism component is missing. For our purposes, we limit our discussion to the Downing and Roush approach, which focuses specifically on feminist development.

According to the Downing and Roush model, feminist identity develops through five stages: passive acceptance, revelation, embeddedness-emanation, synthesis, and active commitment. Although these "stages" seem to represent separate positions, the authors point out that most women will alternately advance and retreat from later to earlier stages as new experiences are encountered.

The feminist identity model proposes that we are socialized to experience the current roles and relative positions of women and men in society as "normal" and the way things ought to be. Thus, in the *passive acceptance stage,* we initially accept or do not deny the subordinate and unequal status of women. However, a crisis or contradiction may occur at some time in our lives that confronts us with personal gender discrimination or prejudice and a realization of our unequal position as a woman. This encounter with the reality of our disadvantaged female status challenges our earlier beliefs and throws us into a position of rage and mistrust of men. As a result, we move into the *revelation stage,* where we question our earlier beliefs. We become angry about women's subordinate roles and guilty about the part we played in accepting our own oppression. As our awareness consolidates, we move into the *embeddedness stage.* Here, we immerse ourselves in issues related to women and reach out to like-minded women who can support us as we shape and strengthen our evolving identity. This emergent feminist identity is articulated in the *synthesis stage,* in which we absorb our new identity into a positive and realistic self-concept. We recognize women's oppression but can function effectively in dealing with discrimination without becoming overwhelmed by it. We celebrate our womanhood and take pride in our journey toward a positive and integrated self.

At the peak of our feminist development, we may reach the *stage of active commitment,* in which action toward social change is the prevailing goal. The full development of a positive feminist identity has been realized. Although it is broad in its definitions, the model is potentially testable and provides a useful organization for conceptualizing feminist commitment for women. Its application to male feminist development is unclear; I believe the process for men might be different but parallel in structure.

The importance of understanding how women arrive at a positive feminist identity has personal, political, and theoretical implications. At a personal level, we try to understand the development and elaboration of our own feminist beliefs. We also struggle to come to terms with these beliefs within a society that remains patriarchal in its conformity with traditional male standards. Self-understanding might be an initial goal. Then, we want to understand how to negotiate this feminist ideal with those in the surrounding culture who remain oppressive or unsympathetic to feminism (see, e.g., Haddock & Zanna, 1994). We strive to maintain our optimism and commitment in the face of negative feedback and barriers to social change. Maintenance and commitment to feminism become a second goal. Finally, we seek to develop relevant research and theories. We want to embrace the feminist movement as a major call for social justice that merits serious consideration in our psychological understandings. Let us turn now to this last goal; a theory begs for research to support its concepts and hypotheses. What does the research literature contribute to our understanding about the emergence of feminist awareness in a traditional culture?

CONTRIBUTIONS TO FEMINIST DEVELOPMENT

The Downing and Roush (1985) model proposes that personal crises or experiences that contradict earlier expectations will impel you toward new stages of feminist awareness and advocacy for social change. A course relevant to women's issues, such as this one, will change many students in many ways. Positive effects of women's studies courses on student attitudes toward endorsement and activism in behalf of feminist values and goals have been found in a number of research studies (e.g., Bargad & Hyde, 1991; Stake, Roades, Rose, Ellis, & West, 1994; Worell, Stilwell, & Robinson, 1991). In the Worell et al. (1991) study, we used the Feminist Identity Scale developed by Adena Bargad and Janet Hyde (1991) to assess two groups of graduate students as they were exposed to experiences and information relevant to women's issues. We found that as exposure to women's issues increased, the 89 women and men in our sample tended to reject passive acceptance and endorsed equally all the advanced feminist identity stages. People did not move clearly from one stage to another and did not explicitly identify with a single stage. We concluded that feminist identity development may represent a dimensional rather than a stage model. That is, with a dimensional model, we may develop relative positions for each stage, and each person can be at several stages at the same time.

In support of our findings, a recent study by Michelle Wolf (1994) also resulted in a dimensional rather than a stage model. The respondents in Wolf's study who were low on passive acceptance were almost equally high on each of the remaining alternatives. Thinking about feminist identity development from a dimensional view suggests an extension of the Downing and Roush model to emphasize relevant experience with a range of encounters.

The critical component for feminist identity, then, may be additional exposure to feminist ideals rather than simply experiencing personal discrimination. Such exposure might move individuals toward endorsement of social action to change institutional structures that support discrimination. This conclusion would answer, in part, the question of how some women want equal opportunities but fail to endorse feminism; they want individual, rather than, collective action and seek to empower themselves rather than advocating for all women. Their identity remains personal rather than socially embedded in a feminist vision of the just society (see Rowland, 1984, for a similar view).

I am proposing here that awareness of one's own discrimination may be insufficient to project women into a feminist identity crisis. Personal discrimination may lead to depression and feelings of helplessness, or to anger and outrage, but its logical outcome is not likely to be identification with a social movement. Rather, I suggest that feminist identity requires communication between women, information about the lives and struggles of other women, and data relating to gender discrimination across a range of situations. All these factors may combine to raise consciousness beyond that of personal disadvantage. The question remains to be explored further; we need additional research that examines the lives of women (and men) in progress. How do attitudes and beliefs change as we encounter differing life circumstances and are provided with diverse opportunities to learn about our past, present, and futures as women and men.

CONCLUSIONS

We started with a broad question about what it means to label oneself as feminist. Through exploring the varied meanings of gender, feminism, and the course of the American feminist movement, we arrived at a point of convergence grounded in theory as well as recent research. It is my impression that feminist identity development is a socially embedded position that depends on both experience and exposure for its emergence and sustenance. It seems to be stimulated by both personal experience and consciousness-raising situations that consolidate toward a new understanding. This awareness is accompanied by a personal determination to reject traditional views of women's and men's social roles based on gendered or dominant culture expectations. As feminist identity is strengthened, the realization of personal disadvantage becomes linked to a developing commitment to social justice and equality for other disadvantaged groups. My personal answer to the question of what feminism means to me is articulated in a commitment to social change. A feminism that is voiced but not lived is bound to decay. A feminist identity that seeks to meet the challenges of injustice with action is determined to endure and triumph.

REFERENCES

BARGAD, A., & HYDE, J. S. (1991). Women's studies: A study of feminist identity development. *Psychology of Women Quarterly, 15,* 181–201.

BEM, S. (1974). The measurement of psychological androgyny. *Journal of Consulting and Clinical Psychology, 47,* 155–162.

BROVERMAN, I. K., BROVERMAN, D., CLARKSON, F. E., ROSENKRANZ, P. S., & VOGEL, S. R. (1970). Sex-role stereotypes and clinical judgments of mental health. *Journal of Consulting and Clinical Psychology, 34,* 1–7.

CARABILLO, T., MEULI, J., & CSIDA, J. B. (1993). *Feminist chronicles: 1953–1993.* Los Angeles: Women's Graphics.

CONSTANTINOPLE, A. (1973). Masculinity-femininity: An exception to a famous dictum? *Psychological Bulletin, 80,* 309–407.

CRAWFORD, M., & MARECEK, J. (1989). Psychology constructs the female: 1968–1988. *Psychology of Women Quarterly, 13,* 147–167.

CROSBY, F. J., & WORELL, J. (1992, June). *The Feminist Teaching Project.* Final report on a Dupont Foundation grant submitted to the Women's College Coalition, Washington, DC.

CROSS, W. E. (1980). Models of psychological nigrescence. In R. L. Jones (Ed.), *Black psychology* (pp. 81–98). New York: Harper & Row.

DOWNING, N. E., & ROUSH, K. L. (1985). From passive acceptance to active commitment: A model of feminist identity development for women. *Counseling Psychologist, 13,* 695–709.

GRADY, K. E. (1981). Sex bias in research design. *Psychology of Women Quarterly, 5,* 628–636.

HADDOCK, G., & ZANNA, M. P. (1994). Preferring "housewives" to "feminists": Categorization and the favorability of attitudes toward women. *Psychology of Women Quarterly, 18,* 25–52.

JAGGER, A. M., & ROTHENBERG, P. S. (1984). *Feminist frameworks: Alternative theoretical accounts of the relations between women and men.* New York: McGraw-Hill.

MILLER, D. T., & PRENTICE, D. A. (1994). The self and the collective. *Personality and Social Psychology Bulletin, 20,* 451–453.

OSSANA, S. M., HELMS, J. E., & LEONARD, M. M. (1992). Do "womanist" identity attitudes influence college women's self-esteem and perceptions of environmental bias? *Journal of Counseling and Development, 70,* 402–408.

OYSERMAN, D., & MARCUS, H. R. (1983). The sociocultural self. In J. Suls & A. G. Greenwald (Eds.), *Psychological perspectives on the self* (Vol. 4). Hillsdale, NJ: Erlbaum.

REID, P. T. (1988). Racism and sexism: Comparisons and conflicts. In P. A. Katz & D. A. Taylor (Eds.), *Eliminating racism* (pp. 203–221). New York: Plenum.

RENZETTI, C. M. (1987). New wave or second stage? Attitudes of college women toward feminism. *Sex Roles, 16,* 265–277.

ROWLAND, R. (1984). *Women who do and women who don't join the women's movement.* Boston: Routledge & Kegan Paul.

SHERMAN, J. A. (1971). *On the psychology of women: A survey of empirical studies.* Springfield, IL: Charles C. Thomas.

STAKE, J. E., ROADES, L., ROSE, S., ELLIS, L, & WEST, C. (1994). The women's studies experience: Impetus for feminist activism. *Psychology of Women Quarterly, 18,* 17–24.

TAJFEL, H., & TURNER, J. C. (1986). The social identity theory of intergroup behavior. In S. Worchel & W. G. Austin (Eds.), *Psychology of intergroup behavior* (pp. 7–24). Chicago: Nelson-Hall.

WEISSTEIN, N. (1968). *Kinder, kirche, kuche as scientific law: Psychology constructs the female.* Boston: New England Free Press.

WOLF, M. S. (1994). *The relationship between feminist identity and body satisfaction.* Unpublished master's thesis, University of Cincinnati, Cincinnati, OH.

WORELL, J., & ETAUGH, C. (1994). Transforming theory and research with women: Themes and variations. *Psychology of Women Quarterly, 18,* 433–440.

WORELL, J., STILWELL, D., & ROBINSON, D. (1991, May). *Feminist identity development: Stages or dimensions?* Paper presented at the seventh annual Nag's Head Conference on Sex and Gender, Highland Beach, FL.

WORELL, J., TODD, J., & CROSBY, F. J. (in press). Have feminists abandoned social activism? Voices from the academy. In M. Lerner & L. Montada (Eds.), *Current societal concerns about justice.* New York: Plenum Press.

SUGGESTED READINGS

BARGAD, A., & HYDE, J. S. (1991). Women's studies: A study of feminist identity development. *Psychology of Women Quarterly, 15,* 181–201.

DOWNING, N. E., & ROUSH, K. L. (1985). From passive acceptance to active commitment: A model of feminist identity development for women. *Counseling Psychologist, 13,* 695–709.

OSSANA, S. M., HELMS, J. E., & LEONARD, M. M. (1992). Do "womanist" identity attitudes influence college women's self-esteem and perceptions of environmental bias? *Journal of Counseling and Development, 70,* 402–408.

ROWLAND, R. (1984). *Women who do and women who don't join the women's movement.* Boston: Routledge & Kegan Paul.